# T.O.B.A. Time

# T.O.B.A. Time

## Black Vaudeville and the Theater Owners' Booking Association in Jazz-Age America

Michelle R. Scott

1 2 3 4 5 C P 5 4 3 2 1
∞ This book is printed on acid-free paper.

Library of Congress Cataloging-in-Publication Data
Names: Scott, Michelle R., 1974– author.
Title: T.O.B.A. time Black vaudeville and the Theater Owners' Booking Association in Jazz-Age America / Michelle R Scott.
Description: Urbana : University of Illinois Press, [2023] | Includes bibliographical references and index.
Identifiers: LCCN 2022028886 (print) | LCCN 2022028887 (ebook) | ISBN 9780252044885 (hardback) | ISBN 9780252086984 (paperback) | ISBN 9780252054037 (ebook)
Subjects: LCSH: Performing arts—United States—Management. | Performing arts—United States—Marketing. | African Americans in the performing arts. | African American theater—History. | Vaudeville—United States—History and criticism. | MESH: Theater Owners' Booking Association—History. | BISAC: HISTORY / African American & Black | SOCIAL SCIENCE / Ethnic Studies / American / African American & Black Studies
Classification: LCC PN1580 .S36 2023 (print) | LCC PN1580 (ebook) | DDC 791.2068—dc23/eng/20220912
LC record available at https://lccn.loc.gov/2022028886
LC ebook record available at https://lccn.loc.gov/2022028887

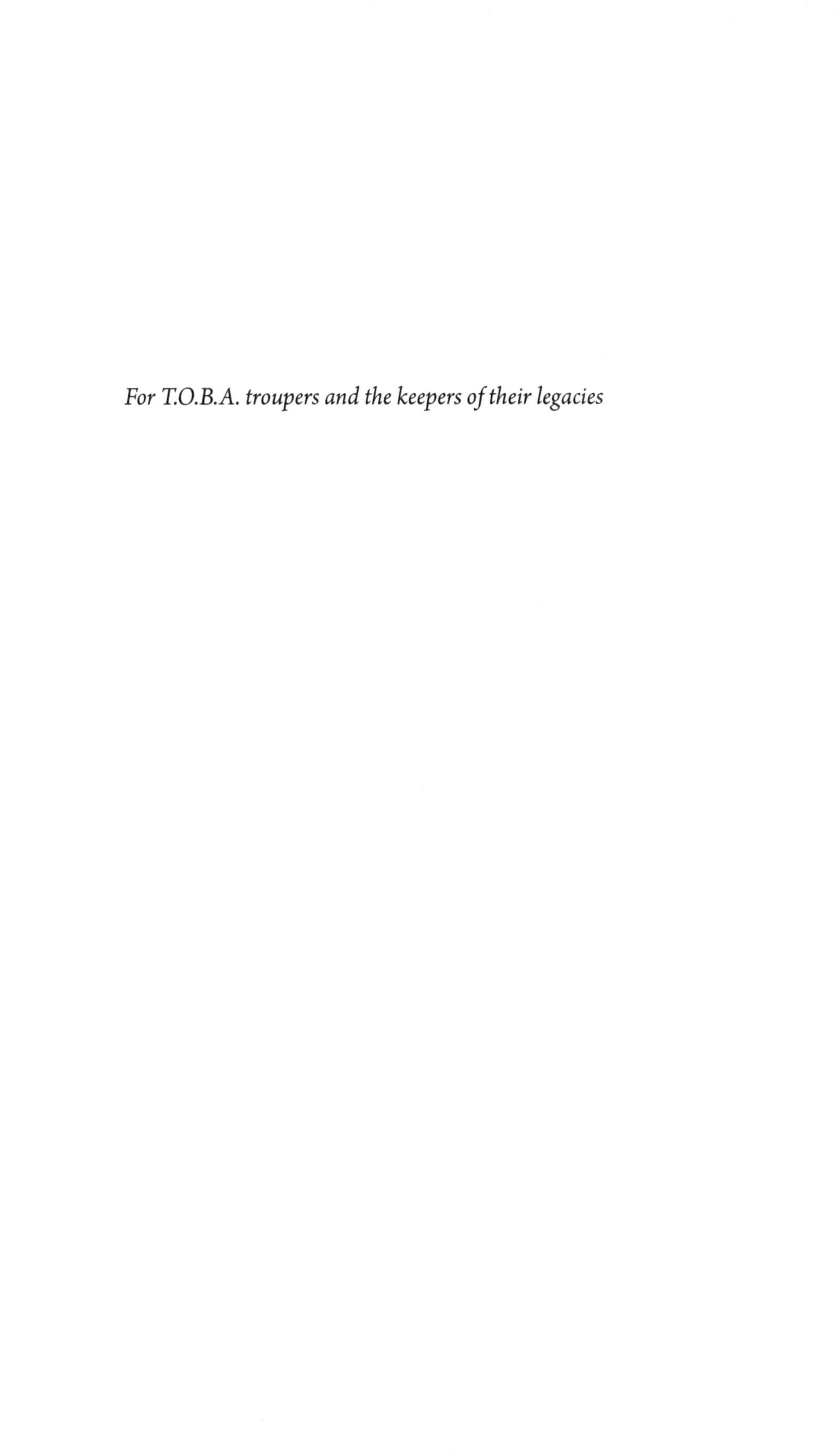

*For T.O.B.A. troupers and the keepers of their legacies*

# CONTENTS

# PREFACE

"Why do you study black vaudeville?" was a question I was often asked when crafting this narrative about a vibrant live theater entertainment genre whose popularity waned nearly one hundred years ago. I began writing *T.O.B.A. Time* in early 2017, when controversy arose concerning the black entertainment performances slated for the presidential inauguration; finished one manuscript draft as global communities used the arts to channel their protests against racial injustice in summer 2020; and completed final revisions in late 2021 when Broadway, concert spaces, and local theater reopened in a society that contended with mask and social distancing requirements created to safely enjoy live entertainment during a health crisis.

Yet my research and fascination with American entertainment history predated this writing span, as I was a book lover and an ardent classic film and musical theater fan even as an adolescent. The original version of American Movie Classics (AMC) and its broadcasts of 1930s–60s films, including *Carmen Jones* and *Stormy Weather*, enamored me, and Donald Bogle's *Brown Sugar: Eighty Years of America's Black Female Superstars* increased my junior high school curiosity about early African American entertainment and history. Fascinated by the full-page photos that vividly displayed Josephine Baker, Ethel Waters, Dorothy Dandridge, Lena Horne, and others who began their artistic efforts on black vaudeville stages, I learned about black women who fought unbelievable gendered economic and political battles offstage to entertain audiences onstage and on-screen. In later years, performing in large, semiprofessional vocal ensembles led me to question what goes on behind the stage to produce a show. How are entertainers paid, who controls the art they produce, and what is involved in the business of entertainment production? How did black performers in the early twentieth century succeed amid open racial and gender subjugation, when travel, lodging, and dining were governed by segregation statutes? These queries propelled me to this detailed examination of African American traveling theater participants and the Theater Owners' Booking Association (T.O.B.A.) theater circuit, the main vehicle for the transmission of black vaudeville performance in the 1920s Jazz Age.

Through studying the professional origin stories of Bessie Smith, Alberta Hunter, and lesser-known black entertainers, I learned that four letters—T.O.B.A.—meant stardom and stability for some and uncertainty and inequity for many others. Like so many subjects in African American history, T.O.B.A. has no dedicated archive, but its story lives in historical black newspapers, memoirs, and oral histories. Casually mentioning to entertainment history buffs that I was writing about T.O.B.A. sparked conversations that included questions like "Did your great-grandmother save a Howard Theatre program?" "Did your great-uncle, the ventriloquist in Indianapolis, perform at the Walker Theatre?" and "Your great-aunt ran a black actors' boarding house in Philadelphia?!" While I was writing, contemporary controversies about black women entertainers embracing their sexuality in music and onstage echoed 1920s black community debates about entertainment's significance and the power of public black images. The 1920s debates were also reflected in the twenty-first-century dismay over entertainers and political figures repeatedly wearing blackface costumes while purporting not to know that blackface minstrelsy, the widely popular nineteenth- and early-twentieth-century entertainment genre that preceded variety theater and vaudeville, was steeped in racist stereotypes of African Americans.

So why do I write about black vaudeville and T.O.B.A. Time? The Theater Owners' Booking Association is a fascinating window into early-twentieth-century American life and a link to a past where black entertainment success was a possible (and/or problematic) key to socioeconomic power for African American artists, managers, and entrepreneurs, as well as a welcomed leisure escape for its 1920s audiences in the aftermath of a global pandemic and socioeconomic uncertainty. Amid all the shimmying, blues music double entendres, and vibrant costumes, I hope T.O.B.A. Time's history will speak to this similar era in the early twenty-first century of the power of black and interracial entrepreneurship and black artistic excellence.

# ACKNOWLEDGMENTS

*T.O.B.A. Time* developed as an idea when I was working on my manuscript on blues singer Bessie Smith and her professional world. What was one or two pages in the story of how Smith became a "Blues Empress" has emerged into this narrative on how artists, managers, and audiences lived on the T.O.B.A. circuit, and it was not a solo effort.

I am very grateful for Dominique J. Moore, Alison Syring Bassford, and Dawn Durante, who are and were at the University of Illinois Press (UIP) when this project began and answered my many questions along the way. Publishing a manuscript during a global pandemic is no easy feat, and I am so thankful that Dawn, Alison, and now Dominique were patient with this "ever-anxious" author. Additionally, I appreciate all the efforts of the UIP production and marketing team, including Jennifer Argo, Kevin Cunningham, Lyric Dodson, Ellie Hinton, Dustin Hubbart, and Roberta Sparenberg. Muriel Jackson at the Washington Memorial Library in Macon, Georgia; Edward Burns with the Carl Van Vechten Estate; Kay Peterson at the Archives Center of the Smithsonian Institution's National Museum of American History; Luke Williams with the Tulsa Historical Society & Museum; and the Library of Congress's Prints & Photographs Division were also essential in helping secure book images.

Much of my primary research was made possible with the aid of former and current curators, archivists, and program specialists at the Smithsonian Institution's National Museum of American History (NMAH), including John Hasse,

Joe Hursey, Omar Eaton-Martinez, Deborra Richardson, Fath Ruffins, and Vanessa Broussard Simmons. I also appreciate the efforts of Chelsea Weathers at the University of Texas at Austin's Harry Ransom Center; Dr. Ida Jones, formerly at the Moorland-Spingarn Research Center at Washington D.C.'s Howard University; Dr. Randall Burkett, formerly of the Manuscript, Archives, and Rare Book Library at Emory University; and Darla Brock at the Tennessee State Archives & Library in Nashville, Tennessee. The staff at the Newspaper and Current Periodical, Manuscript, and Performing Arts Reading Rooms in the Library of Congress as well as the librarians at the Schomburg Center for Research in Black Culture at the New York Public Library were also invaluable. Additionally, my University of Maryland, Baltimore County (UMBC) undergraduate research assistants, Alexis Ashcroft and Tajia Thomas, were very effective in completing digital searches of historical newspapers.

Financially, I could not have completed the research and writing of this study without the resources of the Smithsonian Institution Senior Fellowship and travel and research funding from UMBC, including the College of Arts, Humanities, and Social Sciences Research Fellowship, the Dresher Center for the Humanities Residential Fellowship, and the On-Ramps to Full Professor grant. The financial and intellectual resources of the Mellon Mays Graduate Initiatives Program (MMGIP) also provided me with space and time to write.

Many of the intellectual queries that fueled this project stemmed from vibrant conversations held with UMBC faculty and other colleagues at professional forums. A special thanks to UMBC History Department's Amy Froide, Marjoleine Kars, Denise Meringolo, Derek Musgrove, Susan McDonough, and Anne Sarah Rubin and Eric Brown in INDS who reviewed writing excerpts or counseled me through publication and other woes. During the 2019 Dresher Center Fellowship, Jessica Berman, Dawn Biehler, Katherine Bankole-Medina, Rachel Brubaker, Theresa Runstedtler, and Craig Saper reviewed chapter excerpts and gave critical feedback for which I am grateful. A special thanks to Courtney Hobson at the Dresher Center. Additionally, I appreciate the members of my 2020 writing group from the Dresher Center Summer Research Writing Boot Camp, including Kate Drabinski, Loren Henderson, Kerrie Kephart, Gary Rozanc, and Tracy Tinga. What began as a two-week commitment has evolved into a strong accountability group that still meets today. The physical and virtual writing spaces of Easton's Nook Writers' Retreat and the Association of Black Women Historians (ABWH) Nighttime Writing Sessions helped me get across the writing finish line. Lastly, I want to acknowledge the students in my Mayhem and Murder and Pop Culture Historical Research capstone classes who let me test out my research in class discussions and workshops, as well as the students (shout-out to the UMBC alumni "Scott Squad") who traveled with me to various professional history conferences.

The valuable queries of the UIP anonymous readers were essential to the insights of this final product. At meetings of the Association of Black Women Historians (ABWH), the Association for the Study of African American Life and History (ASALH), the Association for the Study for the Worldwide African Diaspora (ASWAD), the American Historical Association (AHA), the American Studies Association (ASA), the Berkshire Conference of Women Historians, and the Organization of American Historians (OAH), audience members and panelists posed crucial questions to help me shape fragmented thoughts into chapters. At these various forums, the supportive feedback, particularly from Leslie Alexander, Emerald Christopher-Byrd, Samuel Backer, Earl Brooks, Leslie Callahan, Melissa Cooper, Pero Dagbovie, V.P. Franklin, Sharon Harley, Duchess Harris, Robert L. Harris Jr., Nicole Guidotti-Hernández, Reena Goldthree, Wanda Hendricks, Cheryl Hicks, Randal M. Jelks, Martha Jones, Deirdre Cooper Owens, Susie Pak, Gillian M. Rodger, Marlis Schweitzer, Shennette Garrett-Scott, Vijay Shah, Bettye Collier-Thomas, Kristen Turner, Juliet E. K. Walker, Margaret Washington, Jennifer Wilks, and Francille Wilson, helped form *T.O.B.A. Time.* Just weeks before her unexpected passing in 2018, Dr. Rosalyn Terborg-Penn shared encouraging words about this project and gave me a charge to continue paying the mentoring forward. I hope to persevere in what she defined as "the hard work" of archival research and scholarship in African American history.

A circle of family, friends, and loved ones kept me grounded while I completed this manuscript. A big thanks to my MMGIP family of scholars, particularly Dr. Cally Waite. Thank you, Karen L. Hall of the Heritage Signature Chorale, for ensuring I continue singing and for listening to my writing and life escapades. I also thank my Sigma Gamma Rho sorors, (especially Jessica Brewster-Johnson) and friends Chris Roberson and Tommy Voigt for their emotional support. Thank you to all my sister scholars at the Sit & Write writing circle (Drs. Takkara Brunson, Natanya Duncan, Tammy Henderson, Felicia Jemison, Kimberleigh Jordan, Kimberly R. Moffitt, and Felicia Y. Thomas). A special note of deep gratitude to Natanya Duncan (my "Write and Thrive" rather than my "ride or die"), who has led this group of powerful women as we laughed, cried, and prayed our works into being and became a sisterhood along the way. I am forever grateful for all of you.

I am so blessed to have the love and emotional support of my Scott family (love you *so* much, Mom, Dad, Akelah Lisa, Kelli, Ife, and Diallo) and my in-laws, the Hillman, Williams, and Wharton families. During the time between my first book and this one, I have lost several loved ones, and I am especially "wanting memories" of Patricia, Robert, and Michael Ector; Michael Ferguson; Natalie Carter Benson; and Marion Nixon-Vincent. Finally, to my husband, Michael Hillman, thank you for sharing your love, my bonus daughter Macayah, and your large, loving, extended family with me. I am immensely grateful for your continuous support and belief in this project, especially during those times when I thought I could not write another word ("I can't"). Thanks for making me laugh with the imagined monologues, songs, and *dances* of these historical figures along the way, and for reminding me that their stories *need* to be told. I am blessed, highly favored, and so grateful.

# T.O.B.A. Time

# INTRODUCTION

## *"They Called It T.O.B.A."*

Caroline, Caroline, at last they've got you on the map
With a new tune, a funny blue tune, with a peculiar snap!
You may not be able to buck and wing
Fox-trot, two-step, or even sing
If you ain't got religion in your feet
You can do this prance and do it neat

Charleston! Charleston! Made in Carolina
Some dance, some prance, I'll say, there's nothing finer
Than the Charleston, Charleston, Lord how you can shuffle . . .

—Lyrics to "Charleston," 1920. Title quote in Leonard Reed interview by Rusty Frank in 1993.

"To me, they were wonderful," Bessie Dudley proclaimed when she described the black vaudeville shows of the 1920s. At age twelve the future theatrical dancer often played hooky from school in the afternoon to venture to Baltimore's Lincoln Theatre, the black-serving venue on Pennsylvania Avenue.[1] Comedy duo Butterbeans and Susie or music ensemble The Gibson Family frequently filled the Lincoln's all-black entertainer playbill. Blues singers Bessie Smith and Alberta Hunter belted out "Careless Love" and "Downhearted Blues," respectively, wistfully uttering "Love, love, oh careless love" or moaning "Gee, but it's hard to love someone when that someone don't love you."[2] Enthralled by the diversity of acts that graced the stage, an impressionable Bessie Dudley saw them all. She excitedly detailed how the performances began with a line of dancing chorus girls, followed by a comedy skit and blues song sets accompanied by the house band. The spectacle then might end with a crowd-pleasing special attraction of acrobats, an animal act, or a magician. Bessie and her friends remained at the theater throughout the day, without leaving to eat, and just "look, look, looked," as they saw themselves positively reflected on stage by the dancers clad in brightly colored costumes and adorned in feather headpieces.

Over a thousand miles away in Kansas City's local black theater, black vaudevillians shimmying to popular Jazz Age songs fascinated fourteen-year-old "butcher boy" or concessions seller Leonard Reed.[3] In 1922 he could not master tap dancing's precursors of the buck and wing or the jig, but Reed perfected the latest "Charleston" dance, which he performed as a gimmick to attract candy or cigarette customers. By high school Reed transitioned from audience member to professional entertainer and recalled popular traveling black musical shows, like the Charleston Dandies or Hits and Bits. Audience members spent up to $1.50 of their hard-earned income, which might have only amounted to $15 a week, to watch revues featuring the multitalented Whitman Sisters or blues singers, like Ma Rainey and Ida Cox. Eager spectators filled the theater to get some momentary respite from everyday life and join in the music, laughter, and dance.[4]

Bessie Dudley and Leonard Reed were emblematic of the enthusiastic, young, black theatergoers who aspired to be entertainers in the 1920s. Their regionally separate but similar viewing experiences of black vaudeville were linked by an organization known as the Theater Owners' Booking Association (T.O.B.A. or Toby), which garnered wealth for its managers and producers, trained burgeoning black artists, and entertained millions. T.O.B.A. was a theater circuit existing between 1920 and 1931 that specialized in black vaudeville entertainment primarily for working-class black audiences. Vaudeville, the mix of comedy, song, dance, and novelty acts performed before a live theater audience without a set script or theme, was one of the most popular and profitable forms of live entertainment in the United States from the 1880s through the 1920s.

Vaudeville performances offered a window into the microcosm of a newly urban, working-class, ethnically and racially diverse America. Entertainers like the incredibly flexible, heavy-set female aerialist Alfaretta the Great might be on the same bill as Italian comic opera singer Harry Ross or the South American acrobats The Pachecho Family, the Six Chilean Wonders.[5] Not dramatic or high art, vaudeville was mass entertainment that popular culture scholars maintain fostered an "egalitarian atmosphere" and a sense of equality onstage, as a variety of acts could be found on the playbill.[6] The weekly program for New York City's Proctors Theatre on 23rd Street in June 1896 featured contortionists, songsters, serio-comediennes, and bird imitators among its twenty acts. If audience members stayed through act number seventeen, they could watch the Olympia Quartette as the Independent Colored Cadets, the only black entertainers on the bill.[7] Vaudeville's arguably diverse and open qualities were often limited to the talent that appeared onstage. Offstage, vaudeville's business practices were decidedly hierarchal regarding which artists were hired, where they performed, and how they were contracted.[8] Openings for black entertainers in mainstream white vaudeville or the "big time" were few, but black artists had an alternative in their own world of black vaudeville. Although not untouched by the injustices of racial segregation, black vaudeville was a popular entertainment medium that offered African American artists travel opportunities and employment in black-managed theater spaces before predominantly black audiences.

With early antecedents stretching back to pre-1910 Memphis circuits, 1920's T.O.B.A. consisted of interracially owned and managed theaters that booked entertainers into a circuit stretching across the Southeast and Midwest. It reached its height in the mid-1920s, when it included nearly one hundred theaters, and met its end during the Great Depression in 1931. The circuit is familiar to theater historians, popular culture scholars, and jazz, blues, and black musical theater fans, and is mentioned in discussions of African American entertainment origins. Such well-known artists as vocalists Alberta Hunter, Ethel Waters, and Bessie Smith; dancers Bill "Bojangles" Robinson and Clayton "Peg Leg" Bates; and musicians William "Count" Basie and Cab Calloway all honed their crafts on T.O.B.A.'s training grounds before breaking into the recording industry, Broadway, or film. Ultimately, T.O.B.A. served as an essential vehicle for the promotion and transmission of professional live African American entertainment across much of the 1920s United States, except for the West Coast.

Memories and myths of the circuit and its entertainers abound in artist biographies and documentaries. T.O.B.A.'s historical moment has been revisited in musical theater revues, like 1976's *Bubbling Brown Sugar*, 1999's *Rollin' on the T.O.B.A.*,

**T. O. B. A.**
(Theater Owners' Booking Association)
**ALL ACTS, COMPANIES and THEATER MANAGERS**
Communicate with the
**T. O. B. A.**
Suite 442-3-4 Volunteer Life Bldg. CHATTANOOGA, TENN.
SAM E. REEVIN, Manager, Suite 442-3-4 Volunteer Life Building, Chattanooga, Tenn.,
or S. H. DUDLEY, 1223 Seventh Street, N. W., Washington, D. C.

FIGURE 1. T.O.B.A. ad, *Chicago Defender*, May 27, 1922.

and Broadway's 2016 reimagining of *Shuffle Along*, one of the first modern all-black musicals of the early 1920s.[9] T.O.B.A. dancer Peg Leg Bates recalled black audiences and entertainers but mistakenly believed that there were no black theater owners on the circuit, although a third of T.O.B.A.'s owners were African American. Music and theater aficionados incorrectly associate the mid-twentieth-century "chitlin circuit" of juke joints, clubs, and concert spaces that ushered in the careers of many blues, R&B, and rock musicians with the institution, but these venues were not the same as T.O.B.A. theaters. Biographical pieces on comedians, like Dewey "Pigmeat" Markham and Jackie "Moms" Mabley, chronicle the rich experiences of black life that served as their acts' bases but attribute the origins of the circuit to a white-owned agency created in 1907 by F. A. Barrasso that bore little resemblance to 1920s T.O.B.A.[10]

Numerous scholars have chronicled black vaudeville's general development in larger studies of African American theater and entertainment.[11] More recently, T.O.B.A. itself is specifically referred to in black theater texts, cultural histories, and black studies scholarship in discussions of racial and gendered identity politics, the power of black consumer culture between the first and third decades of the 1900s, and the commercial origins of modern blues music.[12] From this vast body of work I build this study of a circuit that provided stages, opportunities, and audiences "for those who could survive the test" of its hardships.[13] Few African American historical narratives distinctly focus on T.O.B.A., an absence I remedy with this chronicle of the black entertainment enterprise.

*T.O.B.A. Time* is a narrative institutional biography that details the origins and business practices of the Theater Owners' Booking Association.[14] It is also a social history that investigates the lived experiences of T.O.B.A. participants and the greater significance of African American vaudeville entertainment in twentieth-century America. While the circuit existed in the 1920s, the conditions that led to its creation developed at the turn of the twentieth century, and the overall scope of the text encompasses the 1890s to the mid-1930s. Drawing from black business history, African American entertainment history, and American popular culture studies, I maintain that, despite negative or mythical portrayals of the institution, T.O.B.A.'s ten-year reign was an incredible feat of black business acumen, black artistic talent, and momentary interracial cooperation amid 1920s America. Quite simply, it was the foundation of twentieth-century black professional entertainment. However, this is not a blindly celebratory history nor a scathing rebuke of the institution. T.O.B.A. was a contradictory organization that *both* empowered and hindered African American men and women entertainers and their entrepreneurial counterparts, onstage and off. Contracted artists often decried T.O.B.A. as an acronym for "Tough on Black Artists" or "Tough on Black Asses" because of its grueling performance pace and pay inequities.[15] But circuit entertainers also lauded the organization as a professional training ground and a community that nurtured black artistic excellence.

This historical study analyzes the circuit as an entity unto itself and recovers the narratives of African American agency in circuit management and theater ownership. I place the organization in the distinct historical context and racial environment of the 1920s, the decade of World War I's aftermath marked by black cultural renaissance, gendered social rebellions, cultural conflict, racial hostility, and generational ideological tensions between a conservative past and an unsettlingly modern present.[16] T.O.B.A. held diverse meanings for various stakeholders, including managers and booking agents, entertainers, and black audiences. I address the perceived lack of criticism of the circuit by examining T.O.B.A. from these participants' distinct perspectives.

By definition T.O.B.A. was a black entertainment *business*, and *T.O.B.A. Time* investigates the industry as such. Yet rather than a strict economic examination of T.O.B.A.'s practices, I investigate the organization against the backdrop of what entrepreneurship and business development signified for early-twentieth-century black America. Early 1900s champions of black business, including W. E. B. Du Bois, Booker T. Washington, and Maggie Lena Walker, saw black economic efforts as a solution to the societal ills that plagued black communities at the turn of the century.[17] These race leaders heralded black entrepreneurship in the aftermath of slavery as inspiring and, in Du Bois's words, a significant "step in social progress worth measuring."[18] Washington particularly contended that successful black entrepreneurs were evidence that African Americans were not shiftless and extravagant nor "vicious and criminal," but a "sober, upright" people who would "gradually advance to all the rights and privileges" of all American citizens.[19] In the first decade of the twentieth century, black women social reformers, like Maggie Lena Walker, also held that the success of black communal reform relied on the strength of independent black financial activities.[20]

I uncover how the T.O.B.A. circuit evolved as an interracially owned, black-serving institution amid the nadir, the low point of black citizenship rights following the end of chattel slavery and the aftermath of Reconstruction.[21] This same era is also what black business historian Juliet E. K. Walker deems as the "golden age of the black business," which saw African Americans at the helm of "million dollar enterprises" made within a segregated "black economy."[22] *T.O.B.A. Time* unearths circuit origins and concentrates on the experiences of black entrepreneurs who shared power with their white counterparts in the circuit's development. Building on the beliefs of Washington and, to a lesser degree Du Bois, the circuit's black founders believed that, as a business, T.O.B.A. could be a vehicle for racial advancement, allowing black theater professionals to have a voice in how, when, where, and why black entertainers performed. This goal was difficult to realize, not because of an inherent ineptitude of black entrepreneurs or a "myth of black business," but because as a black-serving business T.O.B.A. was subject to the same white supremacist violence and economic precarity that plagued its primarily black consumer market.[23] Circuit participant critiques concentrate on the institution's latter years and sharp appraisals of the "unintelligent discrimination, petty jealousy, conceit and (race) prejudice" that contributed to its end.[24] Yet I do not only recount an assumed well-known scenario of how white managers exploited black vaudevillians for economic gain. While I examine the challenges of African American entrepreneurship, I also determine how the circuit achieved success by adopting a tenuous interracial collaboration in an entrepreneurial venture that would not have worked without the coleadership of African American entrepreneurs.[25]

At its heart *T.O.B.A. Time* is a narrative of the foundations of black vaudeville and the African American entertainment industry in the early twentieth century. As T.O.B.A. troupers traveled the country in the 1920s, public discussions arose about the significance of entertainment and the performing arts in black community development. Many of these debates involved questions of how black artistic excellence could help eradicate the growing problems of racial inequality and violence and demonstrate that African Americans were worthy of citizenship, a key ideology behind the Harlem Renaissance.[26] A host of artists and intellectuals, including Alain Locke, James Weldon Johnson, Langston Hughes, and Du Bois, published on black culture's importance at the same time T.O.B.A. was at its height.[27] Locke argued that black "creative expression" must "precede the betterment of race relationships." Likewise, Johnson maintained, "through his artistic efforts the Negro" countered negative stereotypes and demonstrated that African Americans were "helping form American civilization."[28] Yet as these discussions persisted, class-based critiques arose within black communities on whether vaudeville, with its "luscious low comedy" and its dances and songs designed to gratify the palette of the "common element," was indeed "art."[29] While Renaissance participants, like Hughes, wrote positively of the "blare of Negro jazz bands" and the "bellowing voice of Bessie Smith singing blues," much of the popular music and comedy that made T.O.B.A. a success stood apart from 1920s Harlem Renaissance definitions of reputable artistic creation.[30] In contrast, I detail how many legendary black entertainers fought for the opportunity to be T.O.B.A. stars and how the circuit nurtured and redefined black artistic excellence in the form of such acts as the energizing tap dancing of the Nicholas Brothers or the powerful blues vocals of Ma Rainey.[31] This focused examination of the T.O.B.A. circuit highlights the arena where black vaudevillian performers developed their artistic crafts and arguably served as arbiters of American popular culture as they became "central" to the "origins, popularity, and forms" of American music, social dance, and comedy.[32]

Vaudeville performance was much more than popular entertainment for the masses. I use familiar themes in popular culture studies concerning the divisions between high-brow and low-brow culture and the connections between leisure and the consumer marketplace to further examine how T.O.B.A. reflected African American communal life in the 1920s. Gillian Rodger, Richard Butsch, and LeRoy Ashby have each examined American popular culture and variety, or vaudeville, as an entity that has the ability to "reflect and shape the larger society" and often captures the struggles between societal "outsiders and insiders."[33] For audiences, T.O.B.A. performances allowed working-class African Americans to see themselves reflected onstage. Black audience members often viewed a T.O.B.A. show as a needed moment of leisure, and an afternoon or evening performance helped them realize moments of escape, self-definition, and personal freedom. As dancer

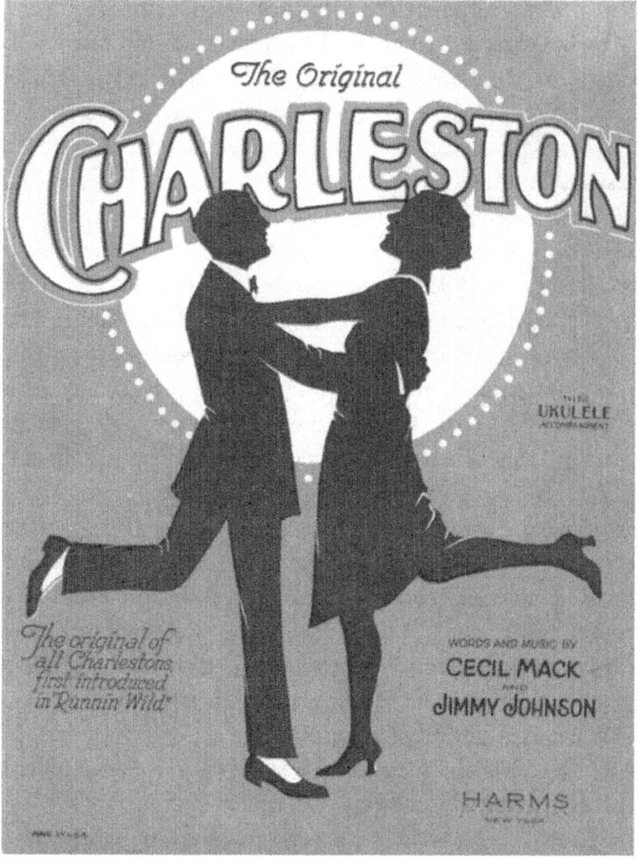


FIGURE 2. "Charleston" sheet music, 1920, Sam DeVincent Collection of Illustrated American Sheet Music, Archives Center, National Museum of American History, Smithsonian Institution.

Bessie Dudley recounted in the opening when she watched the Lincoln Theatre's performances, she made a ritual of going to the show with her classmates and imagining herself onstage. For those hours Bessie was not a young girl living with her grandmother because her mother was too ill to care for her; she was a "Charleston" dancing star.[34] Circuit entertainers mirrored the inner desires, hopes, and aspirations of many of their audience members, and *T.O.B.A. Time* chronicles these exchanges between black vaudeville artists and audiences.[35]

Region and place are characters within this text as much as the artists upon the stage. I investigate T.O.B.A. theaters as spaces where African Americans challenged racial oppression, gender discrimination, and economic decline.[36] How a T.O.B.A. entertainer physically navigated the circuit depended on where their contracted theater was located and the artistic tastes of that region. The black-owned actor's hotel in Washington, DC, might be nonexistent in Galveston, Texas. Chicago had a whole black enclave of institutions near their T.O.B.A. theaters, whereas Macon, Georgia, had one or two restaurants and one hotel open for African Americans. Ultimately, region also proves significant, as I highlight that black vaudeville with T.O.B.A. was not a New York–centered story, as are many narratives of Harlem Renaissance–era artistic production, but rather a story of the Midwest and Southeast.[37]

Collecting the fragments of T.O.B.A.'s narrative has been a formidable task. Unlike the records of large, white-managed corporations, there is no singular archive or collection of T.O.B.A. management accounts. Aside from four valuable boxes of T.O.B.A. documents saved within the Middle Georgia Archives in Macon, Georgia, materials are scattered across the country and initially may not appear to be directly related to T.O.B.A.'s story. For instance, my queries about how black entertainers safely travelled the circuit in the segregated South were fueled in part by ferry ticket stubs and railroad schedules mounted in a white vaudevillian's fragile scrapbook. Although some primary sources are digitized, many are not, making the process of tracking the circuit's origins a far-reaching historical treasure hunt. The stories of the power executive board members or managers wielded to book performers, market acts, and franchise theaters were gleaned from archival records of rarely explored financial reports of theater management executives, annual corporation reports, personal correspondence, advertisements for theater support industries, tax documents, and probate records held in Tennessee, Georgia, and Washington, DC.

As *T.O.B.A. Time* is also a social history of a black entertainment enterprise, I located the stories of the entertainers who fleshed out the circuit's onstage efforts. To examine the lived experiences of theater entertainers in a popular culture medium that cannot be recaptured in its original form, I explored entertainment ephemera in physical archives in Georgia, New York, Texas, and Washington,

DC. I combed through scrapbooks, theater playbills, photos, advertisements, contracts, entertainment oral histories (many held at the Smithsonian's National Museum of American History, Emory University's Manuscript, Archives, and Rare Book Library, and the Schomburg Center for Research in Black Culture), memoirs, census and city directories, maps, vaudeville scripts, sheet and recorded music, film clips, and most prominently, black newspapers and magazines. Once cross-referenced with correspondence or genealogical data, the 1920s black press vividly depicted the early-twentieth-century black entertainment world in theater reviews, routing schedules, advertisements, and gossip columns.

The following chapters are divided thematically and chronologically and survey all aspects of T.O.B.A. life and its origins in the twentieth century's first three decades. The debates concerning the need for an all-black-serving theater circuit managed by black businessmen started in the black entertainment community decades before T.O.B.A. theaters opened. Chapter 1 begins with the rise of vaudevillian and future T.O.B.A. founder Sherman H. Dudley, who publicly called for a black-owned circuit in 1907. Alongside Dudley, the chapter chronicles the backgrounds of black theater managers Charles Turpin, John. T. Gibson, and Emma Griffin, whose individual plans for black-owned vaudeville theaters and circuits in the 1910s led them to contribute to T.O.B.A.'s management structure in the 1920s. Each theater professional attributed sociopolitical power to black-owned entertainment spaces and saw success in black vaudeville as "race work," a larger belief in using the labors and economic rewards of a venture to benefit the uplift of black communities.[38] Through Dudley, Gibson, Turpin, and Griffin's entrepreneurial origins, I illuminate the early-twentieth-century deliberations over whether black theater circuits would be best managed by all-black or interracial entrepreneurial coalitions. These 1910s discussions of the cultural and economic significance of black vaudeville were an essential part of the creation of the T.O.B.A. circuit. The conversations also predated many of the Harlem Renaissance debates about the purpose of art and entertainment in early-twentieth-century black communities and a growing need to have African American theater productions that were "about" black life written "by" black authors "for" black audiences showcased in theaters "near" black communities, as Du Bois expressed in 1926.[39]

While black theater professionals actively debated the social and economic magnitude of black-owned theater spaces, white theater professionals sought economic power as the managers of black-serving vaudeville theaters. Chapter 2 explores the interplay between Jewish immigrant and African American theater professionals in management of black vaudeville between 1910 and 1919. The chapter unearths the professional backgrounds of Chicago's Martin Klein, Chattanooga's Sam Reevin, and Nashville's Milton Starr, Jewish immigrants who joined Dudley and Turpin as T.O.B.A. board members by 1921. To challenge the narrative that T.O.B.A. Time was solely the product of white management and black labor, I examine how Reevin, Starr, and Klein's immigrant and ethnic identities influenced their involvement in T.O.B.A. leadership and chronicle the coalitions they established with black theater managers and black communities just prior to T.O.B.A.'s success.[40] I also explore pivotal moments of ethnic and racial clash in these coalitions.

T.O.B.A. was officially chartered in December 1920 during a frenzied battle among various vaudeville corporations on how to best profit from the centralization of black vaudeville. Chapter 3 examines the economic motivations for creating T.O.B.A. and determines how successful the institution was as a black-serving *business.* After merging with a competing vaudeville circuit, T.O.B.A. established its three regional headquarters, developed a multiracial executive board, and planned to capture a market of black Southerners who remained in the region even after many black migrants relocated to the urban North. By acquiring new theater franchises and following blues music's rising popularity, the circuit rose to new heights by 1925. Yet in this same season, the Colored Actors' Union arose, arguably created in part to contend with the acute labor and civil rights difficulties black entertainers encountered despite T.O.B.A.'s management success.

Artists like swing band leader Cab Calloway, actress Hattie McDaniel, and dancer Peg Leg Bates all successfully contended with T.O.B.A.'s many gendered, racial, and class challenges on their journeys to stardom. In chapter 4 I concentrate on T.O.B.A.'s acts and use the personal recollections of T.O.B.A. entertainers to investigate why being a theater entertainer was such a coveted career, as well as probe the many meanings of "tough" on black actors.[41] For many artists, T.O.B.A. was not only a centralized booking system but rather the primary gateway to American Jazz Age entertainment. Despite auditions, rehearsals, segregated travel, racial violence, and censorship and respectability battles, T.O.B.A. provided a foundational home that sustained "show business crazy" black entertainers. Black vaudevillians endured the "tough" of T.O.B.A. because of its potential for fame, fortune, travel, and the "on-the-job" artistic training that, for African Americans, could not be found anywhere else in the American entertainment industry.

Much of the circuit's prosperity was fostered by the growth of small black businesses in the communities in which T.O.B.A. theaters resided. Chapter 5 views the circuit through the lens of T.O.B.A. audiences and urban black communities. Using a composite of the T.O.B.A. touring schedules of jazz pianist and band leader William "Count" Basie, actor Clarence Muse, actress and vocalist Ethel Waters, and others, I determine how the circuit functioned as an African American entrepreneurial venture within local segregated economies in cities like Chicago, Chattanooga, or Washington, DC. The circuit fostered a reciprocal relationship between its theaters and entertainers and the black communication, transportation, and hospitality industries that catered to the unique needs of T.O.B.A.'s traveling shows.

In October 1927 one of the first sound motion pictures, *The Jazz Singer,* marked a technology shift in American entertainment and coincided with the eventual decline of the vaudeville industry. Chapter 6 documents T.O.B.A. between the 1926–27 season and the onset of the Great Depression. As managers divided their attentions and capital between vaudeville and the growing film industry, black vaudevillians weathered dwindling audiences and found their contracts for forty weeks of continuous billing reduced to ten. Ultimately, T.O.B.A. participant public scandals, managerial infighting, increased segregation in white theater spaces, and economic decline contributed to the close of the circuit.

T.O.B.A.'s end occurred during a production increase of independent, all-black, early sound "race films"; large Hollywood film productions; and popular nightclub revues. Many T.O.B.A. artists, like Bessie Dudley and Leonard Reed, were recast as black Hollywood's ingénues, character actors, or cabaret stars by the mid-1930s. At its conclusion, this study returns to the few preserved 1920s theaters that hosted black vaudeville over a century ago and explores the Theater Owners' Booking Association's legacy in the black entertainment industry in the United States.

# 1

# "WHISTLING COONS" NO MORE

## *Race Uplift & the Path to T.O.B.A.*

> the funniest of all I know
> Is a colored individual as sure as you're alive . . .
> You can talk until you're tired but you'll never get a word
> From this very funny queer old coon . . .
> but he's happy when he whistles in tune.
>
> —George W. Johnson, lyrics to "The Whistling Coon," 1891

> They [colored minstrels] are fast gaining a reputation all over the United States as performers supported by a gentlemanly manner, which is the crown of success . . .
>
> —"The Stage," *The Freeman*, December 18, 1897

Famed minstrel comedian Sherman H. Dudley stood in admiration after he watched the Smart Set show accompanied by the Pekin Stock Company in November 1906. It was not that he was unfamiliar with antics or skits onstage, as he had performed with the Smart Set troupe intermittently since 1904.[1] Rather, it was the sight of an all-black troupe, where "all the plays are written, staged, and produced by Negroes," in a Chicago black-owned theater performing before a predominantly black audience that garnered Dudley's amazement. "Never," Dudley remarked in *The Freeman*, had he "felt so proud of being a colored man" [on] November 23, 1906, "in the only recognized Negro theatre in the world, the Pekin."[2]

Dudley spoke not only of the onstage spectacle, but of the successful entrepreneurial efforts of African Americans at the cusp of the twentieth century. He noted that the Pekin was "a revelation [that showed] just what Negroes can and must do in the near future. . . . Let us hope that in the future every city will have its Pekin."[3] Dudley's enthusiasm for building black-owned theaters across the country was in part due to the awareness he had about the significance of entertainment in shaping the "public identity" of African Americans in the new century.[4] Espoused by race leaders, like Booker T. Washington, Dudley believed the ideology that black entrepreneurship could foster stable and quasi-self-sufficient black communities.

The path to 1920s T.O.B.A. actually began in the 1910s by the hands of a small cohort of black men and women who shared Dudley's passion. This chapter uncovers the efforts of Sherman H. Dudley, Charles H. Turpin, John T. Gibson, and Emma Griffin and the "perfect storm" of socioeconomic motivations that led to black-managed vaudeville.[5] Personal biographical narratives of these theater professionals reveal the ways that race, region, and gender all played a role in the development of T.O.B.A.'s foundation.[6] Each individual was born in the Southern United States near the close of Reconstruction, migrated to burgeoning urban areas near the turn of the twentieth century, and navigated their respective region's rise of increasing racial discrimination. For these vaudevillian entrepreneurs, involvement in black popular entertainment was race work, and they defined themselves as "race" men and women—African Americans dedicated to the uplift and advancement of the black race as a whole amid white supremacist threats of subjugation and repression.[7] Despite encouraging the masks of the happy, carefree, "funniest" individuals as described in "The Whistling Coon," these black theater professionals hoped to use their craft for the greater good of centering African Americans within the business and art of black vaudeville and achieving the "crown of success."

## VAUDEVILLE'S ORIGINS

The drive for autonomous black theater circuits should be seen in the context of the popularity of American vaudeville more broadly. As a genre, American variety and, later, vaudeville theater had been initially popular in Northeastern states. Gillian Rodger notes that variety theater, as vaudeville's immediate predecessor, was born in the 1840s and '50s for a predominantly white, working-class audience and consisted of "miscellaneous amusements" of song, dance, and comedy.[8] Theater historians often note "the dean" or "godfather" of vaudeville as Tony Pastor and acknowledge his establishment of the Tony Pastor's Opera House in New York City in 1865 as the beginning of a move toward "family friendly" variety theater.[9] The beginning of "modern vaudeville" was marked by Boston native Benjamin Franklin "B. F." Keith's efforts in the 1880s to make variety performances more respectable, inclusive of both male and female audiences, and "continuous," with daytime matinees and evening performances.[10] Anywhere from ten to twenty acts could play a matinee or evening's performance and could feature solo musicians, child dancers, animal acts, comedy vignettes, ragtime or blues singers, and anything else in between.[11] A July performance at Tony Pastor's Broadway theater in 1879 brought the "Trick High Kicking" dancing of Sylvester and Everett, the songs of "male soprano" Frank Osborne, and the "tambourine, juggling, spinning" act of The Arnold Brothers. Vaudeville music included novelty song, ballads, brass band music, ragtime, and the precursors to early Broadway musical melodies.[12]

By the first decade of the twentieth century, vaudeville, with its "sole existence" to "give the people what they want," was also one of the most *profitable* forms of American live entertainment.[13] Vaudeville theaters could be found in nearly every city or town throughout the North, Midwest, and West, and although independently owned theaters existed, vaudeville performance was centralized in the late 1890s. By 1907 a conglomerate of managers from the Keith-Albee theaters in New York, the Western Vaudeville Managers Association in Chicago, and the Orpheum Circuit in San Francisco controlled these national theater circuits and formed the United Booking Office (UBO).[14] White theater managers wrote in 1909, with surprise and praise, that in "vaudeville today . . . receipts of $15,000 *a week* are not uncommon; even in ordinary cities like Detroit, the one Vaudeville Theater earns a profit in excess of $150,000 *a year*." A circuit of theaters like Morris Meyerfeld's Orpheum Circuit represented "a cash value of ten million dollars."[15] At the start of the 1912–13 season, the five male leaders of big-time white vaudeville, including E. F. Albee, B. F. Keith, Morris Meyerfeld, Martin Beck, and Percy Williams, could each individually earn between seven million and ten million dollars annually in profit.[16]

Large financial success did not always transfer to the ordinary singer or slack wire performer. The average salary for a basic act depended on its popularity and could range from approximately thirty to sixty dollars for a single novelty performer to $100–$200 for a multiperformer acrobatic act per weekly performance.[17] Artists could perform up to six days a week and play two performances an evening with a matinee on Sundays. As an example of the payment range and the disparity between management and entertainment earnings, a top-billed white headliner in the early twentieth century could receive as much as $2,000 to $4,000 a week on a large circuit, while smaller acts might earn $225 a week and be required to pay for transportation, lodging, costumes, and booking fees from that salary, leaving them with perhaps a third of their earnings after expenses.[18]

Where did African American entertainers fit within the centralization of American vaudeville? Unfortunately, they often found themselves as one or two of the ten to twenty or more acts on a vaudeville playbill. Albeit full of satire and ethnic stereotypes of European and Asian immigrants, African Americans, and Jews, popular culture scholars maintain that vaudeville was a theater of mass consumption for a new ethnically diverse, urban society—a theater of the people and by the people.[19] But one's definition of "the people" differed depending on a theater's ownership or the geographical region. A vaudeville theater in Boston may have seated patrons based on how much customers could afford to pay, with the crowd divided into twenty-five-, fifty-, or seventy-five-cent admission seats. Yet a theater in Norfolk, Virginia, would only allow black customers at a comedy like "King Rastus" to watch from the segregated "gallery for colored people."[20] An all-black act might be included in the playbill of a theater's offerings but featured near the top of the show or the close of the evening. The longer the playbill was, the less the likelihood that an audience might stay to watch performers who played at the very beginning or the end of the bill.[21] For example, in February 1902 when Larkins & Patterson, "a colored couple" of singers who "weren't very good" nor "that bad," played the Providence Theatre, they earned an "early place" on the bill and were the only black act on a bill of ten performers.[22]

While an African American performer could rise to the level of headliner in New York or San Francisco circuits, a "black star" was a rare sighting in white-produced vaudeville. When the future legendary black comedian Ernest Hogan successfully played two Pastor Theatre shows in New York in 1902, hundreds of other black acts were waiting in the wings of a "big-time" theater for the next big break on the playbill.[23] The odds of actually getting to the stage as a black performer increased if those who controlled the doors, advertising, and profits were African American theater professionals.

## BLACK CIRCUIT PRECURSORS

Black-owned theaters of the era that showcased vaudeville included Pat Chappelle's Buckingham Theatre Saloon in Tampa and black financier Robert Reed Church's Park and Auditorium in Memphis, which opened in 1899 and 1901, respectively. Yet when Robert Motts, saloon owner and gambling profiteer, opened the Pekin Theatre in Chicago in 1904, it was one of the more notable black-owned theaters of the early twentieth century.[24] Plans for a black-owned theater in Chicago had been publicized as early as 1901, when black investors of the Northwestern Mutual Life Insurance Company discussed opening Havlin's Theatre.[25] But Havlin's Theatre did not materialize, and Motts took up the initiative on his own three years later. Lauded in death as "a giant in the business and theatrical world among both races," Motts used his gambling income to transform his saloon at 2700 State Street into what would be characterized as "the finest and the largest playhouse conducted by Afro-Americans in the United States."[26] Fire destroyed the original wooden Pekin Theatre in 1905, but by March 1906 the New Pekin opened on Chicago's 27th and State Streets and featured an all-black stock company and African American front managers, stage managers, and ticket-takers. The chances for black employment backstage, onstage, and in the management office abounded with the Pekin's existence, and Motts advertised the establishment as the only "properly equipped Theatre" "owned, managed, and controlled by colored promoters."[27] The Pekin was home to Shelton Brooks, black composer of popular music standards, and hosted black comedians and producers Flournoy Miller and Aubrey Lyles who were "the talk of the town."[28] Robert Motts's modern, "extraordinary," 1,200-seat arena was marketed as an "up to date family theater" that was fully "fireproof" and the most "elegant amusement house on the South Side."[29] While city directories listed other black-serving venues as "5 and 10 cent" amusements, the Pekin was a *theater* in the grand sense, advertised as being funded by "Negro capital and built and equipped entirely by Negro skill and workmen."[30] Thomas Bauman notes that while some elite members of black Chicago society initially refused to patronize the theater and criticized Motts for his ownership of saloons and other vice institutions, Motts overcame many of his detractors and moved "further and further from the notoriety" of his past. For many, the Pekin was a hallmark black Chicago entrepreneurial institution and was a testament to black agency within the vaudeville and dramatic world during its run between 1905 and 1911.[31]

The Pekin was a promising effort in black theater ownership and theater arts education, but the need for a chain of black theaters across the country, particularly in the South, still remained.[32] Prior to the Great Migration of 1915–1940, 89 percent of the nation's African American population lived in urban and rural Deep South and South Atlantic states.[33] Hundreds of black minstrel troupes, circuses, and brass bands traveled through these regions, but many of the groups' black performers were contracted through white-owned and white-managed institutions that did not or could not speak to the unique needs of African American performers. Before one uttered a note or made a dancing gesture, early twentieth-century black artists were thrust into a world of applause and acclaim, ridicule and judgment, and contended with humiliations of segregated travel and inequitable pay and the dangers of racial violence and discrimination.

A circuit was a chain of theaters that shared the same management structure and pay scale, which allowed an artist to be employed for a season without having to negotiate a separate contract at each individual theater. Without some sort of central organizing structure, in midtravel to a performance, a theatrical agency could send an individual artist an urgent telegram asking that one "kindly acknowledge receipt of change in dates . . . you understand that Rockford and Freeport are cancelled" and not offer any compensation to make up these missing performances. In 1901, the Nashville Students, a black minstrel and vaudeville company, was abandoned midseason when their female producer, "an elderly maiden of Chicago," pulled their funds, leaving "twenty-one (actors), all stars" with nothing but a soon-to-be repossessed Pullman railcar and a "hope that they may not starve before someone with money to risk appears."[34] The centralization of black vaudeville could diminish many of these disastrous instances and could be achieved by black theater professionals who had personally survived vaudeville's challenges. By 1907 black vaudevillian and producer Sherman H. Dudley publicly made plans to lead this charge.

## SHERMAN H. DUDLEY

The origin story for the man who music scholars argued "paved the way for the T.O.B.A." is reminiscent of the migration narratives of many of the black performing artists born in the Reconstruction era.[35] Sherman Henry Dudley was born in 1872 to Margaret and Alford Dudley in the Southeast United States. Census reports, estate records, and obituaries dispute whether Dudley was born in Bossier City, Louisiana; Jonesville, Louisiana; or Dallas, Texas.[36] With Sherman as their only living child, the Dudleys resided and worked in Bossier County, Louisiana, by 1880. The Dudleys were semiliterate day laborers who lived in a neighborhood of other black farmers, servants, cooks, blacksmiths, and domestics.[37] By 1888 sixteen-year-old Sherman appeared as a full-time service worker in "his old hometown" of Dallas, Texas, alongside his then unmarried mother, Margaret Dudley. Until the mid-1890s Sherman worked in a variety of domestic service positions in Dallas and Galveston, working for French immigrant banker Jean Baptiste Adoue or as a porter in local saloons.[38] In each of these instances Dudley grew accustomed to serving the elite guests of local financiers and acquired further literacy and organizational skills.

In the midst of all of this daily toil as an invisible manual laborer, Dudley's first exposure to traveling entertainment was a medicine show in Shreveport, Louisiana.[39] Medicine shows were a predominant form of pharmaceutical advertising between the 1850s and early 1930s and told audiences throughout the country, especially in the South and Midwest, of the latest curative product. A medicine company tasked entertainers to lure a crowd into an outdoor tented performance. After a few songs and comedic skits, a show's proprietor, appearing as a learned doctor or professor, came out to hawk his product with his pitch and chants of "Step right up and buy not one, but two bottles of the wonder cure, suitable for your entire household."[40] Occasionally a prearranged "miracle" cure of a customer's ailment that occurred moments after taking just sips of a potion would be the highlight of the night's advertisement.[41] Before the passage of 1906's Pure Food and Drug Act, the products marketed by medicine shows often had little to no true medicinal value and could contain alcohol, colored water, mineral oil, or potentially poisonous substances.[42] Nonetheless, the showmanship of Hamlin's Wizard Oil or the Kickapoo Indian Medicine Company promised audiences that all ailments would be healed with just a few sips of a magical elixir.[43] The Kickapoo Indian Medicine Company hired Dudley in the mid-1890s, and he honed his early comedic skills by working on the "ballyhoo," the preshow that drew customers into the tent for the sale.[44] The sights and sounds of the ballyhoo, the pitch, and the attention of the large crowds all served as precursors to Dudley's place on the stage.

By the late 1890s, Dudley became embedded in the Texas entertainment scene and drew upon the comedic timing acquired as medicine show performer and the organizational talents perfected as a domestic servant. The People's Theater in Houston, Texas, hired him as the stage manager for a black minstrel show in 1895, and he performed as a minstrel at the Olympic Theater in Galveston, Texas, by 1899.[45] Blackface minstrelsy was one of the most popular and profitable entertainment genres between the 1830s and 1910s. In its initial format minstrelsy was an entertainment genre of the Northeastern United States and consisted of ten to twelve white male performers who sang and danced about fictional depictions of black enslaved laborers, all while heavily masked in burnt cork black makeup and overpainted red lips. While its comedic and musical content commented on local labor concerns, political battles, or even interpersonal relationship conflicts, at the center of a nineteenth-century blackface performance was the skill involved in maintaining a "blackface" or achieving "a close imitation of the Negro" with all the stereotypes of black people's mannerisms, character, and alleged "slow wit."[46]

Cultural theorists have noted that the antebellum nineteenth-century genre was "a ground of American racial negotiation and contradiction," as audience members were attracted to the aspects of black culture they glimpsed through blackface characters but often had no connection to, or even great disdain for, actual black people.[47] In the aftermath of slavery, minstrelsy's depictions of blackness and its mythologies of enslaved African Americans carried over into other popular culture song, advertising, and social dance that were often used to justify a restoration of a pre-emancipation racial hierarchy.[48] By the late 1860s and '70s, minstrel shows became full-fledged spectacles containing circus elements, animal acts, full brass bands, operatic choruses, and clog dancers. The largest change to the genre came in the post–Civil War era with the entrance of African American entertainers who, marketed as "genuine Negro" or colored minstrels, also "blacked up" in burnt cork.[49] From white-managed, black participant troupes, like Haverly's Minstrels, the Famous Georgia Minstrels, the W. A. Mahara's Minstrels, and the Primrose and West troupes, came the "finest aggregations of colored minstrels" ever seen who performed songs that were "Sung Where Ever the Sun Shines on Civilization," according to hyperbolic handbill materials.[50]

In many of Dudley's performances, he abided by the minstrel stage traditions and blacked up. Wearing blackface often meant that African American minstrels perpetuated many of the genre's negative stereotypes about black people as lazy, unintelligent, untrustworthy, and inferior beings. Yet the genre also allowed black entertainers to travel and entertain for an often sizeable income. Black minstrel and future blues composer William Christopher "W. C." Handy argued that "historians of the American stage have slighted the old [actual] Negro minstrels while making much of the burnt cork artists who imitated them" and contended that minstrelsy afforded black entertainers a place to display their art.[51] In addition to intermittent success in the larger classical or religious music world, blackface minstrelsy was one of the few professional avenues for black artists of the mid-nineteenth century and "the composers, the singers, the musicians, the speakers, the stage performers—the minstrel shows got them all."[52] The medium-statured, medium-complexioned Dudley cast blackface aside in many of his professional headshots and, as a theater professional, created his own Texas-based Dudley's Georgia Minstrels in the 1890s. He adopted the "Georgia" label to alert audiences that his small ensemble was an authentic "colored" minstrel troupe.[53]

In late 1897 Dudley's efforts warranted national attention, and he was cast in P. T. Wright's Nashville Students and Colored Comedy Company.[54] A long-standing troupe with a twenty-year run in the late nineteenth century, the Students made P. T. Wright's name "a household word in every nook and cranny of this continent."[55] Soon after becoming part of the company, Dudley built on his Texas experiences and became the Nashville Students' stage manager. Known for his "wide-spread reputation" and "an active brain," Dudley wowed crowds and theater critics alike with his singing and reorganization of the Nashville Students' repertoire.[56]

Rapidly working up the entertainment hierarchy, Dudley added musical arranging to his stage management and comedic skills, making himself indispensable to the groups he worked with for with his off- and onstage contributions. Reportedly he did everything from "playing the trap drum in the monster street parade to leading comedy stunts 'on the end.'"[57] He simultaneously crafted his image as a blackface comedian, crooning tunes like "Done Said All I Had to Say," with his role as an entrepreneur who created "unique and original conceptions."[58] Dudley traveled the standard minstrel circuit with the Nashville Students and worked with independent shows during the summer seasons, including a 1901 stint on the white B. F. Keith circuit.

In 1902 Dudley joined the white-owned, black minstrel group Richards and Pringle's (R&P) Famous Georgia Minstrels as a comedian and stage manager. Dudley was hired to rehabilitate the show's onstage content and public image in the aftermath of the violent death of company member and trombonist Louis T. Wright at the hands of a Missouri mob. While the details cannot be fully chronicled here, white townsmen in New Madrid, Missouri, lynched Wright on February 17, 1902, for allegedly cursing at local white youth in response to their harassing antics and racial slurs. Wright's murder became national news and remained in the media throughout much of the year. Dudley joined the troupe that October as the group mourned its loss and attempted to rebuild its image.[59] Much of Dudley's urgency in transforming black vaudeville can be attributed in part to his time with R&P and the belief that the creation of a black theater circuit might offer black performers stability, safety, and perhaps protection from racial violence.

Pausing during this professional climb, Dudley married fellow entertainer, Ohio-born Alberta Mae Ormes. Born in 1879 in Warren, Ohio, Ormes's rise to fame did not appear quite as arduous as Dudley's. A fair-skinned African American chorus girl, or "soubrette," and vocalist, Ormes emerged in black musical revues in the late 1890s and early 1900s. Early reviews in industry periodicals praised her rapid success in just two years "before the footlights."[60] Dudley and Ormes met as cast mates in white producer John Isham's *King Rastus*, "a serio-operatic comedy surprise," in the summer of 1900.[61] Ormes performed with *King Rastus* until it folded in May 1901 and continued to be a featured player in many of the same playbills as Dudley even after their 1902 marriage.[62] In publicity material Ormes initially included her maiden and married names and won praise in her own right as a "sweet singer and graceful dancer" apart from her husband. Ormes became Dudley's vital but quiet partner, allowing him to establish a family in Chicago with the birth of their son Sherman H. Dudley Jr. while he simultaneously ventured out to explore the growing black vaudeville world.[63] Dudley's image as a stable family man would benefit his later efforts to market black vaudeville as respectable entertainment worthy of financial investment.

The years between 1903 and 1912 marked an era of increased performance and entrepreneurial activity for Dudley. He was involved in various projects, including Texas vaudeville shows, Chicago black businesses, and theatrical productions in New York City.[64] Black theater journalists crafted the narrative of Dudley as a consummate showman onstage and a skilled black businessman offstage. In a review of the Famous Georgia Minstrels, Nagol Mot commented, "without a doubt, S.H. Dudley is one of the best comedians on the stage. His droll wit, his genuine humor and refreshing eccentricities, is exemplified in everything he says or does, and he compels his audience to laugh in 'self defence' [*sic*]."[65]

When Gus Hill's Smart Set, one of the nation's largest black traveling troupes, needed an immediate substitute for its ill headliner, Tom McIntosh, Dudley subsequently began performing intermittently with the nationally lauded company and won a permanent role after McIntosh's death in late 1904.[66] Just as he refashioned the bill of the Nashville Students, Dudley did the same with the Smart Set Company. According to Lynn Abbott and Doug Seroff, the Smart Set troupe was "a singular vehicle for constructive change," as it bridged the gap between traditional minstrel troupes and more "pure vaudeville" and created a company that showcased "Vaudevillized Minstrels," which lasted over forty years.[67] Again, Dudley did not just perform, but very quickly began to write, manage, and produce annual playbills for the traveling Smart Set shows, starting with *The Black Politician* in 1904 and continuing through *Dr. Beans From Boston* in 1912. He increased the novelty aspect of his blackface musical skits by adding Patrick, his mule, to his act, which became a hallmark in Dudley's self-marketing.[68]

Throughout the Smart Set years Dudley never stopped working, not even when he produced independent works, like *Jolly Ethiopians* or off-Broadway black musical revues that fell in with popular "coon song."[69] Coon song, a subset of vocal ragtime songs, began in the 1890s and was named after a derogatory Southern term for African Americans: "coon," short for "raccoon."[70] These comedic songs were full of stereotypical images and language about black communities that often proved to be utterly racist in their humor. Prevalent themes included descriptions of violent, razor-toting black men; fair-skinned, sexually promiscuous African American women; and gambling, alcohol use, social mishaps, and unrequited love scenarios. The coon song increasing in popularity just as segregation became more prevalent in the 1890s speaks to popular culture's attempts to "standardize the stereotypical profile" of African Americans. Many black community members rightly argued that the genre failed to represent African Americans as diverse, moral, upright citizens and further fueled many of the negative depictions of blackness that were used to justify segregation and racial oppression as it was being federally sanctioned.[71] Yet, coon song was prominent until the 1910s on both white and black stages, and while white lyricists were the majority of the genre's writers, black professional lyricists also briefly capitalized on the phenomenon.

Dudley composed the music for his own coon songs, including "Mr. Coon, You'se Too Black for Me" and "Dat Coon Done Put the Rollers Under Me," although he moved away from these stereotypical compositions as he became more heavily involved with the Smart Set productions.[72] Early recordings of Dudley's novelty tunes appeared in Victor and Edison phonograph catalogs in 1906, which allowed Dudley to join the ranks of other black entertainers, like vaudevillians George W. Johnson, Bert Williams, and George Walker, in experimenting with the new medium of recorded sound.[73] Yet for all the apparent frivolity onstage or the mocking tunes on record, Dudley was a master at gaining access to the power of theater organization behind the scenes.

## *"With the Eye of a Prophet": The Plans for a Dudley Circuit*

Dudley set forth plans for a black theater circuit in 1907, just a year after watching the Smart Set at the Pekin. His efforts were preceded by Florida-based black theater professional Pat Chappelle and his plans to "revolutionize vaudeville" through black-operated vaudeville touring companies in 1900. Chappelle's efforts in Florida were not fully realized, and Dudley in part picked up his mantle in Chicago.[74] In a key interview in the *Indianapolis Freeman*, the writers described Dudley as "a modest, unassuming gentleman, genial in temperament and well-versed upon all the topics of the day . . . willing to descant eloquently upon the merits of his fellow professionals." After ten years as a professional, "with the eye of a prophet," Dudley confidently outlined the possibility of "a chain of Negro theatres, controlled by a syndicate of Negro managers, duplicating in every city in the country where there is a considerable colored population, the triumph that is being achieved by the New Pekin in Chicago."[75] Dudley maintained that "white people like pure Negro comedy, up-to-date Negro music and folk lore, so if the entertainment at a Negro house is one of the best quality and good order is maintained, they (whites) would give generous support and of course the Negroes will be there early and often."[76]

As he continued with the Smart Set, this "prophecy" of theater ownership would not leave Dudley's mind. In 1910, courted by Charles Barton, the white new owner of the Smart Set Company, Dudley became a "colored manager" of "three colored companies" and would "organize, produce, and stage all three musical productions" of the Smart Set Company.[77] The *Freeman* acknowledged this transformative moment saying, "just think, these thespian magnates [Barton and Wiswell] will give employment to over one hundred colored performers, and place S.H. Dudley in a position that has *never* been filled by a *colored man* in the history of modern comedy productions."[78] Dudley's move to company manager preceded his becoming a trustee in the newly formed Colored Vaudeville Benevolent Association, or the C.V.B.A., which ensured he had a hand in supplying jobs for black entertainers as well as gathering resources to help black entertainers navigate moments of unemployment and financial hardship.[79]

As an extension of his focus on the betterment of black vaudevillians, Dudley subleased his first theaters and opened a management office. With the profits saved from his management position, crossover appearances with the popular black actress Aida Overton Walker on white vaudeville stages, and the financing of local black business leaders, Dudley eventually fully opened his business in Washington, DC, although his primary residence and family remained in Chicago. Dudley recognized African Americans' ability to expand and control their own theaters, much in the same manner as the white theater syndicates had been doing in Chicago with the Western Vaudeville Managers Association: start with ownership of a few local theaters and build outward. Advertisements in the Spring 1911 issues of the *Indianapolis Freeman* called performers, investors, and managers to "Get Together" in "Oklahoma, Texas, Tennessee, and Georgia, we are booking Theatres in your vicinity." All those who wanted to collaborate in a black circuit could "get in on the ground floor" of what would be Dudley's enterprises.[80] Versions of this advertisement ran intermittently through the rest of 1911 as Dudley amassed a small team to help him bring his vision to fruition.

With Washington, DC, as the hub of his operations, the fledgling "S. H. Dudley Circuit" opened in the summer of 1912. Dudley's "modus operandi" involved cultivating "colored men with money," leasing empty theaters to be "operated by colored men and *not backed by white* men" in cities like Philadelphia, New York, and Chicago but also Southern venues like Baltimore; Washington, DC; and Norfolk, Virginia. The circuit was meant to be an operation of "business men of the race," aimed at keeping the doors open "365 days per year." Dudley planned to use former "white only" motion picture and dime show theaters (discarded because of physical building decline and neighborhood racial demographic shifts), which were a "vast amount of theatrical property" in segregated cities, and refashion them into African American venues.[81]

Wanting to start fresh, perhaps without the Pekin's successes or failures in mind, the District of Columbia was a smaller city to navigate than Chicago.[82] It possessed a burgeoning black community that was near New York but also close enough to the larger black populations of the deep South. The District could be a promising yet risky location to create a national African American theatrical enterprise. In 1903 black theater critic Sylvester Russell outlined geographical plans for black performers' success amid the overt repression in the aftermath of the *Plessy v. Ferguson* segregation decision and did not advise "the brightest performers of the North and West to immigrate South." Rather Russell encouraged Southern performers to develop their talents in the South: "start out [performing] through the West, and end up in Chicago, when they have captured Chicago, it's time enough to think of going East."[83] By 1912 much of Russell's suggestion still proved true, and if artists wanted to reach big-time white circuits, they looked to Chicago and ultimately New York. But Dudley was invested in bringing shows to his black audiences, and a majority of African Americans lived in the South.

Dudley was familiar with the black Washington, DC, theater scene from various performances in the early 1900s.[84] With a black population of over ninety-four thousand people and only fourteen vaudeville and motion picture theaters, the DC move was a sound investment as a hub for a black circuit.[85] The District was home to its own version of the Pekin, the Howard Theatre. While the Baltimore-based, white-operated National Amusements company owned the Howard, within two years of its opening the company hired Andrew Thomas, a black theater professional, as its manager. Built as an alternative to the overcrowded, worn-down venues that segregated African American patrons to a balcony or gallery, the Howard was meant to be a venue that showcased black drama and vaudeville for predominantly black audiences, and it was "one of the most beautiful, modern theaters in Washington."[86] Its opening further cemented Dudley's investment in the city as a location of black business opportunity.

Dudley's first theater in the District was a far cry from the opulence of the Howard and had once been the Minnehaha Theater on 1213 U Street. Dudley only slightly refurbished the stage and seats of the three-year-old building in 1913 and transformed the Minnehaha from "a 5-cent theater building" into the S. H. Dudley Theater.[87] A year later Dudley leased an office at 1853 Seventh Street NW as the headquarters for his theatrical agency, just blocks away from the Howard Theatre.[88] The Seventh Street corridor was home to black-owned and black-serving commercial establishments in the increasingly racially segregated city. The selection of both U Street and Seventh Street fed into Dudley's plans about bringing his ventures to the black communities they served. He laid the cornerstone of his theatrical circuit in the midst of what was a thriving black urban enclave in the early twentieth century.[89]

## *Praise and Critique of the Dudley Circuit*

Soon after Dudley relocated to DC, black community members publicly praised his vision for a black theater circuit. In 1912 *Freeman* reader John R. Thomas wrote to the editor and lauded Dudley's business acumen. Thomas commended Dudley's "long years of experience in the theatrical business" and held faith that Dudley's venture was clear advancement for the "race," as Thomas "never considered any theater that is owned by white men a colored theater."[90] While other Dudley believers joined Thomas, the "Lone Star Comedian" had one prominent detractor: African American theater critic Sylvester Russell.

Briefly a minstrel vocalist with the Al G. Field troupe in the 1890s, Russell was an active theater critic in the black periodicals the *Freeman* and the *Defender*.[91] He labeled himself as the "Foremost Dramatic Critic" regarding all things concerning African American theater and took issue with the proposed Dudley Circuit and with Dudley himself.[92] As Dudley's contemporary, Russell fairly reviewed Dudley's work throughout much of his Smart Set work and independent summer productions. Although not an entrepreneur nor a professional vaudevillian, Russell had his own proposal for black theater advancement that put him at odds with Dudley. Arguing that "we have reached an age where money goes ahead of all things," Russell made his own designs for an integrated "Consolidated Managers Alliance" circuit in which "managers white and colored, should come together and invest."[93] Additionally, Russell thought that Chicago, as a core of the black theatergoing community, should be the hub of his newly proposed circuit, not Washington, DC.[94]

By 1912, when Dudley sought to put his plan into action, Russell readily denounced him in part because of a lack of faith in Dudley's plan but also because of personal animosity between them.[95] Russell demanded that before Dudley receive any more praise, "he has to convince us of three things," which included evidence of dedicated funding; Dudley's ability to work with "men of his race who are *his superiors* in business ability, tact, educational qualifications, and ready wit as essentials to success"; and finally that Dudley incorporate a black theater circuit.[96] Sylvester Russell's objections to Dudley's entrepreneurial ventures stood out and mirrored the white vaudeville landscape that abundantly praised Dudley as "a popular and talented negro comedian" but said little about his potential as a businessman.[97]

Dudley responded to critics primarily through his actions. The S. H. Dudley Circuit opened in the 1912–13 season as a heavily Southern enterprise, managed by "men of the race," and Dudley was the first African American to operate a successfully functioning circuit of black theaters. In August 1912 the Dudley Circuit included theaters in Washington, DC, and Norfolk, Richmond, and Newport News, Virginia. Two months later Dudley expanded to Indianapolis's Crown Theatre; Cleveland's Oriole Theater; Columbus, Ohio's Dunbar; Winston Salem, North Carolina's Rex Theatre; Rex Theater in Wilmington, Delaware; and the Circle Theatre in Philadelphia.[98] As more managers responded to the persisting advertisements in the *Freeman* that remarked "Some are Wise, Some are Otherwise, managers who are *wise* are booking through S. H. Dudley's Theatrical Enterprise," the Dudley Circuit steadily grew.[99] Dudley hired other African American men to manage his theaters and extended employment to a theater's surrounding black community for managers, cashiers, and concessions salespersons.

There was nothing smooth about the growth of the Dudley Circuit. Dudley's business tactics were a combination of economic self-interest and racial uplift work, and they did not always succeed. While African American residents in Chicago commented that "we are glad to see Dudley have such a kindly progressive feeling for his race," Dudley's circuit was not an altruistic mission but meant to be a profit-generating business. He reportedly was "offered $500,000 to work with white theatrical managers but was not selling his interests *yet*."[100] In reflecting on his early years as a theater owner Dudley lost $16,000 in revenue during the first year of his circuit buying theaters in Virginia that were physically substandard and whose houses did not always attract patrons.[101]

Dudley relied on his professional connections and reputation as a veteran performer to transform that difficult first year and grow the circuit. His ability to talk with former castmates and get them to sign on as acts with the Dudley Circuit eventually made him a successful booking agent and theater owner. Dudley continued to publicly recruit African American theater managers using advertisements in the *Freeman* or the *Chicago Defender* and personally cajoled them into supporting the need for a centralized circuit by pointing out the poor salaries and large jumps in between bookings on other circuits. Dudley visited black theaters that were just being built or refurbished, like Nashville's Majestic Theatre, and publicized that, should the theater "come up to standard," he would include it in his growing circuit.[102] The circuit owner also took on occasional jobs as a performer, funneling the profits earned entertaining in the "Frog's Follies" back into the Dudley Circuit.[103]

As "a strong believer in race pride and progress," Dudley confidently observed that no matter what the economic climate, African Americans spent money on amusements and leisure activities, and "with the proper inducements they will see the necessity of supporting their own institutions of all kinds."[104] After a few years of work on the circuit, he booked such acts as the vocalist duo The Griffin Sisters; the Musical Spillers, an instrumentalist ensemble; and a yet-to-be-known vocalist, Bessie Smith, then called "the Southern Nightingale."[105] By 1915, Dudley Enterprises represented the Howard, Dudley, Foraker, Chelsea, and Fairland Theatres in Washington, DC, along with theaters in Detroit, Cincinnati, Louisville, Pittsburg, Philadelphia, and Memphis. In the 1915 *Colored Theatrical Guide and Business Directory of the United States* Dudley promoted his circuit as a racial uplift vehicle, and the guide advertised businesses "whom the Race should Patronize, THOSE WHO MEAN US GOOD."[106] He continued his litany of frank remarks on the urgency for economic race work and spoke of the need to "elevate" the show business in the face of all critics who thought vaudeville was low-brow amusement. In 1916, Dudley purchased the previously white-owned Mid-City Theatre and, after he assured the black public that it had been "taken over by Race people," made its offices his new headquarters.[107] Ultimately, Dudley pushed for "more Race people working and more *Race capitalists* to invest in this field before it is too late."[108]

## CHARLES H. TURPIN

While Dudley laid claim to the Southeast, equally prominent African American entrepreneurs found their way into black vaudeville theater in other regions of the nation. The Dudley Circuit left a good deal of the Midwest open for business, and politician, entrepreneur, and race man Charles H. Turpin worked to fill the needs of that region. More commonly known as "C. H.," Turpin was born between 1870 and 1872 in Columbus, Georgia. Similar to Dudley, Turpin's family also migrated after Reconstruction's close, and St. Louis, Missouri, became the Turpin family's home by 1880.[109] Yet, Turpin himself was no musician or vaudevillian, and black theater ownership became what he used to become more critically engaged in political and economic race work.

John L. (Jack) and Lula Turpin, along with their four children—C. H., Tom "Million," Eleanora, and Nannie—settled on 62 Saint Charles Street in St. Louis in the city's sizeable black enclave in 1880.[110] Although moving frequently, the Turpin family remained together as a tight family unit with all able children working alongside their parents to maintain the household. After Lula Turpin's death in the 1890s, Jack became the primary financial head of household and settled in as a saloon operator. Just six years later, a sixteen-year-old C. H. worked in the saloon alongside his father.[111] Two factors foreshadowed C. H.'s move to black theater management by the 1910s: the organizational experience developed as a city government employee and his financial partnership with brother and ragtime composer, Tom "Million" Turpin. In 1897, the same year Sherman Dudley became a professional minstrel, C. H. moved from saloon laborer to City Assessor's office clerk and worked with real estate assessments and property taxes.[112] A student of a local business college, C. H. Turpin maintained his bookkeeping work at the City Assessor's office for the next three years.[113]

Living near the commercial docks, Turpin navigated a line in St. Louis's black enclaves between respectable ventures in city employment and labor in the entertainment and leisure districts that celebrated "the pleasures of the flesh." Romanticized as the "happy go lucky negro roustabouts," African American manual laborers flooded into the hundreds of St. Louis saloons on break from their backbreaking work at the docks.[114] In 1893 Jack operated a saloon at 425 Twelfth Street, and the family lived on Targee Street, the infamous street in St. Louis's Chestnut Valley, where porters, steamboat workers, hostlers, and hack drivers mixed with gamblers, madams, and sex workers.[115] Chestnut Valley resident, band leader, and blues composer William Christopher "W. C." Handy remembered the area with its black men in their "high roller Stetson hats" alongside "beautiful" black women, who, adorned in "diamonds," sat "for company in the little plush parlors under gaslights."[116] In Chestnut Valley, the "capital of the sporting world," Tom Turpin began his career as a ragtime musician, and C. H. Turpin learned the foundations of the black entertainment business alongside his brother.[117]

A uniquely American musical genre, ragtime is a fusion of syncopated music inspired by African "ragged" rhythms and European harmonies, often composed for the piano.[118] Historians debate exactly where it was born regionally, but early copyrighted ragtime compositions came from Midwest cities, like St. Louis and

Chicago, and Tom Turpin was among its earliest composers with "Harlem Rag."[119] As the 1900s approached Tom opened his own saloon, The Rosebud, on 2222 Market Street. The Rosebud became a hub for royal battles, or "cutting" contests, between ragtime composers for instrumental superiority, and ragtime piano players including Louis Chauvin, Joe Jordan, and the legendary Scott Joplin who lived in St. Louis between 1901 and 1904 frequented the space.[120] Tom continued to compose ragtime compositions, like "St. Louis Rag" and "A Ragtime Nightmare," and participated in the music's rising popularity that occurred after ragtime was showcased at the World's Fair in Chicago in 1893 and the Louisiana Purchase Exposition in St. Louis in 1904. As popular tunes cataloged with every conceivable form of "rag" in their titles reached the sheet music and piano rolls markets, Tom Turpin helped foster the genre, which advertised to popular musicians that "you're not 'in it' if you don't play the Great Cake Walk, Rag Time and Coon Characteristic Pieces."[121] C. H. learned the mechanics of the black entertainment business as he aided Tom with Rosebud's management while also holding his job at the Assessor's office.

### *The Political and Theatrical Stages*

While C. H. Turpin might have been a part-time financier of ragtime's central hub by night, by day he embedded himself in the world of black politics. In 1910, Turpin became the first African American elected official in the city when he won a seat as constable of the city's Fourth Ward.[122] He ran as a Republican for a position that gave him the responsibility of maintaining law and order, mediating property disputes, and enforcing debt collections in his ward with the help of deputy constables. Turpin held the position between 1910 and 1914 and won a strongly contested race for a second four-year term in 1918.[123] The dedicated support of African American religious and economic institutions in Turpin's election demonstrated that the black community respected his political efforts despite, or perhaps even because of, Turpin's ties to black leisure environments, like The Rosebud. As a constable, Turpin was *both* a peace officer potentially policing leisure and amusement environments as monitor and judge of "respectable" expression as well as an entrepreneur who built black amusement spaces.

It was with this same complicated concept of racial uplift that Turpin opened the Booker T. Washington Theatre on Market Street, the first black-owned vaudeville and motion picture theater in the city, in 1913. So intertwined was his theater entrepreneurship and political efforts, that in the immediate aftermath of the theater's opening, pleased St. Louis residents pledged that they would re-elect Turpin as constable as a "reward" for the theater's creation. Although a laudatory biographical article on Turpin maintained that he single-handedly opened his theater with "50 cents down," the Washington Theatre actually began as an air dome or an open-air amphitheater in 1910. After running into debt, Turpin tented the amphitheater during the winter, heated it with stoves, battled the climate, and used the facility for motion pictures until a financial backer could be found to build a brick-and-mortar theater.[124]

With the guidance of real estate specialist Sidney Schiele and the financial backing of the Adler-Goldman Commission Company, Turpin completed negotiations in March 1913 to build a theater at the southeast corner of Market and Twenty-Third Streets.[125] The forthcoming theater was discussed by entertainment industry periodical *Billboard* and was constructed by architect J. M. Hirschstein for an estimated $25,000.[126] Finally, black St. Louis residents had a theater of which to be proud, one "owned and operated by one of our race." The Washington Theatre was further advertised as an example of racial progress, where black performers were "nothing but clean, classy" and black patrons deserved and received "courteous treatment" within a city that either possessed shabby segregated theater balconies for black patrons or promoted theaters that were closed to African Americans entirely.[127] The Washington would soon be known for featuring new performers, like East St. Louis native and dancer Josephine Baker and blues music stars Mamie Smith and Bessie Smith.[128]

Three years after opening the Washington Theatre, Turpin traveled to the annual session of the National Negro Business League (NNBL) in Kansas City, Missouri, to discuss black theater ownership and economic racial uplift. Founded by Booker T. Washington in Boston in 1900, the NNBL was meant "to promote the commercial and financial development of the Negro" and concentrated on racial uplift through black economic independence and prosperity.[129] Turpin's presence at the first NNBL session after Washington's passing in 1915 and the naming of his theater spoke to the connection he saw between his business practices and the economic components of Washington's ideologies. Turpin contended that he named his theater after the emblematic leader because "Mr. Washington had spent his life in helping to upbuild our Race," and his name was "a synonym of industry, self-respect and racial progress."[130] Three years after its opening, the Washington Theatre seated nine hundred to twelve hundred patrons, employed thirty to forty black vaudevillians a week, and pulled in $475 to $600 a week on ten- and twenty-five-cent admissions. Turpin prided himself that he operated a modern, ventilated theater with "clean amusement" for the enjoyment of the "Race." The theater was an investment in the economic success of black St. Louis, and other black entrepreneurs heralded Charles Turpin as one of "the most energetic and enterprising members of the St. Louis community."[131]

Turpin's theater was an economically profitable black racial enterprise. However, he did not close himself to participation in interracial ventures. Just months after opening the Washington Theatre in 1913, Turpin joined an interracial consortium of theater owners in Chicago, the Colored Consolidated Vaudeville Exchange (C.C.V.E.). Members of this collective, who marketed themselves as the "best in vaudeville," included black vaudevillian Tim Owsley, Jewish entrepreneur Martin Klein, and S. H. Dudley, all initial management participants of T.O.B.A. Time.[132] Turpin's collaboration with the C.C.V.E. and Dudley would ready him for an active leadership role in black vaudeville management in the upcoming decade.

## JOHN T. GIBSON

While Charles Turpin explored the interracial vaudeville management network in Chicago in 1915, John T. Gibson celebrated the first-year anniversary of his Standard Theater in Philadelphia. John Trusty Gibson rose from relative obscurity to a vaudeville leader on the East Coast over the course of four years. Born in Baltimore, Maryland, between February 1872 and 1878, Gibson's background mirrored that of his vaudeville manager contemporaries in several ways.[133] He was a product of the post-Reconstruction era, labored for a time in a southern urban environment, and migrated northward by the late 1890s. Unlike Dudley or Turpin, Gibson was not a professional entertainer nor was anyone in the immediate Gibson family. Rather, for Gibson, the theatrical world represented a sound business investment and an opportunity to work for the "race" after an influx of Southern black migrants moved to Philadelphia in the 1890s.

John T. Gibson was the son of hack driver George H. Gibson and domestic laborer Elizabeth Jones Gibson.[134] He was one of four living Gibson children, including William, Albert, Harriet, and himself as the youngest.[135] Gibson emerged in his own right in the local records in 1890 when he served as a waiter and resided on 1130 Lafayette Street in Baltimore.[136] He toiled in Baltimore's hospitality industries off and on until 1895 when he migrated to Camden, New Jersey, with his elder brother William and sister-in-law, Ella.[137] After a few months of working in New Jersey, Gibson pulled upon his small savings to return to Baltimore and enroll in college courses at the historically black institution Morgan College as a member of the first-year class in the college preparatory track of the 1895–96 school year.[138] Formal education and attendance at a historically black college shaped the ways in which Gibson viewed his responsibilities to African American communities, honed the organizational skills needed to run a business, and influenced how he viewed black theater ownership as a method of racial uplift.

After his attendance at Morgan, Gibson moved to Philadelphia with his brother's family in 1905. The Gibsons were part of a larger migration movement of blacks to Philadelphia from Southern states in general, but specifically from Maryland, Virginia, and New Jersey.[139] By late 1910, Gibson finally found his entrepreneurial niche in the theater world and, with local black painter Samuel Reading, became a comanager of the North Pole Theatre at 1426 South Street.[140] He and Reading selected a theater on South Street to manage in an effort to capture a growing black migrant audience in a location that had become a commercial and residential enclave for African Americans and European immigrants by the 1890s.[141]

Renamed the Auditorium in 1911, Gibson and Reading's theater featured both silent motion pictures and select novelty vaudeville acts, earned profits for almost three years, and was prominently reviewed among black periodicals, including the *Freeman* and the *Philadelphia Tribune*. Gibson continued on as a manager of the Auditorium even as his collaboration with Reading came to an end in the 1910–11 season. For the next few years, the theater featured acts as varied as Maud Thompson, a "New York soubrette"; George and Williams, the Musical Monks; Carrie Stithe, an operatic vocalist who "trilled and warbled equal to any prima donna"; and Anita Bush, a vocalist whose "array of costumes out-dazzles anything that has been seen."[142]

When Gibson began managing the Auditorium, there were few, if any, black-owned vaudeville or motion picture theaters that catered exclusively to African American audiences in the city, and even fewer black managers. At the turn of the twentieth century, black Philadelphia entrepreneurs labored as barbers, grocers, saloon operators, bakers, and undertakers, but not as commercial entertainment providers. The city had been a hub for African American blackface minstrels in the nineteenth century, and select vaudeville venues around the city hosted black performers, including the Trocadero and Circle Theatres.[143] Yet, in 1910, a national theater guide listed only twenty theaters (listed by address, stage dimension, seating capacity, and price) for the city's 1.5 million total residents.[144]

Although not bound by the de jure segregation standards that permeated Southern communities, Philadelphia institutions did not always welcome African American residents. Housing reform advocate Helen Parrish wrote in her 1888 diary that the Fifth Ward's black residents were vice-ridden people upon whom she tried to impart morality and respectability, often with "failing" results.[145] In the late 1890s, when the color line in the nation was more explicitly drawn after the *Plessy* decision, both native-born African American and whites' disdain for the influx of "uncultured," working-class black migrants was palpable. In his sociological treatise of the city's Seventh Ward, *The Philadelphia Negro*, W. E. B. Du Bois commented that new masses that fled into already crowded black enclaves "with their low standard of living and careless appearance" were "unwelcome to the better class of blacks and to the great mass of whites."[146] Nonetheless Du Bois argued that these black residents, from the "families of undoubted respectability" to the "respectable working class" and the "honest" poor and "very poor," all needed forms of "some rational means of amusement" for the youth beyond prayer meetings and church socials.[147] Providing a place to view "polite vaudeville" is where Gibson's venture met a need in African American Philadelphia society.

### *"The Most Popular" Theater Proprietor*

Black Philadelphians praised Gibson's management efforts at the Auditorium, and it was during his tenure there that he fused his concepts of racial uplift with black theater management. Gibson was involved in every aspect of managing the Auditorium, from booking the talent to ensuring the satisfaction of the audience. As with all theater managers, Gibson booked acts on a trial basis. For example, the comedy team that was great for an audience in Newark, New Jersey, might not suit the tastes of black Philadelphians. By 1911, African American theater reviewers noted that Gibson "got wise to the fact that a good show means good business, and in fact the shop here has eclipsed all previous records with S.R.O. matinees and night performances."[148] Enjoyable talent in a continuous cycle of performances every evening and twice on Saturday and Sunday prompted large satisfied audiences of "the most respectable clients among the residents of Philadelphia and vicinity," whom Gibson and his employees treated with "polite attention." Gibson's successful run managing the Auditorium continued through 1913, and he became known in black periodicals as the rare manager who succeeded in "getting together five acts without showing two of a kind" and "always meets you with a smile."[149]

After leaving the Auditorium in late 1913 as "one of our [black Philadelphia's] most successful theatre managers," Gibson managed an establishment that served as the economic foundation for his further activities as a race man in Philadelphia: South Street's New Standard Theatre.[150] Before Gibson's involvement, the New Standard opened in April 1913 and was operated by black New York entrepreneur Gibson L. Young and the Standard Amusement Company. The grand opening was well attended and "packed from pit to dome," with hundreds of people kept in line to "await the next performance" that featured both black and white acts, like black comedic musical duo Cole and Johnson and the white juggling act, the Three Millers, billed as "the fastest of its kind."[151] Like mainstream white vaudeville, the Standard's playbill itself was integrated, but the individual acts on stage were not. Gibson became the New Standard's manager in Fall 1913 and, by January 1914, purchased the theater from the New York-based Standard Amusement Company.

As the owner Gibson remodeled the theater with a seating capacity of 1,800 and included "modern appliances for safety and comfort of patrons and employees." Gibson renamed it Gibson's New Standard Theatre and employed the techniques he had developed when managing the Auditorium. He soon reopened the Standard for continuous vaudeville, with an amateur show every Friday, evening shows for ten, fifteen, and twenty cents, and a Saturday and Sunday matinee for

FIGURE 3. John T. Gibson, Standard Theatre, Philadelphia, PA (1919) in Clement Richardson, ed., *The National Cyclopedia of the Colored Race* (Montgomery, AL: National Publishing Co., Inc., 1919).

ten cents. Just as with the Auditorium, Gibson's New Standard did "extraordinary business and had packed houses both afternoons and evenings." Successful operation of the Standard allowed "Mr. John T. Gibson" to be the "most popular theater proprietor in Philadelphia."[152]

While Gibson financially achieved the status of those "best class of Philadelphia Negroes," those "fairly educated, and liberally trained" who lived throughout "the better parts of the city," whom Du Bois praised in *The Philadelphia Negro,* Gibson remained a man of the people in terms of how he ran his theaters.[153] As a migrant himself he made sure the theater was open to all patrons and not "one of the Jim Crow" theaters that regulated black customers to an upper balcony, while white patrons were seated on the first floors.[154] Advertised as the "finest Colored Theatre in America, playing the best acts in the Country and Europe," Gibson's

New Standard became the "big time theater" that African American performers aspired to play before moving to black theaters in New York City.[155]

Gibson used his theater as a decided weapon in challenging racial discrimination in the city. Although the theater was black managed before Gibson's tenure in 1913, it still operated under racially discriminatory policies that would normally be openly found in Southern cities. In October 1913 African American patron Walter Flournoy bought a ticket to a Standard show and was escorted to the "extreme rear of the balcony," causing him to warn others in the black Philadelphia community to "stay away from the Standard Theatre as it has been plainly shown that their money is not wanted."[156] While it might be assumed that, despite Philadelphia's northern status, white-owned theaters might practice segregation, Gibson challenged segregation as a civil rights abuse in a black-*owned* theater. When Gibson initially subleased the New Standard from the Standard Amusement Company, he fired all the previous employees who willingly practiced segregation, promising citizens "they need not fear being insulted when they attempt to go to the Standard in the future."[157] Establishing an open seating policy was just the beginning of Gibson's attempts to model race work and uplift through black theater ownership.

Gibson's connections to the wider black vaudeville world only strengthened in his role as the owner of Gibson's Standard. While starring in the Smart Set, Dudley played the Gibson's New Standard in 1914, and the network between the legendary vaudevillian and rising black theater magnate began.[158] Gibson joined the Dudley Circuit by 1915 and cemented his explicit mission of being a businessman that meant the "race good." John T. Gibson was well on his way to becoming "one of the great theatrical managers of the country, [and] undisputedly the greatest in the Colored Race," a position that would align him to become a consultant in the plan for a national African American vaudeville circuit.[159]

## EMMA AND MABEL GRIFFIN

In the same years when John T. Gibson labored to make his New Standard Theatre one of the hallmarks of the Philadelphia black community, two black Chicago vaudevillians labored to become theater entrepreneurs. Despite the male dominance in the realm of vaudeville management, Louisville, Kentucky, migrants Emma and Mabel Griffin, "the Griffin Sisters," desired to control their offstage management dealings as well as their onstage comedy and vocal act.[160] Professional entertainers since they were adolescents, the Griffin Sisters were singers, comedians, and dancers who carved out a career beginning in 1895. The sisters, particularly Emma, the ensemble's businesswoman, held definitive ideas about how black vaudevillians should be booked and contracted, and after consulting with S. H. Dudley and contracting with the Dudley Circuit, the Griffin Sisters made plans to be black theater owners in late 1913.[161]

Born in Louisville, Kentucky, in 1874 and 1877, respectively, Emma and Mabel were the oldest and middle of four children of laundress Blandina Montgomery Duncan and laborer Henry Griffin.[162] By 1880, Blandina Duncan had four children under the age of ten: Emma, Henry, Mabel, and George.[163] Blandina worked as a laundress in residences across town, often residing as a live-in laborer, and at other times noted as a live-out laundress and boarder. By 1894, a nineteen-year-old Emma also became a laundress to supplement the family income.[164]

Bound by chronic underemployment and trapped in a community that faced rising racial hostility and discriminatory practices, eventual migration and entrance into the entertainment industry would prove to be a glimpse of economic and social freedom for the Griffin children. By the early 1890s, Emma and Mabel were drawn to the music of traveling entertainment productions. They fell into line as chorus girls on the variety stage after having acquired basic musical skills by singing in church, taking music classes at Louisville's black higher education institution, State University, and soaking in the traveling shows that visited Louisville.[165]

After relocating to Chicago in 1894 with mother, grandmother, and brothers in tow, Emma and Mabel made their first public performances in the newly opened Kohl & Middleton's Dime Museum.[166] Popularized by amusement impresario P. T. Barnum's American Museum, nineteenth-century dime museums were the precursor to twentieth-century sideshows or "freak shows."[167] They were exhibitions that promised patrons a glimpse of unseen human oddities and curiosities combined with live music and dance, all for the price of a ten-cent entrance fee. In his 1913 memoir Middleton remarked that the dime museum "was a strange business . . . with strange curiosities."[168] A general Kohl & Middleton playbill might beckon patrons to step right up and view the wondrous "woman born without arms, an Ossified Man, a beauty show of fifteen or sixteen fairly good looking ladies," or black conjoined twins "Mille Christine, the Double-Headed Nightingale."[169]

As chorus girls, the Griffins were participants in Kohl & Middleton's beauty pageants and capitalized financially on their beauty and "exotic" phenotype. The *San Francisco Call* described Emma with a "countenance several degrees duskier than that of Mabel" and incorrectly believed the two to only be "sisters in stageland." The *Call* characterized Mabel as the taller sister with "hair slightly 'kinked' and deeply dyed a beautiful antique gold hue."[170] From black-and-white photos both women were relatively fair-skinned African Americans who perhaps had the ability to "pass" for some other ethnicity besides black yet chose not to. Yet the Griffin Sisters rose to success in white-managed vaudeville because of the exploitation of their racial and gender identities. They became chorus girls in John Isham's *The Octoroons* and gained acclaim in New York in 1895. *The Octoroons* was a production that featured fair-skinned or mixed-race black women in "an organization of fifty colored performers . . . performing selections from grand and comic operas."[171] The Griffins left the dime museum circuit to be a part of this production, performed in the chorus for nearly two years from 1895 to 1897, and were among Isham's select "fairest daughters of the Sunny South."[172] The Griffin Sisters rose through the ranks because of their racial ambiguity and ability to satisfy an audience's curiosity and erotic fascination for the exotic "other."[173]

## *From Performers to Entrepreneurs*

Between 1900 and 1909, Emma and Mabel evolved from nameless "fairest daughters" in the chorus to skilled and recognized performers in white vaudeville theater. The Sisters contracted with the Western Vaudeville Managers Association (WVMA), or what some theater critics labeled as "real vaudeville'" in comparison with Isham's musicals.[174] Incorporated in Chicago in 1905, the WVMA was one of the three large conglomerates of white vaudeville in the nation. The WVMA controlled the vaudeville bookings for at least two hundred theaters across twenty-five states and formed a monopoly in the vaudeville booking industry with the Orpheum and Keith circuits in 1907.[175] Two of the leading WVMA partners were Charles E. Kohl and George Middleton, producers from the Sisters' dime museum years, giving the women a familiar management framework with which to work. When the management side of vaudeville became more integral to the Griffin Sisters, Emma acknowledged that it was her start in the industry with "Mr. Cole (Kohl), Mr. George Castal (Castle), and Old Pap Hedges of the Western Theatrical Vaudeville King" and work in the "best houses" that began the Griffins on their entrepreneurial path.[176]

After the Sisters used the better part of a decade to entrench themselves in white vaudeville and the WVMA circuit, they left white vaudeville for more personal autonomy offered by black-owned theaters in African American vaudeville. The Griffin Sisters made Chicago their permanent home in 1910 and soon took their act to Chicago's black Monogram Theatre and Indianapolis's Crown Garden.[177] They expressed excitement in turning to black stages to "entertain our race for 'we are, who we are,' there" and not just "another colored act."[178]

The Sisters began their foray into vaudevillian entrepreneurship, undeterred by the glaring absences of many women in management, and entered a level of the entertainment industry that was decidedly white, male, and hierarchal. In 1900 African American women over the age of ten comprised just over a third of the African Americans doing wage work in the nation. Ninety-two percent of those black wage-working women performed domestic labor and agricultural work for low wages, primarily in Southern states. Emma and Mabel Griffin were among the 262 black women across the United States working as "actors, professional showmen, etc."[179] In the mid-1910s, there were only two other notable African American women in vaudeville management: Sissieretta Jones (born Matilda Joyner) of the Black Patti Show and Mabel Whitman of the Atlanta-based Whitman Sisters. Jones, a lyrical classical soprano, led her own "Black Patti" Show (so named because Jones's voice was said to be reminiscent of Italian classical soprano Adelina Patti) in the 1890s. Musicologist James Graziano illustrated how Jones headlined her own "Black Patti' show in vaudeville under white managers Rudolph Voelckel and John M. Nolan from 1896 to 1915.[180] The Whitman Sisters—Mabel, Alberta, Essie, and Alice—began producing their own musical comedy revue in 1900 and persisted for over thirty years, a tremendous feat of stamina and skill. Mabel Whitman remarked, "We rely upon no one but ourselves as far as the administration of our business affairs is concerned, and at the same time every effort in our power is made to make each and every engagement booked stand out."[181] As theater scholar Nadine George-Graves chronicled, Mabel Whitman was eventually able to "demand top dollar, garner the best acts, fight corruption, and desegregate theaters."[182]

As the Griffin Sisters' act increased in its popularity from 1910 to 1913, Emma and Mabel gave periodical interviews detailing the behind-the-scenes lives of black vaudeville performers. In these exclusives they called for greater autonomy in black theater and eloquently connected the struggles of black entertainers to the larger struggles of the race as a whole. As established performers the Griffins did not hesitate to criticize white managers who asked actors servicing black theaters "to work for such salaries as $35 for teams, $50 the limit, some singles as low as $10 per, expecting them to change acts twice a week . . . while making thousands of dollars yearly off of these colored theaters."[183] Fresh from the WVMA entered the Griffin Sisters, who declared it was "time" we let "the white man see that we can do it without him."[184] Emma posited that unless black artists were able to control their own theaters and booking agencies, black performers would never reap the financial reward for their artistry.

In the Griffins' eyes, black performers on white stages were essentially spectacles with little authority or control over their places in the entertainment arena. When early twentieth-century racial uplift advocates held "a fervent desire" to "substantiate something of a higher and cleaner quality in the standard of music and entertainment" for black audiences, Emma folded these concerns into her plans for an autonomous black vaudeville industry.[185] As the 1913–14 theater season approached, the Griffin Sisters signed on with one of the few black theater owners and producers in the country, Sherman H. Dudley, with "splendid results" as performers.[186] The Griffins' alignment with Dudley provided them with the industry support they would need to branch off and launch their own booking agency.

The Griffin Sisters Theatrical Agency opened in Chicago as the "first and only colored women's theatrical booking agency in the United States" in December of the 1913–14 season.[187] The Sisters announced they were "hanging out their shingle" and created an agency that contracted black entertainers and attempted to provide them with consistent work at competitive salaries on par with the $70 to $250 a week that white acts might have received on the Keith or Orpheum circuit. The Sisters commented that they "opened up [their] agency and school of vaudeville so that [they] may promote the colored show business, as it is at a standstill and the acts have no protection."[188]

Agency advertisements explicitly promised to "furnish first class acts . . . and help to build up any house that has a tendency to run down in receipts."[189] While the Sisters could have merely lent their name to an agency and had no direct management contact, they instead were integral participants in the Agency's functions. Emma applied for a formal license to open as a free employment agency, and for approximately twelve dollars a month, she rented a room at 3159 State Street as their office.[190] The Sisters played upon their connections with the WVMA circuits and argued that they had "been so well taught by big white managers, [that] we know just how to build up our own theaters."[191] Crafted to book and train black artists, the Agency also recruited for domestic service jobs, where migrants could work as seamstress, grips, dressers, and porters in road shows.[192]

By 1914, the Sisters worked with the management of the Alamo Theater in Chicago and booked attractions there from talent recruited at the Griffin Sisters Agency. In a booking agency income was earned from the 5–10 percent commission taken from the salary an entertainer received from an individual theater. The Sisters only increased their profits by helping acts, like Fisher & Fisher or Babe Brown, negotiate higher salaries from thirty-five to sixty dollars a week.[193] In declaring the motive behind the agency as one of providing black artists with the stability, consistency, and employment that white theaters and agencies had failed to provide, Emma Griffin specifically made the Griffin Sisters Agency a force in racial self-help and black pride.

After opening the Agency, the Griffins set up a second residence in Washington, DC, at 1907 Ninth Street NW during the 1914–15 season and moved into the District's black theatrical world. Rather than build from the ground up, the Sisters planned to sublease existing black theaters in the model of Dudley. In a sophisticated attempt to draw up support, Emma continued to use the black press to express how much the Sisters loved Washington, DC, and its positive environment of racial uplift. She maintained that it was "a pleasure to play DC as [it] was destined to become the theatrical center of the country as far as the colored artists were concerned," for the theaters that wanted black patrons were "actually *controlled by managers of our own race*." For the Griffins, "*race pride* was one of the many essentials in the permanent uplift of the negro in the theatrical arena."[194]

Emma continued the successful techniques that had allowed the Sisters to open the Agency in Chicago and create a social network to garner capital by calling out to other black entrepreneurs and defining black theater investment as race work. Washington, DC, hotel owner James Ottaway Holmes eventually answered Emma's call for "colored gentlemen" investors and was listed as one of the Sisters' key backers by mid-1915.[195] With Holmes's investment and their continued performances throughout the 1914–15 season, the Griffins subleased the District's Majestic, Blue Mouse, and Fairyland Theatres, all in Northwest Washington, DC. The *Defender* praised the Sisters as "business women from the heart [who] will win, if given half a chance."[196]

The Griffin Sisters' business practices and intertwined ideologies about race work and vaudeville labor activism were explicit. They were among the few entrepreneurs of the genre who had actually seen the industry from both the stage and the production office and had survived on white vaudeville stages for ten years. Emma did not hold her tongue nor speak in appropriate "lady-like" language while demanding higher wages or more effective managers of color. She asserted that voicing her concerns was the obligation of true race women. As a result, in 1915, the *Broad Ax* referred to the Sisters as "aggressive colored women of the 20th century who are doing much for the Colored actors."[197] The characterization of "aggressive" could be read in two ways: as praise for the Griffins being modern women who fought for change, but also as black women who were domineering and overly forceful. For example, when Emma met with members of the Colored Vaudeville Benevolent Association (C.V.B.A.), the premier black and predominantly male vaudeville guild, to further promote a systematized all-black vaudeville circuit, theater critic Sylvester Russell chastised her for racial "radicalism."[198]

Despite Emma's seemingly antagonistic behavior she was not without outspoken champions. By the 1914–15 season, even her critics noted that season Emma Griffin was "a figure that all managers of colored theaters and booking agents will have to reckon with . . . whether her missions will prove available or not, all depends on her upon her business ability, rather than her ambition or assertiveness."[199] The Griffin Sisters became a force in vaudeville management and their beliefs in black economic nationalism would not be easily dismissed.

As the 1920s and New Negro era approached, there were a wide variety of ideologies regarding the next steps that should be taken to centralize and stabilize black vaudeville as a national entity and how these efforts would be linked to uplift. After 1916 and the stabilization of the Dudley Circuit, S. H. Dudley adhered to a plan for a theater enterprise that perhaps unconsciously mirrored Sylvester Russell's 1910 vision: an integrated circuit where African American talent was promoted by any and all theater management figures who supported the race. The possibility of a more centralized, interracially managed but black-serving circuit was not an anomaly for C. H. Turpin, as he had already begun collaborations with white Chicago theater manager Martin Klein by the 1910s. John T. Gibson patiently gathered the resources needed to craft a black theatrical hub in Philadelphia and used his influence to combat discriminatory practices in the theater world. As the only woman featured prominently in the discussion, Emma Griffin lambasted black theater managers for their lack of nationalist pride throughout the 1910s. But even Griffin recognized that whoever was at the helm of African American vaudeville needed to improve black theater circuits for the sake of black management, artists, and audience members. By 1914 all found themselves still vying for creation and control of an effective system of black vaudeville management. These black vaudevillians persisted in their theater racial uplift actions, even if it meant calling on the cooperation of nonblacks as new partners in the path toward vaudeville centralization and T.O.B.A.

# 2

# "HEBREW, NEGRO, AND AMERICAN OWNERS"

## *Black Vaudeville and Interracial Management*

> Dukes and Lords and Russian Czars
> Men who own their motor cars
> Throw up their shoulders to that raggedy melody
> Full of originality
> Italian opera singers have learned to snap their fingers
> The world goes 'round to the sound of the International Rag . . .
>
> —Irving Berlin, lyrics to "The International Rag," 1913

As Martin Klein read the stage sections of *Indianapolis Freeman* in winter 1913, he was disturbed by the Griffin Sisters' most recent opinion pieces. Black "business women to the core" who planned to "make the theatrical world 'sit up and take notice,'" Emma and Mabel Griffin were quick to denounce any vaudeville manager that they did not feel had the best interests of the race at heart.[1] Emma, the more vocal of the duo, determined that Klein, the Monogram Theatre's manager, would be like other "outsider" managers who served black theatrical community needs, only to extent that it was economically profitable to white management. Griffin generally called out white managers in the black press and had specifically critiqued Klein in personal correspondence, wary about his plans for a Chicago-based black theater circuit. Klein openly challenged the Griffins' critique and replied that the women managers "had written in a tone that was not only *unbecoming* but makes them liable to court proceedings." In commentary that was both racialized and gendered, Klein condemned "these two young women" and accused them of "race prejudice" against him for being white.[2]

A first generation Jewish American, Martin Klein had managed black theaters in Chicago since 1910 and, with black theater owners S. H. Dudley and Tim

Owsley, created the interracial Colored Consolidated Vaudeville Exchange in 1913, whose theaters would be incorporated into T.O.B.A. Klein was one of several European immigrants involved in the creation of a national black vaudeville circuit. This chapter chronicles the ramifications of interracial and multiethnic leadership in black vaudeville at the onset of T.O.B.A.'s formation. Industry leaders noted that T.O.B.A. was a "chain of Colored vaudeville theaters, owned by a combination of Hebrew, Negro, and American owners," a composition that drew praise from black theater professionals who believed that interracial coalition was necessary in the centralization of black vaudeville and concern from others who wanted black vaudeville to be led by African American entrepreneurs.[3]

Martin Klein, Samuel Reevin, and Milton Starr were all immigrant or first-generation Americans who rose to prominent leadership positions on the T.O.B.A. board in the 1920s. A chronicle of their professional origins reveals how they developed their positions and crafted relationships with black theater communities. This trio had so much visibility and power that even some black entertainers were unaware that African Americans also held executive board member positions and circuit shares. White Jewish immigrant entrepreneurs negotiated relationships with black theater owners in Northern and Southern cities, who, in turn, wrestled with the concept that an interracially controlled institution could retain some black racial uplift and economic nationalism components. These often fraught relationships formed the networks upon which T.O.B.A. would be built as a "mixed membership" race business.[4]

## RACIAL INTERACTIONS IN VAUDEVILLE

From the 1890s to the 1910s national vaudeville employed a diverse roster of male and female entertainers from various racial and ethnic backgrounds who were either native-born Americans or recent immigrants, a reflection of the growing diversity of the nation. The genre was *both* inclusive with room for all acrobats, singers, or ballerinas *and* segregated, with each ethnically diverse act separated from each other on the bill. Many variety and later vaudeville participants of the 1890s and 1900s imitated racial, cultural, and gender differences onstage as a regular part of their comedic acts. Artists engaged in ethnic humor and perpetuated images of "happy Italian rascals"; drunken Irishmen; conservative Germans; lazy, slow African Americans; or "canny" or too clever Jews—a collection of characters who would have shared in "The International Rag" chronicled in the chapter's opening. Theater historians suggest that this mocking, while at times "aggressive," was an acknowledgment of the entertainers' and the vaudeville audiences' cultural diversity at the dawn of the twentieth century, arguably with humor in mind.[5]

African Americans and Jewish immigrants shared vaudeville spaces since the late nineteenth century. Jewish entertainers Eddie Cantor, Al Jolson, and Sophie

Tucker "blacked up" as blackface minstrels and used pseudo-Southern dialect in comedic skits. Tucker, Nora Baye, and Fannie Brice sang "coon songs" to great audience acclaim.[6] Conversely, fair-skinned African American actor Harry L. Gilliam adopted mannerisms, dress, and faux Yiddish to pose as "the original Acrobatic Hebrew" in 1900. Gilliam gained great popularity with this character and promised that if he was "no hit," then he expected "no pay."[7] African Americans and Jews regularly borrowed elements of each other's musical inflections, rhythms, and mannerisms in ragtime, jazz, and blues songs; comic skits; and popular dance numbers.[8] Famed composer Irving Berlin fused the tones from traditional Jewish songs with African American rhythms and pseudoblack dialect to create such pieces as "Alexander's Ragtime Band" in 1911. With its promises to hear the "Swanee River played in ragtime" by the "bestest band, what am," the tune garnered as much acclaim as the actual African American ragtime songs that gave the song its moniker and became an American popular music standard.[9] Yet some of these moments of appropriation or "emulation" in vaudeville crossed the line to cultural theft and "plagiarism."[10] As cultural theorist Eric Lott contends white blackface minstrels had both "drew up and crossed racial boundaries" and displayed a contradictory "love and theft" of black culture by embodying and exaggerating the music, mannerisms, and humor of African Americans in the 1850s and '60s.[11]

By the 1890s and the inclusion of actual black performers in American musical theater, many black vaudevillians critiqued the continued use of blackface and white imitations of black performers as a threat to African American entertainers' livelihoods and the humanity of actual African Americans. Many of these white blackface entertainers were Jewish immigrants who literary scholar Irving Howe argued "took the genre over almost entirely" by the 1910s.[12] Emma Griffin called out "big time white women" who asked her "to teach them how to do a coon song as she does," for which these white female performers might be paid "six hundred dollars" per week, while Griffin, as the act's originator, would only receive "fifty dollars."[13] Griffin and a generation of black vaudevillians wanted to create acts that infused the humor and music of their own communities while reaping the financial reward from those performances and upholding their professional and personal integrity.[14] She feared that Klein and his proposed circuit might threaten those desires for a measure of black autonomy in black vaudeville.

## MARTIN KLEIN

While concerns about African American autonomy in black theater spaces arose, white Jewish immigrants saw the management of black vaudeville theaters as a prosperous new business opportunity. In the 1910s S. H. Dudley and his contemporaries performed in black-owned and segregated theaters, and many African

Americans were locked out of theater ownership due to inadequate financing and racial restrictions in property sales.[15] Yet in these same years, immigrant entrepreneur Martin Klein rose to prominence in Chicago with an idea of an interracially controlled black vaudeville circuit. Unlike black theater managers Dudley or Emma Griffin, Martin Klein came to the black vaudeville with no theater experience as a performer either in mainstream theater or the rapidly growing Yiddish theater movement of turn-of-the-century New York and Chicago.[16] Klein fell into theater management because of a lucrative business opportunity created when he married into a family that owned property in Southside Chicago.

Born on July 31, 1883, in Illinois, Martin Klein was a first-generation American and a representation of what many new settlers hoped to achieve amid the golden age of immigration in the United States.[17] Klein's parents, Phillip Klein and Gizella Green Klein, were born in the Austro-Hungarian Empire in 1859 and 1861, respectively. Naturalized as US citizens, the couple met and married in Cook County, Illinois, in May 1883, and Martin was born three months later. Martin was soon followed by three younger sisters: Bertha, Daisy, and Jesse Klein, and by 1900 the Klein family found itself living on 3148 Union Avenue, not too far away from the Southside community in which Martin would eventually begin his theater management career.[18]

After marrying first-generation immigrant Lillian Nissel in 1905 and welcoming a son in 1906, twenty-two-year-old Martin Klein needed a greater income than his store clerk job to support his young family, and it was this need and coincidence that propelled Klein into theater management.[19] Klein's new brother-in-law, H. B. Miller, owned and operated a saloon at 3501 S. Halstead Street, and he hired Klein as a manager after 1906.[20] The saloon business included managing the bar and the small-time musicians and vocalists who entertained customers as they imbibed. Miller soon bought property on State Street, which began to serve an African American clientele by the early twentieth century. Business was profitable, and by 1910 Miller purchased an additional State Street property, which Klein managed.[21] The State Street sites quickly evolved from saloons to small theaters, and Miller's "5 and 10 cent" establishment at 3028 S. State Street reopened as the black-serving Monogram Theatre. "Manager Klein" began his new career between 1909 and 1910.[22]

How did Jewish immigrants come to invest in predominantly black-patronized businesses? That can be answered by the change in Chicago's demographics, both as a result of increased European immigration and African American migration prior to World War I, and the racial restrictions in the Chicago real estate market. In 1910, Jewish residents totaled over two hundred thousand people, and African Americans equaled 46,226 out of 2.1 million residents in the nation's second-largest city.[23] As both immigrants and migrants fled into the city their potential residential neighborhoods were often governed by social custom or contractual racial covenants that prevented the sale or renting of property to "undesirables." In many cases desirability was governed by race and class, and contracts included language that barred native-born white owners from selling their property to African Americans, Jews, or other ethnic and racial minorities, depending on the area. After the influx of African American migrants increased the city's black population by 148 percent, Chicago was on its way to becoming one of the "most segregated cities in the country."[24] In the case of black Chicago, both old settlers (those who had resided in the city before 1900) and new migrants flooded into neighborhoods in the South Side in the 1910s, which had been previously inhabited by Irish and German Jewish immigrants. John Levy, a black migrant and future talent manager, described his own family's motivations in moving near St. Lawrence and 49th Streets in a previously Jewish South Side as a "search for a better neighborhood" with space for all family members and potential boarders.[25]

White Chicago journalists described black migrants' search for home and stability with words like "swarm," "invade," and "infect," and newspaper headlines chronicled the "half million darkies from Dixie" swarming into the city.[26] Some African American journalists, wary of increased black migration, described the new South Side in the same manner as their white counterparts. In the same years Miller and Klein moved from running saloons to managing vaudeville spaces on State Street, a *Defender* journalist remarked that African Americans had "invaded the Jewish neighborhood" between Thirty-First and Thirty-Ninth Streets near "State and Cottage Grove avenue" like a "flock of sheep." Revealing the class and generational tensions within black South Side communities, the journalist further asserted that, before the black migrant influx, "the better element of our race" lived in the neighborhood but, in the 1910s, it was full of "men and women half clothed" and "ragtime piano players" who did not know that the South Side was "not the slums of some Southern town."[27] With migration, new Black Chicagoans encountered Jewish immigrants who remained involved in the South Side's economy as commercial property owners, landlords, and merchants and worked with the 101,594 African American "black belt" residents.[28] Klein joined the hundreds of other white entrepreneurs who sought active involvement in "big black businesses."[29]

## *"Manager Klein"*

The Monogram Theatre operated as a live entertainment and motion picture venue in the burgeoning black belt, and advertisements claimed that "all first-class acts" and "the very best" orchestra could be found at the 3028 State Street site.[30] Racial segregation was practiced in many Chicago neighborhoods despite that "Negroes were entitled by law to the same treatment as other persons in restaurants, theaters, stores, and other places of public accommodation."[31] Yet black Monogram audience members did not have to worry they would be told "that there were no seats reserved for colored people."[32] The theater hosted industry favorites like the Griffin Sisters and Shelton Brooks, while local Chicago acts, like vocalist Ethel James, dancer Dude Kelly, or comedian Anson Davis, rounded out the early playbills.[33] Klein handled all the talent and stage-managed many of the all-black acts that led to "splendid bills" at the Monogram. The theater claimed a space in the array of black theaters and clubs on State Street and was a foundation of the street's reputation as the "Dahomey Stroll" in the 1910s and the "Broadway of the Black Belt" in the 1920s.[34]

On the Dahomey Stroll, the African American commercial district on State Street between Twenty-Sixth and Thirty-Fifth Streets (which eventually extended to Thirty-Ninth Street) and the Monogram faced viable competition from a select group of theaters that featured African American talent.[35] Upon its opening the Monogram was thought to be one of the upstart "toy houses" or vaudeville theaters that were small, crowded, and frequented by the black working classes. It was no competition for the black-owned Pekin Theatre at Twenty-Seventh and State Streets, referenced in chapter 1. As "one of the most beautiful structures in this section of the city," the Pekin was a goal for which to strive, but the Monogram's true competition was the Grand Theatre.[36] The original Grand was established in 1908 on 3100 State Street. It grew in popularity as a variety entertainment theater and hosted acts that left patrons wondering "what's on the Grand, let's go to the Grand."[37] Black producer Marion A. Brooks left the Pekin to manage the white-owned Grand in 1908, a move which soon made the Grand the Pekin's closest rival in the 1907–1908 season. With five hundred seats, the Grand "gave the public what it demands, namely a high-class bill."[38]

With Brooks as manager the Grand brought in vaudeville talent from magicians to dancers and was soon remodeled into the New Grand by the 1911–1912 season. Enlarged to encompass the space between 3110 and 3112 State Street, the New Grand marketed itself as the "Finest Theatre in America," that played continuous vaudeville and moving pictures. With the "business system of this house now nicely regulated" the Grand hosted African American, white, and multicultural vaudeville acts, including singers from the Famous Georgia Minstrels, like Sidney Kirkpatrick; the Namba Japanese Troupe; and singer Carita Day.[39] The multicultural bookings at the Grand, although enjoyable, raised some concern, as the theater was still a Stroll staple with a black clientele who liked to see themselves represented on the stage at some point. When the Grand booked successful black acts, even theater critics mentioned how it "did our hearts good to see a colored act at the Grand," as if the presence of black talent was not as frequent as audiences would have liked.[40] The New Grand slowly overcame these concerns by booking more black musical acts and successfully persisted into the 1920s, where it featured early jazz and blues artists, like Mamie Smith, Bessie Smith, and Clara Smith (no relation).[41]

The racial demographics of the Monogram's playbills did not raise complaints, and much of this was due to Klein's leadership. Although the Monogram was white owned and managed, Klein was very deliberate in making continuous inroads in the Chicago black theatergoing community. Critic Sylvester Russell argued that if a theater's playbill provided "a good show for the money," then the theater owner's race didn't matter. Nonetheless Russell also acknowledged that "to retain the patronage of the Negro race" amid increased black migration to Chicago, a theater on the Stroll had to "play one or as many colored acts as possible." Klein managed to do just that and "supplied almost exclusively colored performers."[42] Miller and Klein hired African American William Dorsey as the orchestra leader, who generally pleased the Stroll crowds. Klein was so involved with the local African American performers that when George Walker of the famed Williams & Walker comedy team died suddenly in January 1911, he sent flowers of condolence on "behalf of the Colored actors of Chicago."[43] Klein took out advertising space in key black periodicals like the *Defender*, *Freeman*, and *Broad Ax* and ensured that both Sylvester Russell in the *Freeman* and journalists in the *Broad Ax* reviewed the Monogram's billings almost weekly in the 1911–1913 seasons.[44] Furthermore, Klein also dealt with the poor physical logistics of the theater itself. Despite being located close to the city's elevated train tracks, attracting a less than refined crowd of patrons and what Jacqueline Stewart documents as the Monogram's "shabby conditions," Klein made noted efforts to keep the theater running. The Monogram remained open throughout much of the winter and in the extreme heat of Chicago summers, moments when other theaters shuttered and businesses lost profit as patrons avoided the poorly insulated and ventilated, pre-air-conditioned structures.[45]

Yet still some performers and other black theater managers did not completely embrace Manager Klein as part of the black entertainment landscape. Black Chicagoans praised the local Jewish community for protesting discrimination and segregated seating in downtown theaters and their general communal success "attained by sticking together and helping one another."[46] *Defender* editorials suggested the black communities should "emulate the Jews" and similarly patronize *black owned* businesses to "make opportunities for the employment of *your* sons and daughters."[47] This praise of the Jewish community was used to support racial uplift within the African American community and promote black entrepreneurship. In this environment of growing economic black nationalist spirit, Klein's efforts at the Monogram were also questionable when the black-owned Pekin Theatre stood blocks away on State Street.

Historian Cheryl Greenberg argues that "most relationships between African Americans and Jews were deeply unequal," and while they might have lived "parallel" lives to some extent, "many interactions between them were hierarchal."[48] Several black Chicagoans recoiled at the prospect of Jewish immigrants filling economic niches in black communities that could be filled by black residents themselves. Aware of this unease, it took years for Klein to gain the trust of the community. By 1913 the *Freeman* finally entreated hesitant black theater participants to be more receptive to the relative newcomer stating, "if the managers as well as the actors would give him [Manager M Klein] his consideration . . . they would find him responsible for more good deeds than bad ones."[49]

### *The Colored Consolidated Vaudeville Exchange*

In 1913 Klein's brother-in-law, H. B. Miller purchased the Merit Theatre property on Thirty-Fifth and State and named it the New Monogram Theatre. Miller tapped Klein to be the manager of both Monograms and was "well pleased with his new theatrical venture along the stroll." [50] Yet, more importantly for the T.O.B.A. narrative, Klein's expanded management efforts caused him to reach out to African American vaudeville managers to cocreate the Colored Consolidated Vaudeville Exchange (C.C.V.E.). The C.C.V.E., developed by Klein and S. H. Dudley, was a predecessor to T.O.B.A. Time in which theater owners organized African American performers to be exclusively booked at a predetermined circuit of black-serving theaters across the country. While still based in Chicago, Dudley came into contact with Klein in the local black entertainment circles of the Stroll. Even within Jewish immigrant circles Dudley was "recognized as the foremost mirth-provoker of his race."[51] When Dudley formed his own circuit in Washington, DC, in 1912, the talent that frequented his theaters in the Southeast were also available for booking in the Midwest. Yet there was no formal vehicle to ensure that an act playing the Dudley Theatre on DC's U Street would play the Monogram in Chicago three weeks later. Salaries, access to transportation, and the popularity of an act varied from theater to theater and region to region. The C.C.V.E. was initially created with a "hope to book acts for the entire Dudley circuit" in June 1913 and proposed to book the "best and most catchy acts on the road."[52] This initial partnership was a noticeable change from Dudley's "race capitalist" and uplift strategies that he publicly discussed as he planned for Dudley Theatrical Enterprises.[53] The beginning of Dudley's racially inclusive work efforts toward a black circuit began in earnest with his collaboration with Klein.

While Dudley's name carried more weight in the industry as a vaudeville veteran, Klein took on the daily work of recruiting theater managers to the C.C.V.E. who may have not been affiliated with the Dudley Circuit. Klein again relied on the black press and traveled to Indianapolis to enlist the aid of *Freeman* journalists.

Weeks after announcements about the impending exchange went out in June 1913, Klein traveled to Cincinnati, Cleveland, and Pittsburgh.[54] By July the C.C.V.E. had recruited twelve theaters in total, including three theaters in St. Louis, Cincinnati, and Pittsburg that were not already formally part of the Dudley Circuit. Manager Klein became the leader of D.O.K. (Dudley, Owsley, and Klein), the alternative moniker of the C.C.V.E. under the leadership of Dudley, black theater veteran Tim Owsley, and Klein himself.[55] As the 1913–14 season approached, Klein further showcased his interracial collaboration skills and crafted a C.C.V.E. board that was primarily composed of African American men. The organization held three offices, with Klein in Chicago, Owsley in Indianapolis, and Dudley in Washington, DC. The team included Owsley as president, Dudley as secretary, Klein as manager and treasurer, and a board of directors that featured African American theater owners Charles Turpin, William Lowhorn, Ollie Dempsey, Bob Slater, Onis Williams, E. B. Dudley, and A. A. Moncrief, as well as Italian immigrant theater professional Anselmo Barrasso and Jewish professional M. Edelman. In keeping with the difficulties that the Griffin Sisters had experienced in breaking into the business side of black vaudeville, the only African American woman associated with C.C.V.E. management was Miss Lillian Smith, "stenographer for the Colored Consolidated Vaudeville Exchange."[56]

Klein and the C.C.V.E. continued to recruit members throughout the Midwest and the East, declaring they were "not the first, not the oldest, but the *one* that gives out more work to actors" and the one that all "responsible managers belong to."[57] The first theater professional to publicly critique the C.C.V.E. was Emma Griffin. Her opposition stemmed from her black economic nationalist ethos, a belief in "race pride," and her own entrepreneurial efforts. The Griffin Sisters had opened their own booking agency only five months after the C.C.V.E.'s opening and defined their motivation as an effort by race women to tackle racial salary inequities and "make some of the money" that "white men" were making "off of colored acts and colored people." Emma further argued that "if a white man runs a colored theatre, let him book his acts from *our* colored agencies," in an attempt to correct what she believed was the growing imbalance of power between black and white management in black vaudeville.[58]

Klein believed his interracial efforts would result in booking the best black acts to ensure the largest profits for all managers of black vaudeville, regardless of their race. His many supporters in the theatrical world combatted the Griffins' valid critiques of the industry from a gendered perspective, diminished the Sisters as emotional "pretty young women," and objectified adult black theater professionals as childlike, "less capable human beings" because they were black women.[59] The *Freeman* defended Klein against the Griffins and praised his longevity of "five years" in the business and his ability to employ "a number of colored men and women." The newspaper contended that "there is no way possible for anyone to stop its (C.C.V.E.'s) progress."[60] In the same *Freeman* edition black critic Sylvester Russell described Ms. Griffin as "pretty" in "pink pouts and angry blushes."[61] Russell, an ardent supporter of an interracially managed circuit, downplayed Griffin's attempts to air her concerns about white managers because of his personal belief that color did not make a "difference" in the pursuit of "honest" booking agents.[62] But of equal significance, Russell critiqued Griffin based on her gender and the belief that women were not as rational and business-minded as men. He argued that in "disputing with individuals" like Klein and others, Emma Griffin was simply "irrational," which negated her long-term work in white and black vaudeville.[63] Russell's public commentary fit the larger narrative of the wariness many men had about the "woman's role in a man's business" and exemplified the beliefs of black Chicago activist Fannie Barrier Williams who maintained that a "colored woman" in early-twentieth-century America was the "only woman without sufficient defenders when assailed."[64]

Instead of responding to Russell or Klein, the Griffins continued their entrepreneurial endeavors. Klein and Griffin persisted on their two divergent paths toward employing more African American performing artists and general laborers. The Griffin Sisters opened their own black employment agency in Chicago in January 1914. Klein followed right behind and started his employment agency for black laborers in February 1915.[65] Throughout the development of the C.C.V.E., the Griffin Sisters stood out for being among the few African American women to successfully break into the overwhelming white and male world of vaudeville management as demonstrated by their agencies and stints as theater managers.

Although Klein slowly commanded respect as "Manager Klein" of the Stroll, Klein's motives were not completely altruistic, as his goal was to forge ties with managers who would further the *business* of black vaudeville. He traveled to black communities in much of the Midwest to build the Consolidated Vaudeville Exchange and included the next generation in the "family business," as he involved his eleven-year old son, Walter, in some of his vaudeville meetings. Just as S. H. Dudley had done with S. H. Jr., Klein sought to teach Walter the business from the ground up, and the C.C.V.E.'s expansion persisted.[66] The Old Monogram closed in 1916, and the following year the C.C.V.E. made new collaborations with theaters inching into the Southern United States, a move which allowed Klein to "furnish steady work for double the number of acts that are loyal to the old Consolidated."[67]

At some point between during 1914 and 1915, Klein became the only manager advertised with the C.C.V.E. Dudley focused on his own DC-based circuit, and Owsley continued performing onstage and managing the New Crown Theatre in Indianapolis.[68] In November 1914 Sylvester Russell commented on the C.C.V.E.'s management change and disparaged S. H. Dudley as a "detriment to the advancement of colored actors financially and otherwise" for reducing his connections to Klein. Russell claimed Dudley failed to pay actors a livable salary and questioned the commission percentage booked actors paid upon the Dudley Circuit.[69] In one of the few articles that made specific reference to the racial and religious identities in the Dudley, Owsley, and Klein collaboration, Owsley chastised Russell for his rebuke of a fellow black theater professional:

> It is a well-known fact that Negroes never go hand in hand nor stick together at the head of the class when it comes to sticking together. And I dare say if Mr. Sylvester Russell was a Jew and Mr. Klein was a Negro, Mr. Russell's article would have read different . . . No man could ask of me to use my standing with the best Negro paper in denouncing one of my own race for his glory . . . No matter what Klein says, Dudley says, Owsley says, or what Sylvester says you will find that every man is running his own business to suit his own convenience, be he Jew or Gentile.[70]

In this scathing op-ed in the *Freeman*, Owsley did not so much as chastise or ridicule Klein as the white proprietor of a black business as he denounced Russell for not engaging in public racial uplift practices. Owsley frankly criticized Russell as a "good slave" for speaking ill of another African American theater professional who adopted the same business practices as any white or Jewish theater professional.[71] Three years after this public moment of infighting, Dudley still supported the concept of interracial black vaudeville management, as he was "not selfish." If he couldn't handle a booking, he wanted to "let the Consolidated Vaudeville Manager [Klein] book it." For Dudley these shared management efforts were movement toward "harmony and elevation for his people," even if it meant conceding bookings to Klein and sharing power across racial lines.[72] Other prominent black managers came to accept Klein's efforts as long as they were financially profitable for all involved, regardless of race.

The C.C.V.E. and Klein contended with a different set of concerns with the entrance of the United States into World War I, the "Great War" in 1917. The draft disrupted vaudeville playbills, as many male performers and audience members were called to join the American Expeditionary Forces. Rations and reductions in income meant that regular theater attendees reduced their theater outings, and as a result the C.C.V.E. held a convention to discuss "war conditions," both "pro and con—mostly con."[73] Misguided displays of patriotism revealed themselves in many American cities as anti-German sentiment, and Chicago was no exception. Many American citizens strongly resisted German propaganda beliefs or the superiority of German "kultur" and taunted and harassed members of new and established German American communities. Some Chicago ordinances banned teaching German in schools, renamed frankfurter sausages and sauerkraut to "hot dogs" and "liberty cabbage," banned music by German-born composers, fired German employees, and generally painted German Americans as the enemy.[74]

As an American-born child of immigrant German-speaking, Jewish parents, Klein weathered the anti-German environment of Chicago and enlisted in the draft. Although not selected to serve, Klein also reduced his public role in the C.C.V.E. and promoted African American leadership. Consequently, African American vaudevillian Chinz Moore, manager of Dallas's Park Theatre, was brought on to run the Southern division of the circuit 1919. The C.C.V.E. continued until mid-1920, and Manager Klein continued to run the New Monogram, known in the pantheon of 1920s Chicago black theaters as the place "where they had *all* the comedians."[75] The relationships Martin Klein cultivated with black communities and managers in the C.C.V.E. would result in him being a Midwest leader in the future T.O.B.A.

## SAMUEL REEVIN & SOUTHERN BLACK VAUDEVILLE

Martin Klein's efforts to centralize northern black vaudeville were matched in the urban South by theater manager and entrepreneur Samuel Reevin. In 1910 when Klein became the manager of the Monogram and his African American partner S. H. Dudley became the director of the Smart Set Company operations in New York, Reevin, the future charter member of T.O.B.A., was just adapting to life in the United States.[76] While the interracial Klein-Dudley partnership had its controversies, it was not forbidden in the Chicago vaudeville world. But public policing of race and ethnic hierarchies in the United States South were much more restrictive, and Reevin's relatively equal interracial partnerships were not easily constructed. Reevin began his theatrical career in black vaudeville with no theater management experience, little English, and few previous contacts with African Americans. Yet by 1920, he was the T.O.B.A. Southern manager.

As a white manager of a southern African American vaudeville theater, Reevin was preceded by the Barrasso Brothers, theater entrepreneurs who opened sites in Memphis in the 1910s, and Charles P. Bailey and L. D. Joel, managers who pooled resources to build Atlanta's 81 Theatre in 1909.[77] An Italian immigrant family, the Barrassos proposed a theater owners' booking agency in 1907.[78] The Barrasso brothers—Frederico, born in Italy in 1883, and Anselmo, born in St. Louis in 1889—settled in downtown Memphis and opened saloons, jewelry stores, and tailor shops at the turn of the century. They managed the black-serving New Savoy, Metropolitan, Venus, and Palace vaudeville and motion picture theaters and "spared no pains" to make their enterprise "a grand success."[79] The brothers promised black performers jobs in Memphis and other nearby Tennessee towns, but the Barrasso-owned theaters did not evolve into a network that could address black performer concerns on a national scale. Anselmo Barrasso, who called for "first class acts of all kinds" for his sites near Memphis's Beale Street, would eventually become a Theater Owners' Booking Association board member.[80]

Charles P. Bailey, a native-born white Southerner who became a very vocal and controversial T.O.B.A. board member, will be discussed in further chapters. His business partner, British Jewish immigrant L. D. Joel, was more of an entrepreneurial model for Reevin than Bailey or Barrasso. Lionel "L. D." Joel was born in England in 1880, immigrated to the United States in 1890, and was quickly naturalized. After working in salvage and as an auctioneer in Ocala, Florida, Joel became a theater proprietor in Jacksonville, Florida.[81] In December 1910, L. D. Joel, the "theatrical king" of black vaudeville, created the Southern Vaudeville Circuit, a short chain of five theaters in Pensacola, Florida; Montgomery, Alabama; Mobile; and Atlanta that catered to African American talent. Performers who "had the goods" were promised anywhere from twelve to twenty-four weeks of employment "without losing a day."[82] Joel collaborated with African American vaudevillians, like Billy King, who was his assistant manager and amusement director in his Atlanta theaters, as well as worked with an all-black management staff of cashiers, property men, electricians, and orchestra leaders.[83]

Joel's entertainment circuit mirrored the Northern efforts of Klein and the C.C.V.E., albeit on a smaller scale. Whether or not Joel's Jewish immigrant background was of importance to his African American partners is not clear, yet Joel's personality, expertise, and disdain for traditional hierarchal Southern race relations was discussed by black vaudevillians in the informal entertainment networks of actors' boarding houses, barbershops, and "green rooms" or performer holding spaces in black theaters.[84] In these spaces, black performers and managers alike shared that Joel was a fair manager and further noted in the black press with letters that gave "notice to all performers in the South . . . if signed by L.D. Joel, you are fine."[85] L. D. Joel remained a theater manager throughout the 1930s, even after the Southern Vaudeville Circuit was subsumed by T.O.B.A. Sam Reevin found similar success in this same entertainment world.

## *Refugee in Chattanooga*

Born in Repke, Chernigov, Russia, on January 15, 1881, not many details are known about Samuel Elias Reevin's life in Repke prior to his 1906 emigration to the United States. Reevin resided in the Pale of Settlement—the segment of Western Russia, Poland, and Ukraine in which Jews in the Russian Empire were forced to reside from the late eighteenth century until 1917—where he worked as a carpenter and a journeyman.[86] After marrying young Sarah Lebovitz, the Reevins' departure from Russia in 1906 coincided with a rash of violent pogroms between 1905 and 1906. Between 1881 and 1906, genocidal violence and destruction plagued sixty-four towns in the Pale, "including Odessa, Yekaterinoslav, Kishinev," Sarah's home of Kiev, and Samuel's home of Chernigov.[87] Enduring untold destruction of property, livelihood, and loss of life, "the worst pogrom year" of 1906 resulted in the flight of more than "200,000 Russian Jews," of which "154,000 fled to the United States."[88] Schmuel and Soro Rivin (Samuel and Sarah) were two of these 154,000 who fled and sought passage on Hamburg's *SS Patricia* in April 1906 to land on Ellis Island in New York Harbor on May 17, 1906.[89]

The Reevins differed from many of the fellow passengers on the *Patricia* in that they knew New York City was not going to be their final destination. Private philanthropic American Jewish organizations, like the Industrial Removal Office (IRO), attempted to sort the hundreds of thousands of Eastern European Jewish immigrants and move them from the overcrowded New York City boroughs to less-populated urban and quasi-urban locations throughout the United States. Sponsored by a "Gedolye Bere," the Reevins decided to make Chattanooga their home upon arrival in Ellis Island.[90]

At the onset of the twentieth century, Chattanooga city boosters labeled Tennessee's third-largest city as the "gateway to the South" and promoted it as a developed, modern New South city.[91] With its growing manufacturing industries, rail transportation centers, and natural resources, the city wanted to entice many "Northern capitalists" to upbuild the city as a monument to the "thrift, industry and energy of men—southern and northern" dedicated to making the region an "inland metropolis of the South."[92] Civic leaders wanted to recruit laborers and entrepreneurs willing to work and invest in the city, and migrant and immigrant populations relocated to Chattanooga by 1900. While many of these newcomers were formerly Northern residents, a small European immigrant population began to seek out the city after 1910.

Although Tennessee only had a 9 percent immigrant population in 1910, Samuel and Sarah Reevin joined a Chattanooga Jewish community of eight hundred persons out of an estimated forty-four thousand city residents.[93] With roots dated back to the 1870s, Chattanooga's Jewish community was home to three Jewish congregations, including two Orthodox congregations, B'Nai Zion and the Gates of Zion, and one Reform congregation, the Mizpah Temple. Jewish social clubs, a Young Men's Hebrew Association and Hebrew Ladies Aid Society, and a Zionist organization all rounded out the offerings of the Jewish community in the years between 1900 and 1920. Refugee settlement works maintained that Chattanooga was a "growing industrial town," with a Jewish population that was largely "very happy and contented."[94] Despite some immigrant complaints that "Chattanooga was fifty years behind civilization" in comparison with New York City, Samuel and Sarah "put their shoulders to the wheel" and dedicated themselves to becoming Americans and Chattanoogans.[95] In 1907, just a year after their arrival, the Reevins declared their intent to be naturalized and renounced "absolutely and forever all allegiance" to Russia. After the birth of their two daughters, Goldie in 1908 and Frieda in 1911, the Reevins were granted citizenship in July 1911.[96]

### Working in the Black Chattanooga Community

In between 1906 and 1914, Sam Reevin labored as a cabinetmaker, an employee at the Chattanooga Furnace Company, and finally as a grocer.[97] The Reevin family worked and lived among small established Jewish neighborhoods in the city near fellow merchants who worked on Market and West Main Streets, near the Orthodox congregation of B'Nai Zion on Carter Street.[98] Reevin's move from laborer-merchant to a theater entrepreneur was a gradual seven-year process that allowed for him to more firmly acquire English language skills and develop community connections with other Jewish merchants who worked near or in African American enclaves.[99] The other merchants, who would all eventually be charter members of the original Theatre Owners' Booking Association in 1920 along with Reevin—M. H. Silverman, Benjamin Silverman, and Abraham Slabosky—were connected with the B'Nai Zion congregation.[100] The Silvermans and Slabosky eventually participated in the segments of Chattanooga commerce that catered primarily to African Americans, including the drugstores and nickelodeon theaters that dotted East Ninth Street.[101] But Reevin was one of the first in this group to become involved with variety and silent film theaters.

Sam Reevin joined the white and immigrant merchants who served Chattanooga African Americans because it was a financially lucrative business decision. Yet arguably Reevin also saw the similarities between his refugee immigrant group and the black clients he served. Early twentieth-century Tennessee practiced de jure racial segregation just as the rest of the Southern United States did, but black Chattanooga and East Tennessee in general were regarded as anomalies because of their antebellum past. Tennessee had not wanted to join the Confederacy, was the last state to secede from the Union, and Chattanooga was home to few slaveholders. The city's immediate post–Civil War, black-white racial relationships reflected a not-yet-fixed racial hierarchy, in that African Americans could still serve in elected and law enforcement positions, even after the *Plessy v. Ferguson* decision and federally approved racial segregation.[102] Yet when the Reevins moved to the city, a white mob lynched African American laborer Ed Johnson on Walnut Bridge for an assumed assault on a white woman, Nevada Taylor, a rare and well-publicized display of horrific racial violence in the city. The Chattanooga of March 1906 would have been reminiscent in some ways to the cities from which the Reevins had just fled. Racially violent incidents occurred throughout Chattanooga in the months after Johnson's lynching, and the city remained on guard for months, fearing that African Americans would retaliate for Johnson's demise.[103]

Tenuous comparisons to and "a vague sense of empathy" between Southern Jews and African Americans aside, what drew Reevin to African American

Chattanooga commerce was its growing prosperous nature.[104] By 1910 African Americans were nearly one third of Chattanooga's overall population of 17,944 residents.[105] There were "few Negro loafers" as the unemployed and vagrants were "offered employment in many factories and public works."[106] Even local white newspapers concurred that the "superiority of negro labor in such occupations (unskilled and semi-skilled) seems to be undisputed."[107] Class conscious black Chattanoogans were quick to tout the commerce opportunities that the city's growing manufacturing institutions afforded. Black periodical articles noted the "business Negroes" of Chattanooga and lauded how working-class African Americans in the city saved money to buy homes, attended institutions of higher education, and "engaged in business of their own, catering to members of their own race."[108] Even prior to the early years of the Great Migration there appeared to be a decided effort on the part of both black and white city leaders to retain residents and laborers in Chattanooga and encourage even more growth.

Chattanooga's local center of black commerce was East Ninth Street, or the "Big Nine." Nearly 155 black commercial and professional establishments and residences permeated the twelve- to fifteen-block stretch between Market Street and the city's National Cemetery as early as 1900.[109] East Ninth Street was no "Dahomey Stroll" of Chicago, for it was much smaller. Yet the "Big Nine" was a vibrant commercial district where black Chattanoogans satisfied many of their shopping, leisure, and employment needs and where supposedly a "Negro had more business and better business than any other town in the state could boast."[110] Chattanooga's black entrepreneurs created a chapter of the National Negro Business League in the 1910s, and their efforts warranted enough success for the city to host the annual NNBL conference opening at the city's Lyric Theatre in 1917.[111]

While white theater venues either excluded or segregated black customers in upstairs balconies, vaudeville and motion picture theaters along East Ninth were marketed as the only "houses for colored people."[112] The Ivy Theater at 329 East Ninth opened in May 1910 and boasted of the "highest class Colored Vaudeville obtainable," safe for "Ladies and children." Just a block down the street the Casino Theater stood at 403 West Ninth Street, "the only one of its kind that is owned, controlled, and patronized exclusively by the colored people."[113] As these theaters attracted patrons and revenue, Reevin observed the prosperity of these institutions and made the switch from managing his grocery store on West Ninth Street to becoming a theater manager.

## *An Extra-Large Heart for the Theatrical World*

Nothing in his previous occupation history indicated that Reevin had the faintest idea of what it took to manage a theater or book live acts for local black

Chattanoogans. Hiring a suitable buck and wing dancer to perform in between short reels of the latest silent film was nothing like managing the produce inventory of a grocery store. While small nickelodeons that occasionally showcased live acts existed, seven black-serving theaters had come and gone between 1910 and 1913.[114] Nonetheless, Reevin became the manager of the Leader, Eagle, and Queen Theaters all along East and West Ninth Streets by 1914.[115]

Reevin's engagement with black Chattanoogans began with managing the Queen Theater. Most of Chattanooga's black-serving theaters were white owned and managed in the late 1910s, and the Queen was no different. Yet the black periodical the *Crisis* advertised the institution as an example of racial uplift, where "only *Negro talent* will be employed" in a site with a seating capacity for "700 with luxury boxes" to be "equipped for *first class* vaudeville," owned by the Sword Brothers.[116] Reevin was expected to help the theater perpetuate its "first class" goals of quality entertainment for the up-and-coming black Chattanooga community. He did so first by increasing the theaters' publicity in the national black press. While the Eagle or Leader might have advertised in local black Chattanooga *Blade*, Reevin sought out advertisements for the Queen in the entertainment section of the national *Indianapolis Freeman*.[117] The *Freeman* listed Queen Theater advertisements for much of the latter half of 1914 until the February 1915 season, with an average frequency of about twice a month.[118] Reevin angled to have his advertisements placed in the same row as those theater advertisements from Chicago, Philadelphia, or St. Louis, hoping to attract the same top-notch performers who might have sought work on the Dudley Circuit or at the Gibson's New Standard.

Reevin dove into management as an independent booking agent and was quick to use the black press to clear his name should there be misunderstandings about salary, booking, or contracts. While he was not yet adept at selecting the most talented singer or novelty act, Reevin garnered a reputation for organization and kept meticulous records. When the black vaudeville novelty team Washburne and Piper told other vaudevillians to "beware of the Queen Theatre" in early October 1914 in print and characterized Reevin as shortchanging them ten dollars for a performance, Reevin did not ignore these allegations. Rather as a new manager, Reevin wrote an editorial for the *Freeman*, in which he publicized the correspondence between himself and the duo with the agreed-upon salary, chronicled Washburne's public drunkenness, and convinced an African American public of his trustworthiness as a manager.[119] While the back-and-forth continued on until November, with no further negative or contradictory commentary from other vaudeville groups, Reevin was later lauded in the *Freeman* as "a prince of a fellow, notwithstanding reports to the contrary." Black theater professionals encouraged performers to seek out Reevin, as he would pay what the contract stated, and "everybody there (Chattanooga) was happy."[120] In the latter half of 1914, the Queen Theater joined the *national* black vaudeville conversation, and popular acts began to view Chattanooga and the South more generally as an attractive booking location.

While Reevin made no known attempt to cross racial boundaries by having social relationships with fellow black theater professionals, he was praised for his "sagaciousness" as much as he was critiqued for not being free flowing with actor salaries.[121] Scholar Eric C. Goldstein's maintains that many Jewish newcomers to the early-twentieth-century South tended to "affirm their whiteness by negating the comparison between themselves and African Americans." Reevin departed from this characterization and cultivated collegial professional relationships with African American theater managers and later publicly declared his disdain for the "humiliation" of "Jim Crowism" with its "special side entrances" for the "colored."[122]

In 1918 Reevin briefly opened his own theater circuit, mirroring Dudley and Klein's efforts. Booking agent Reevin joined forces with fellow Chattanoogan Benjamin Silverman and Joseph M. Shallet of Louisville, Kentucky, and created the Mutual Amusement Company in the 1917–1918 season. Incorporated in Kentucky for $10,000, Mutual Amusement became Reevin's project, although he only owned twenty-five shares of the company. A year later M. H. Silverman and Abe Slabosky also joined the executives.[123] Mutual Amusement was physically based on East Ninth Street in Chattanooga, "booked eleven theaters in the South," promised "good commissions, with no layoffs," and covered the same geographic areas the L. D. Joel circuit had—Nashville, Chattanooga, Atlanta, Macon, Savannah, Jacksonville, and Pensacola. Reevin handled the vaudeville booking for theaters that had both live shows and film reels. With the company's promise to "place tickets anywhere," Reevin booked acts for the black-owned Douglass Theatre in Macon, Georgia, and the white-owned, black-serving Bijou Theatre in Nashville, Tennessee.[124] Eager to display his dedication to his newfound nation, Reevin also donated Mutual Amusement revenue to support the city's push for war bonds and other home front support measures during World War I.[125]

After a season of running Mutual Amusement Co., Reevin also returned to the theater management business as the proprietor of the new Liberty Theater at 312 East Ninth Street. He helped build the Liberty Theatre from the ground up and "struggled with it" in those first few years.[126] Opening amid wartime, the Liberty hosted black community events and was used primarily for African American wartime outreach. In the 1918–1919 season the Liberty welcomed former Chattanooga resident and black classical tenor Roland Hayes, held a public lecture on the Civil War by an African American veteran, hosted a religious organ recital by

Professor Carl Ditton, and held the commencement exercises of the "colored" Howard High School.[127]

While the war effort damaged the vaudeville community because of drafted and absent performers and the dwindling leisure incomes of audience members, Reevin used the Liberty to make inroads into the social and cultural lives of African American Chattanoogans. He honed a connection that would encourage the community to return to the Liberty Theater once entertainers resumed theater travel. Reevin also resided just blocks away on E. Fourth Street, within walking distance of the local downtown African American community.[128] On the cusp of the incorporation of T.O.B.A. Sam E. Reevin was on his way to becoming the one whom some black vaudevillians called a "medium-sized person with an extra-large heart for the theatrical world . . . and a keen eye to business."[129]

## MILTON STARR

Rounding out the trio of Jewish immigrant entrepreneurs who rose as part of the interracial management team of 1920s T.O.B.A. was Milton Starr. Starr's background story differed from both Klein's and Reevin's, in that he was the youngest of the three, was born in the Southern United States to Russian-Jewish immigrant parents, and had a family background in theater management. Born in 1896, Starr arguably was more a product of twentieth-century America than the nineteenth century like his counterparts Klein, Reevin, Dudley, and Turpin.

Born on May 17, 1896, Milton was the seventh of Joseph Starr and Sarah Lusky Starr's eight living children, including Birdie, Solomon, Michael, Rose, Jacob, David, Milton, and Alford.[130] By Milton's birth in 1896 the Starr family settled into Nashville at 229 Main Street. Joseph Starr supported the family as a peddler and was soon joined by his three eldest children in the workplace.[131] With a home of twelve people in a duplex at 146½ N. Sumner Street by April 1900, all combined income was needed to feed and shelter the family, which also included Sarah's parents.[132] Nashville's Jewish community had slightly deeper roots than Chattanooga's. Individual Jewish residents called Nashville home in the 1840s, and the first Jewish congregation was established by 1861. Most of the Nashville Jewish community in the early twentieth century resided in the "downtown areas of Market, Cherry, and Summer Streets," close to Jewish commercial districts and the town's first synagogue.[133]

Unlike his older three siblings, Milton was allowed to complete his public school education without simultaneously working at a trade or office. Starr graduated from high school and pursued higher education at the prestigious local Vanderbilt University.[134] During the 1913–14 theater season Milton's father, Joseph, embarked on the new occupation of amusement theater proprietor, and the new family business was born—a business for which Milton eventually left Vanderbilt to help develop. In 1913 Joseph Starr opened the Starr Theater on Cedar Street in the heart of Nashville's black community and became one of several Jewish proprietors of black-serving businesses in the US South.[135]

## *Black Business on Cedar Street*

The Starrs operated their theater in the city's vibrant black enclave. In 1910 Nashville was a robust urban center of black life in the New South.[136] The city's African American past was rooted in Middle Tennessee's investment in slavery. While large-scale plantation slavery was atypical, historian Bobby Lovett noted that the city of Nashville itself owned slaves who labored on civic infrastructure projects in the 1830s and '40s. Slave auction houses had been on the very same streets that would be home to black-owned establishments a half century later.[137] With a population of 36,583 African Americans by 1910, the post-Reconstruction Nashville black community that the Starrs encountered was dedicated to racial uplift through the establishment of black educational institutions, churches, and commercial businesses. City tour manuals argued that "Nashville was the center of influence for more than two-thirds of the negro inhabitants of the country."[138] The city served as the headquarters of the National Baptist and African Methodist Conventions; hosted the National Baptist Publishing Board; was home to black colleges, including Fisk University, Walden University, and Meharry Medical College; and was the location of Greenwood Park, one of the region's few public parks for the "pleasure of colored people only."[139] As scholar Christopher Scribner notes, the city boasted its prominent black weekly newspaper, the *Nashville Globe*, dedicated to black community narratives and "the Negro in business."[140] It was not unusual to find black-owned grocers, milliners, restaurants, hairstylists, or drugstores along N. Main or Cedar Streets.[141] Black commerce further flourished in Nashville, as it was the site of one of the earliest local chapters of the National Negro Business League (NNBL), hosted its third annual conference in 1903 and was the hometown of the NNBL's second national president, J. C. Napier.[142]

## *The Starr Family and the Amusement Business*

The Starr Theater opened in April 1913 and promised the "best moving pictures," as they were under "new management." The Starrs joined two other black-serving theaters, the Majestic and the Twelfth Avenue Theatres, out of the city's fourteen theaters overall.[143] Located at 412 Cedar Street, the business was housed among black real estate offices, a barbershop, and a billiards hall. Nearly every business and residence on Cedar Street between the 400 and 1200 blocks was owned or managed by or served African Americans. The Starr Theater hired an African American staff and immediately advertised its playbills in the *Globe*.

Joseph Starr's first year as a theater entrepreneur was far from smooth, and there was resistance to his initial presence on Cedar Street. Part of this resistance may be due in part to Starr's rapid move to manage both his own named theater and the nearby Majestic. In the next season, the Majestic faded as a separate entity and became the Starr Theater #2 at 426 Cedar, while Starr #1 was at 412 Cedar. Son, Solomon Starr, was placed as the Starr #2 manager, while J. Starr negotiated the building of the Starr Amusement Co. In one year, Joseph Starr took over two of the three black-serving theaters in the city, suggesting that the family's presence would be broad and sustained in the black Nashville community.[144]

While the majority of the staff was African American, racial conflict in Starr's Cedar Street theaters was not unknown, and black manager E. E. Rice accused J. Starr of a physical confrontation with one of their young black patrons in November 1913.[145] Rice's account of J. Starr roughly removing a black teenage boy from the theater made the first page of the *Globe,* demonstrating behavior that could incite a black boycott of the Starr Theater. Joseph Starr used his new connections to the black community commercial district to refute these charges in the *Globe* and offered a class-based excuse, claiming that the young teenager had disrespectfully treated a "colored people's place of entertainment" like "some back alley." J. Starr concluded that as "the life of our business depends on the patronage of the colored people," he would never insult or assault African American patrons.[146] Black readers interested in race uplift and respectability might have been swayed by Starr's contentions that his venues would "preserve order" and provide a "good clean show in a clean house."[147] Yet the discrepancy between Rice's and Starr's narratives of what happened to the unnamed black teenager highlights historians' accounts of the conflicts that occurred as Jewish employers moved into black communities and outwardly "affirmed their whiteness" and regional racial hierarchies. It also points to some white owners' paternalistic behavior toward black managers, even in black-serving spaces.[148] The *Globe* publicized nothing else about this incident, and the Starr family went on to manage a second theater in the 1914–15 season.

While the two or three other black-serving theaters came and went in Nashville after this incident, Joseph Starr hired another manager, George A. Gary, and the Starr Theater concentrated on "high class moving pictures" while remaining at the 412 Cedar address.[149] By 1916, fifty-five-year-old Joseph no longer managed the theater that bore the family name, and twenty-year-old Milton Starr left Vanderbilt to follow in the family business. Although the racial tension had diffused from the 1913 incident, Milton offered a younger, fresh perspective infused with native Nashvillian knowledge and college training. Milton Starr began his tenure in Starr Amusements by acquiring an additional theater.

The Bijou Theatre at 421 Fourth Street did not serve black patrons, but when Milton Starr took control in 1916, Friday night became "Colored Society Night," and soon the Bijou argued it was "the largest house in the South operated exclusively for negroes."[150] With Milton's involvement there was increased connection between the professional relationship of the Starr family, the Nashville black community, and the national black entertainment scene. Trade journals, like *Motography* and *Moving Picture World,* took note of Milton's industry moves in Nashville, and national black periodicals recognized the Bijou. The *Chicago Defender* noted that Starr deserved "a vast amount of credit" for spending extra money to seek out the world's best in African American produced films or "race productions" and not just re-release white film reels for black movie houses.[151]

As World War I approached and shifted the Nashville entertainment landscape, as it did in the rest of the nation, Milton Starr registered for the draft. Starr was selected for service, and he served in the Signal Corps, while his brother David served in the United States Navy.[152] Anticipating his official release from the Corps in January 1919, Starr announced plans for a major expansion of the Bijou in December of 1918. Throughout the running of the Starr Theater and the takeover of the Bijou, Milton and his family occasionally worked with live entertainers but devoted much of the business to film screenings. Starr, like Reevin in Chattanooga, used his theater space to make greater connections with the surrounding black community. In 1917, for example, the Bijou hosted a YMCA fundraiser with the Invincible Concert Company from Chicago and screened a film on "The Life of Our Savior."[153] When the Bijou hosted Madame Rose's Octoroons and the Original Georgia Minstrels in 1917 with its cast of thirty people including an orchestra and a brass band, the booking made the local *Nashville Globe* as "the greatest theatrical event of the season."[154]

In 1918, Starr and his brother Michael bought a former white opera house and converted it into the new Bijou Theatre on Fourth Avenue. The new Bijou still screened films, but vaudeville for the masses often led the playbill. The *Globe* covered the opening of the Bijou with nearly a full-page article in December 1918 and heralded its promise of being a theatrical center for colored patronage, both Nashville natives and visitors.[155] The *Globe* raised no concerns that the new Bijou would be owned and operated by the white Jewish Starr family, and rather made more of an issue that this local theater was essentially rescued from a "New York concern" of real estate professionals that had no roots in Tennessee.[156] As the 1920s approached the Bijou was thus accepted by African American community leaders as a part of black Nashville life. Milton Starr held a celebratory preview of the 1919 season by holding a "special vaudeville" on Christmas that year. Subsequently in the first few years of the T.O.B.A. circuit even some black vaudevillians mentioned that the "soft spoken" Starr treated black artists with respect, and Ethel Waters noted that Starr was the first white manager to refer to her as "Miss Waters," as if she was "already a star."[157]

The new theater brought the Starr siblings together as members of the Bijou Amusement Company in 1918. With Milton Starr at the helm, Bijou Amusement was a theater management company that acquired motion pictures and live entertainment theaters for African Americans, capitalizing on the growing black leisure entertainment market.[158] Ultimately, work with Bijou Amusement facilitated Milton Starr's introduction to Sam E. Reevin in 1918. As president of his Mutual Amusement Company, Reevin handled the live entertainment booking for the new Bijou. With a formal Starr and Reevin partnership, all the key southern players were in place to battle for control of national African American variety theater organization. Milton Starr's work with Nashville black communities gave him a small example of what it would be like to be a white immigrant manager of a black-serving corporation.

One of the key players absent from the post–World War I black vaudeville battles was Emma Griffin. By 1915 both Emma and Mabel battled debilitating respiratory infections and reviewers noted when they were "suffering with a cold" yet still commanded the stage or when they traveled separately due to illness of one or the other.[159] The rapid physical pace of performing combined with infrequent healthcare respites proved overwhelming and detrimental to their business plans, and they were forced to return to Chicago in 1916. As illness kept them from the stage, they faced mounting medical and housing expenses they could not surmount. After hospitalizations and failed medical procedures, Emma Griffin died of acute bronchitis in August 1918, and the Griffin Sisters act never performed again.[160] Emma did not live to see the charter of the T.O.B.A., but her general wariness about the interracial management of black-serving theaters permeated the board's discussions throughout T.O.B.A.'s tenure.

Critiqued by some black theater veterans, like the Griffin Sisters, and accepted by theater critics who sang their praises in the black press, Martin Klein, Sam Reevin, and Milton Starr built a tenuous familiarity with local African American communities that allowed them to be at the forefront of a black-serving theater empire. Although S. H. Dudley and John Gibson spoke of black theater as uplift through race capitalism, these immigrant newcomers maintained that they "deeply appreciated the patronage" of their black customers but also acknowledged that "every nickel counts" in the amusement business.[161] As the 1920s approached and black uplift advocates and the "outsiders" joined forces, centralized black vaudeville evolved into a show business enterprise and the multimillion dollar industry that was T.O.B.A. Time.

# 3

# T.O.B.A. FORMS

## *The Interracial Business Plan for a New Negro Business*

There is nothing sure but death, and nothing *so* uncertain as show business.

—S. Tutt Whitney, "Retrospection," *Freeman*, July 9, 1910

"Performers Will No Doubt Profit," "Incorporating in Florida," and "Headquartered in Chattanooga" were all among the litany of announcements made about black vaudeville circuits in 1920. The 1920–21 theater season was the period where all the major players in African American theater management fought to take control of the field in the Midwest and Southeastern circuits. When black intellectuals argued about the aftermath of World War I and the New Negro figure with his "self-consciousness, new desires, and hopes for the future," many black theater owners simply wanted these New Negro men and women to fill theaters.[1] Managers longed to reclaim the performers who had survived the World War I battlefields, restore theater buildings that had been repurposed for civic needs, and retrieve audience members who might have the leisure income to attend a vaudeville performance. Black periodicals announced the opening of the Dudley, Klein, and Reevin United Vaudeville Circuit in June 1920, and entertainment trade journals declared the incorporation plans of the Florida-based Southern Consolidated Vaudeville Circuit in July of that same year. Months later the Theater Owners' Booking Association wrote of its December 1920 incorporation date in Tennessee and its plans to solve the "discontentment" felt by "Negro performers."[2] The players in all these interracial organizations overlapped, and the infrastructures were very similar. Yet when the flurry of announcements and articles on "vaudeville wars" subsided, only T.O.B.A. remained.

T.O.B.A. developed as a profitable entrepreneurial venture in the early 1920s, and that journey is this chapter's focus. The circuit evolved from the vestiges of various black vaudeville centralization plans to a viable organization worth five million dollars by 1926, with African American and immigrant theater professionals like S. H. Dudley, C. H. Turpin, Sam Reevin, and Milton Starr all at the helm. The executive board developed a successful business strategy that straddled the often conflicting interests of both its African American and white participants in an effort to garner maximum profit for management and stability for entertainment laborers. The newly incorporated Theater Owners' Booking Association emerged from the "uncertain" realm of show business to become a flourishing institution only through the joint efforts of its African American theater veterans, who fashioned essential networks with black artists and audiences, *and* its white theater professionals, who helped navigate financial obstacles in the segregated business world.

## BUILDING A VAUDEVILLE CORPORATION (1921–22)

As a black-serving institution with a multiethnic, interracial executive board, T.O.B.A. charted a complicated path. In the 1920s African American scholar E. Franklin Frazier noted that definitions of the New Negro largely focused on the "creative artist" who expressed the "aesthetic emotion of the race." Yet Frazier also noted that a New Negro could be defined as a black entrepreneur dedicated to "the salvation of the race in economic enterprise."[3] T.O.B.A. embraced both definitions, as the production and dissemination of creative black art was its business. As a product of the Great Migration and New Negro struggles for advancement and progress, the circuit stood at the intersection of commercialized entertainment and race entrepreneurship. If planned correctly, T.O.B.A. held the promise of black community advancement through black popular culture and art and entrepreneurial opportunity for theater owners and booking agents. Ultimately, as an interracially managed organization the circuit addressed these conflicting goals with moments of brilliant success and clear mishaps along the way.

T.O.B.A. was incorporated when there was still debate among some white entrepreneurs over the existence and profitability of a black consumer market. Robert Weems reveals how white advertisers, doubtful of the economic vitality of African American communities, posited on how to use strategic advertising in the late 1920s and early '30s.[4] Racially biased advertisers held that consumers were "preoccupied, often stupid, and always lethargic." Marketing publicists argued that of the American consumer base of "twenty-one million families," the lowest strata included the "the illiterate, indigent, criminal, foreign-born, the Indian and the *Negro*."[5] In contrast through his encounters with the National Negro Business

League, race leader Booker T. Washington estimated in 1915 that African Americans owned a diverse range of property valued at $1 billion and operated between forty-three thousand and forty-five thousand "Negro businesses" with at least thirty thousand of those businesses in Southern states alone.[6] Between 1900 and 1930 the development of industries owned or operated by African Americans, like bakeries, grocery stores, milliners, hair care salons, truck farms, and banks, illustrated that black citizens could locate the funds to support the businesses that most interested and best served their communities, and that included the black entertainment industry. Working-class African Americans who had the leisure income to spend on commercial amusement were the primary audiences for black vaudeville performances. In 1920 Sadie Tanner Mossell discovered that some black Philadelphia consumers were so devoted to entertainment consumption that they attended their vaudeville or motion picture theater regularly, spending anywhere from twenty-five to sixty-five dollars of their annual income, which might have been just over $700.[7] An African American market for T.O.B.A.'s potential theaters and performances was clearly apparent.

T.O.B.A.'s leaders incorporated the circuit officially as the Theater Owners' Booking Association on December 8, 1920, in Chattanooga, Tennessee, and charter members included familiar vaudeville management participants, like Sam E. Reevin and Milton Starr. The other official T.O.B.A. charter members were not as known at the national level. Reevin, the one constant executive board member during the entire ten-year tenure, and Nashville theater owner Milton Starr were joined by brothers Morris Hillel Silverman and Benjamin Silverman and the Silvermans' brother-in-law, Abraham Slabosky.[8] M. H. Silverman was the owner of the Chattanooga black-serving movie theater the Lincoln, while brother Ben owned the Rose Drug Store in the city. Abraham Slabosky owned the Grand Theatre, an additional black-serving theater in Chattanooga. The Silverman and Slabosky properties were all located on Chattanooga's black commercial center of East Ninth Street or "the Big Nine," confirming their familiarity with black Chattanooga markets.[9] As discussed previously, black periodicals briefly mentioned that M. H. Silverman, Reevin, and Slabosky had formed the Mutual Amusement Company in early 1917 as a booking company primarily focused on distributing silent film.[10]

Reevin selected the Silvermans and Slabosky as charter members to fulfill a Tennessee incorporation law which mandated that "five or more persons above the age of twenty-one" must unite to execute an incorporation. Despite their previous theater collaborations, the latter three entrepreneurs faded from the T.O.B.A. story after signing the charter.[11] Reevin was the only one who physically signed the charter and attested to knowing all the "bargainors."[12] For a thirty-dollar filing fee and provisions for capital stock of "$20,000 to be divided into two hundred shares valued at $100 a share," as of December 1920 the Theater Owners' Booking Association was officially a for-profit theatrical entity.[13]

T.O.B.A.'s incorporation charter legally defined the business as a theatrical booking institution and included provisions to buy real estate, erect new theaters, and rehabilitate existing spaces into T.O.B.A. theaters. It also tellingly made room for operating motion pictures, whose golden age was just on the horizon.[14] Yet African American entrepreneurs were not included as signers of the charter, and there was the glaring absence of Reevin's previous partners, S. H. Dudley and Martin Klein, absences that would not be publicly discussed in any detail until mid-1921. T.O.B.A. was not identified as an African American-serving business in corporation documents, nor was there any overt discussion of race or ethnicity in the filing records. T.O.B.A. was a for-profit business, and its standard incorporation language specifically followed the template for theater or opera house corporations as mandated by the state of Tennessee as well as the language set forth for domestic corporations according to the federal government.[15] The charter stated that the Theater Owners' Booking Association operated as a

> theatrical booking company to furnish Theatre Owners and Operators with vaudeville sets, stock companies and theatrical attractions of *all kinds*, and to make contracts and agreements relating thereto, and to contract with vaudeville performers, stock companies, and theatrical troupes and companies *of all kinds*, for their services, and to do all sets necessary of incident to the conduct of a theatrical booking agency; And for the purpose of erecting, purchasing and leasing buildings for the use of and occupation as opera houses and theatres, for the purpose of furnishing theatrical and motion picture entertainment; and for the purpose of buying, leasing, and sub-leasing, producing, and presenting motion picture films.[16]

This formulaic language was a commentary on all the varieties of theater attractions that could be booked legally and the types of real estate that could be used for theatrical entertainment, rather than a meaningful mission of black vaudeville. Yet it established T.O.B.A. as a business with the ability to franchise theaters and distribute shares to stockholders around the country—the purpose of a corporation.[17]

How T.O.B.A. became a "race" business and the details of how the institution functioned as an interracially managed institution are not found in its incorporation charter but in the annual tax reports and stockholder meeting summaries connected to the organization's chartering. The all-white charter membership was not unusual given that Reevin chartered the circuit in Tennessee. While interracial business partnerships were not explicitly illegal, the 1918 Tennessee legal code made provisions for segregated schooling, street cars, railcars, hotels, hospitals, and parks and gave specific fines and jail time for each instance of race mixing.[18] Furthermore, T.O.B.A.'s charter membership fit with national practices in black entertainment management. In his 1899 edit of *The Negro in Business*, W. E. B. Du Bois lauded the economic significance of "traveling Negro vaudeville" and observed that many black vaudeville companies were "compelled" to have white management in order to conduct business with white-owned theaters, banks, and other segregated entities. Du Bois maintained that traveling black theater was "largely under Negro control" and was a sizeable "investment of Negro capital."[19] Twenty-one years later, T.O.B.A.'s summaries of its initial stockholder meetings and executive board selection echoed Du Bois's previous sentiments.

When T.O.B.A. held its first stockholder meeting in February 1921, its purpose of creating a business for black consumers with the inclusion of black management was clear. The consistent representation of African Americans as officers and board members kept the circuit from being an entirely white-owned business that capitalized off the black consumer market, but rather an interracially managed institution with a black consumer focus. The mention of race officially entered the tax summary reports by 1922 when the organization defined itself as an operation "to supply vaudeville attractions to colored theaters."[20] Yet, from its inception, theatrical presses referred to T.O.B.A. as a "colored" vaudeville circuit and commented on the "New Combine of Southern Negro Houses."[21] The election of African American theater veteran Charles H. Turpin as vice president and the appointment of T. Spencer Finley and Charles H. Douglass as Board of Directors members also further cemented the interracial management nature of the enterprise, as all three had worked with Reevin and Martin Klein as part of C.C.V.E.[22]

Turpin and Douglass were long-standing members of the National Negro Business League (NNBL) and adhered to its arguably "militant" and black "nationalistic" belief that black business was a mode of racial uplift and community advancement.[23] Both black entrepreneurs brought to T.O.B.A. the contention that black theater managers should have at least a shared economic investment and profit in black vaudeville theater with white investors. As the owner of St. Louis's Booker T. Washington Theatre, Turpin was no stranger to interracial business partnerships as previously discussed. He served as T.O.B.A.'s first vice president to build on his legacy of "furnishing clean, decent public amusement" while keeping "some profits spent for pleasure and edifying entertainment" within his "own Race."[24] Likewise as a theater owner in Macon, Georgia, Douglass joined the T.O.B.A. board to expand on the success he had with his own theater in securing "colored patronage" for the "best attainable" predominantly black vaudeville acts he booked.[25] T.O.B.A. was an interracially managed black-serving business from the start.

Through close examination of black vaudeville organizations between 1910 and 1920, it is apparent that T.O.B.A.'s executive membership and business plan was essentially an amalgamation of all circuits that had immediately preceded it. The initial T.O.B.A. board looked very reminiscent of the board of the National Managers' Protective Association (NMPA), a short-lived black vaudeville managers group created in May 1920. The NMPA deliberated on the combined "interests of managers, theater owners, and performers" of black vaudeville, and its board was entirely African American, with Turpin as president, Finley as secretary and treasurer, and Reevin as an informal part of the NMPA's initial planning meetings.[26] T.O.B.A. franchised many of the previously promised forty-eight theaters of the Dudley, Klein, and Reevin United Vaudeville Circuit, a theater-booking collaboration that S. H. Dudley, Martin Klein, and Sam Reevin proposed in June 1920.[27] United Vaudeville's three regional management design in turn had been based upon Martin Klein's Colored Consolidated Vaudeville Exchange in Chicago and the S. H. Dudley Circuit in Washington, DC. T.O.B.A.'s first season would be a test of how well it assembled all of these various strategies and participants from the previous attempts at centralization.

Within months of T.O.B.A.'s official incorporation, its first president and charter member, Milton Starr, advertised the circuit's importance to theaters, performers, and audience members alike. The company's resources were valued at "about $2,000,000" with room for tremendous growth.[28] Steeped in his seven years of experience managing Nashville's Bijou Theatre, Starr announced that T.O.B.A. had formed to redeem the "colored theatrical industry" from "greed, gross mismanagement, and unfair dealings" and restore some power to theater owners. Again, he spelled out T.O.B.A.'s purpose as an African American–focused business and invited "any theater owner in America" to become a "member of this organization" by purchasing three shares of stock "at par value of $100" or the face value of the share. With this purchase, a T.O.B.A. theater owner ensured that he or she had "one vote" in "all affairs of the association" and became the "recipient of a franchise for life."[29] Starr believed in the new professional management style so much that he encouraged interested theater owners to travel to the Chattanooga headquarters, meet with Reevin "at the expense" of T.O.B.A., and check out the organization. Subsequent advertisements in 1921 made a pitch for "every desirable theater in the South and Middle West" and "All Acts and All Companies" to write to Sam E. Reevin for more information.[30] In black periodicals, the circuit placed a special emphasis on highlighting well-known African American theater veterans, like C. H. Turpin or C. H. Douglass, as circuit leaders, again reassuring performers and audience members that T.O.B.A. indeed was in part a black business venture.

The first theaters to sign on with T.O.B.A. included twenty-five stockholder theater houses, while seven more promised to sign franchise contracts by the end of 1921. As mentioned, many of these theaters, especially those in St. Louis, Charleston, Louisville, and Memphis, had already been promised to the unrealized United Vaudeville Circuit and moved with Reevin to T.O.B.A.[31] Not yet a national circuit, southern houses were represented by theaters in Alabama, Arkansas, Georgia, Kentucky, Louisiana, Florida, North Carolina, South Carolina, Tennessee, and Texas; and the Midwest was represented by Indianapolis, Michigan, Missouri, Ohio, and Oklahoma. Just over a third of these initial theaters were black owned and managed. Harking back to the sexism the Griffin Sisters experienced in theater ownership and management, only two African American women, Zelia Breaux and Loula T. Williams, owned theaters on the circuit.[32]

T.O.B.A.'s first fiscal year had a slow but promising start and showcased emerging novelty performers, like tap dance team Roy White's Stylish Steppers, comedian Tim Moore and his Chicago Follies, and Henry Dixon's Jazzland Girls.[33] Vaudeville veteran Frank Montgomery praised T.O.B.A. as a "circuit" conducted "in a business manner," where "all the directors are business men and gentlemen . . . and they treat everybody as *gentlemen and ladies*," alluding to the ongoing racial tensions in white-managed black vaudeville that professionally "killed" black vaudevillians "every day," as previously described by Emma Griffin.[34] But the 1921 summer season was fraught with the effects of a national depression. Economic historian James Grant estimated that unemployment rates were as high as 19 percent or between "two million and six million" Americans out of a population of 31.5 million in 1921. T.O.B.A. president Milton Starr argued that rising unemployment rates were reflected "in the amusement business in the form of a marked falling off in attendance."[35] Twenty-five of the thirty-plus theaters closed with promises to "open by Labor Day" and either screened film reels or were dark altogether.[36] Performers either played fairs, carnivals, or non-T.O.B.A. theaters to make ends meet, and audiences were left wondering if their favorite acts would indeed come back to town come the fall.

## DUDLEY JOINS T.O.B.A.

It was this unstable season that moved Starr and the board of directors to include theater magnate S. H. Dudley in their advancement discussions. In mid-1921, theater veteran Frank Montgomery wrote in the *Defender* that although "money is tight all over the country and [the depression] is "hurting business all over," "T.O.B.A. is still going on." Montgomery believed T.O.B.A. would persevere through economic decline because S. H. Dudley was "fixing to join."[37] With T.O.B.A.'s slow growth the organization needed someone with the expertise and inroads with the black vaudevillian community to help revitalize the circuit, and Dudley was that expert. While many of the franchised theaters that first season had

**TABLE 1.** Initial Stockholders in 1921

| Location | Theater | Owner or Manager |
|---|---|---|
| Alexandria, LA | Liberty | F. C. Holden |
| Beaumont, TX | Lincoln | Clemmons Brothers |
| Birmingham, AL | Gay | H. J. Hury |
| Charleston, SC | Milo | J. J. Miller |
| Chattanooga, TN | Liberty | Sam E. Reevin |
| Cincinnati, OH | Lyceum | **T. Spencer Finley** |
| Columbia, SC | New Royal | H. W. Tolbutt |
| Dallas, TX | Park | **Chinz Moore** |
| Detroit, MI | Vaudette | **E. B. Dudley** |
| Galveston, TX | Lincoln (Liberty) | Lee & Moore |
| Houston, TX | American | **C. H. Caffey** |
| Jacksonville, FL | Strand | **W. J. Stiles** |
| Little Rock, AK | Plaza | M. A. Lightman |
| Louisville, KY | Lincoln | **William Warley** |
| Macon, GA | Douglass | **C. H. Douglass** |
| Memphis, TN | Palace | A. Barrasso |
| Mobile, AL | Pike | C. C. Schreiner |
| Montgomery, AL | Majestic | Bennett and Gordon |
| Nashville, TN | Bijou | Milton Starr |
| New Orleans, LA | Lyric | Boudreaux and Bennett |
| Shreveport, LA | Star | Charles F. Gordon |
| St. Louis, MO | Booker T. Washington | **C. H. Turpin** |
| Waco, TX | Gayety | W. H. Leonard |
| Wilmington, NC | Brooklyn | E. C. Foster |
| Winston-Salem, NC | Lafayette | **W. C. Scales** |
| PROMISED THEATERS as of February 1921 | | |
| Cleveland, OH | Grand Central | O. J. Harris |
| Indianapolis, ID | Washington | **E. S. Stone** |
| Kansas City, MO | Lincoln | Lawrence Goldman |
| Muskogee, OK | Dreamland | **L. T. Williams** |
| Oklahoma City, OK | Aldridge | Breaux and Whitlow |
| Savannah, GA | Pekin | **W. J. Stiles** |
| Tulsa, OK | Dreamland | **L. T. Williams** |

Note: African American owners are listed in bold.
Source: Milton Starr, "Milton Starr Makes Statement," *Chicago Defender*, February 12, 1921.

been previously pledged to the former Dudley, Klein, and Reevin United Circuit, personal infighting resulted in Dudley being excluded from T.O.B.A.'s charter. Nonetheless, Dudley had maintained a thriving management career throughout the 1919–20 and 1920–21 seasons. He strengthened Dudley Enterprises and hired fellow vaudevillian George Day as a new general manager to help organize his DC offices.[38] In June 1920 the entrepreneur formed the Dudley-Murray United Theater Corporation in Alexandria, Virginia, with other prominent local DC African American entrepreneurs, lawyers, and real estate developers. The corporation's purpose was to open the lavish, "thoroughly modern" Douglass Theatre on the 1800 block of U Street NW.[39] Dudley pursued the Douglass development while simultaneously continuing business dealings with white and black theater professionals in Chicago's Colored Consolidated Vaudeville Exchange (C.C.V.E.). The Exchange later transformed into plans for the United Vaudeville Circuit, with S. H. Dudley, Martin Klein, and Sam Reevin at the helm.[40]

When the United Vaudeville plan seemingly fell through in mid-1920, Dudley publicly announced in the theatrical industry press the creation of the Southern Consolidated Vaudeville Circuit, in partnership with white Florida theater manager Ernest L. Cummings.[41] Dudley's theaters in DC and Virginia, as well as Atlanta's 81 Theatre and Winston-Salem's Lafayette Theatre, were franchised to the Southern Circuit, and the business made plans to incorporate in Pensacola, Florida. Although a local white Pensacola paper mistakenly portrayed Cummings as the founder and primary shareholder of the Southern Consolidated Circuit, Cummings and Dudley as president and vice president, respectively, owned "three $100 shares each" of the Southern's stocks.[42] Sam Reevin was the secretary of the Southern Circuit before leaving to charter T.O.B.A. five months later with the Southern's basic proposed incorporation statement: "the business to be transacted is the booking of vaudeville acts and theatrical stock companies of *all kinds* in any city or town in the United States."[43]

Ultimately, in surveying the 1920 "war" in black vaudeville, Dudley was not only a participant but an officer in at least five of the black-serving organizations publicly discussed in the theatrical press. Those organizations that actually opened and appeared to be profitable, like the Southern Consolidated, had Dudley-franchised theaters and booked acts attached to them. Many industry insiders agreed that for T.O.B.A. to truly succeed, S. H. Dudley had to be included, and recruiting him was evidence that "T.O.B.A. managers must know their business." Dudley's addition was the imperative "right thing at the right time" and promised to put the circuit "on the square."[44]

Cultural historian W. Fitzhugh Brundage notes that Dudley was known for "speeding the economic integration of what had been an unsystematic and decentralized industry" of black vaudeville.[45] Dudley's potential success with T.O.B.A.

was extremely significant, as it was evidenced that black entrepreneurs could retain some autonomy in black vaudeville even after consolidation and interracial corporation. Upbuilding T.O.B.A. was incremental and built upon all the knowledge and network connections Dudley had gathered in creating his own circuit nearly a decade prior to T.O.B.A.'s formation. His veteran status afforded him with a host of knowledge on black entertainment markets, plus he had the added advantage that, as a performer himself, he could speak to the concerns of T.O.B.A. entertainers. Starr and Reevin specifically needed Dudley's management skills to recruit additional theater managers and fend off competition from the Southern Consolidated. They eagerly invited him to meet at T.O.B.A.'s Chattanooga headquarters in May 1921.

The theatrical press viewed Dudley's visit to Chattanooga with hope that it meant an end to the managerial infighting so the circuit could return its focus on entertainment.[46] While detailed records of this meeting no longer remain, Dudley had an advantage as the eastern booking director of the Southern Consolidated. The bookings of over two thousand black performers were caught up in the battle between the Southern and T.O.B.A., for if an entertainer was booked with one circuit, they could not perform in a competing circuit's theater.[47] If singer Ethel Waters was booked at the 81 Theatre in Atlanta on the Southern, she could not be booked at T.O.B.A.'s Douglass Theatre in Macon just an hour and a half away. Either circuit stood to lose a good act to an independent theater or lose money on a forfeited booking when the physical distance between contracted theaters proved too wide and expensive for entertainers to navigate. Dudley's response to the creation of T.O.B.A. without him was to "call in his acts to report" to Dudley Enterprises and away from potential T.O.B.A. theaters.[48] After deliberations about the personal infighting that had continuously occurred among all parties since 1913, what most likely occurred was a frank discussion about the loss of profits on two competing circuits and the great economic benefits of a merger. As T.O.B.A. president, Starr did not have the long history with Dudley as the other partners did and likely was able to act as a neutral figure. Subsequently, soon after Dudley's crucial Chattanooga meeting with Reevin and Starr in May, "the war between the two corporations came to an end" and the Southern Consolidated was added to T.O.B.A.'s Eastern branch with Dudley's aid.[49] T.O.B.A. marketed the merger, which nearly doubled its size, as a "decisive victory," and the operation expanded to include cities in every region except the West Coast. T.O.B.A.'s gain was also Dudley's, as he became eastern booking director for T.O.B.A. following the merger.[50]

By 1922 Martin Klein, Dudley, and Reevin's partner in prior dealings joined the management team and rounded out T.O.B.A.'s three regional headquarter systems. Reevin led the finances of the organization as the treasurer and director of the Southern branch based in Chattanooga; Dudley directed the Eastern branch headquartered in Washington, DC; and Martin Klein advised the Midwestern branch based in Chicago. As an entrepreneurial venture T.O.B.A. rose from the 1922–23 season and, "free from the anxiety that prevailed" in the previous fiscal year, was hopeful that "perhaps [managers would be] able to devote more time to the strictly professional."[51]

The constant possibility of mergers and acquisitions of smaller black-focused theater circuits continued throughout much of the tenure of T.O.B.A. and made for great fodder for both the entertainment and business sections of black and industry periodicals.[52] Newspapers crafted vivid narratives of the "air of *mystery* that surrounds colored theater combines," yet these reports merely relayed the ebbs and flows of the volatile business of American amusement.[53] Behind the speculations lay an institution that continued to add stockholders and became even more transparent in financial documents regarding its interracial management structure.

In its 1922 annual report filed with its state corporation taxes, circuit secretary W. S. Scales noted that the "colored vaudeville" corporation paid its taxes in full and issued $17,300 of its $20,000 capital stock. According to the charter rules $17,300 equated with the issuing of roughly fifty-eight separate stockholders who managed and owned at least one theater.[54] Incoming T.O.B.A. president Clarence Bennett, white owner of New Orleans' Lyric Theatre, made the annual report details a bit clearer when he attested that he was to preside over an organization that, after just a year, was worth five million dollars, with plans to expand into "Mexico, Canada, Porto Rico, and the Bahamas."[55]

## "HARMONIOUS SESSIONS" AND "BAD BUSINESS": T.O.B.A. BUSINESS STRATEGIES (1922–26)[56]

Although T.O.B.A.'s international expansion was not as forthcoming as incoming president Bennett may have hoped, the stabilization of the corporation proved beneficial for all involved for a time. T.O.B.A. business practices reflected elements of Dudley's and Turpin's NNBL-related beliefs about the promotion of economic racial unity through black business development, particularly in its efforts to center the circuit in black communities and hire African American managers. For Dudley, T.O.B.A. was still in part race work, as he was dedicated to "race capitalism" as a way to empower black communities.[57] He was also invested in black middle-class discussions of respectability onstage and how acts should conduct themselves to best represent the "race," as will be detailed in the next chapter.[58]

T.O.B.A.'s creation coincided with an increase of black business institution building as a response to growing racial hostility and discriminatory policies after the legalization of segregation. In black business's golden age, a host of "national business associations" developed after 1900 and the NNBL's establishment. These institutions and business associations increased in number between 1920 and 1930 and included black banks, insurance companies, and real estate corporations; artisan guilds for tailors, undertakers, hair care specialists, and builders; and men's and women's local business leagues. The development of black leisure spaces, including parks, recreation centers, and theaters, was part of this institutional growth and demonstrated what Juliet Walker argues was a "defiant" symbol of resistance to the segregationist attempts to make African American citizens solely subordinate laborers.[59] As an interracially managed institution the circuit could not fully meet black business associations' calls for racial "economic independence," but rather reached out to any and all managers of black-serving theaters to make the circuit a nationally known entity.[60] T.O.B.A.'s multi-tiered strategy focused on recruitment of seasoned management, clear advertising, and continued acquisition of Southern franchised theaters, forming a consistent headliner roster and using the black press to be transparent about the circuit's business practices.

The board created an advertising campaign that depicted T.O.B.A. as the "best" and biggest circuit in the industry and began recruiting vaudeville management veterans as well as other nationally prominent black entrepreneurs to invest in the circuit. In 1922, the T.O.B.A. board of directors added John T. Gibson of Philadelphia's Standard and Dunbar Theatres as a "special representative."[61] With Gibson's role as an early leader in black vaudeville, T.O.B.A. further fostered an image of success and of being the "best as usual."[62] In that same year, the officers and board of directors added W. S. Scales, a black North Carolina banker, as secretary, adding his banking, real estate, and theater management skills to its ranks.

While recruiting management veterans, T.O.B.A. refined its general circuit marketing plan. Jason Chambers chronicles the work of 1920s black entrepreneur Claude Barnett, who argued that advertisements for black consumers should concentrate on "image, distribution, and product awareness."[63] Barnett stressed that successful black marketing should foster racial pride, advertise products that were accessible even in segregated communities, and run advertisements frequently within the black press. The circuit followed all these principles. With Dudley as part of the team, T.O.B.A. "want ads" for managers and performers were clear and reminiscent of the ads for the Dudley Circuit in the 1910s that encouraged managers to "get wise" to the "oldest" and "best" colored circuit.[64] T.O.B.A. advertisements all promoted the same message: T.O.B.A. was the foundation of black show business, and every *worthy* black act should be "booked exclusively" upon its stages for the most favored bookings, better pay, and short jumps between shows.[65]

Management executives had no problem using the legal system to maintain its growth. When T.O.B.A. franchised theaters were found using noncircuit vaudevillians in 1922, Milton Starr and T.O.B.A. filed a $5,000 breach of contract lawsuit against Globe Indemnity of New Jersey. The circuit continued this practice the following year when they alerted "All Acts" that select theaters in Cleveland and Kansas City were not T.O.B.A. houses, and that any T.O.B.A. acts would be subject to "inconvenience" and "lay-off" if they accepted an engagement with a non-T.O.B.A. theater.[66] Out of 132 black-serving vaudeville and vaudeville-equipped theaters in the United States in 1922, T.O.B.A. had issued franchises and stock for at least fifty-eight of them and was rapidly taking over the market.[67]

Another layer of T.O.B.A.'s strategy was that it constantly fought to acquire new stockholders and theater franchises, particularly in black Southern theaters, echoing the tactics that vaudeville managers Emma Griffin and Dudley had employed nearly a decade prior. From 1921 until 1929, the circuit called for all "desirable theaters" and ran an advertisement in the *Chicago Defender* seeking the attention of "all acts, companies, and theater managers," particularly those in Southern states.[68] Beginning in 1915, the Great Migration, with its large black demographic shifts from southern states to northern states, edged the black consumer market into a northern urban center. Yet despite these shifts, many black consumer markets still resided below the Mason-Dixon line in the 1920s.[69] In 1921 advertising industry periodical *Advertising and Selling* held that Southern wealth was on the rise, with resources increasing by over 1,400 percent and noted that it was "a logical market for your product . . . a product that can be reached most effectively and economically" through Southern newspapers.[70] With Reevin and Starr already acquainted with Southern African American consumer populations from their pre-T.O.B.A. efforts, the southern recruitment plan was sound.

Vaudevillian and future film star Clarence Muse vividly described T.O.B.A.'s connection to the South in his 1932 semiautobiographical work, *Way Down South*. After a successful late 1920s performance of the show *Charleston Dandies* in Durham, North Carolina, protagonist Dusty McClain (Muse) "experienced, moreover, with acute keenness, the tremendous 'feeling' of the South about him, this strange, mystical South so different from all the rest of America, so richly endowed . . . with such a perfectly grand historical past unlike that of any region in the universe."[71] The "mystical South" that Muse romanticized was full of willing and waiting audiences who could not or would not patronize the existing live performances provided by a Keith-Orpheum "big time" type of circuit that had either segregated seating for African Americans or excluded black customers entirely. T.O.B.A. sought the patronage of the loyal spectators who had the resources to visit a theater frequently and found among them foundry workers, entrepreneurs, or music lovers of Birmingham, Memphis, or New Orleans.[72] Accordingly, during the circuit's lifetime, sixty-seven of the one hundred T.O.B.A. franchised theaters were in urban Southern centers, like Tampa, New Orleans, or Dallas. Following the tent show, minstrel, and circus routes in Southern states ensured T.O.B.A. had familiar and stable audiences that were willing to pay on average twenty-five, thirty, or fifty cents to attend shows in floor seats or eighty-five cents to one dollar for box seats.[73]

In addition to theater franchises, T.O.B.A. made its primary income from a 5 percent commission on entertainer contracts, and that commission was only collected if performers were popular enough to fill theaters throughout a three- to five-day schedule of regular performances. This 5 percent commission was paid from the "amount received by the party of the second part" (the contracted performer) and was taken out by "theatre manager weekly."[74] Theater managers made their profit off the door, with income often being paid from a percentage of the house receipts of an individual show, while T.O.B.A. took its percentage off the top.

Developing a stable roster of headliners was a pivotal T.O.B.A. strategy to garner commission. The circuit regularly considered audition requests from newcomers who sought fame on the stage. Regional district booking agents as well as individual theater owners received letters from talented boxers, like Bartling Norfolk from New Orleans, who wanted to try his luck as a novelty performer. Even family members of trusted race leaders wanted a T.O.B.A. "try out," like musician Joseph Douglass, grandson of Frederick Douglass and former head of the violin department at the Washington Conservatory of Music at Howard University.[75] Yet for every brief notice for a dance team, like Emmie Croft and Charles Snow introduced as an unknown "new act" on T.O.B.A. Time, there were many more advertisements aimed at drawing more veteran performers that might have a greater chance of filling the four-hundred- to two-thousand-seat theaters of the circuit.[76] Reevin told theater owners that he "didn't just pick up companies just because they write for work." Just like on larger white vaudeville circuits, T.O.B.A. managers wrote a "report card" on acts on their stages to determine further hiring.[77] An untested act could be dropped from the roster in midrun for failure to receive positive reviews from the stage manager in the theater they just played, with dismissal telegrams meeting potential performers as they emerged from the train. Yet what mitigated this report card system for headliners was the network and knowledge of booking agents like Dudley and Klein, who could attest to the quality of an act if they had been previously booked on the Dudley or C.C.V.E. circuits. When blues singer Ma Rainey and Company missed a performance at Macon's Douglass Theatre, T.O.B.A. booking directors assured the Douglass manager that Rainey, as an "old, reliable performer," would "positively make it good," pay back any outstanding debts, and be ready for the next T.O.B.A. booking.[78]

While devoted attention to the specifics of entertainment acts will be found in later chapters, headliners included many of the performers made popular on black vaudeville circuits, tent shows, and minstrel spectacles prior to T.O.B.A.'s incorporation. Comedy teams like Butterbeans and Susie, dance teams like Drake and Walker, or tabloid shows or abbreviated musicals led by the trusted singer-dancer-comedy ensemble, the Whitman Sisters, were all acts that could draw an audience. Tab shows produced by Irvin C. Miller gave managers "record breaking business," while Salem Whitney and Homer Tutt produced *Smarter Set* comedic revues that warranted them the title of "theatrical architects par excellence" with shows that touched "every American city."[79] After the 1925–26 season, tabs like *Shufflin' Sam from Alabam,' The Chocolate Dandies, Plantation Days,* and *Brown Skin Models,* among others, all maintained a successful basic format until "it had exhausted itself."[80]

While women were absent from T.O.B.A. board leadership, among the most popular individual acts on the circuit were black women performers of classic or vaudeville blues.[81] As suggested by scholar Daphne Duval Harrison, the increased popularity of blues music furthered the growth of the circuit and vice versa, for the earliest recordings of blues women coincided with T.O.B.A.'s chartering in 1920.[82] T.O.B.A. and black vaudeville theaters were the professional homes of Ma Rainey, Ida Cox, Ethel Waters, Victoria Spivey, and Bessie Smith before Paramount, Black Swan, Okeh, and Columbia found them, and the press reflected this popularity. New Negro intellectual critics clamored that "the heavily advertised Blues singers" were prisms through which "the songs of our people" were transmitted "by radio to remote corners of the world."[83]

Even beyond the individual performances on its stages, T.O.B.A. attached itself to the fame of the "blues queens" in its advertising placements. The circuit often placed its "all acts, managers, and theaters" advertisement right below the latest phonograph hit of a blues vocalist, whether it was Ethel Waters with Black Swan Records or Bessie Smith with Columbia Records. The advertisement placement conveyed that while black blues women might have appeared on white variety stages, especially after their recordings of "race music" became profitable outside of black consumer markets, T.O.B.A. booked "the best shows in the business," and these women were the best.[84] Blues stars filled the seats at even higher prices than the comedy or tab shows. The Howard Theatre could book musical revues, like an all-black cast of *Salome,* at the evening prices of thirty-nine, fifty-five, and eighty-nine cents a seat. However, Philadelphia's Standard Theatre, with its 1,200 seats, could play the "incomparable" Mamie Smith and her syncopated Review for sixty cents per floor seat and one dollar per box seat, and audiences attended regardless of these increased prices because of the popularity of these blues women.[85] African American female talent funded the rise of T.O.B.A. success.

The 1924–25 season exemplified the circuit's growing success. The annual stockholder meeting of 1924 was reportedly the "most harmonious meeting yet held by the association," and 1925 followed with the corporation's most viable organizational structure, franchise expansion, and measurable profit increase. In 1924 Chicago-based Martin Klein became the official director of the Midwest region and took over the management of theaters in Indiana, Illinois, Michigan, Missouri, and Ohio, expanding T.O.B.A.'s focus of being predominantly a Southern circuit. Following Southern migrants into the Midwest, T.O.B.A. expanded its reach as far west as the Mississippi River and grew to include over sixty theaters. Organizationally, the circuit solidified its stable roster of acts, for "when one office gets through with a show it turns it over to the next one" and "assured consecutive bookings" to artists.[86] Annual domestic corporation reports for 1925 demonstrated that $18,200 of the $20,000 capital stock had been issued, resulting in the purchasing of 182 shares of T.O.B.A. stock, or approximately sixty franchised theaters. The organization had filed and paid all taxes on time by June 29.[87]

In midseason, industry critics approvingly remarked that, despite growth, the organization had not been consumed by some larger entertainment conglomerate and was "owned and operated by owners and managers of the theaters forming the circuit."[88] Out of the 132 African American–serving vaudeville and vaudeville-equipped theaters listed in 1922's *Julius Kahn Directory*, a national theater industry service directory, or the *Negro Year Book*, the annually compiled encyclopedic and statistical reports of black life, T.O.B.A. effectively managed nearly half of the black vaudeville establishments in the nation. T.O.B.A. Time consisted of "upward of 63 theaters on the circuit, playing more than 25 tabloid and review attractions and 106 singles, teams, and trios, and showing to [a minimum of] 4,500" people daily in 1925.[89]

## THE VAUDEVILLIANS ORGANIZE: PROTEST & UNION ORGANIZATION

As a result of T.O.B.A.'s attempts to maintain steady rosters of headliner performers, an unintended but necessary consequence occurred: T.O.B.A. troupers organized their own vaudevillian union. While 1924 and 1925 proved to be the most profitable years for the circuit at the stockholder level, with profit and growth came increased tensions between management and performers, who rightfully wanted those benefits to filter down to them. As part of T.O.B.A.'s strategy of counteracting negative publicity quickly and publicly, the circuit's involvement in the journey to create a black vaudeville union was all covered in the African American press.

When debates on the New Negro, black capitalism, and entrepreneurship occurred in black intellectual circles in the 1920s, writer J. A. Rodgers argued that a sign of black progress was when the "New Negro joins unions either of his own or forces whites to take him in and once in never rests until he gets fair play."[90] If negotiations between management and labor were a hallmark of New Negro advancement, then the stabilization of the Colored Actors' Union (C.A.U.) was evidence of black theater progress. Formed initially in 1921 in Washington, DC, (with a second office briefly in Chicago), reorganizing in 1924, the C.A.U. became black vaudevillians' key vehicle to fight for change within the T.O.B.A. structure. C.A.U.'s creation was bolstered by the existence of the Colored Vaudeville Benevolent Association (C.V.B.A.), "the oldest, most active benevolent association of Colored theatrical people in America." The C.V.B.A. formed in 1909 in New York City with the "express purpose of bettering the condition of the colored vaudeville performer . . . as far as his work and general deportment."[91] After the creation of a female auxiliary group by 1915, the C.V.B.A. counted Dudley, Sylvester Russell, and the Griffin Sisters as early members and provided a "safety net" for ill and infirm colored vaudevillians when other forms of such insurance did not exist in the profession. The C.V.B.A. persisted through the early 1930s, but "the association modestly kept itself in the background, contending as it were, only every once in a great while for the favor of the public's attention."[92] For example, when novelty performer Ollie McDow died of "acute indigestion" in his rooming house in February 1923, those with C.V.B.A. membership, along with "other theatrical folk," raised the money to cover McDow's burial. Through the Great Depression, the C.V.B.A. continued to hold benefits to honorably bury black vaudeville legends who had no family or community aid. A separate organization, the Negro Actors' Guild (NAG), took over the C.V.B.A.'s efforts in 1936 with a promise "to foster and promote the spiritual welfare of Negro Actors and Actresses in every branch of the theatrical profession."[93]

Segregation within or open exclusion from white theatrical societies fueled the C.V.B.A. and later the C.A.U.'s creation. While class divisions between "legitimate" American theater and other forms of live entertainment, including "vaudeville, burlesque, circus, carnival, fairs, ballet, or concert recital," prevented genre-unified actors' unions in the late nineteenth century, racial prejudice further ostracized African American performers from vaudeville unions.[94] The aptly named White Rats Actors' Union of America was created by eight white male performers in June 1900 in New York City as a "brotherly" association with hopes of promoting "a higher form of entertainment," "protection of original material," and "abolition of commissions on salaries." Yet for all the talk of lofty ideals of "Freedom and Advancement, Enlightenment, Fairness, and Kindness," the White Rats bylaws clearly stated that membership would be extended to "every *white* actor, performer, or entertainer in the amusement world, male or female, of good moral character, and in mental and physical condition satisfactory to the Lodge, irrespective of religion or nationality, who is now and has been a bona-fide actor . . ."[95] With gender, religion, and physical and mental maladies addressed, the membership statement essentially included almost *any* actor besides an African American actor.[96]

The birth of the C.V.B.A. in part addressed this glaring racist exclusion of black vaudevillians from union activity, yet it lacked the ability to ameliorate troubles between black vaudeville management and labor. As the White Rats gained national union representation and recognition by the American Federation of Labor and its affiliation with the vaudeville branch of the Associated Actors and Artistes of America, or "4As," black vaudevillians were still in even greater need of an organization they could shape to address their contract, travel, and salary concerns.[97] This is where the C.A.U. entered. If T.O.B.A. performers found themselves on the road and could not acquire railway tickets or get a transfer company to ship scenery for a reasonable price for black traveling revue members, they took these concerns to the C.A.U. With four payments of $2.50 to total the ten-dollar annual dues, C.A.U. members, both men and women, became card-carrying members who agitated for a "living salary" and to build a colored actors' home.[98]

Both T.O.B.A. management and performers negotiated in the shadows of mainstream vaudeville battles of 1919 and 1920, battles that had taken the White Rats and later the Associated Actors and Artistes of America all the way to the Federal Trade Commission. In February 1919, members of the White Rats accused the mainstream white vaudeville conglomerate—the Vaudeville Managers' Protective Association; the National Vaudeville Artists, Inc.; the United Booking Offices; and the Vaudeville Collection Agency—among others, of a "monopoly of the vaudeville business" that had not "only dealt with the question of dollars and cents," but with the "destines [*sic*], bodies, and wills of men and women."[99] Between February and late May 1919, lawyers for each representative group amassed nineteen volumes and thousands of pages of testimony. Artists alleged that the national theater syndicates committed basic labor violations, from blacklisting (refusing to hire any vaudevillian affiliated with an industry union) to more lurid crimes of violent harassment against actors who "were dangerously kicked, assaulted and left in the streets" for "dead" in pursuit of vaudeville commissions, "amounting to 90 percent of vaudeville actors' salaries."[100] The Federal Trade Commission and later the Department of Justice threw this extensive case out of court in May 1920 on the basis that "theatrical entertainment" was not "commerce" and therefore "vaudeville combinations" did not "violate the Sherman anti-trust law."[101]

In the similar but separate universe of black vaudeville, T.O.B.A. management and C.A.U. fashioned its own tenuous relationship. C.A.U. members shared the woes that plagued White Rat or Equity actors, including complaints of long hours, little pay, shifting contracts, and temporary layoffs. With its reorganization in February 1924, the C.A.U. grew into a more formidable force and formally located itself in the S. H. Dudley Enterprises office in Washington, DC, at 1233 Seventh Street NW. Members elected a full slate of officers, including President Jules McGarr, Vice Presidents Paul Carter and Chinz Moore, Secretary Telfair Washington, Chief Deputy Bart Kennett, and Treasurer S. H. Dudley. The organization published an eight-page bulletin informing the membership of monthly happenings and, by 1925, crafted a seventy-two-page handbook with a member directory, history, railway rates, and an agent list.[102]

The proposed handbook provided the information for black vaudevillians that was already readily available for white vaudevillians in standard industry guides, information that was only occasionally published in supplemental "colored" guides. This infusion of centralized organization propelled performers to consistently voice their protests to management on issues of salary and travel and use the black press to keep their concerns alive. Black theater critic Kennard Williams lauded C.A.U. participants: "though they unfairly receive no more than the shirk, they resolutely refuse to be beaten, and [fight] to surmount all obstacles to their advancement."[103] C.A.U. leadership constantly fought for increased membership via advertisements and Dudley-authored articles in black periodicals that proclaimed that the union would do "some big things soon" and that it would be an artist's "only salvation" in the ongoing struggles with management.[104]

Despite a seeming conflict of interest with S. H. Dudley both being a T.O.B.A. regional booking director and board member and the initial C.A.U. treasurer, potential members apparently trusted Dudley to focus on his role as a performer first. As performance studies scholar Nadine George-Graves contends, consistently "Dudley made a concerted effort to remedy the problems of Toby," even if that meant returning to his performer roots. Black theater veteran, journalist, and integral T.O.B.A. management player who will be discussed further in upcoming chapters, James "J. A." Jackson remarked, "despite [Dudley's] present day capitalistic status he remains at heart a performer" and that "confidence in his integrity and his business acumen is perhaps the greatest asset the Union has with which to promote membership."[105] Dudley offered his services and the use of his offices as C.A.U. headquarters for free. While Dudley continued to use the press, President McGarr drummed up membership rolls directly. By contacting performers on-site in black traveling revues across the T.O.B.A. territories, McGarr earned a positive reputation as a "traveling delegate hustling the revival of real interests."[106] Transparent in their budgeting and the actual benefits they promised future members, Secretary Telfair Washington listed the names of each of the forty-three dues-paying members in the *Chicago Defender* and the 1924 expense budget as a plea to future participants to "work hard and make a fight."[107]

The multiple membership appeals paid off, and by 1925 C.A.U. grew from forty-three to eight hundred black members.[108] The organization's next action step was to strive for participation in T.O.B.A.'s semiannual stockholder meetings. While individual performers could be members of actors' guilds or local musicians' unions, like the "colored local of the American Federation of Musicians," the C.A.U. fought to be recognized as *the* black vaudeville and variety union organization.[109] Motivated by a stated goal of supporting "the Race" and the realization that it simply could not exist without performer talent, T.O.B.A. made moves to include the C.A.U. at the negotiating table in March 1925. Dudley took to the press again to assure C.A.U. members that the union was "positively not conceived for the purpose of becoming factional to the T.O.B.A.," but that it was an independent entity meant to ensure the betterment of manager- performer relations, as well as providing the best shows for the public.[110] After constant talks and separate meetings of its constituents, the Colored Actors' Union became the premier-recognized union by T.O.B.A.'s executive board and board of directors in July 1925:

> Whereas the Theater Owners Booking Association has for the past several years been Recognized as . . . the only reputable booking offices for the Race theatrical attractions for race theaters and Whereas the Colored Actors Union has, for a considerable time, been recognized as the only reputable organization of the race performers and actors, and, Whereas it is now the spirit of the Board of Directors of the Theater Owners Booking Association to give official recognition to and to lend and to solicit the co-operation of the Colored Actors Union, now therefore, be it Resolved by the Board of Directors of the Theater Owners Booking Association, legally assembled of the purpose of transacting the business of the Association, that official recognition be given to the said Colored Actors Union.[111]

With this recognition, the C.A.U. first placed *Billboard* journalist and black theater industry veteran J. A. Jackson as their liaison on the T.O.B.A. board, and later C.A.U. President Jules McGarr. Members looked at Jackson as "one of the best informed theatrical men in the country," who would present union demands "sensibly and forcefully."[112] If the selected union representative was unavailable, the C.A.U. made provisions that "a representative of the actors union will also be present at [board] meetings" with the continued goal that the circuit and the union should strive to work "together in harmony."[113] The achievement of "harmony" between management and the union was fraught, but the C.A.U. achieved incremental changes that slowly remolded the T.O.B.A. management-performer relationship into something manageable for the next years of the circuit. Even Reevin professed "his un-camouflaged approval" for the demands for shorter rail jumps and the need to protect entertainers caught in the fight amid circuit-franchised theaters that hired non-T.O.B.A. performers.[114]

T.O.B.A. management constantly refined its business strategies to meet new markets, stabilize its profits, and contend with its entertainment laborers. Between 1920 and 1925, the circuit rose from the bits and pieces of former black vaudeville organizations to become the driving management and booking institution of the entire industry. While Reevin and Starr initially led incorporation efforts, after the inclusion of S. H. Dudley, the business of making T.O.B.A. a successful black-serving institution was a racially cooperative management effort. As the business grew, T.O.B.A.'s artists, the heart of the enterprise, contended with the benefits and challenges of the circuit.

# 4

# THE MULTIPLE MEANINGS OF T.O.B.A.

## *The Performers' Perspective*

> Driggs: Okay, tell me about the TOBA.
> Calloway: You know . . .
> Driggs: I know what it means.
> Calloway: *You* know the meaning of TOBA?
> Driggs: Theater . . . Theater Owners . . . what? Booking Association, right?
> Calloway: Yeah.
> Driggs: But it also had . . . what's the other . . . what's the other name?
> Calloway: TOBA *Tough* on BA! It was, it was great though . . .
>
> —Cab Calloway interviewed by Frank Driggs, September 10, 1992

By mid-March 1927 Cabell "Cab" Calloway traveled to what he hoped was fame and freedom from a traditional family life in Baltimore. As a burgeoning vocalist in a T.O.B.A. show Calloway left high school and adolescent escapades involving gambling and drinking to follow his elder sister Blanche into traveling black vaudeville. Between 1921 and 1927 Blanche Calloway rose from adolescent chorus girl to a noted performer in musicals in New York and Chicago, like *Shuffle Along*. Okeh Records, the recording company for several burgeoning blues music stars, had even recorded Blanche in 1925.[1] With Cab's contract for *Plantation Days*, a musical revue originally staged for Chicago's Plantation Café that also featured Blanche, Cab had his first experience with T.O.B.A.[2] Decades later, after emerging as an energetic band leader known for his powerful tenor voice, dapper fashion sense, and signature call-and-response tune "Minnie the Moocher," Calloway referred to the Theater Owner's Booking Association circuit as "tough" on "BA" or black actors. He spoke of the circuit in same manner as the "incorrigibles

FIGURE 4. Cab Calloway, 1933, by Carl Van Vechten © Van Vechten Trust. Carl Van Vechten Papers Relating to African American Arts and Letters. James Weldon Johnson Collection in the Yale Collection of American Literature, Beinecke Rare Book and Manuscript Library.

among Colored Vaudevillians" had in 1929.[3] But what did being "tough" on African American performers entail?

The diverse lived experiences of contracted T.O.B.A. performers are the center of this chapter. Through oral histories, memoirs, playbills, and theater reviews, how performers entered the black entertainment world, what opportunities they had for artistic growth, travel, and community building, as well as their concerns about performer autonomy and respectability are all unearthed. Daphne Harrison maintains that T.O.B.A. had a "reputation that ranged from laudable" to "despicable depending on who was telling it."[4] From the artists "who told it," T.O.B.A. was both a rewarding and exhausting gateway into the American entertainment world. T.O.B.A. promised artists who had participated with previous fleeting black vaudeville circuits a stable income and increased performing opportunities on the largest black circuit in the nation. Yet those assurances panned out differently depending on where an artist performed, their entertaining specialty, their popularity, and the unpredictable nature of the traveling entertainment industry. Black vaudevillians like musician Cab Calloway, blues vocalist Ma Rainey, dancer Peg Leg Bates, or comedians Butterbeans and Susie weathered the challenges of segregation, low pay scales, and racial discrimination to realize aspirations of travel, artistic development, fame, and the prospect of wealth—all aspects of T.O.B.A. life.

## WHO WAS THE T.O.B.A. PERFORMER?

By the mid-1920s hundreds of performers had dazzled audiences across the eighty to one hundred theaters that formed the T.O.B.A. circuit. No matter juggler, blues singer, or tap dancer, the publicity staff of one, W. R. Arnold, made sure the black press wanted to know more about circuit performers.[5] Articles that addressed countless details of T.O.B.A. bureaucracy contended that there was "more acute interest in the lives of actors than there is in any class of our citizens," and a glimpse into the life of a black vaudeville star just might make a theatergoer pay that twenty-five cents to a dollar to see their favorite performer live on stage.[6]

The circuit's potential entertainers were products of the sociocultural environment of 1920s America and the aftermath of World War I. The decade was imbued with narratives of the rebellious youth of the Jazz Age alongside images of Prohibition, speakeasies and subsequent rising gang violence, and narratives of young men and women who tested sexual and class boundaries in a nation on the cusp of modernity.[7] Popular culture historian Lucy Moore asserts that the 1920s were "an age of iconic events and people, of talismanic names and episodes that have entered our consciousness more like myths or morality tales than historical occurrences."[8] For African Americans, the decade was equally marked by increased repression and racial violence in the aftermath of World War I; heightened migration to urban enclaves in Chicago, New York, or Philadelphia; and new forms of political and artistic resistance as demonstrated by the New Negro Movement and the Harlem Renaissance.[9] New Negro participants were black citizens in the post–World War I environment, "ready" to dedicate themselves to the "ceaseless fight for right, the safety of home, and for betterment of the race."[10] For many new Black performing artists, the question came of how to best undertake this New Negro "ceaseless fight" in music, dance, and comedy while also enjoying the excitement of stage performance and travel.[11]

T.O.B.A. categorized performers by their entertainment genre and their tenure in the industry. Circuit artists included African American children, adolescents, and young adults between eighteen and twenty-five years old, or veteran minstrel and vaudeville entertainers in their late twenties and beyond. Entertainers varied in class status, educational background, arts training, region, and religious background. The playbill breakdown included individual acts or "singles"; double or triple ensembles that might include sibling or male/female partnerships; novelty performances (animal, child, acrobatic, or psychic acts); and abbreviated musical revues or tabloid "tab" shows, which featured upward of thirty dancers, singers, and musicians.[12] Performers could either be "rookie" newcomers, consistent regulars who filled out chorus lines or stage bands, or standout entertainers who headlined a T.O.B.A. show. Comedians who had honed their skills in the minstrel-like shows of the Smart Set at the height of S. H. Dudley's performing years in the 1910s might have earned a headliner spot on 1920s T.O.B.A. Likewise an entertainer who began as a chorus girl on the Dudley Circuit might have evolved into a blues music queen like Bessie Smith or Ida Cox by the height of Toby Time.[13] Entertainers welcomed the supposed changes that T.O.B.A. advertised in industry periodicals and took to heart the promises of "Better Booking Conditions in the South."[14] Ultimately, the draw of a circuit where a black performer would not be the only act of color on the bill and could be paid well and respected had an appeal for black vaudevillians of all genres.

## THE PUSH AND PULL OF THE STAGE

Early twentieth-century black theater critics had long spoken of the lure of the stage for "the Negro vaudevillian, playing to Negro audiences." *Freeman* journalists, half in jest, warned that if a vaudeville show auditioned local residents there would be "no more cooks in the kitchen" or "no more hands in the field" as many Black youth longed to be entertainers.[15] Black veteran comic Tom Fletcher thought "on nothing but the stage" in the late nineteenth century after watching a preshow circus or minstrel parade with its brightly colored banners, vibrantly costumed dancers, and shiny instruments. When parade participants handed him a banner to carry or a red band coat to wear, for a few moments Fletcher moved from spectator to entertainer, which sparked his lifelong pursuit of show business.[16] Yet just like any other profession, a series of preliminary steps, including auditions and on-the-job training, had to be taken before instant fame.

By 1921 hundreds of potential entertainers answered T.O.B.A. advertisements and wired Sam Reevin in Chattanooga or S. H. Dudley in Washington, DC, to see if the call for "all companies and all acts" applied to them.[17] Veteran vaudevillians searched trade periodicals, like *Variety* and *Billboard*, as well as the entertainment pages of the *Freeman* and the *Chicago Defender* for auditions for single acts, ensembles, and abbreviated musicals or "tab" shows. Aside from published audition listings, first-time vaudevillians often tested their luck with a T.O.B.A. show when it played the local theater. Baltimore-born dancer Bessie Dudley pushed her way into vaudeville as an adolescent because she was "show business crazy." As a child she left school and visited the local T.O.B.A. theater, the Lincoln, almost daily during the 1922–23 season. At twelve years old, Bessie and her friend Evelyn Paine lingered for as many shows as possible once they had run enough errands to earn the dime for admission. Dudley remarked "we'd stay there all day . . . we didn't come home to eat or nothing, we just set in the show."[18] Scholar Saidiya Hartman describes this realization that came over many aspiring entertainers, who, as they watched a show thought, "I want to be up there. *I* can do that."[19] Bessie Dudley watched the vaudeville acts so often that when The Gibson Family, a family musical comedy act that included child dancers and instrumentalists, came to the Lincoln, Bessie begged the vaudevillian family to grant her a tryout. She auditioned with no set routine and told the accompanist just "to play" at the stage door while she did the Charleston and other popular social dances in the back alley. Bessie Dudley won a coveted spot with The Gibson Family during the same tour where they performed to rave reviews, putting the "house in a riot" of laughter. "Somebody gave her a coat" and Bessie went with "what she had on" to the next tour date, initially without her guardian grandmother's consent.[20]

Similarly, in 1923 blues pianist Sadie Goodson stumbled into professional entertainment when the "Empress of the Blues," Bessie Smith, starred as the featured headliner of a T.O.B.A. revue in Pensacola, Florida. After Smith's piano player fell ill at E. L. Cummings's Belmont Theatre, an adolescent Goodson at age "old enough to know how to play the blues" won an audition with Smith and the accompanist job by playing Smith's signature "Gulf Coast Blues."[21] Novelty performer and dancer Clayton "Peg Leg" Bates arrived at his audition for a T.O.B.A. show at age sixteen after hitchhiking from Fayetteville to Winston-Salem, North Carolina, in a torrential downpour. Given that Bates had lost a leg in an industrial accident at age twelve, tap dancing with a wooden prosthesis, let alone traveling, was a feat of persistence. Producer Eddie Lemons reported after watching the drenched Bates board the tour bus that coincidently picked him up, that "if you dance with that peg leg, I'll give you a job right now."[22] These vivid oral history accounts mirror the dozens of stories of other T.O.B.A. newcomers who entered the circuit after watching shows and envisioning themselves being the artists rather than audience members.

In some instances, show business was the family business. It was not out of the ordinary for Sherman H. Dudley Jr. to become a vaudevillian dancer and producer in the early 1920s, as he followed the footsteps of his mother, dancer Alberta Ormes Dudley, and father, theater magnate Sherman H. Dudley Sr. But for many potential T.O.B.A. participants, their choice of stage entertainment was met with family and community curiosity at best and skepticism or derision at worst. In environments where African American occupational parameters were often bound by agricultural, industrial, and domestic or service industry opportunities, families wanted their children to pursue formal education first so they would be "equipped for better things" than manual labor.[23] Many simply could not envision their loved ones as profitable stage entertainers.

Several aspiring performers who weathered family or community concern shared conservative religious foundations that defined amusement or leisure activities as worldly or ungodly. Black Christian periodicals of the 1910s warned congregants against the evils of dancing and argued that "the only real reason people danced was for sexual arousal."[24] For some black Protestant and Catholic practitioners, the very act of listening to secular music like blues or jazz with their barely veiled themes of sexuality or alcohol consumption was a sinful act. Many of these same religious conservatives frowned upon attendance at minstrel-like comedy shows that celebrated the crude humor found in everyday life situations or promoted black stereotypes. Yet dancing, music, and comedic skits were at the heart of a T.O.B.A. career. Although some seasoned black vaudevillians argued that there were "a great number of Christian families earning their living upon the stage," new T.O.B.A. artists who longed for the excitement of what might be a "haphazard career" willingly crossed the line between church teachings and the desire to be on the stage.[25]

While some churches "barred theatre-going, card playing, and dancing as works of the 'devil,'" some black adolescents pushed against traditional proscriptive teachings and nearly left the church entirely in the 1920s and '30s.[26] Both her Catholic background and her granddaughter's young age factored into dancer Bessie Dudley's grandmother, Mrs. Selby, having a negative initial reaction to the circuit. A parishioner of Baltimore's St. Mary's Church, Selby understandably did not approve of a twelve-year-old girl frequenting the alleys of Pennsylvania Avenue at a T.O.B.A. theater's stage door or working for spare change to attend vaudeville shows with their "low" amusements.[27] Mrs. Selby's objections did not prevent "dance crazy" Bessie from dropping out of Druid Hill School in seventh grade to join a T.O.B.A.-booked Gibson Family act, and only when Mrs. Gibson later promised to be Bessie's chaperone did Selby relent.

Playing blues music sparked Sadie Goodson to leave her Pensacola, Florida, home and her parents' Baptist traditions. The raw, comic lyrics of longing, loss, and open sexuality in blues music was appropriate for what cultural critics referred to as the lively and spirited "Saturday Night Function" of juke joints, tent shows, or rent parties. While juke joint patrons and Sunday morning congregants might be one and the same in some circles, publicly performing the "devil's music" was definitely not suitable for a virtuous Christian woman like Goodson.[28] Sadie's

Baptist father, Hamilton Goodson, purchased a piano for the home and encouraged all six of his children to learn to play instruments for church worship.[29] Goodson trained to play sacred music, like "Nearer My God to Thee," but she also would "sneak and play the blues" she overheard being played on neighborhood phonographs.[30] All of her private music training did not prepare Goodson to vamp to the lyrics "some of you men, you sure do make me tired, you've got a mouth full of gimme, a handful of 'much obliged'" in Bessie Smith's "Gulf Coast Blues" in 1923.[31] But Goodson's hidden blues-listening prompted her to move from playing piano hymns for Pensacola funerals to accompanying Bessie Smith's tab shows, a coveted role that eventually led Goodson to become a New Orleans jazz musician.

Other potential T.O.B.A. performers' entertainment aspirations were met with critique because vaudeville was considered "low-brow" amusement. Lawrence Levine maintained that vaudeville houses were entertainment centers for the masses and, although racially segregated, were thought to have an inclusive environment for working-class audience members.[32] For some black professionals who sought to climb social hierarchies within black communities and maintain what Willard Gatewood defined as "genteel performance"—the exercise of public and private self-restraint conducted by wealthy, educated, and well-born African Americans—supporting loud, raucous vaudeville amusement would not have been practiced. Likewise, black citizens who desired to prove themselves "respectable" and virtuous as a tool of resistance to racial subjugation strove to disassociate themselves from uncultured entertainment.[33] Theater critics had debated mainstream vaudeville and variety theaters' immoral qualities since the 1860s, and this debate only intensified when black professionals at the turn of the century lamented black vaudeville's "disrespectable" stereotypes and base humor.[34]

Cab Calloway argued that vaudeville's low-brow characterization prompted his family to not fully support his pursuit of T.O.B.A. fame. Calloway's family was part of Baltimore's rising middle-class African American community. Although his sister Blanche had become a blues singing star, Calloway's mother, music teacher Eulalia, and stepfather, realtor James Fortune, hoped that Cab would be interested in medicine or law.[35] While the Fortunes provided Cab with private musical training, they did not expect him to "pawn his drums" to join sister Blanche after she played Baltimore's Royal Theatre.[36]

Buck and wing dancing, tap dancing's predecessor, had mesmerized South Carolina dancer Clayton "Peg Leg" Bates since he was five years old, but Bates had to "dance on the sly."[37] His mother, Emma, nearly disowned him when she caught him at age seven dancing for tips in front of a barbershop in 1917. Bates recalled, "I was dancing, I was going to town and the white folks was going crazy and clapping their hands." Emma retrieved and physically punished Bates, as she was very angry at the thought of the white crowd "making a monkey out of my kid."[38] Although a working-class woman, Mrs. Bates was agitated not only that her son was performing "ungodly" dances but that the crowd treated Clayton as a toy for their amusement and not as a respectable young black boy.

Oklahoma-born, Los Angeles-raised clarinetist Marshal Royal Jr. was quite familiar with the shows that traversed the T.O.B.A. circuit, as his musician father, Royal Sr., traveled and trained with acts like Drake and Walker and the Whitman Sisters.[39] Despite being raised in a family of traveling musicians, Royal Jr., too, was taught that there was a hierarchy of music performance, and he "studied legitimate music" on classical violin since "he was five years old." Royal Jr. eventually became a member of Count Basie's swing band and blurred this constructed boundary between legitimate and "illegitimate" music, but he still held on to his fondness for "round-backed, beautiful, inlaid mandolins."[40] While performers navigated these individual instances of religious and class resistance to participation in African American vaudeville, as T.O.B.A. grew, it would devise its own campaigns to infuse black theater performance with its own definitions of virtue, morality, and respectability.

## THE BENEFITS OF T.O.B.A. TIME

In a 1925 article black theater journalist Kennard Williams maintained that "God must have loved the Negro who travels the T.O.B.A. for he made so many of them and has endowed them with more vitality and endurance than any single group on earth."[41] T.O.B.A. performers had the energy and strength to travel the nation to share their artistry with enthusiastic audiences. For "show business crazy" artists talented or lucky enough to move beyond their local benevolent club or state fair, T.O.B.A. offered black performers the possibility of fame, financial reward, and artistic community on a national level. The number of black entertainers who made a living as performing artists was not high. By 1925 there were 1,075 working black actors (out of 28,361 total) or nearly 4 percent; 878 gainfully employed black "showmen" (out of 19,811 total) or 4.5 percent; and less than 1 percent of the nation's theater managers and owners were black, with just 175 African American managers out of 18,395 throughout the country.[42] T.O.B.A. management's continued promises of "brightening" conditions or tales of circuit headliners who have "graced the big stages along Broadway" muted this reality and encouraged novice black entertainers to seek the stage and stardom.[43]

### *Marketable Fame and Notoriety*

Although veterans warned show business newcomers about the "dapper stage sheik" with his "flowery promises and praises" and the delusion of "spectacular notoriety and the glittering lights," entertainers joined the T.O.B.A. circuit with hopes of fame and fortune.[44] Fame was seductive, and the more theaters joined the circuit, the more opportunities urban and small-town-dwelling African Americans had to encounter traveling black vaudeville. Blues scholars argue that T.O.B.A.'s many challenges failed to "dampen the spirits" of those who "pursued the glamor and glitter which they *perceived* that the TOBA offered."[45] "Stage struck" youth could write to theater advice columnists and be told that "show business is a good business for people with ability, plenty of grit, and the backbone to withstand hardship. . . . if you have the talent then 'fight for your place and don't give up until you get it.'"[46]

When promising newcomers came to the circuit, they were often "presented" to the black vaudevillian world with a short introductory note in a local black periodical that announced that they would be seen "next season" or that they were "going over in fine shape."[47] After Cab Calloway joined *Plantation Days*, the *Afro-American* lauded him as the "popular local entertainer" from whom a "great deal was expected" before the show moved out West.[48] By the early 1930s, aspiring musicians had witnessed Calloway's rise from an impoverished traveling performer who pawned drums to purchase luggage in Baltimore in 1927 to a headlining big band leader. By the time guitarist Danny Barker left New Orleans on his own path as a professional musician in the 1930s, "every guitar player in America white or black, would like to be with Cab Calloway."[49]

Not only did managers and critics claim that T.O.B.A. and the "amusement game" would only continue to prosper and take on "a great spurt" by the mid-1920s, but the stars themselves were further rewarded with advertisement endorsements for products and industries of all kinds.[50] Just as the circuit's rise followed the social movements of the New Woman, New Negro, and Jazz Age, it also fell in line with an increased promotion of American celebrity culture. Rather than political figures or intellectuals, 1920s celebrities, entertainers, and sports figures assumed the roles of success symbols of the era. In a "mixture of consumerism and fandom," some audience members looked to popular entertainers as models on how to dress, socialize, and be.[51]

While it is commonplace for social figures of the late twentieth and early twenty-first centuries to market everything from products to philanthropic deeds and social justice causes, the entertainer-focused celebrity culture of the 1920s was a product of what popular culture scholars argue was a new consumer age.[52] The early cosmetic industry had used the images and names of white stage actresses to market their products, and these stars became part of the cultural shift of beauty treatments formerly only associated with "worldly" oversexualized figures to viewing cosmetics as the trappings of young modern womanhood. Likewise, T.O.B.A. women headliners were particularly targeted to advertise cosmetics and hair products to New Negro women.

Although companies who marketed to African American women did not necessarily get involved in the 1920s debates that posited whether makeup fostered "artificial beauty," they did profit from the increased presence of black residents in the consumer marketplace. Both the white-owned and black-owned cosmetic companies observed the rising success of black stage actresses, blues singers, and comedians, and sought the endorsements of T.O.B.A. women as "examples of ideal beauty" in black communities.[53] In turn, black vaudevillians used the endorsements to further their notoriety with hopes that consumers would not only buy the products but show tickets, sheet music, and recordings. Statuesque and brown-skinned blues singer Bessie Smith found the "Golden Brown Vanishing Cream" from Madame Mamie Hightower "indispensable," while actress Ethel Tyler *only* used "Golden Brown Cold Cream."[54] Famed *Shuffle Along* and *Blackbirds* performer Florence Mills was an international black vaudevillian known for her soprano voice, "petite stature," and "frenetic dance movements." Mills's popularity was such that she marketed her own "beauty preparations" at Flo Mill Chemical in New York. Singer Blanche Calloway's smiling face told consumers that everyone could have her "long, silky, beautiful hair" if they only used Wavine Hair Dressing.[55] In 1929 Calloway attested that her "rich, velvety-smooth skin tone" could be achieved by using Madam C. J. Walker's Face Powder, available for just one dollar for three boxes.[56] Comedy headliners Butterbeans and Susie (married couple Jodie and Susie Edwards) developed their own cosmetics line that included makeup preparations and a hair straightener, "ok'ed by great Race artists," based at Race Supply Co. in New York's East Forty-Second Street.[57] Marketing told audience members that if they used the right product they could look like the beautifully dressed, glamorous, talented singers and dancers they saw onstage. "Race" advertising offered T.O.B.A. performers fame onstage and off while they developed the potential to become "tastemakers" for African American communities.

## *Salaries and Travel*

Although fame was an eagerly sought benefit of T.O.B.A. participation, being an entertainer was a profession, and a chance to earn an income from the stage was paramount. Dancer Leonard Reed mentioned that black artists on white circuits could earn more than a T.O.B.A. performer, and the "pay scale was no comparison," as "white vaudeville was a step up" economically. But few black vaudevillians had the opportunity to break into white vaudeville and the number of those crossover performers, like tap dancer Bill "Bojangles" Robinson, could be "counted on one hand."[58] T.O.B.A. distributed salaries according to a hierarchical scale. A chorus member or bit player made little in comparison to headliners, but even low-level circuit artists earned more than agricultural laborers, domestic servants, industrial workers, or clerical staff. In the 1920s, where anywhere from 30 to 60 percent of the American population (depending on region, race, and ethnicity) was considered impoverished in terms of income and "lived a modest and insecure existence," T.O.B.A. performers could make a sustainable salary as long as they kept working and audiences poured into the theaters.[59] The key issue was how much take-home pay an entertainer might retain after lodging costs, travel fees, and paying a 5 percent commission to the circuit.[60] It was to the entertainers' advantage to sell as many tickets as possible. Reportedly, veteran performers, like blues singer Ma Rainey, whose many pre-T.O.B.A. years in the business had taught her not to idly trust a male manager to handle her money, paid someone in the ensemble to watch each paid patron as they went through the door. This ensemble insider was meant to ensure that the percentage receipts matched the number of paid customers in the seats.[61]

After 1921, T.O.B.A. was the largest circuit of black-serving theaters, and as brass band leader P. G. Lowery argued, if an entertainer "hustled," there was decent money to be made, particularly in the more successful years of the circuit between 1925 and 1927.[62] Featured soloists in tab shows fared well. For his first T.O.B.A. show in 1927, *Plantation Days,* Cab Calloway earned thirty-five dollars a week, and "that's good money! $35 a week, man."[63] Working forty-eight weeks of the year, Calloway had the potential to earn $1,680 a year. In comparison, the average American farmworker earned just over $300 a year, while a black female laundress might earn the same. Even an experienced coal miner in 1926 only had the ability to earn an average of $1,447 a year for arduous manual labor.[64]

Novelty performers on the circuit could earn a bit more than Calloway had as a newcomer depending on the popularity of their act. Contortionist DeWayman Niles earned forty-five dollars for a week of performances in 1924, as did "nostril harmonica blower" Shoestring Willis in 1925. Charles Nickerson, who performed on the southern branch of the circuit as comedian "Mr. Bozo," earned as much as fifty dollars a week.[65] Chorus members and bit players in large traveling revues, like *Hits & Bits,* were at the very end of the pay scale. These shows could have a band, chorus line, dramatic actors and actresses, child stars, and comedians who all needed a salary.[66] Manager Jesse Cobb negotiated $300 a week for Mae Wilson and her "Brown Beauties" in 1924, and since the act contained ten performers, each performer might earn thirty dollars a week if the pay was distributed equally (which was not often the case).[67]

Headliners' salaries were higher to ensure their loyalty to T.O.B.A. Time and encourage other veteran players to join the circuit. The Bessie Smith Revue captured as much as $600 a week in 1925, while Whitney and Tutt's Smarter Set Company also earned the same in January of 1926. As performers worked their way through the circuit, grew in popularity, and began to record or play exclusive engagements in white venues, their earnings grew accordingly. Cab Calloway started at thirty-five dollars a week in 1927 ($521 in 2020), but by 1933 he was earning over $3,300 a week ($65,900 in 2020) at the Lafayette Theatre in Harlem.[68] Sideman Danny Barker explained that Calloway had paying gigs every week at two different jobs in the 1930s. The band played the Cotton Club cabaret at dawn hours and another "theater in the daytime," and "all them theaters, were loaded with people . . . Cab Calloway was doing all that."[69] For the lucky few veterans and headliners who knew how to manage their earnings, T.O.B.A.'s salary potential might be enough to mitigate many of the circuits' trials and tribulations. T.O.B.A. income could serve as the foundation for financially uplifting a performer and his extended family for some time.

A T.O.B.A. performer had the potential to earn these salaries while traveling throughout much of the nation. Prior to the early twentieth-century, opportunities for working-class African Americans to travel were often curtailed because of lack of time, funding, and social or citizenship status.[70] Even after World War I, while African Americans may have visited family members across state lines, or even spent time in Europe, Cuba, or the Philippines because of military activity, widespread leisure travel for average African Americans was infrequent. Yet for T.O.B.A. performers travel was the foundation of their working life. Segregated travel was humiliating, dehumanizing, and at times dangerous, but at least it was *possible*.

For T.O.B.A. performers, show travel mirrored the paths Great Migration participants made before finally relocating to the urban North and West. Isabel Wilkerson maintains that leisure travel exposed migrants to the "freedoms" previously in one's hometown and "emboldened" migrants to make permanent moves.[71] New York's Harlem was an attainable destination for Fountain Inn, South Carolina-born Peg Leg Bates, or New Orleans-born guitarist Danny Barker because of vaudeville travel. Hattie McDaniel played the T.O.B.A. circuit in Denver and eventually resettled in the film world of Los Angeles, while S. H. Dudley Sr. left the medicine shows of Texas to make a home in Maryland and Washington, DC. Not all T.O.B.A. performers made their relocations permanent, but circuit travel opened a window to the possibilities of geographic mobility and alternative, albeit contested, employment.

### *Training Ground and Arts Education*

After navigating T.O.B.A. to reap the rewards of potential fame, salary, and travel, the road is where artists went to train and perfect their craft among seasoned entertainment legends. While the fortunate individuals had some formal training, like Sadie Goodson or Marshal Royal, many T.O.B.A. entertainers learned their roles by first imitating and then building upon what they witnessed "year in and year out," according to comedian Dewey "Pigmeat" Markham.[72] *Defender* theater advice columnist and vaudevillian Vivienne Gordon Russell (no relation to Sylvester Russell) lamented the lack of artistic training for young entertainers because of the fears of African American parents who failed to see the stage as a "legitimate method of earning a living." She argued that music and dance education should be as viable an option for "talented" high school age youth as a trade school or domestic science. While Vivienne spoke of the "social advantage for your son or daughter to be accomplished, preferably in music," the absence of arts education fortunately could be remedied through the "on the job" training and informal mentoring received on the circuit.[73]

Many burgeoning artists who were marginalized in everyday society because of their gender, sexuality, race, or class status viewed the theatrical world as a space to attempt to "build a beautiful life," as outsiders were more readily accepted within entertainment circles.[74] Entertainers socialized, networked, and built complicated families, sometimes intimate relationships, with the only other people who may have understood how one spent an average day that sometimes spanned two geographical states. After traveling all night and grabbing a few hours of "snatched" sleep, T.O.B.A. artists could begin the day with breakfast at noon in an Alabama boarding house if there were any accommodations for "Race folk in town."[75] An afternoon meal might be followed by a rehearsal, two performances on stage, and break time in a theater basement "green room." The day might close with midnight dinner in a bar and a return to the train destined for Tennessee. T.O.B.A. artists, like "all good troupers," spent their time off the stage in a world of "alternate singing and dancing" and "quarreling and loving."[76] They built a community of entertainers who mentored and critiqued each other in a world that was uniquely their own.

Mentoring occurred across gender and rank lines, as performers traded tips and created informal networks. Jazz trumpeter Adolphus Anthony "Doc" Cheatham taught himself to play cornet and saxophone by listening to early jazz recordings, yet his true "school" was Nashville's Bijou Theatre. As Cheatham argued, when there was not enough music instruction for African Americans in Nashville schools, owner and T.O.B.A. president Milton Starr allowed Cheatham to practice in the pit for free. Cheatham strengthened his skills, watched musicians from the traveling shows, and was picked up by T.O.B.A. revues that included the John Williams' Broadcasters and the Frederic "Sunshine Sammy" Morrison show in 1926. These circuit travels eventually took Cheatham to Chicago, where T.O.B.A. headliner Ma Rainey took him into her band.[77] Georgia-born composer and pianist Thomas Dorsey, later known as the Father of Gospel Music, perfected his craft in the backyard of Atlanta's 81 Theatre as an amateur artist known as "Barrelhouse Tom" in the 1910s. Dorsey learned music theory by playing with seasoned musicians in Atlanta in the same ways that Cheatham did in Nashville. By 1924 Dorsey became Ma Rainey's band director, and as a composer he worked his way up through the blues music industry hierarchy. Songs like "It's Tight Like That," with its lyrics of "the gal I love, she's long and slim, and when she whip it, it's too bad Jim," or the other fifty-nine risqué compositions he wrote with guitarist Tampa Red, bore no resemblance to the gospel songs, like "Precious Lord," Dorsey would become known for by the 1930s. Yet the fundamentals of performance, composition, and the discipline of constant rehearsal were staples of the T.O.B.A. environment for all those who "learned the business" on the circuit.[78]

The circuit also educated performers in multiple genres of entertainment. Vocalists perfected comedy sketches, musicians became adept at several instruments, and according to dance scholar Jacqui Malone, dancers became "singing dancers" in their T.O.B.A. "apprenticeships."[79] When Dorsey practiced in the 81's backyard, he spent time with a young Bessie Smith who was then a dancing chorus girl in 1917. By the time T.O.B.A. began in 1921, the dancing Smith had learned enough to know that the chorus line was not her strength, and she became the partner of Wayne "Buzzin" Burton as she developed into a blues music vocalist and a circuit headliner. Future film actress Hattie McDaniel began on the circuit as a comedienne and by the late 1920s she emerged as a blues singer at T.O.B.A.'s Chicago and Cincinnati theaters, composing her own tunes like "Boo Hoo Blues" and "Any Kind of Man."[80] Versatility ensured performers were ready for any available part in a tab show or a novelty act, even beyond the confines of T.O.B.A.

Tap dancer Leonard Reed began his career in carnivals and Charleston contests in Oklahoma before he landed on the T.O.B.A. circuit in 1926. For Reed "TOBA was the stepping ground for all the [larger] black theaters, the Lincoln and the Howard in DC, the Earle and the Pearl in Philadelphia." In the absence of professional training, the circuit offered a space for entertainers to hone their craft as "you went from one theater to another" and "you built your reputation."[81] For three shows a night, Tuesday through Saturday and two on Sunday, a dancer learned those basic chorus line steps and developed their own signature style. An adolescent entertainer while on T.O.B.A.'s circuit, Fayard Nicholas of the famed acrobatic dance duo, the Nicholas Brothers, was born on the circuit. Fayard recalled T.O.B.A.'s arts education component, as he and brother Harold had no dance training but practiced their fast-paced taps, fluid arm movements, and audience interactions by watching from the wings. Nicholas recalled how Alice Whitman, (of the Whitman Sisters) "was outstanding. They used to travel in the I guess they call it, T.O.B.A., . . . and Alice oh, she was so beautiful, . . . and Bill Robinson, he is the greatest, his taps were so clear."[82]

## *From the "Pickaninnies" to the T.O.B.A. Stage: Black Child Stars*

The training component of T.O.B.A. could also be a family affair when black vaudevillians placed their children in their acts. In late nineteenth-century- and early twentieth-century vaudeville, black children had performed as "pickaninnies" alongside "coon shouters," white women, often in blackface, who mimicked the cadences and postures of African American women vocalists in the popular racialized genre of coon song. May Irwin, Josephine Gassman, Marie Cahill, and others were known to add two to three black children to their act as street children or enslaved children, depending on the nature of the song.[83] The vestiges of minstrel-like performance were not entirely eradicated with the arrival of T.O.B.A. Time. But circuit parents focused on the artistry of musical and dance entertainment and made room for child prodigy entertainers. Praised as one of the most skilled and diverse entertainers of the twentieth century, Sammy Davis Jr. was raised in the black vaudeville circuit. He began his career onstage with his father Sammy Davis Sr. and godfather Will Mastin, while Davis's mother Elvera was a chorus girl in tab shows and nightclubs. Davis noted that if you were an entertainer and "you had a kid you brought them on (stage), that was their proving ground." At three years old Davis took to the stage, dancing and singing age-inappropriate tunes, like "I'll Be Glad When You're Dead, You Rascal You," and learned his craft from the bottom up, although it is debatable how much "childhood" he experienced.[84]

From the 1910s onward regional regulations about the age, education levels, work hours, and payment of child entertainers abounded but were more lenient in states like New York as opposed to Illinois or Louisiana, for example.[85] Reformer Jane Addams acknowledged the "direct appeal" and novelty of child entertainers, but begged the question of "why is it that stage people insist that a child should appear upon the stage prematurely?" Addams argued that children "too young to understand" about sexualized stage humor and antics should be protected against the undue "powerful" influences of the stage.[86] However, raising children as entertainers allowed T.O.B.A. performers, particularly women, to keep their families intact without having to constantly seek outside childcare or quit their profession entirely.

Parents and guardians addressed the issue of a lack of formal education for child entertainers by arranging road tutors who taught fundamental math and reading basics or by sending youth to school in between bookings. Some child stars also acquired music or dance training from private instructors, professional family members, or in public school.[87] Future female swing trumpeter Valaida Snow started her career in her father's traveling show, "John V. Snow's Pickaninny Troubadours," as a child prodigy violinist in 1913. She would later take this early training and apply it to her work as one of the few women big band leaders in the country by the 1930s.[88] Similarly, The Gibson Family children were formally trained musicians, and parents Albert and Corinne placed them in the act before age five. As the older children matured, they gained more responsibility for managing the act, and The Gibson Family lasted as a "wholesome" family-friendly ensemble for nearly two decades.[89]

Children who were not explicitly part of their parents' acts but accompanied the parents backstage often nurtured their own independent entertainment careers in later years. Clarinetist Marshal Royal Jr. was exposed to T.O.B.A. green rooms and rehearsal spaces when he was still an infant. Royal's father, mother, and uncle had a pit band for black vaudeville revues like the Whitman Sisters. To keep her child with her and still stay "in the band," mother Ernestine brought Marshal along. Marshal "slept behind the piano from the time I was 2 or 3 months on my father's overcoat. Anytime [my parents] would go out of town or across town or anywhere else, to keep her in the band, I was the baby back in behind the piano on the overcoat."[90] The value of musical performance and the difficulties of road travel remained a part of Royal's background as he moved from an early California jazz scene to a member of Count Basie's band by the late 1930s and early '40s.

Fayard and Harold Nicholas's parents, Ulysses and Viola, performed as theater-based pit musicians in "an orchestra that was independent" of a specific show. Fayard recalled that his parents played for jazz trumpeter Louis Armstrong, dancers Leonard Reed and Buck and Bubbles (Ford Washington and John Sublett), singers Adelaide Hall and Willie Bryant, "and many, many other artists." Both Fayard and Harold were born on the road in Alabama and North Carolina, respectively, and Fayard noted that he was literally raised in the pit:

> And she [Mother] was playing in the orchestra pit with my father and the rest of the musicians had me in the bassinet right beside the piano where she was playing . . . so, there she's playing, and puttin' a bottle in my mouth as she's playing . . . all this music around me.[91]

With "all the music" around them, Fayard and Harold became tap dancers at Gibson's Standard Theatre in Philadelphia at the ages of fourteen and seven, respectively. Ulysses and Viola left their careers as musicians to manage and travel with their sons as they rose from T.O.B.A. to Broadway and eventually to film.[92]

Some child performers used T.O.B.A. as a "middle school" of sorts. Child comedian Ernest Frederic "Sunshine Sammy" Morrison Jr. started his career in silent films in 1917 at age five. Father Ernest Morrison Sr. worked as a chef to Los Angeles's incoming elite and networked his children to early stardom in film. "Sunshine Sammy" played the T.O.B.A. circuit when the film market for "America's first black child star" slowed between 1924 and 1926 and used his time on the circuit to supplement his income.[93] Morrison's T.O.B.A. stints were bookended by appearances in Hal Roach's *Our Gang* or *Little Rascals* films that began production in 1922.[94] For many of these "children of the business," T.O.B.A. often allowed entertaining families to remain together on the road, helped child entertainers learn the business, and fostered a performing arts educational community.

## THE CHALLENGES OF T.O.B.A. TIME

Despite the circuit's many benefits, T.O.B.A. Time did not come without its unique challenges. New vaudevillians spoke of employment uncertainty, poor salaries, and substandard theater conditions, particularly in the southern regions of the circuit. Concerns of racial violence, gender discrimination, and respectability battles loomed large for all T.O.B.A. entertainers.

A circuit booking was meant to ensure anywhere from thirty to forty straight weeks of performance opportunities and secured routing throughout much of the nation. As comedian Pigmeat Markham remarked, T.O.B.A. booked these shows "all through the middle West all the way up to Baltimore, MD," following the pattern of vaudeville networks established by "big time" black-owned theaters like Philadelphia's Standard or Washington, DC's Howard.[95] The performance season officially began in September and ended in June, with an alternate routing of summer shows dependent on the availability of open T.O.B.A.-contracted theaters during the sweltering "hot summer months."[96] T.O.B.A. management and stockholder meetings were held in January and July and often influenced routings. The acquisition of a new theater might shorten the distance an act had to travel. For example, McGarr & DeGaston's Ragtime Steppers might be able to play a city in between their Birmingham, Alabama, and Louisville, Kentucky, acts, increasing their salary but also necessitating a change in their travel plans.[97]

A contract, secured bookings, and the promise of a consistent routing schedule was often *just* a promise that might not be realized. Due to miscommunication or travel delays, Smarter Set Comedy producer Salem Tutt Whitney acknowledged that some "performers were never sure of the next date until they had reached the place booked and the curtain went up on their first performance."[98] While the details of segregated travel and lodging will be detailed in a subsequent chapter, insecure bookings compounded the problem of unstable salaries, especially for newcomers. Leonard Reed was paid "$15 a week, and a meal ticket" and "paid his room" from his paltry salary.[99] For many T.O.B.A. performers Reed's situation was familiar, as a typical salary for a new vaudevillian might provide "two meals per day and lodging, obtainable at two of the better class houses catering to the profession, in this city [Baltimore] for $10 per week," and "laundry and other requisites quickly gobble up the remainder, preventing any coupon clipping."[100] Expenses were paid from a performer's *projected* salary, which meant that a T.O.B.A. performer's livelihood was dependent on credit extended from a theater manager or booking agent. In the worst cases, performers left lodging with debt and gave black hotel owners "I.O.U.s" to be paid by individual theater managers. In 1927 performer G. M. Howell did just that when he booked a show at Macon's Douglass Theatre and asked the theater manager to pay his bill at Atlanta's Hotel DeMonte on credit.[101]

## *"Call the Health Department": Theater-Building Standards*

A T.O.B.A. theater's physical condition varied depending on the location and manager of the establishment. While generally located in urban black neighborhoods, T.O.B.A. theaters were not always the most modern or sophisticated in construction. Some of the initial T.O.B.A. theaters added to the circuit in 1921 were just a step up from the tent shows and open airdome theaters that permeated the nation in the 1910s. Lacking in electricity, plumbing, or actual walls, many of these "theaters," seen to be appropriate for black working-class patrons, were little more than elevated platforms with benches for the audience. As the 1920s approached, some theaters like the Bijou Theatre in Nashville, owned by T.O.B.A. president Milton Starr, had originally been white-only vaudeville houses or silent motion picture theaters that white owners sold for the use of black audiences once migration remapped a city's black population or a theater was in a state of near disrepair.[102] At times with only cosmetic renovation, these theaters were reopened as T.O.B.A. jewels.

In 1924 theater critic Tony Langston took up the issue of the physical maintenance of T.O.B.A. theaters in the *Defender* and reported a wide spectrum of results. In Chattanooga, a circuit headquarter city, the Liberty Theatre had "the three dressing rooms, toilet and running water and was very clean," while John T. Gibson's Philadelphia Standard and Dunbar Theatres "were both clean and up to date." Yet Nashville's Bijou Theatre had plenty of "filthy dirty" dressing rooms that were "ready to fall on you." Pensacola's Belmont Theatre suffered an invasion of "bedbugs," and Baltimore's Star Theatre was "in need of everything, including a call from the health department."[103] Eastern Regional Director S. H. Dudley responded to these reports with surprise and sincere hopes that theater managers who had "never been in their own dressing rooms" would soon rectify the situation. Ever the performer, theater magnate Dudley praised Langston's "interest shown to the welfare of the performers."[104]

Two years later in 1926, Dudley's desires still had not been met, and the *Defender* again published critiques of the physical state of T.O.B.A. theaters, this time exposed by fellow producer and T.O.B.A. performer Salem Tutt Whitney.

While Langston had been at a "loss to understand why members of the profession will wallow in the filth and dirt of germ and vermin laden, disease spreading dressing rooms without protest," Whitney asked how performers could show off their artistry and give the audience a "first class" experience in what appeared to be third-class or lower conditions.[105] Actors had difficulty creating the illusion of a moment if a theater was devoid of appropriate staging. Whitney discussed how a "bedroom loses much of its realism when the bed is missing. The audience does not expect to see kitchen chairs in the parlor scene or parlor chairs in a kitchen," but "this often happens and the show was not to blame."[106]

Issues persisted still when "sixteen or more" actors attempted to crowd into as few as two available rooms. Whitney joked that "by the time they [performers] have finished stepping on each other's feet, mixing up their costumes, and stumbling up and down the narrow stair case to the stage . . . they're as amiable as a bunch of bolshiveks [*sic*] at a capitalist meeting."[107] Further building concerns included the cleaning and treatment of the actual stage itself, for if it wasn't covered when not in use, it could damage or soil costumes. Many backstage areas were stifled by poor ventilation and were either damp and cold or full of coal smoke. Often musicians had difficulties with the configuration and resources in the orchestra pit, for if there was "no orchestra pit and the piano not furnished, a show was then truly up against it."[108]

Overall, Whitney strongly suggested that to improve the manager's profits and the performers' spirits "each theater should have at least three sets of scenery in good condition, proper facilities for lighting effects, and furnish the properties so necessary for a first-class performance."[109] The persistent poor physical conditions of select theaters prevented the booking of key headliner acts, contradicted the purpose of a centralized theater circuit, and eroded the morale of the average T.O.B.A. performer. Some of these concerns were addressed in a piecemeal fashion in individual cities in the circuit's early years, but arguably only after customer complaint and a decline in attendance. Many managers did not have any real incentive to repair T.O.B.A.'s crumbling theaters until they faced formal complaints from the Colored Actors' Union or lost patrons in the overall industry shift to motion pictures.

## *"Fiendish Mobs": Racial Violence on the Road*

In the first decades of the twentieth century, the threat of racial violence was consistent for any African American who disobeyed the rules of deference—the appearance of obeying supposed white authority—in a racially segregated society. Male members of 1910s minstrel groups had actually been lynched in Missouri and Arkansas for such infractions as being dressed too well, defending the virtue of black women, and not being appropriately submissive to whites in their behavior.[110] While lynching threats slackened for individual T.O.B.A. performers in the 1920s, artists were still subject to the racially discriminatory policies of circuit theaters, especially those in Southern states. White Atlanta theater owner Charles Bailey was a known staunch supporter of segregation and unspoken deference rules. He reportedly ran the 81 Theatre much like a "plantation," and artists were told when and where to eat and dress. As early as the mid-1910s black theater managers Emma and Mabel Griffin professed their desire to "drown out such men" as Bailey for his discriminatory practices. By many other performer and theater manager accounts, he was one of the most difficult personalities of the circuit and was viewed as a "gun toting, Caesar of Atlanta's Black Belt."[111]

Bailey's treatment of performers did not improve after he became a T.O.B.A. manager and stockholder, and he was known to denigrate certain performers that did not meet his expectations of deferential behavior. He cast out entertainers amid their circuit-contracted tours, which disrupted performer travel and caused for bigger jumps between cities. Bailey "refused to play" the Johnnie Reddick Company from Atlanta in 1924 and attempted to do the same to the Whitman Sisters in early 1925.[112] Even the rising star Ethel Waters encountered Bailey's blatantly racist demeanor at the 81 Theatre. Angry that Pennsylvania-born Waters criticized his theater's substandard equipment when she offered to pay to have his house piano tuned, Bailey retorted with "no Yankee nigger bitch is telling me how to run my theater." He then called circuit president Milton Starr and demanded the removal of that "black bitch of the T.O.B.A. time."[113] Bailey's demands were ignored, and his entertainer-alienating antics resulted in a failed attempt to form his own circuit apart from T.O.B.A. in the late 1920s.[114] Additional discriminatory and racially violent incidents followed T.O.B.A. performers along the circuit and included tales of white Chicago gangsters forcing black jazz musicians to perform until dawn at gunpoint or even the racially and sexually motivated, police-instigated murder of Clinton De Forest, a black vaudevillian female impersonator in New York.[115]

The most egregious case of racial violence directed at T.O.B.A. performers occurred amid the Tulsa Massacre in 1921, one of the largest US racial massacres of the twentieth century.[116] In the early 1900s Tulsa, Oklahoma, was a vibrant well-populated city due in part to a flourishing oil industry. Although the city was staunchly segregated, Tulsa's African Americans created their own residential and economic neighborhoods, most notably in the city's Greenwood District. By 1920, eleven thousand African Americans across the class spectrum called Tulsa home, and Greenwood earned the title "Negro Wall Street."[117] Over fifty black-owned or -managed establishments, including restaurants, tailors, drug stores, bakeries, barbers, and newspapers, lined the "Tulsa Colored Business Directory" in the 1920s black periodical the *Tulsa Star*. W. H. Phillips' Livery, C. H. Perkins and his "Real Mexican Food," the "leading Colored hotel" the Stratford, and the headquarters of the *Tulsa Star* could all be found on Greenwood Avenue alone. The silent motion picture and vaudeville house Williams' Dreamland Theatre on 127 N. Greenwood Avenue rounded out the black-owned establishments in the district.[118]

Owned and operated by married couple John W. and Loula T. Williams, the Dreamland opened in 1914 on Greenwood Avenue and soon advertised itself as having the "latest motion pictures and high-class vaudeville," where only "first class performers" need apply.[119] With J. W. Williams's pleasant demeanor and "good smile" and Loula's organizational abilities as proprietor, the Dreamland soon became a rousing success.[120] T.O.B.A. included the Dreamland as one of its theaters as soon as the circuit opened in 1921, and while not the only theater for black audiences in Tulsa, it was one of the few black-*owned* theater institutions. The Dreamland succeeded in attracting top-notch entertainment, for reviews discussed its "successful engagements" and its hundreds of "pleased patrons."[121] In the initial six months preceding the massacre, T.O.B.A. acts in Tulsa included Davenport & Davenport; comedy group Mills & Frisby's Tar Babies; dancers Lemons & Brown; musicians the Grant, Jones & Burney Trio; and Ridley's International Players, among others.[122] The Dreamland was on target for a robust 1921–22 season, with the summer set to open with the appearance of the Cleo Mitchell's Jazz Repertoire Company. Managed by her entertainer husband Joe Carmouche, dancer and actress Cleo Mitchell's ensemble included "some of the best looking girls," "comedious comedians," and a host of "talented" and "experienced performers."[123] Poised to perform at the Dreamland on Wednesday, June 1, 1921, the Mitchell troupe found itself surrounded by mobs that leveled the Greenwood District and left ruins of "cinder and ash" in their wake.

Between the evening of May 31 and June 1 two days of arson, looting, and murder directed at Tulsa's African American residents became known as the Tulsa Massacre. The Tulsa events followed in the wake of devastating racial turmoil in Atlanta, Georgia, in 1906; Springfield, Illinois, in 1908; in East St. Louis, Illinois, in 1917; and 1919's Red Summer, which ripped through such locations as Washington, DC; Chicago, Illinois; and Elaine, Arkansas.[124] The scale of human and physical destruction was much larger in Tulsa than in these previous attacks. Additionally, Tulsa's outnumbered black community members met white violence with armed resistance, and the local and state governments were complicit in black destruction, as "police officers deputized and armed a bloodthirsty mob."[125] At the crux of the chaos was a seventeen-year-old white Sarah Page, who falsely accused a nineteen-year-old black Dick Rowland of attacking her in the elevator of Tulsa's Drexel Building on May 30.[126] When word got out in the black community that Rowland had been arrested on suspicion of assault on May 31, a small group of black Greenwood residents armed themselves and marched to the courthouse to prevent Rowland's lynching. The resulting clash of fifteen hundred to two thousand armed white citizens against "fifty to seventy-five" armed black men devolved into ritualistic carnage when a white man attempted to forcibly disarm a black man and gunfire was exchanged.[127] In the violent exchange, Rowland and Page were forgotten, and the throngs of white citizens at the courthouse turned their attentions to the residences and commercial establishments of Greenwood District, the visible symbol of Tulsa's black community prosperity. The Dreamland and its evening's principal players Cleo Mitchell's Jazz Repertoire Company were swept along in the turmoil that leveled the Greenwood District.

As the carnage and destruction crept along the Greenwood Avenue block by block throughout the daylight hours of June 1, it became apparent that the complete annihilation of Tulsa's black community was the mob's goal. In the early dawn hours of the first, Cleo and her company sheltered in place, and the company's belongings remained safe in the theater as the invasion had not yet hit the Dreamland. Yet the violence only escalated despite the activation of the Tulsa branch of the National Guard. In the midst of the morning, rioters murdered prominent African American citizens, male and female, when they attempted to defend their property or physically resist. Dr. A. C. Jackson "was killed on his doorstep," while John Wheeler, a black bank employee, "was killed by a stray

FIGURE 5. Dreamland Theatre, Tulsa, Oklahoma, 1921, courtesy of the Tulsa Historical Society & Museum.

bullet" on the way to the bank. John Wesley Williams, "the wealthiest Negro in Tulsa" and co-owner of the Dreamland was assumed among the black dead, as his wife Loula witnessed his kidnapping and the destruction of their home at 102 North Greenwood Avenue.[128] African American eyewitnesses watched as ordinary white citizens, deputized by the city police, looted and torched the Dreamland.[129] The Red Cross Disaster Relief group sent to take care of the newly homeless summarized that "what had been a prosperous, peaceable, and fairly well-ordered negro business and residential district was transferred into a burned and devastated area."[130]

When the white mob members set the Dreamland on fire, Cleo Mitchell and her Company were allowed to escape and were "forced off stage while in costume" as the city's "most elaborate pleasure house . . . laid in ruins."[131] Cleo Mitchell, Sweenie Price, Edna Young, Frank Tansel, William Cole, Emma Hawkins, and the rest of the "company lost by fire or were despoiled of every possession but the clothes they wore at the time." The Mitchell Troupe lost "$6000 worth of costume and wardrobe," but they left with their lives.[132] The Associated Negro Press argued that "whatever [Greenwood] enjoyed in the matter of thrift, enterprise, and a fair name had been destroyed by a wanton, fiendish mob actuated by jealousy and race hatred, for the simple reason that [black] prosperity and intelligent development was becoming too evident to suit the wishes of a certain element of whites."[133]

National Association for the Advancement of Colored People (NAACP) executive Walter White argued that although two black-serving theaters lined Greenwood Avenue, the Dixieland and the Dreamland, only the Dreamland was black-owned and "always well filled," while the white-owned Dixieland "was poorly patronized." As "economic racial solidarity" was strongly expressed in Tulsa, black citizens effectively boycotted white businesses and made the best of the legally imposed self-sufficient community.[134] In the eyes of white Tulsa citizens black Greenwood residents economically benefitted from the very segregation policies that had been established to make sure African Americans knew their "place" on the racial hierarchy. The carnage experienced in Tulsa resulted in the leveling of thirty-five residential and commercial blocks in the Greenwood District, ten thousand black homeless residents, over seven hundred wounded black citizens, and the deaths of forty white citizens and anywhere from sixty-seven to three hundred murdered black citizens.[135]

Cleo Mitchell and her company rebounded due to financial donations asked for in black periodicals like the *Defender* and the *Afro-American*. The Cleo Mitchell Jazz Repertoire Company resumed performances a month later at T.O.B.A.'s Pensacola, Florida, theater, the Belmont, though not without the scars of Tulsa imprinted in their immediate consciousnesses.[136] The violent destruction of a prominent T.O.B.A. theater in the circuit's founding year could have upended

T.O.B.A. in the Southern District. Eight years prior, black vaudevillian Emma Griffin had tried to promote black vaudeville tours to the "Sunny South," promising fellow vaudevillians that, beyond segregated travel and select white supremacist theater managers, the South was worth the risk. The highly publicized, devastating violence in Tulsa could have destroyed all of Griffin's promises. Yet fortunately the Dreamland's Mrs. Loula Williams, a witness and an assumed grieving widow, was also a change agent. After it was determined that her husband, J. W. had been gravely injured but was still alive, Loula and he set upon rebuilding their fortunes. Mrs. Williams sued the local government and her insurance companies for property losses and rebuilt the Dreamland by 1922 at 127½ N. Greenwood Avenue.[137] Williams stayed active in T.O.B.A. management for several more years, as she remained the owner of the Dreamland Theatres in Muskogee, Okmulgee, and Tulsa, Oklahoma.

## *Those Wicked Chorus Girls: Gendered Concerns & T.O.B.A. Women*

The potential for racial violence leveled at T.O.B.A. performers knew no gendered boundaries. Yet in many other aspects, T.O.B.A. women often encountered gendered restrictions in ways their male counterparts did not. The policing of female entertainers' bodies and moral characters predated T.O.B.A.'s rise as chronicled in the narrative of the Griffin Sisters as vaudeville managers. Soon after Sam T. Jack cast African American women in their first theater performances in the burlesque review *The Creole Show* in 1890, theater critics and some African American audience members alike questioned if black women really belonged on the stage. Black musical revues that followed, such as John Isham's Octoroons or Oriental America in 1895 and 1897, respectively, had names that encouraged and perhaps mirrored an audience's appreciation for fair-skinned, "exotic" looking black women on stage.[138] Yet, regardless of phenotype, being a theater performer did not fit the societal expectations and roles that Black "virtuous women" were expected to fill as wives, mothers, or service laborers.

Many critics characterized all actresses as barely a step above the women who frequented nineteenth-century urban theaters, the paid escorts and roving sex workers of a theater's famed third tier.[139] Facing challenges about their integrity and assumed sexual promiscuity, many black women's rights advocates in the early twentieth century sought to promote "negro womanhood" as "pure and virtuous."[140] Black progressive leaders discouraged leisure activities, like secular music, dance, and theater that could potentially further immorality and vice, particularly among working-class black women. Female vaudevillians were often unmarried, childless women who wore makeup and "provocative" dress—women who did not fit their socially proscribed "place." In New York in 1902 Christian missionaries made their field of service not a community overseas but local black vaudeville stages. These missionaries offered bible classes to combat the "widespread superstition" of "the inherent and *universal wickedness* of stage people and particularly *chorus girls*."[141] In a 1909 *Freeman* column, black vaudevillian Harry Brown asked "can girls of our race be moral on the stage?" and again raised the issue of virtuous black womanhood being incompatible with the theater profession.[142] Another reader directly addressed Brown and commented that "immoral colored girls" would not be "immoral" if "colored men" of the stage did not lead them "astray." This discussion of female vaudevillian virtue was not resolved in the *Freeman*, and a continued conversation about female morality persisted in the theater industry throughout the New Negro, New Women, and flapper movements of the 1920s.[143]

As T.O.B.A. rose along with these social movements, theater managers and producers with an apparent need to manage female entertainers' duties and behaviors, especially chorus and background performers, often included gendered demands into individual performer contracts. The Musical Spillers, a black instrumental troupe that performed both in black and white circuits from 1906 to 1940, were very specific in their contracts and stated, "the *ladies* must help dress the stage and see that everything is clean" and "no ladies are allowed to frequent clubs, dives, and places of ill repute."[144] The ladies referred to in the contract were not Spillers staff but adult female musicians and paid cast members. Yet management still patrolled their offstage behavior as if they were young children and did not hesitate to reinforce a gendered hierarchy. Infractions of this code could result in fines, loss of pay, and finally termination of the contract. There were no provisions made for the offstage behaviors of the Spillers's male members.

The industry's conflict between the creation of protected spaces that safeguarded T.O.B.A. women's morality and a fundamental belief in the stereotype that all women entertainers were somewhat debased and sexually promiscuous often ignored the reality that female T.O.B.A. performers faced a host of pressing concerns on the road, including colorism, the practice of associating higher social status and privilege with African Americans who were fair-skinned. Managers' overt preference for fair-skinned women in 1890s musical revues continued in many T.O.B.A. shows in the 1920s. In 1922 Charles Turpin of the Booker Washington Theatre vented in the African American press that "we could stand a lot more good looking women in the game" and that he could "write volumes about the good looking women we DON'T see in colored show business."[145] Orchestra leader Benton Overstreet of Gibson's Dunbar Theatre vehemently disagreed with Turpin's comments on women performers and unmasked Turpin's terminology to decipher that, by "good looking," Turpin meant "fair skinned." Overstreet shared that John T. Gibson wanted to hire good "talent, regardless of color and looks."

The orchestra leader also warned fellow theater staffers that if they failed to hire "your dark women and your browns," you would not have a show, alluding to an African American audience who wanted to see themselves represented on the stage in all their hues as long as they presented "real material."[146] An audience's desire for diversity in representation could also be found in tunes popular on T.O.B.A., like "Brown Skin Gal" that purported that "a brown skin gal is the best gal after all." And yet still the color divide persisted, as exemplified by singer Bessie Smith being cast out from tab shows that "Glorified the Brown Skinned Girl" for she was "too dark" or dancer Bessie Dudley recalling that she was the darkest dancer in the lineup at the Alhambra Theatre in 1930s New York and had to wear light makeup to make the lineup.[147]

Stereotypes about physical beauty also plagued women vaudevillians in their attempts to find offseason employment. In between seasons many T.O.B.A. performers secured employment that had no connection to entertainment. Pit musician and drummer Ulysses Nicholas worked as a clothes presser when not in the theater's orchestra, while a young blues singing Hattie McDaniel labored as a domestic when not with the circuit. Even blues singer Bessie Smith worked in a Birmingham laundry in the offseason, before she became the "Empress of the Blues" who filled T.O.B.A. theaters in the late 1920s.[148] Yet, many T.O.B.A. women found it difficult to supplement their incomes in these ways, as the *Defender* reported "a strong prejudice against engaging a former stage girl." Prospective female employers believed stage performers too *fragile* for serious manual household labor and too *attractive* to dim the "fatal fascination" of a household's husband, father, brother, or son.[149]

While the image of the seductive domestic might make for good gossip or have explained the occasional consensual affair between male employers and their female "help," historians and fiction writers have illuminated that black female domestics were clearly more at risk of their employer's sexual harassment rather than the other way around. Rather than acknowledge the predator-like behavior of their husbands or sons, many a female employer would just rather avoid hiring a "good-looking colored wench."[150] Compounded with these employment difficulties, African American female entertainers also had issues securing housing on the road. While a local citizen might convert their home for boarding young teachers, secretaries, or students, women entertainers contended with boarding home operators who argued that "*thoughtless* chorus girls cause a great deal of trouble" ... "therefore" they will not be "accepted ... as roomers."[151] The pervasive unjust image of T.O.B.A. chorus girls as flighty, sexually promiscuous, or argumentative only made road life that much more difficult.

The public visibility of T.O.B.A. women performers increased the threat of unwanted sexual attention, attempted assaults, and sexual violence from black and white, male and female assailants alike.[152] Bessie Dudley recalled that as she attempted to audition for the Gibson Family Troupe in 1923, a piano player, only referred to as "Steve," tried to "get fresh" with Dudley and dragged her "in the alley" behind Baltimore's Lincoln Theatre. Thankfully, Dudley managed to run away and avoid sexual assault but explained that there was little to no protection for a young woman on the road.[153] After Bessie Dudley secured a position as a chorus girl with the Gibson Troupe, she remained a target for inappropriate unwanted sexual attention. Sherman H. Dudley Jr., son of the theater magnate, pursued Bessie when she was still an adolescent. Bessie had falsified her age on their wedding license and said she was twenty-one when she was actually between the ages of twelve and thirteen. She further commented that S. H. Jr. was both unfaithful and physically violent from the wedding night onward: "My husband loved other women, he would beat me and then go sleep with other women in the same hotel." This abusive treatment continued throughout their marriage until Bessie escaped Dudley Jr. in New York when he left the United States to stage a show abroad. As Dudley Jr. waited for Bessie at the dock she hid, "went to another girl's house and stayed there until the boat pulled off," effectively ending the abusive relationship, as Dudley Jr. did not seek to reconnect with Bessie when he returned from France.[154]

Ultimately, even consensual heterosexual relationships could also prove difficult if the risk of pregnancy could not be avoided. While a married entertainer might find a home for her child as an eventual youth performer, an unwed black mother who worked as a chorus girl could be a triple affront to respectability politics. In 1920s American society, single or divorced white mothers were socially stigmatized and had great difficulties gaining and keeping wage jobs once employers knew of their status.[155] It was that much harder for a black unpartnered mother to continue her career in the absence of familial support and in the face of gendered racism. The narrative that blues singer Bessie Smith's "adopted" son, Jack Gee Jr., was simply "given" to her by a chorus girl in the Smith Revue who couldn't care for the child, is a testament to the lengths women might be forced to go to remain employed on the stage.[156]

Former chorus girl and 1920s theater columnist "Vivienne" at last came to the rescue of African American chorus girls and T.O.B.A. women in a series of *Defender* articles in 1925 and 1926. Using her experiences in pre-T.O.B.A. shows like Will Marion Cook's *In Darkydom* and J. Leubrie's *Darktown Follies*, Vivienne Russell maintained that the women's chorus line was the "very *source* of the theatrical profession." She asked theatergoing audiences to suspend their judgment and "stop to consider how strenuous (female) parts are and how little credit they get." She detailed that chorus girls often rehearsed without pay, working hours after the headliners and male cast members had gone, like "little Trojans" with "empty

FIGURE 6. Effie Mae Moore Troop, 1920s, Scurlock Studio Records, Archives Center, National Museum of American History, Smithsonian Institution.

stomachs."[157] Leonard Reed echoed Vivienne's descriptions when he recounted how chorus girls could perform up to six shows a day at New York's Apollo Theater, and that was the "hardest job he'd ever seen for girls."[158]

The constant physical entertaining while challenging the stereotype of not being as serious an artist as a male comedian or musician took a mental toll on T.O.B.A. women. Vivienne spoke directly to black women entertainers and asked them to "put your whole heart into your work" and "make your failures stepping stones to success." She implored vaudevillians to keep entertaining, even when it seemed as if theaters were half empty, as a dedicated work ethic could be a path to other genres of performance even beyond T.O.B.A.[159] Although Vivienne discussed entertainers' offstage behavior, she suggested that a respectable image could make it easier for an entertainer seeking adequate lodging, a key booking, or even ensure that mainstream stages paid black entertainers "the same wage" as white entertainers. Reforming current stage acts placed black artists in a "position to demand" economic equality on any stage.[160] Yet Vivienne did not publicly criticize nor address black women entertainers' interior lives, consensual sexuality, or the communities they created among themselves. Rather, Vivienne concluded that hard-working chorus girls were "the very backbone of our shows" and as such should command respect and be given opportunities to excel in vaudeville.[161] Could women of the race maintain their morality on the T.O.B.A. stage? The answers were both "of course" and "whose definition of morality?" Yet the discussion permeated larger circuit-wide battles and attempts to redefine black morality in general that extended over the life of T.O.B.A. Time.

## "Cut the Smut!": Censorship Battles and Respectability Wars

In 1926 Milton Starr, T. O. B.A.'s president, promised "many good things" for next season if only the "actors did their part in giving Mr. Starr first class acts. Cut out the smut, the patrons don't want it anymore."[162] The continuous discussions of the need for respectability in entertainment and black leisure culture at large had migrated from sermons, speeches, and periodicals into the management discussions of the T.O.B.A. circuit itself. Again, the morality battle was not new, and theater scholar Karen Sotiropoulos examines how black vaudevillians at the turn of the century "managed to make stage life an acceptable sphere" for middle-class African Americans by highlighting entertainers' personal morality and virtue apart from their onstage characters.[163] In the 1920s and the Harlem Renaissance era, the sustained morality debate had a decided effect on how T.O.B.A. performers constructed their acts, the wording in their contracts, and the bookings they could receive. Black theatrical veteran and journalist J. A. Jackson argued that black vaudevillians were "perhaps the greatest advocates on the court of race relations," but often only if they were a positive example of black civility.[164] For many black theater owners, managers, and performers who saw show business as an extension of New Negro race work, the efforts to entertain yet not offend audiences was a constant struggle. As T.O.B.A. plans arose, race critics who argued that "the rise of the race is obstructed and . . . the pathway to progress waxes more difficult unless we develop a community sense strong enough to drive vice into its grave" pressured managers and performers to shape their acts accordingly or run the risk of not being employed.[165] Even fellow black vaudevillians contended that some of the most popular and skilled entertainers in the business could be found in "T.O.B.A. houses," if only the circuit would "get their acts arranged" to repel potentially vulgar material.[166]

Exactly what was objectionable or "smutty" material transformed over T.O.B.A.'s life span and varied depending on community taste, convention, and region. The most problematic material for show critics contained references to overt sexuality, alcoholism, and gambling in a song, skit, or dance performance. Additionally, the minstrel performances and blackface that were acceptable in 1900 or 1910 were often criticized by many African American audiences by the late 1920s. In the 1899–1900 season, Bert Williams' and George Walker's *The Policy Players,* which included songs like "Broadway Coon," with Williams in blackface and a plot that focused on the winner of an illegal local lottery or policy game, earned praise as the first Williams and Walker black musical theater production.[167] By 1925, the "low comedy" of Bert Williams was considered "passé" by many, and black theater critics asked performers to discover a new "corkless" comedy that would not be performed "at the expense of the Race."[168]

Blues music was an artistic genre that helped the circuit thrive due to its popularity, but it also challenged circuit critics. Bessie Smith's *Downhearted Blues,* with its lyrics of "I'm so disgusted, heartbroken too, I've got those Downhearted Blues," was revered by audiences in 1923 and sold 780,000 sides for Columbia Records.[169] Yet other more overtly sexual, comic "hokum blues" songs of the later 1920s sung by a cadre of blues musicians with titles like "Shake That Thing" or "He Like It Slow" filled juke joint and rent parties, with patrons sensually dancing the "Slow Drag" or the "Black Bottom." These bawdy blues songs that celebrated sexual freedom purposely contained elements of "protest and rebellion" to middle-class aspirations of respectability and consequently received negative backlash from black theater critics and conservative audience members alike.[170] This backlash was clear in letters to the *Defender*'s editor that questioned "will the time ever come when our vaudeville actors . . . stop dancing so vulgarly and springing such vulgar jokes . . . in the places where young girls and boys attend for wholesome recreation?"[171]

T.O.B.A. headliners Butterbeans and Susie's 1927 "I Want a Hot Dog for My Roll" was a key example of potentially questionable material:

SUSIE: I want a hot dog for my roll.
BUTTER: Well, here it is, here it is.
SUSIE: I want it hot, I don't want it cold.
BUTTER: My dog's never cold.
SUSIE: Give me a big one, that's what I say, I want it so it will fit my bread.
BUTTER: Now here's a hot dog for your roll.
SUSIE: Now is it young, I don't want it cold.
BUTTER: My dog never cold.
SUSIE: I sure will be disgusted if this dog ain't full of mustard. Don't want no excuse, it must have lots of juice, I want a hot dog for my roll.
BUTTER: Come and let me straighten you out. Now here's a dog that's long and lean.
SUSIE: Oh-oh, that ain't the kind of dog I mean.
BUTTER: Now here's a dog, Sue, that's short and fat.
SUSIE: But I sure need somethin' different from that.
SUSIE: Now here's my roll.
BUTTER: Where's your roll?

SUSIE: Now where's your dog?
BUTTER: Oh-oh, sister, that roll you got will hold a half a hog, yes sir!
SUSIE: Hey listen, Butter, can you fit it?
BUTTER: Why, sure I can.
SUSIE: Why, boy?
BUTTER: Why, Sue, I'm known now as a champion hot dog man.[172]

The married couple compiled much of their act of slightly risqué comedy skits from the complexities of romantic relationships, including sexuality. Yet "I Want a Hot Dog"'s double entendres were quite transparent and conjured up images that left no doubt that the couple boldly sang of sexual prowess, a topic that some conservative critics maintained was unsuitable for a respectable public.[173]

FIGURE 7. Butterbeans and Susie, 1920s, Photographs of Prominent African Americans. James Weldon Johnson Collection in the Yale Collection of American Literature, Beinecke Rare Book and Manuscript Library.

T.O.B.A.'s first attempts to solve the issue of respectability in performers' material involved the concept of "censor directors" as a measure of centralizing and shaping the acts of the circuit to fit the tastes of the New Negro era and leave the sentiments of minstrelsy and vulgarity offstage. The censor director proposal did not stem from white T.O.B.A. managers, who may have had no problems with black vaudeville's blackface past. Rather, eastern booking director, S. H. Dudley, in his continued pursuit of "race progress," promoted strategies that he believed would aid the industry and support artists. In 1923 Dudley maintained that "acts continue to submit the same material they have been using in some cases for ten years or more." Dudley surmised that T.O.B.A. "have one man invested with full and complete authority as an adjuster and *overlord* to the business . . . with the ability to suggest reforms and the courage to adhere to them."[174] Dudley suggested that this overlord should be J. A. Jackson, black theater critic for *Billboard* magazine. Jackson declined, but Dudley's request foreshadowed ongoing concerns about the quality of T.O.B.A. shows and revealed the constant struggle performers would have over the autonomy of their own performances. Dudley's suggestion that one person possess the ability to monitor the quality and moral character of hundreds of acts across the nation was logistically unrealistic. It was also problematic in terms of the balance of power between the circuit and its performers, as well as being a way for the circuit to continue to promote its middle-class definitions of morality for audiences that simply wanted to be entertained, even by comedy characterized as "low brow."

When the circuit overlord and censor directors did not pan out, Dudley arranged a meeting of forty performers and several T.O.B.A. managers in his Washington, DC, Mid-City Theatre in 1924. The group discussed troubling issues regarding "the originality of acts," "costumes and their maintenance," and "deportment" of actors. The gathered body concluded that reform plans should include a "try-out house" on the circuit wherein all acts "would be inspected and censored before presented on the time."[175] That Dudley included over forty actual entertainers in his meeting illustrated that he had moved past the concept of complete managerial control of artist behavior to including performers in monitoring their own stage material. Yet management's views on censorship and morality greatly influenced the decisions actors made in selecting comedic material and costumes for new revues.

Beyond discussions of outdated individual acts came the question of the prevalence of tabloid shows or shortened musicals on the circuit outselling the mainstays of traditional vaudeville—novelty acts, comedic duos, and specialty singers. Where a proposed "try-out" house might review and suggest reforms for a singular act, little could be done to transform the entire script of *Shufflin' Sam from Alabam'*, for example, without the show's producer and managers' consent.

As tab shows became more prevalent on the T.O.B.A. schedule, more traditional vaudevillians shared their concerns. Babe Townsend wrote a letter to the *Defender's* theatrical editor in 1925 and asked, "Does T.O.B.A. give Tabs preference over other acts?" Townsend complained that "all tab shows were identical," hosting comedians in blackface who "mistaking vulgarity for art, simply wallow in filth." Townsend believed that by "diversifying" the bill and not allowing tabs so much routing space, "the Race" would be given a chance to view the uplifting art it deserved.[176]

Managers like Dudley agreed that tabs shows, as well as individual acts, needed reform. Yet his conflicting roles as manager, entrepreneur, and entertainer prompted his argument that if audiences wanted tab shows, with their familiar skits and headliner performers, then managers had to give audiences "what they wanted" to stay popular and relevant. Vaudeville theaters should continue with tab shows, Dudley added, and as "show business was the same as any other business," there would be no need for the supply without the demand.[177] Henry T. Sampson revealed that tab shows performed in both T.O.B.A. houses and white theaters. Tabs often had to retain enough of the "plantation element" (or minstrel show structure) to appeal to audiences in white theaters, yet not so much as to repel black audiences in T.O.B.A. theaters.[178] T.O.B.A. manager correspondence corroborated tab shows' popularity, as Macon theater manager C. H. Douglass vented to Southern Director Sam Reevin that there were "no vaudeville acts to book, only 'musical tabs.'"[179]

Absent in this discussion of tabs versus traditional vaudeville was the performer's view about vulgarity onstage and in their offstage public personas. How did the unrelenting concerns about vulgarity and reform trickle down to T.O.B.A. entertainers? In mainstream vaudeville, like the Keith-Orpheum Circuit, the respectability issue had long been handled by written morality clauses included within individual entertainer contracts. Variations of the standard "morals clause" in performance contracts stemmed from this respectable transformation of the industry into "polite vaudeville" by the late nineteenth century. Such contracts stipulated that "no suggestive remarks or vulgarity in dress, words, or action or intoxication will be permitted in said theater. A violation of this clause by the Artist will mean instant dismissal and this contract will become null and void."[180]

T.O.B.A. performer contracts followed the Keith-Orpheum model. Most of the Southern District contracts held a clause that stated, "It is especially agreed that incompetency or drunkenness shall be considered a sufficient reason for annulling this contract without notice. Manager reserves the right to cancel any act after the first performance."[181] While the drunkenness clause was self-explanatory, individual theater managers decided what was considered "incompetency" after the first performance. If the Johnny Lee Long Company performed successful jokes in Chattanooga's Liberty Theatre yet failed to earn rousing applause in its next placement in Macon, then manager C. H. Douglass of Macon's Douglass Theatre could cast the company out, invalidating the contract.[182] The fight for morality meant that performers lost income if they did not adhere to policy. The pursuit of respectability arguably transformed some compliant T.O.B.A. performers into racial uplift activists. The result was that a host of novelty acts billed themselves as "clean" or family-friendly, such as Sam H. Gray and Virginia Liston, Okeh music recording artists who wrote "all clean hits." Other artists spoke of their reformed ways, like T.O.B.A. comedian Lonnie Fisher, whose performance was cancelled in Chicago for "using smut" and he "never told a double meaning or suggestive story since."[183]

Although critics and T.O.B.A. management made performers feel as if bawdy jokes and or suggestive lyrics were a "yoke and a burden" and that "wholesome" shows gave T.O.B.A. performers the power to "help the Race . . . to lift the stamp of inferiority," many audiences embraced the circuit's stars, raunchy acts and all.[184] Given the numerous times the issue was raised in private correspondence, public reviews, and letters to the editor through 1931, definitions of morality and vulgarity were clearly inconsistent among managers, audience members, and T.O.B.A. artists. While some managers focused on uplift, reform, and profit, many entertainers just wanted to share their definitions of art throughout the nation with lively, paying crowds who enjoyed the ribald vibrant entertainers of T.O.B.A. Time.

Was T.O.B.A. "tough"? Yes. The hard-won triumphs of carving out a space for African American artistic performance and training black artists despite the segregated American entertainment system was accompanied by a host of obstacles, including the humiliations of discriminatory travel, racial violence, gendered oppression, and censorship battles. However, when Cab Calloway recounted that T.O.B.A. stood for "tough," he also enthusiastically remarked that, as a professional foundation, "it was great though."[185] Apart from these many individual narratives, the true triumph of T.O.B.A. was that it socialized and professionalized performers into the African American vaudeville industry. The circuit paid performers to travel, influence popular culture, and "to have the privilege of entertaining." Additionally, T.O.B.A. allowed black vaudevillians to "get together and have *a good time*" while entertaining audiences.[186] These same audiences and communities played a prominent role in T.O.B.A. Time's success, and the resulting reciprocal relationship often thrived.

# 5

# A "RESPONSIBILITY" TO COMMUNITY

## *Circuit Theaters and Black Regional Audiences*

I'll be down to get you in a taxi honey, please be ready bout half past eight
Honey don't be late, I wanna be there when the band starts playing
Remember when we get there, honey
Two steps I'm gonna have 'em all, gonna dance out both my shoes
When they play the "Jelly Roll Blues"
Tomorrow night at the Darktown Strutters Ball . . .

—Shelton Brooks, lyrics from "Darktown Strutters Ball," 1917

"They *all* came to the Lyric," according to New Orleans guitarist Danny Barker. "All" in this instance were blues singers, like Ma Rainey, Bessie Smith, and Clara Smith; early jazz musicians; and tabloid shows. Barker ventured to T.O.B.A.'s Lyric Theatre to hear "mostly blues and old love ballads" and a "whole lot of cabaret songs . . . which were risqué." New Orleans audience members, like so many others, were people who went out "for a good time, to laugh at themselves, and laugh at the world," and the local T.O.B.A. theater provided this escape.[1] Philadelphia resident Idelle Truitt Elsey vividly recalled her attendance at the Standard Theatre on South Street, "right around from us." John T. Gibson's neighborhood vaudeville house was one were Elsey could "run around" and see shows for "like, fifteen cents, you know."[2] Macon's black Douglass Theatre was all Viola Turner knew, and she gave "no thought" to the all-white theaters on the same street because she was "too busy getting to the Douglass." Unlike the Macon Opera House, where she saw Black Patti's Troubadours, Turner did not have to "climb all those steps" to the segregated balcony because the Douglass, with its "three and four shows every afternoon . . . of the best class," was an entrepreneurial venture created for Macon's African American community.[3]

Black artists made their careers performing upon circuit stages from Chicago to Chattanooga, and the communities in which these theaters resided were arguably equally transformed in their connection to T.O.B.A. This chapter examines T.O.B.A.'s appeal to black audiences and reveals how the circuit's successes were intertwined with the regional economies where they traveled. In 1924 theater critic Kennard Williams defined the relationship between the Theater Owners' Booking Association and its hosting black communities as a symbiotic one. As T.O.B.A. had a "monopoly" "in much of the east, (mid) west, and north," it had a "*responsibility*, therefore, to those patrons . . . who are segregated in their own houses by custom or law."[4] As a fulfillment of this responsibility, T.O.B.A.'s development often furthered communication, hospitality, and uplift industries in urban black communities that, in turn, allowed the circuit's traveling shows to navigate early 1920s segregation policies.

## "THE PUBLIC HOLDS THE ACE": T.O.B.A. AUDIENCES

In the relationship among performers, managers, theater owners, and the masses, many black theater journalists argued that the "public holds the ace," for without the surrounding community there would be no audience, no consumer, and no need for a professional show.[5] By their presence in theaters across the country, T.O.B.A. audiences influenced ticket prices, the genre of acts hired, and the popularity of specific entertainers. Viola Turner recounted that visiting a black theater was a rare experience, something "your Mama didn't let you go to every week," but "once in a while" because of the cost involved in supporting leisure activities.[6] Yet still the circuit evolved into an impressive $5 million quasi-national corporation made from the literal nickels and dimes of working-class African Americans. In one black Philadelphia family three young men visited Gibson's famed theater every week in 1920, collectively spending over $500 that year alone, when an average black migrant family only earned between $770 and $1,970 a year.[7] Having an income that was robust enough that funds could be spent on entertainment and leisure was evidence of a black consumer's growing financial stability. In the case of T.O.B.A. audiences, spending on commercial leisure was also indicative of a black working class that prioritized recreation in defiance of a larger society that defined them primarily as marginalized laborers and these crowds had an increased number of theaters and cabarets open for black patronage in urban environments.[8]

American entertainment audiences in the nineteenth and twentieth centuries were often divided along class lines between an elite audience who passively and formally viewed dramatic productions versus a working-class vaudeville audience, which was lively and more informal. Scholars contend that the latter evaluated an act's success by giving an immediate vocal and visceral response of approval or disdain.[9] T.O.B.A. spectators were the epitome of active audiences, and artists fostered an informal, family feel with their viewers. Entertainers noted that the Baltimore black vaudeville theatergoers ran up and down the aisles before the show, "yelling greetings" and sharing food with each other—actions that garnered the disapproval of elite African Americans who warned theatergoers not to "make loud expressions," "chew gum loudly," or get up and mill about during performances. Yet artists were rewarded with some of the "most appreciative audiences in the world," who applauded "'til the building shook" if they approved of a performance. In contrast, T.O.B.A. audiences could also "freeze up" an act by offering polite, hesitant applause, little reaction, or vocal disapproval.[10]

At a T.O.B.A. house, urban audiences listened to vaudeville blues music that captured emotions of love, loss, journey, despair, anger, or joy. Watching bejeweled blues headliners in lamé gowns or feather headdresses accompanied by chorus girls in alluring costumes gave audience members glimpses of glamour that counteracted their own everyday wardrobes. But these artists were more than beautifully adorned entertainers. Blues songs reflected the circumstances of an individual spectator, and listeners related to complaints about an untrustworthy lover or thinly veiled praises of a partner's sexual capabilities. Daphne Harrison maintains that audience members grasped a vocalist's "identification with anxieties, alienation, and disaffection" of urban African Americans, even in the delivery of a blues piece. When headliner Bessie Smith belted out how her "sweet man" threw "her down" and now she was "bound for Black Mountain, me, my razor and gun" in pursuit of her unfaithful lover, empathetic listeners felt free to reply openly and loudly with shouts of "that's right" or "yes." These call-and-response moments between the artists and the audience were an example of the community created in the theater and captured why many spectators longed for the next T.O.B.A. show once the evening concluded.[11]

Audiences flocked to T.O.B.A. shows to see the most current entertainers in the country without having to leave their local urban community. All the visiting African American vaudeville acts could be found at T.O.B.A.'s "old Booker T," theater on St. Louis's Market Street, as Nathaniel Sweets fondly remembered, and residents did not have to travel to New York or Chicago. In a Whitman Sisters or Drake and Walker revue, dancers often showcased rhythmic, skilled acrobatics or performed stage versions of the Charleston, "Ballin' the Jack," or "the Shimmy," bringing the latest dances into the local theater.[12] Circuit spectators invested their time and money in performances that reflected their whole identities, whether humorous, profane, sorrowful, or joyful. Communities paid to be entertained and experience moments of escape from music that Ralph Ellison argued had the ability to "transcend" the discriminatory conditions caused by a "denial of social justice" in African American communities.[13] If performed well, T.O.B.A. shows afforded theatergoers opportunities to be entertained and enjoy a moment to "delight in sheer physical existence" without worries of labor, income inequities, and discrimination that often stood beyond the theater doors.[14]

## THE CIRCUIT AND THE PRESS

T.O.B.A. communicated the details of upcoming performances with potential audiences, artists, and managers in both white and African American weekly and daily national newspapers. New York–based *Billboard* magazine had more direct coverage of T.O.B.A. than any of the other white periodicals. Founded as an entertainment advertising journal in 1894 and now a twenty-first-century recorded music and entertainment trade periodical, the weekly *Billboard* marketed itself as "indispensable to the professional entertainer and allied interests."[15] Between 1920 and 1925, James A. Jackson narrated all the business details that T.O.B.A. wanted to share. From board meeting details to the opening of new tab shows, it was all on his "J.A. Jackson's Page," which focused on "colored entertainment."[16] With Jackson as the "Page's" manager, T.O.B.A. had a mainstream voice, as Jackson was a black entertainment world veteran and the Colored Actors' Union representative to the T.O.B.A. board of directors in the 1924–25 season. Despite *Billboard's* targeted window into black entertainment until 1925, many predominantly white periodicals lacked the dedicated coverage needed to draw focused attention to T.O.B.A. stages, aside from select articles in the trade journals the *Clipper* and its successor, *Variety*.[17]

As it was the primary communication vehicle between the circuit and its audiences, the black press was essential to T.O.B.A.'s and black business's general productivity. Booker T. Washington championed the long-standing cooperation of the black press and black business and argued that "the owners and editors of the Negro newspapers of this country" worked tirelessly "toward the uplift of our race."[18] In the entertainment industry, productions advertised their routing information, theater critics reviewed individual performances, and managers listed employment and audition opportunities all within black press periodicals. *Billboard* might provide notice of an upcoming show on the "colored circuit," but a black weekly periodical shared the exact wording of a T.O.B.A. resolution and sent correspondents to cover the mood of an annual meeting, the demeanor of the board members, and what was on the menu for that afternoon's "delicious" luncheon.[19] The black press both facilitated a commercial exchange of goods and services and, as historian Jason Chambers contends, provided an "important outlet" for black journalists who served as a source of "pride and information for their readers."[20] It also served as a bridge between the Midwest, North, and South as black migration surged in the 1910s and '20s.

The *Indianapolis Freeman* had an early starring role as the essential African American theater periodical over its 1884–1927 tenure. The periodical, published by Louis Howland until 1892 and George Knox between 1892 to 1927, had at least two of its eight-page weekly publication dedicated to "The Stage."[21] *Freeman* journalists featured wide genres of entertainment, including minstrelsy, marching band music, and circuses. Readers could explore everything from the early performances of a young Sissieretta Jones (aka the Black Patti) to news of a potential purchase of a new local black theater. Although based in Indianapolis, the *Freeman* was a national black weekly with correspondents who captured the political, economic, and social news of black America. Columns in the Stage section might be dedicated to the happenings in Cincinnati, New Orleans, Chattanooga, or Detroit at any given moment. As the first African American illustrated weekly, *Freeman* articles on dance team Walker and Drake or the Smart Set comedy troupe gave readers the first photographs of these stage stars, often in full costume.[22] The *Freeman* encouraged traveling revues to write monthly columns that offered an inside look at show business for the public. Audience members were able to get word of a performance, build a visual connection with these artists, and finally get a glimpse of the background and social life of those artists, albeit a manufactured glimpse. All of these layered reminders that the Smart Set or the Williams and Walker company was coming to town drew in potential paying audience members.

Performers also used the *Freeman* as a literal home base. Show managers finalized the results of large regional auditions and, via the Stage Page, informed all the performers from the Nashville Students or Mastodon Minstrels to report for summer rehearsals and "leave the trunks at home."[23] Traveling revue participants listed their mailing address as the *Freeman* on business cards and in a weekly list in the newspaper itself. This mailing list was not merely a gender-divided directory of performers but at times became the only way booking agents, managers, and even family members could find an entertainer who rarely stayed in a city longer than two to three days.[24] Performers themselves sent personal greetings to each other within public columns on their traveling revues, and announcements of entertainers' weddings, anniversaries, obituaries, and memorials were listed for all to read.

The *Freeman*'s Stage and Gossip of the Stage pages also offered focused discussions on what black theater performance meant for racial uplift in many of the columns of black theater critic Sylvester Russell. Russell was a staunch promoter of black self-help within the theater community, as seen in his discussions of the C.V.B.A. and the memorials he wrote to fallen black variety stars.[25] *Freeman* readers were rightly assumed to be politically astute consumers who were aware and interested in the life and political meanings of the African American stage. Readers turned to the Stage to read debates about the virtue of a black theater circuit, the demands for racial equality in black vaudeville, and the early wars over the various incarnations of what eventually became T.O.B.A.

While the *Freeman* was a foundational model for the cooperative efforts of black theater and media, the *Chicago Defender* and Baltimore *Afro-American* made specific partnerships with T.O.B.A. Founded in 1905 and 1893, respectively, both of these periodicals maintained robust entertainment sections since their inception and carved spaces in their widely circulated papers for T.O.B.A. in terms of routing lists, performance reviews, advertising, and articles discussing the intricacies of management. In the *Defender* and the *Afro*, journalists, like Sylvester Russell, Tony Langston, Kennard Williams, and later performers and producers-turned-columnists Frank Montgomery, Salem Tutt Whitney, Clarence Muse, and even circuit founder S. H. Dudley, kept T.O.B.A. alive for audience members from Chicago to New Orleans.[26]

T.O.B.A. itself fostered these relationships by hiring its own white media liaison and director of publicity, W. R. Arnold, in the 1924–25 season.[27] Arnold wrote his own columns and helped circulate T.O.B.A. information across the country. When performers raised potentially damning concerns Arnold addressed them in public with columns like "Arnold's TOBA News," or helped facilitate board members' columns to the public, like "Reevin Writes," "Starr Speaks," or "Dud's Dope." Even T.O.B.A. directors reiterated the value of the partnership with the press in both public declarations and private correspondence. Reevin publicized key happenings in black newspapers and told other theater managers of the "boost for T.O.B.A" from publicized board-related news, "especially when it comes from one of our Directors."[28] When there were dramatic changes made in terms of contracts, salaries, new acts, etc., all news was "broadcast through the channels of the colored press."[29]

Between 1921 and 1926, the *Defender* published three hundred full articles or columns devoted to T.O.B.A. Time, and this did not include the targeted advertisements for the circuit itself, revue reviews, or individual performer marketing. T.O.B.A. details could be found under headlines, like "T.O.B.A. Doings," "A Note or Two," "T.O.B.A. Mentions," or "On the T.O.B.A."[30] The *Afro* also promised "to review" black vaudevillians' acts, followed the *Defender*'s lead, and published nearly one hundred circuit articles in that same five-year period, including Arnold-facilitated pieces, like "Arnold's Dope from the T.O.B.A. Circuit" and "T.O.B.A. Dope."[31] Again these pieces were more than just routing guides, as the *Defender* and *Afro* shared *Freeman* writers' beliefs that the theatergoing crowd could combine a known desire for "sensationalistic" and "lurid" with an interest in critical columns on the greater social significance of African Americans in entertainment production.[32] Although the partnership with T.O.B.A. was not quite as defined or robust, other black periodicals, including the Pittsburgh *Courier*, *Philadelphia Tribune*, and the New York *Amsterdam News*, also included Arnold's articles and notes from the semiannual T.O.B.A board meetings. Overall, journalists heralded the relationship between T.O.B.A., the press, and black entertainers, asserting that "the Negro press is also an important ally" that takes "delight in the accomplishments of the worthwhile artist" while "tempering their justice with mercy" and serving as the audiences' window into the industry.[33]

## THEATER EMPLOYMENT

By the early 1920s the construction of new vaudeville and motion picture theaters held the promise of employment for "hundreds of laborers, both skilled and unskilled," in terms of construction and management. Once in operation, theaters could hire "hundreds of others" and help stimulate the regional economy of "its particular community, improving living conditions."[34] Theaters like the Howard Theatre, associated with Dudley Enterprises in Washington, DC, had "given employment to 75 or more persons" by 1928.[35] Aside from the performing roles onstage and the positions within a traveling revue, there were a host of other jobs, from custodian to lighting technician, that beckoned 1920s laborers. As community employers, T.O.B.A. theaters often called on African Americans to fill these positions, even if the theater itself was white owned. St. Louis resident Nathaniel Sweets saw this for himself in the Midwest District and praised Turpin's Booker T. Washington Theatre. Sweets recalled that "naturally most all" Turpin's employees were "Negroes." When the Washington Theatre closed in the early 1940s after T.O.B.A.'s demise, many of the employees left in black-serving theaters were "white operators."[36]

What were these essential supplementary theater positions? A "best practices" guide of the era, *The Vaudeville Theatre, Building, Operation, and Management*, included over fifteen areas within an elite theater's management staff, from the treasurer and the cashier, "the heart of the business," to doormen, night watchmen, special policemen, porters, cleaners, ushers, electricians, stage managers, dressers, property men, stage crew members, and house orchestra musicians. While a midsize T.O.B.A theater seating five hundred patrons might not employ a "ladies maid," who was "neat clean" and "preferably white," most of the other positions would be necessary for successful theater function.[37]

In keeping with the New Negro mission of "respectable" black entertainment, T.O.B.A. houses often publicized their backstage staff right alongside the artistic talent. S. H. Dudley set this precedent with Dudley Circuit theaters. Publicity was often deliberate and included both men and women employees and named all the staff members of the house as well as printed their photographs. Staff jobs could be coveted positions often filled by retired performers, family members of performers, or just general valued members of the black community. Women workers were often titled with the respectful "Mrs." or "Miss" to symbolize that virtuous, married African American women and young single girls did indeed work for the theater.[38] Often women laborers were the most trusted employees and were selected to be the treasurer or cashier of a theater, responsible for the nightly till. Mrs. S. B. Carter was noted as the "faithful and efficient" cashier of Nashville's Bijou. Ushers Misses Mildred Kelley and Ruth Johnson were featured in the black press right alongside the director of the Indianapolis's New Crown orchestra, V. A. Kelley, in the 1910s.[39] T.O.B.A. shows continued this Dudley Circuit policy and also noted the backstage staff in addition to artistic talent. Programs from Washington, DC's Howard Theatre in the 1920s named the property manager Andrew J. Thomas, music directress Mrs. Alice Randolph, and projectionist John H. Miller. A playbill may have advertised a "wonderful chorus of bronze beauties" on the inside, but on the outside the skilled theater professionals listed told the T O.B.A. public that the circuit brought stable black employment opportunities to the community.[40] With four hundred black vaudeville acts on the road, new T.O.B.A. theaters could also give way to building more black theatrical hotels or restaurants and the labor positions that went with them.[41]

## REGIONAL TRAVEL AND HOSPITALITY INDUSTRIES ON TOUR

When black comedian "Jolly" John Larkin played the predominantly white Gus Hill Enterprises in 1917 in Providence, Rhode Island, white stage managers gave him a call sheet with a train schedule and a list of five available hotels to patronize after that night's performance.[42] Yet choice in lodging or travel often did not exist for performers on T.O.B.A. Time. Tom Fletcher recalled that after his performance in predominantly white towns at the turn of the twentieth century, "townspeople made it very plain" that they had no further use for black performers and encouraged their swift retreat. Aside from a few residential black service workers these "sundown towns" and suburbs purposely and coercively fostered an all-white demographic and "prominently displayed" signs that Fletcher noted read, "Nigger, Read, and Run" or "Nigger Don't Let the Sun Go Down on You."[43] T.O.B.A. still contended with this blatant racial hostility in the 1920s.

At its height T.O.B.A. had nearly one hundred theaters in three vastly disparate geographical regions, all governed by different degrees of Jim Crow segregation. Each district had its own institutions, including restaurants, boarding homes, and social clubs that serviced traveling black vaudevillians based on that locale's policies and customs. T.O.B.A. built relationships with black businesses all over the country, and its management might suggest to performers which railroad lines to take or which lunchrooms to use to try to avoid discrimination. While *The Negro Motorist Green Book* existed in the 1930s, the valuable guide meant to "give the Negro traveler information" to prevent "difficulties, embarrassments and to make his trips more enjoyable," post-dated T.O.B.A.'s existence by five years.[44] Instead circuit professionals, like *Billboard* journalist J. A. Jackson, collected information on black-serving theaters and support industries and shared it with other black periodicals and mainstream theater directories, like *The Julius Cahn-Gus Hill Theatrical Guide*. By 1922 the white *Cahn-Hill Directory* even published a separate supplement, the "Colored Theaters and Attractions," which listed a state's black population statistics and the location and managers of black-patronized theaters.[45] Yet often black travelers navigated the journey from the Midwest through the South and up the East Coast following the unwritten rules of negotiation during Jim Crow—community word of mouth.

### *Navigating the Midwest*

Artists often began tours in T.O.B.A.'s Midwest District, which included cities in Illinois, Indiana, Kansas, Michigan, Missouri, and Ohio and set upon an experience that many younger artists remembered for the excitement and fun of "traveling and living with the company."[46] Tour experiences between 1924 and 1928 in Chicago and St. Louis shed light on some of the unique transportation, lodging, and social institutions open to black troupers. Under the guidance of T.O.B.A. board member Martin Klein from 1923 to 1928, the Midwest office was headquartered in Chicago. Klein moved the T.O.B.A. office around Southside Chicago until finally locating it in the Overton Building on S. State Street, a black "locus of economic power" in the 1920s.[47] Chicago itself had very few black-serving vaudeville theaters given the size of its black community, and the three affiliated with T.O.B.A.—the Grand, Monogram, and Apollo—were white owned and often white managed at the onset of the circuit.[48] Chicago's T.O.B.A. theaters dotted the densely populated Southside, a section of the city nineteen blocks long inhabited by ninety-two thousand people in the 1920s, many of whom were black migrants.[49] When the *How Come* revue came to play the Grand Theatre in September 1925, its star Eddie Hunter and "a company that would do credit to any theater in the country" did not have far to search for welcoming institutions.[50]

Theatrical businesses were among Chicago's many black-serving industries, and they contended with "temperamental kinks" of vaudevillians, including the odd operating hours of customers who rose at noon due to late-night performances.[51] Each of these establishments listed themselves as black theatrical institutions in industry directories and employed local black residents. Chicago held eleven hotels that catered to black entertainers, and the Columbia Hotel and Monogram Hotel were just blocks away from T.O.B.A.'s theaters on S. State Street. Cooks and wait staff earned money from the late afternoon breakfast crowd who frequented Jasper Taylor's Barbecue on 3634 S. State Street. The Dreamland Café at 3520 S. State Street served "American and Chinese meals" after hours when fledgling performers, like Alberta Hunter, left the stage.[52]

Before he became a "Count" and a nationally recognized swing music band leader, rising pianist William Basie spent much of his off time on a Chicago T.O.B.A. tour visiting the Apex, Plantation Cafe, and Dreamland Ballroom; listening to fellow jazz musicians Earl Hines and drummer Zutty Singleton; and meeting legendary trumpeter Louis Armstrong. The patronage at surrounding cabarets and nightclubs on the Southside increased when a T.O.B.A. troupe was in town, as troupers visited fellow musicians and dancers performing in the city. The city was a jazz music recording hub in the 1920s, and musicologists argue that T.O.B.A. was an early catalyst in the black music recording industry, as it brought entertainers in close physical contact with Paramount, Victor, or Okeh

FIGURE 8. Count Basie, 1947, William P. Gottlieb, *Portrait of Count Basie, Aquarium, New York, N.Y., Between 1946 and 1948.* United States, 1946. Monographic. Photograph.

recording studios. T.O.B.A.'s vaudevillian musicians used extended show layovers during the day to record tunes popularized in their shows before their evening performances, in turn strengthening the Chicago record industry.[53]

After earning money playing Chicago theaters, T.O.B.A. entertainers often traveled to St. Louis, the first stop on the road between the T.O.B.A. Midwest and Southern Districts.[54] There was a distinct intraracial class dynamic entertainer Clarence Muse observed in St. Louis's audiences between black working- and middle-class "Market Street" residents and the elite black professionals or "dicties" of "La Belle Street," who generally opposed the course, bawdy antics of a black vaudeville performance. These class stratifications were not unusual, as mentioned in previous chapters on respectability battles and artist censorship. Yet in St. Louis T.O.B.A. navigated this separation by personally inviting black upper class "dicties" to the Washington Theatre at the request of theater owner and elected official C. H. Turpin. Turpin made a display of these "special evenings" designed for the regional black elite and the working class. Muse noted that these combined evenings were known for a "happy carnival spirit "and a "joyous carefree mood" marked by audiences "applauding most heartily."[55]

St. Louis's black businesses benefitted from T.O.B.A.'s arrival and vice versa. The black record industry thrived when T.O.B.A. artists shopped at the record shops that were "steps from the Booker T. Washington Theatre" on Market Street. Likewise, the city's black Grand Central Hotel was large enough to host a traveling revue of thirty-five black performers in Muse's *Charleston Dandies*, employing custodians, maids, laundresses, wait staff, and hotel managers in the process.[56] Even the underground economy of speakeasies and cabarets flourished amid Prohibition when T.O.B.A. troupers came to town. The discreet, "ordinary private houses" where "liquid refreshment" was readily obtainable welcomed entertainers and their counterparts.[57]

## *The Southern District*

The Southern District was T.O.B.A.'s largest and included theaters in Alabama, Georgia, Kentucky, Louisiana, Oklahoma, Tennessee, and Texas. Many Southern T.O.B.A. venues were white owned, but black managed. Because of the very visible and at times violent ways white Southern society enforced segregation and policed blackness, as discussed in the previous chapter, African American vaudevillian spaces were even more crucial. Occurrences in Chattanooga and Macon exemplify how Southern District black businesses developed to serve incoming entertainers. With Sam Reevin as regional director and national booking manager, Southern T.O.B.A. headquartered in Chattanooga, Tennessee, in the Volunteer Life Building at the corner of East Ninth and Georgia Streets. T.O.B.A. made its initial home in the heart of the city's early-twentieth-century African

American commercial district amid black-managed drugstores, barbershops, and restaurants.[58]

A tremendous obstacle in the Southern District was the injustice of segregated transportation.[59] For most interstate travelers of the 1920s and '30s passenger trains were the predominant mode of travel, and rail service was often demeaning, unsanitary, and crowded for African American passengers. As segregation did not emerge as a complete fixed system in the 1890s, states often attempted to regulate color boundaries in the transportation arena first, as it consisted of confined spaces used by all races and genders. Kenneth Mack contends that white Southerners crafted late-nineteenth- and early-twentieth-century legal statutes regarding rail travel to assert their supposed dominance in society and force African Americans into literal inferior "places" in rail cars and terminals.[60] Transportation segregation laws were unique to each state, often requiring a black passenger to switch from an integrated first-class car in some Northern cities to a "colored" car in Deep South states or the "colored" portion of a car in other states. An 1897 Alabama statute mandated "that all railroads carrying passengers in this state shall provide equal but separate accommodations for the white and colored races by providing two or more passenger-cars for each passenger-train," while a 1917 Mississippi statute mandated segregation by "dividing the passenger cars by a partition to secure separate accommodations."[61]

At the onset of T.O.B.A., performers could not always depend on headquarters to wire or mail rail tickets in time for a show's opening and often had to directly contact headquarter directors or even individual theater managers in an attempt to ensure passage. When Bowe and Lindell, a "singing, talking and dancing" duo, wanted to be booked into Macon, Georgia's Douglass Theatre in 1926, they wrote manager C. H. Douglass directly, inquiring about travel and asking to "please send tickets in plenty of time" to avoid any concerns with missed trains or a lack of "colored" seating.[62] Black insurance executive Viola Turner described how segregated seating reinforced beliefs about black inferiority regardless of a black passenger's gender or economic class. When traveling through Georgia, a black porter forcibly removed Turner from the first-class section of a café car for which she paid and seated her with an amiable "white prostitute" in complete disregard to Turner's first-class fare. Neither the white sex worker actively pursuing clients nor Turner, an African American female professional sitting quietly, was "virtuous" enough to warrant seating in the "ladies' café," according to the Southern Railway.[63] A troupe of fifteen to thirty performers could not run the risk of having just one performer justifiably protest racial deference laws if it meant violence, arrest, and imprisonment. Rather than withstand the constant humiliations of segregated travel, prominent acts in the early years of the circuit, like the Bessie Smith Revue or the Madame Rainey and Company Show, exposed "the cracks" of segregation and leased private railcars outfitted just for the troupe. The railways may have publicly ostracized African Americans, but they gladly took black headliners' money for these private transactions that allowed performers to sit, eat, and sleep wherever they liked on individual railcars.[64]

As the circuit persisted, Salem Tutt Whitney noted that when he and the Smarter Set traveled on Toby Time in 1928, "many of its [travel] discomforts and humiliations" had been alleviated in "every city where a T.O.B.A. house was located," as "passenger agents for the different railroad companies made arrangements for the movement and accommodation of the company."[65] After the mid-1920s growth of the circuit, a tab show manager could purchase rail tickets in bulk in advance, so while troupes did not lease a series of private railcars, performers had separate seating as a unit apart from the rigors of racially segregated train travel.[66] Performers could arrive in New Orleans, do a show at the Lyric Theatre, frequent the many black-owned establishments in the city, and be assured a ticket on the train out to the next performance date as a troupe.

Positive relationships between the circuit and the local railway could occasionally physically protect troupers. Because of pre-purchased group rail tickets, Basie recalls that Gonzelle White's tab show was able to quickly flee the 1927 Mississippi River flood as it reached New Orleans, when "water was all the way up to the trestles and bridges" of the rail station. In mid-1920s Atlanta an altercation between notoriously racist white theater owner Charles Bailey and a boldly defiant Ethel Waters (who called Bailey a "cracker sonofabitch") resulted in Bailey prohibiting the rail station from selling Waters a ticket to escape his physical retaliation. A local conductor of the Louisville and Nashville (L&N) railway in connection with T.O.B.A. management helped Waters travel to Nashville, defying Bailey's orders.[67]

In terms of lodging and food service while traveling, Myra Armstead suggests that nationally, 1920s black-owned institutions, like the Sterling, Gordon, Banneker, Holmes Cottage, and the Vincennes hotels, "functioned as insular leisure residences" within racially hostile environments. Yet residences for average African American visitors to the South were generally infrequent, and their absence was one that activists lamented the most regarding black travel.[68] As T.O.B.A. grew in the Southern District, its presence sparked an increase in boarding homes, actor's hotels, and restaurants that located themselves near local theaters to meet this need for black lodging. Black boarding house operators tended to be widowed women who rented out a series of rooms in their homes to supplement income for rent or mortgage payments. The status of being widowed perpetuated the image that these women entrepreneurs were stable and nurturing women whom young artists, particularly chorus girls, could trust with their welfare while in town. Mrs. Marie Williams in Chattanooga promised performers at black-serving theaters that they would "be well protected and treated right" at 309 East Ninth Street, just steps from the Queen, Eagle, and later the Liberty Theatres.[69] Artists touring in Chattanooga praised "Mother Bella's" right next to T.O.B.A. headquarters, run by a "genial old Negro" lady who made "downhome food" served on family tables. Troupers welcomed the convenience of these accommodations and praised these lunchrooms as "the swellest in the South." As many of these eateries were "entirely run by colored folk," T.O.B.A. artists supported a segment of the black economy.[70]

Macon stands out in the Southern District as an example of the community-circuit connection. African American entrepreneur and T.O.B.A. board member Charles H. Douglass owned the city's circuit franchised theater. Douglass opened his namesake theater in 1911 and refurbished it in 1921 for $100,000 to seat "one thousand people."[71] Not only did Douglass employ African Americans (and whites) in the Douglass Theatre, but in his bank, hotel, and local café. Vaudevillian Annie Fritz wrote C. H. Douglass directly to "save" her specific room in the Douglass Hotel when she arrived from the 81 Theatre in Atlanta in March 1926, praising its comfort and close location to the rail station. Troupers moved from the Miles Killen Café to the theater, the hotel, and then to the adjoining Douglass Bank to meet any financial needs.[72] As many of the Douglass-owned establishments were built from the income of the T.O.B.A.-backed theater, cooks, maids, cashiers, tellers, landlords, and even film projectionists each shared the benefits of a regional economy supported by black entertainment proceeds.

## *The Eastern District*

T.O.B.A. revues rode the Southern Railway from the deep South states to T.O.B.A.'s Eastern District, which included cities in Pennsylvania, Maryland, Virginia, the Carolinas, and Florida. Artists' tour experiences in Philadelphia and Washington, DC, serve as a microcosm of eastern T.O.B.A. experiences. Although its social customs and laws did not exactly mirror the practices of the deep South, the Eastern District was not absent from racism or discriminatory segregation that operated without physical "colored" and "white" signs. Racial segregation in southeastern cities of the district might allow white and black passengers to ride together on a streetcar without segregated seating but did not assure an African American performer lodging at one of the downtown Philadelphia or Washington, DC, hotels.[73]

The Eastern District was often the last step for performers before they launched into theaters and cabarets in New York City, the pinnacle of national vaudeville success or "1st heaven," as it was known to dancer Peg Leg Bates.[74] Once in the East, traveling revues made use of the Baltimore and Ohio Railway lines. Although segregated seating came to an end in Washington, DC, T.O.B.A. revues still purchased bulk railway tickets to travel as a unit, while headliners traveled independently. *The Official Theatrical World of Colored Artists* guide of 1928 even included a railway "lowest fares" table in the same manner as the white vaudevillian guides, suggesting that individual acts in the East could book their own fares rather than solely rely on T.O.B.A. to navigate through segregated practices.[75]

With travel accomplished, artists in the East sought lodging and restaurants that catered to theatrical troupers, whether they be black-owned or black-serving establishments. Many theatrical boarding home operators were "themselves thespians," who created employment opportunities for other former entertainers.[76] As Philadelphia was home to John T. Gibson and his Gibson and New Standard Theatres, regional theater support industries flourished. Gibson used his theaters as African American employment clearing houses, where "thousands of colored actors and house employees yearly were given employment."[77] Although many Philadelphia theaters practiced segregation just when African American travelers thought they were "free at last" when they crossed the Mason-Dixon line, the Gibson establishments did not.[78] The city hosted eight theatrical hotels, and the Douglass Hotel, marketed as "The Finest Colored Hotel in America," was home to many T.O.B.A. regulars, like comedian Jackie "Moms" Mabley.[79] If the Douglass was full, then "Mother Havelow's," close to the New Standard, was a welcome respite for young musicians. Bassist Milton John "Milt" Hinton recalled that Addie Havelow had "a nice living room for the piano in there, and a sitting room and a bedroom. This was where all the bandleaders [including] Duke [Ellington], and [Count] Basie stayed," while company musicians lodged in theatrical hotels.[80] Just as in the Midwest District, a T.O.B.A. tour fostered additional patronage of local black nightclubs and dancehalls. In 1926, vaudevillian Basie and his counterparts performed at the Standard, then got into "little musical competitions" with the local club musicians after hours. Philadelphia night club musicians were surprised that the young Basie was much more than just a "jive show-biz musician," but a burgeoning jazz music standout.[81]

Out of all the cities in the Eastern District, T.O.B.A.'s efforts in fostering black business opportunities were perhaps the most effective in Washington, DC, and this was attributed to S. H. Dudley. Dudley managed the Eastern T.O.B.A. office at the Mid-City Theatre on 1223 Seventh Street—Washington, DC's black commercial hub—where the elites met the black working classes, the "ordinary Negroes, who made a living with their hands."[82] In 1920 Washington, DC's black population reached roughly 25 percent of the city's overall population, and many of those 110,711 black residents patronized black theaters, many of which were black owned and/or black managed.[83] *Variety* magazine noted that Dudley had no need for New York or "sideline" jobs because "he made it pay in Washington D.C."[84]

FIGURE 9. Mid-City Theatre, 1933, Scurlock Studio Records, Archives Center, National Museum of American History, Smithsonian Institution.

As evidenced by the full-page, Dudley-sponsored advertisement in the 1928 *Official Theatrical World of Colored Artists* guide, DC black entrepreneurs often opened hotels and cafes that catered to the black theater crowd.[85] When Jules McGarr and his Ragtime Steppers played the Dudley Theatre in the mid-1920s, members of the company could have lodged at the black-owned Whitelaw Hotel, whose patrons included the black social and political elite. But more often, T.O.B.A. entertainers patronized Bart Kennett's Summit Hotel on Seventh and N Streets NW, "one of the most popular and attractive hotels on the circuit."[86] In 1926, Julian "Jules" McGarr, president of the C.A.U. asked his wife Mabel McGarr to take over the management of his Ragtime Steppers dance troupe so he could assume the management of the Summit Hotel in Washington. With Dudley's financial support, McGarr opened the newly named Mid-City Hotel, replete with "a rehearsal room and other conveniences for professionals."[87] The Mid-City became a working-class alternative to the Whitelaw and evolved into a residential and theatrical hotel by 1930. Its main guests were white immigrants and African American domestics, wait staff, and barbers who lived alongside actors and actresses.[88] When there was downtime between rehearsal and performance, a troupe visited the Mid-City pool room next door to the theater, managed by Dudley leasee, Spiros Demetriou, or crossed the street to a Dudley-supported lunchroom.[89] Through the late 1930s, Dudley Enterprises continued to upbuild black businesses in the District, including restaurants, soda fountains, pool halls, apartments, photography studios, and savings banks, all steeped in the capital of black vaudeville.

## COMMUNITY UPLIFT INDUSTRIES

When asked in the 1970s about the supposed dearth of black social life and exclusion from amusements due to segregation, president of the black-owned North Carolina Mutual Life Insurance Company, Asa T. Spaulding, responded with pride that this was not the case in the early twentieth century, as "well you see, we had our *own* black theaters."[90] Beyond the service industries developed to support circuit theaters, T.O.B.A. houses also served as sites of community uplift, racial philanthropy, and political support. The same racial uplift motivations that led C. H. Douglass or S. H. Dudley to use theater profits to open banks and real estate ventures also prompted select managers on the circuit to open their spaces to benefit the community beyond that evening's entertainment.

Theaters were some of few free-standing spaces, outside of churches, large enough to hold community gatherings. In St. Louis, Turpin's race work ethic prompted him to use the Washington Theatre to aid victims of racial strife. In July 1917, Turpin took a decided political stand, and the Booker T. Washington Theatre dedicated all profits of an evening to the refugees of the nearby East St. Louis racial massacre in hopes that they would rebuild after white supremacist violence.[91] Nashville African Americans had their own private celebrations at Starr's Bijou Theatre when the end of World War I and the Armistice came in 1918. Black Nashville residents had already participated in the public celebration, and the Bijou gathering was for them to acknowledge black participation and honor African American patriotism without running the risk of angering white supremacists who wanted to quench the spirits of the New Negro.[92]

Using theaters as sites of political resistance continued after T.O.B.A. franchises opened in 1921. In early 1921 A. J. Smitherman, editor of the *Tulsa Star*, used Tulsa's Dreamland Theatre to hold clandestine meetings about how to best resist the city's escalating violence toward African Americans. Only months later white supremacists in the Tulsa Massacre murdered hundreds of African Americans as previously discussed, and T.O.B.A.'s Dreamland and hundreds of black-owned businesses were targeted because these institutions symbolized black Tulsa's wealth and economic prominence. Observing the prominence of the Dreamland in the community, it was not surprising that Loula Williams rebuilt and opened the theater as soon as possible after the violent destruction.[93]

Ethel Waters highlighted the political prominence of black theaters when she recounted in her autobiography how white terrorists chose Macon's Douglass Theatre as the site to dispose John Glover's mutilated body in summer 1922. Glover, a twenty-two-year-old black Macon resident allegedly killed a white deputy sheriff and wounded two black men in a fight at the Douglass Pool Hall next door to the T.O.B.A. theater on August 4, 1922, and then escaped. After a three-day man hunt, in which Macon's downtown black businesses were shuttered and innocent black families violently harassed, a mob captured, murdered, and displayed Glover's body in front of the theater. Reportedly, white onlookers cheered and horrifically took souvenirs of Glover's clothing and person. The Douglass Theatre and C. H. Douglass himself were also deliberately targeted to strike fear into the progressive black community and diminish the success of the city's most prominent and independent African American entrepreneur. But Douglass's prominence also brought national attention to Glover, police brutality, and lynching during the same months that the Senate evaluated the Dyer Anti-Lynching Bill. The publicity of the Glover case with its Douglass Theatre connections and public community protest contributed to the pursuit of an indictment of at least four members of the white mob that murdered Glover, although there were no convictions made in the racially hostile court system of 1920s Macon.[94]

In Philadelphia, John T. Gibson opened his theaters for conversations and mass meetings on black community concerns. At Gibson's Dunbar Theatre, regular community conversations on racial uplift, migration, and electoral politics were held on Sundays in late 1923 to gain "the support of the community" and make advances toward black social justice in Philadelphia. Facilitated by Dr. Henderson, these meetings were conducted before entertainment matinees, and attendants were so grateful for Gibson's space, they loosely referred to sessions as "St. John's Open Forum." Similarly, music historian Frederick Jerome Taylor contends that Gibson's Standard Theatre was known in the city as an alternative "conference center" for African American organizations hosting black professional societies, like the "National Medical Association, Madam Walker's Hair Culturists Association, the Perry C. Bradford Company, and the Irvin C. Miller Corporation." Overall, Gibson's theaters were a hallmark of Philadelphia's black community.[95]

In the District of Columbia, S. H. Dudley matched Gibson's efforts and lent his resources to similar fundraisers. In 1924 Dudley performed at a benefit for the local Y.W.C.A, sponsored by the black women's group the Pollyannas, and held it at the Lincoln Theatre on U Street. In the same month, George Martin, owner of T.O.B.A.'s Foraker Theatre, provided the entertainment for a Christmas fundraiser for needy children sponsored by the Blaine Invincible Republican Club, an African American political group.[96]

Finally, individual T.O.B.A. theaters reached out to surrounding communities in times of natural disaster. When the Mississippi River flooded the Delta in 1927, the lives and homes of hundreds were devastated in the wake of the waters. Six T.O.B.A. theaters existed in the flood area, and the "fear of breaking levees" left theaters, from the Palace in Memphis to the Lyric in New Orleans, "almost empty." T.O.B.A. houses outside the danger zone pooled together to aid the refugees, and Baltimore theaters, including the Star, Regent, and Royal worked with the Red Cross to give "special performances" to raise proceeds for disaster relief.[97] When necessary, a T.O.B.A. theater could add stability to a black community, represent "Black pride and progress," or be an uplifting space for social change.[98]

Musician Danny Barker was correct; they *all* came to the Lyric in New Orleans and to T.O.B.A. Time theaters in Chicago, St. Louis, Chattanooga, Philadelphia, and Washington, DC.[99] As the 1927–28 theater season approached, T.O.B.A. was on its way to being one of the most profitable black entertainment businesses with interracial management in the nation. T.O.B.A. sparked job creation in the theaters themselves and in supplemental institutions that allowed the circuit to function and navigate racial segregation. Circuit audiences benefitted from the amusement and escape provided by the artists' performances and in turn individual communities shared a reciprocal relationship with the black vaudeville institution.

# 6

# "TROUBLE IN MIND"

## *The End of T.O.B.A. Time*

I'm all alone at midnight and the lamps are burnin' low
Never had so much trouble in my life before . . .
Trouble in mind, I'm blue, but I won't be always
The sun gonna shine in my backdoor someday.
—Richard M. Jones, lyrics from "Trouble in Mind," 1924

It was a small notice in the *Defender* placed just diagonally from the weekly T.O.B.A. advertisement on the entertainment page. Aside from the "NOTICE" headline in bold letters the excerpt would be easy to miss: "the theatrical department holds mail addressed to the following from the United States district court, calling a meeting of the creditors of Ethel Waters, who was recently duly adjudicated *bankrupt* on September 19, 1928."[1] Black periodicals recounted how Waters, billed as the "World's Greatest Colored Phonograph Star," was able to "gratify her every wish where money is concerned" by 1921. In the mid-1920s she reportedly earned between $1,250 and $2,220 per week. In July 1927, Waters opened *Africana,* her first Broadway musical, at New York City's Daly's Theatre on Sixty-Third Street. *Africana* showcased songs from Waters's T.O.B.A. acts, like "Dinah" and "Take Your Black Bottom Out of Here," and employed a cast and crew of sixty members of "the race."[2] Yet, after nearly a year on the road the show abruptly closed in May 1928 when the musicians went on strike from lack of payment. Where did the money go? Was there mismanagement on her producer's part? As debts loomed with $10,000 owed to Daly's Theatre and $50,000 owed to her theater manager, Waters's management team advised her to file for bankruptcy. While her fortunes would shift in two years, Ethel Waters braced for mounting financial and legal troubles in 1928.[3]

FIGURE 10. Ethel Waters, 1932, by Carl Van Vechten © Van Vechten Trust. Carl Van Vechten Papers Relating to African American Arts and Letters. James Weldon Johnson Collection in the Yale Collection of American Literature, Beinecke Rare Book and Manuscript Library.

Waters's troubles in the late 1920s were a herald for T.O.B.A. Time's end. For Waters, bankruptcy and decline came from one poorly produced show in one theater season. For T.O.B.A., decline was a bit more gradual. It is this process of the circuit's concluding years that is this chapter's story. By uniting the management skills of African American and white managers, T.O.B.A. as the interracial experiment had done rather well by the 1925–26 season. Communication was smooth, receipts were relatively high, and the union that performers had crafted to fight for better salaries and bookings was officially recognized by T.O.B.A. management. But the continued promises of bigger and better shows halted near the end of the decade when "show business" momentarily came to "a standstill."[4] T.O.B.A.'s end involved the interests of all stakeholders, including management, artists, and audience members, and started all the way at the top. Highly publicized management and entertainer scandals affected audiences' perceptions of the respectability of vaudeville performance. Infighting between managers and booking agents spread beyond board meetings to the front pages of the black press, while competition from the cheaper "talkie" motion pictures emerging after 1926 influenced the popularity of vaudeville itself. Ultimately, all these issues were compounded by the difficulties in negotiating the segregated economy as the Great Depression approached. During the last few seasons of T.O.B.A. Time the epigraph lyrics rang true, as the organization and black vaudeville faced "trouble in mind."

## DUDLEY'S SCANDALS

The same usage of the national African American press to positively promote T.O.B.A. also resulted in negative press that threatened the circuit's promises of respectable entertainment.[5] Detailed discussions of improprieties, mishaps, and outright crimes in the T.O.B.A. ranks titillated consumers and shocked conservative critics. Immediately following its banner 1925–26 season, the first of many such controversial incidents involved the Eastern District manager S. H. Dudley. Dudley was involved in every aspect of T.O.B.A., from the Washington, DC, booking office to the Colored Actors' Union and later occasional stage performances with his *Ebony Follies*.[6] Rarely did a news story on Dudley fail to mention T.O.B.A. or black vaudeville theater. Flattering pieces in the *Defender* and the *Crisis* invited readers to explore Dudley's world and marvel at how the former minstrel man "with the mule" had become a wealthy theater magnate. Most articles remained at the surface level and avoided a deep discussion of Dudley's family. However, a January 1925 article in the black monthly *The Messenger* concluded with discussion of how S. H. and Mrs. Dudley, "a Georgia girl," were newly married and that he "gave her credit for all success."[7] Readers might have been surprised to see the "Dudley Denies Divorce Rumor" headline in the *Baltimore Afro-American* just a year later.[8]

Entertainment romances came and went all the time, yet loyal vaudeville followers might have known that Mrs. Desdemona Barnett-Dudley was not the same Mrs. Dudley, who was the mother of S. H.'s only child, S. H. Dudley Jr. The second Mrs. Dudley was far younger than S. H. and was not an entertainer as the previous Mrs. Alberta Ormes Dudley had been. Fair-skinned, young, and "pretty,"

Desdemona was between twenty-four and thirty years old when she wed fifty-one-year-old Dudley. She had worked as the cashier and stenographer for Dudley Enterprises since 1914, her first professional clerical position, after stenography courses.[9] While the details of the cliched "boss has affair with secretary" scenario are slim, Dudley and Barnett's entanglement resulted in marriage on December 2, 1924, in Oxon Hill, Maryland.[10] However, the grumblings of mistreatment on both sides leaked out to the press just months into the marriage.

What made the Dudley-Barnett divorce murmurings take hold of the public imagination was the space these articles were given. Divorce, while not common in the United States in 1920s, was not completely unforgiveable in the entertainment world.[11] Dudley was already a divorcee when he married his young secretary, and his previous separation from Ormes was arguably civil and was not widely discussed in public. Yet the Dudley-Barnett proceedings that had been on page six in black newspapers in February and March 1926 soon crept to the first page by May, and details became more lurid and T.O.B.A.-centered. Barnett accused Dudley of physical assault, while Dudley accused his wife of property destruction. Still Dudley publicly denied that he was filing for divorce and spoke of reconciliation in an effort to defuse the gossip reports.

Not even a full year prior, Barnett had been characterized as a sweet young girl from north Georgia, not a high-spirited woman emmeshed in the flapper or New Woman culture of the 1920s. By May 1926, the separation murmurings filled front-page articles, like "S.H. Dudley in Sensational Suit: Scandal Rocks DC as Dudley Demands Divorce." These articles named co-respondent George S. Davis, a black District of Columbia police officer, in the divorce petition and noted each alleged incidence of Barnett's infidelity by date and location.[12] The most damning thing about this publicity to T.O.B.A. was that articles also mentioned Dudley as a "director and one of the three general booking managers of the Theatre Owners Booking Association," the last type of publicity the organization needed.[13]

Dudley prided himself on being the elder statesman of black vaudeville theater, the manager who called for censor panels while at the same time advocating for entertainers' pay rights. The theater magnate championed black entertainment, yet his personal relationships jeopardized T.O.B.A. Because Barnett worked for T.O.B.A., the divorce lawsuit stated that she retaliated against the petition by "succeeding in destroying several indispensable records, books, and papers" in the circuit's Eastern District office.[14] Would actors be paid? Would the personal correspondence between the managers in Macon and Nashville be leaked? The Dudley divorce scandal worsened as the accusations and counter accusations made headlines, op-eds, and satirical cartoons for months and included discussions of domestic violence, sexual intrigue, "profane" behavior, and Dudley's supposed worth of $200,000 ($2.9 million in 2020) in stocks, insurance, residential and commercial property, and racing horses.[15]

While the divorce played out for the world to see, Dudley and other African American theatrical producers scrambled during those hot months of June and July to try to keep ticket sales up and get ready for the 1926–27 season. Lurid narratives of Dudley's misfortunes earned black press sales, but they did not ensure a tab show a full house at the theater. Even in the midst of the proceedings, Dudley still regularly wrote theatrical columns for the *Afro-American* and *Chicago Defender*, advising performers to refine their acts and give the "managers what they want" "to stay in the game."[16] These columns revealed Dudley's struggles to keep all eyes on the circuit's performance efforts and not his personal exploits.

All came to a screeching halt when front-page headlines of "Wife of S.H. Dudley Slain By Lover" emerged after September 21, 1926.[17] After news of a Dudley couple reunion, Davis asked Desdemona if she was indeed "through with him," which she confirmed. Subsequent to this brief exchange, Davis shot and killed Desdemona Barnett-Dudley on September 21, 1926 before turning the gun on himself.[18] The immediate aftermath of the murder rendered S. H. Dudley, T.O.B.A. magnate, "mute." Any public discussion of the Dudley-Barnett-Davis affair was forever connected with press reports of "Sherman H. Dudley," "theatrical magnate" and "proprietor of several colored theatrical enterprises." Murder became associated with stories of the T.O.B.A. management. S. H. Dudley could not escape the violent end to his marriage, and Davis won infamy and notoriety as the "D.C. Killer Cop," a series of events that threatened T.O.B.A.'s self-image as an upright business.[19]

## THREATS TO BLACK THEATER RESPECTABILITY

T.O.B.A. entertainers' publicized disgraceful behavior plagued the integrity of the circuit's family vaudeville mission just as much as the actions of circuit management. When T.O.B.A. actor and producer Clarence Muse allegedly slapped and threw chorus girl Frances Walton out of Howard Theatre, he was arrested and formally accused of assault. The Muse incident demonstrated the growing power that black women utilized as they openly challenged physical assaults and demanded respect, as Walton later dropped the criminal charges in exchange for payment for civil damages. But the incident also had the potential to ward off aspiring entertainers who feared the very real dangers of being young, unchaperoned women in black vaudeville.[20]

Publicized negative interactions continued in the last few seasons of the circuit. The all black Miles Dewey troupe was accused of "enticing" two presumably non-black women and was arrested after a beach concert in California in 1925. While

Dewey was not contracted by the circuit at the time the incident occurred, even this consensual activity resulted in a petition "to ban any Race group of professionals from playing the beach" in Southern California. As the presumption of interracial sexual activity was a prime motivation for racial violence targeted at African American men throughout the late nineteenth and early twentieth centuries, entertainment critics lambasted the Dewey ensemble for its effect on black vaudeville in general. Journalists remarked that "the profession must be saved" and could not afford to lose the "ground which has been won by hard effort and plugging" by those stepping across the color line.[21]

T.O.B.A. and black vaudevillians wanted to conceal personal scandal in the same ways Donald Bogle maintains that black Hollywood actors desired to "protect the public perception about the morality of the movie colony" and the "box office."[22] When accounts of a violent assault against Bessie Smith emerged in 1925, T.O.B.A.'s publicist, W. R. Arnold announced it before the local authorities could do so. Rumors of Smith's "bootleg liquor" habit, quick temper, and sexual behavior already abounded, even in her song lyrics of "Empty Bed Blues" or "Gimme a Pigfoot."[23] But Arnold and the T.O.B.A. board did not want actual police reports regarding violence or sexual activity to hurt ticket sales. The Arnold-written story read that Smith, one of the "biggest drawing cards on the T.O.B.A. circuit," was horrifically attacked in her Chattanooga hometown by local criminal Buck Hodge. Arnold's piece conveyed sympathy for Smith, while an expose on an intoxicated *female* vocalist caught up in the aftermath of a 4:00 a.m. bar brawl in T.O.B.A.'s headquarter city would not.[24]

Publicists spun tales about offstage skirmishes, but nothing could mitigate incidents that resulted in death. A year after the Dudley murder scandal, another case of infidelity leading to death hit the Washington, DC, newspapers in the Wiggins-Sturdivant case. John "Ginger" Wiggins, wife Velma Wiggins, and fellow castmate James Sturdivant were all known T.O.B.A. performers and members of the Nehigh Musical Company when it was booked by DC's Foraker Theatre in 1927. During the revue's run, Sturdivant allegedly attempted to seduce the recently separated Velma Wiggins in her hotel room. Unaware that Mr. and Mrs. Wiggins were in the same hotel room, an uninvited Sturdivant forced open Mrs. Wiggins's door after midnight and was met by Mr. Wiggins, who shot and killed Sturdivant instantly.

As an institution T.O.B.A. was enmeshed in the case. The incident occurred in Jules McGarr's Summit Hotel, an actor's hotel, owned and operated by president of the Colored Actors' Union, and was the second fatal shooting at the Summit since McGarr had purchased it.[25] One of S. H. Dudley's personal lawyers, George E. C. Haynes, was Wiggins's defense attorney when he was sentenced to manslaughter.[26] In the minds of DC journalists, the George Davis and Wiggins cases were so closely related that the sentencing for both came out in one article in the *Washington Post*.[27] These multiple incidents further tarnished positive perceptions of the circuit, and the organization could not quite keep control of T.O.B.A.'s narrative of progress.

## MANAGEMENT INFIGHTING, BOOKING STRIFE

Increased internal T.O.B.A. participant complaints compounded the effects of these publicized scandals.[28] In the Southern District, Sam Reevin, as both national treasurer and overall booking manager, was simply overtasked. Reevin wrote to each theater manager with a forthcoming act's "report card" as well as handled entertainer queries about contracts and salaries. He was responsible for everything from filing corporate taxes to chasing down delinquent commission fees from individual managers. All these responsibilities resulted in Reevin being the center of most T.O.B.A. booking complaints. His personal correspondence addressed this stress in the tone of his words to various managers. When Reevin wrote that "you may not realize it . . . but there is a lot of detail attached to this office and sometimes it is impossible to remember everything" in trying to negotiate a contract with Macon's Douglass Theatre, he revealed the mounting pressure in the office of a two-to-three-person staff.[29] In a professional conflict with Douglass, Reevin appeared to be personally offended, as he extended the "desire to have the good will of the Managers" and had considered African American manager C. H. Douglass "a friend" before whatever misunderstanding occurred.[30] By mid-1926, exhaustion and severe illness prohibited Reevin from working at all, and the smooth function of the entire Southern District headquarters appeared at risk.

Interestingly in Reevin's absence much of the Chattanooga office was handled by his secretary Mrs. Louise Nason, T.O.B.A. stenographer since 1924.[31] While personal details about Mrs. Nason are few, she was a wage-working woman in 1920s Chattanooga, married to a prominent civil engineer, Roy S. Nason.[32] T.O.B.A.'s booking operations were under Nason's control for much of 1926, and the board did not bring in another male theater professional from one of the South's other membership theaters to run the main office. Reportedly Reevin had contracted tuberculosis sometime in early 1926, and without disclosing his illness or the specifics T.O.B.A.'s publicist acknowledged that Reevin was "a mighty sick man," as he was hospitalized in Chattanooga's Erlanger Hospital for a period of "five weeks" between May and July of that year.[33] Reevin's trips to and from Erlanger Hospital were covered by African American, Jewish, and industry periodicals throughout much of 1926.[34] As a testament to her skill, Louise Nason made decisions on how to negotiate salaries, contract new bookings, and even evaluate talent in acts while Reevin fought to recover.[35] Yet, Nason's time as the de facto head of the

Southern region was brief, and she faded from the city directories as T.O.B.A.'s stenographer by 1927.[36] Industry managers reported that Reevin's illness had so weakened him that he and his family relocated from his downtown residence on E. Fourth Street to Signal Mountain, where he was "domiciled in his mountain top home" in search of better air quality.[37] T.O.B.A. continued to advertise that the Southern District office was in the downtown Volunteer Building, but Reevin "virtually lived in his pajamas" and undertook the bulk of his business from his Signal Mountain home.[38]

While the Southern office functioned during Reevin's intermittent absences, vaudeville, and by extension T.O.B.A., faltered as a mass entertainment genre in general. Numerous reports from the 1927–28 season contended that "show business" again was "at a standstill."[39] This claim about a stagnant market was not new, but in 1927 more voices echoed these valid manager and agent complaints publicly. Paying audiences for T.O.B.A. shows declined in number. Theaters like the Douglass that had done prime business in the mid-1920s just barely broke even or reported losses of almost a $1,000 a week.[40] A comparison of the routings listed for T.O.B.A. in 1925 and 1927 further demonstrates these stark differences. While a week in late October 1925 in the Midwest might have contracted fourteen different acts, including boxer Jack Johnson, tabloid show the Smart Set, and blues singer Clara Smith, a week in the mid-1927 Southern region boasted one tabloid show, the Brownskin Models.[41]

What was the cause for this rapid falloff in audiences and diverse acts? Theater owner C. H. Douglass openly blamed T.O.B.A. for its own demise and lamented that managers took on too great a risk by hiring unproven talent. Douglass declared that "owners will go broke, the companies will have to disband and seek employment on the tent and carnival" circuit if the consistent losses persisted. He warned that unless T.O.B.A. management was reconfigured "one group of the profession will become obsolete."[42] By this "one group" Douglass meant vaudeville acts rather than tabloid shows, but also arguably independent black theater owners. Privately Douglass supported his views, maintaining that "business is bad" but "a real vaudeville will make things better" rather than the mix of tabloid shows and silent film reels that played at many T.O.B.A. theaters.[43] As his dealings with T.O.B.A. continued to dissolve, Douglass "surrendered his 3 shares of stock" and subleased the Douglass Theatre to white manager Ben Stein.[44]

Douglass was joined by black theater veterans who marked 1927 as one of the "worst" theater seasons since T.O.B.A. began but for different reasons. *Defender* theater journalists argued that "the producers must bring some new ideas if they expect a lucrative beginning in the fall."[45] For veteran Tim Owsley the fault lied in "*our* show business, still trying vainly to succeed in these modern times with unintelligent discrimination, petty jealousy, conceit and prejudice."[46] Ultimately,

Dudley blamed it on the "very little new material" from T.O.B.A. performers and the theaters that tried "to book shows independently" and strayed from T.O.B.A.'s centralized structure.[47]

In the same theater season, T.O.B.A. board member Charles Bailey attempted to lease theaters and form his own circuit. The proposed Bailey Circuit threatened the fragile interracial co-operation within the T.O.B.A. board, for Bailey, along with Joe Spiegelberger, wanted to host a "new circuit [that] will fast gain popularity with the acts if they start in right to treat the gang *white*."[48] This proposal could be read as Bailey wanting to treat black vaudeville acts in the same way that white vaudeville managers treated their headliners: with better pay and more autonomy. Yet based on his previous racist interactions, Bailey arguably wanted to reduce the influence of African Americans at the management level and work with the "gang" of white managers within the circuit. Operating a black-serving institution while not even superficially treating black managers with respect proved to be a problem for T.O.B.A. Privately, even Milton Starr conceded that "Bailey is having a battle with the T.O.B.A." and hoped "he will quit his so-called opposition to us" if other T.O.B.A. managers refused to work with him.[49]

As Bailey tried to create his own circuit, both Douglass and Owsley intimated that the hierarchal structure of the circuit, with its rarely fluctuating executive board, must be altered before significant changes could be made to T.O.B.A. shows. Milton Starr had remained the president of T.O.B.A. throughout much of its tenure. This dominance of a white president was a problem for a circuit that pushed the concept of an interracial membership model. Although Starr was reelected year after year, his once promising leadership beginning in 1921 was soon at odds with his own family's attempt to create a monopoly in black-serving or "colored" motion picture theaters in the South. With the same players who had made up the Bijou Amusement Company in 1914, Starr acquired formerly white motion picture and vaudeville theaters and reopened them for African American consumers throughout the 1920s. While expanding his business interests was productive for the Bijou Amusement Company, other T.O.B.A. board members accused Starr of using his T.O.B.A. connections to staff these side businesses.

By 1926 Dudley and Reevin deemed Starr's outside acquisitions as a threat to T.O.B.A., particularly as some of the theaters hosted motion pictures instead of vaudeville.[50] Dudley himself owned or operated multiple theaters both before and during his T.O.B.A. tenure, but all his theaters appeared to host circuit productions. Starr's conflict of interest was also clear as he was the circuit president, responsible for negotiating commissions with the unions and financial terms with theater managers while also becoming a multi-theater owner and manager himself. In essence he negotiated with himself in the name of the T.O.B.A. circuit. Reevin and Dudley argued that Starr had been "appropriating his time and money to his own interests by launching his own attractions and leaving T.O.B.A. interests to pine and perish in non-attention" and charged him with neglect.[51] Starr's response was to not change his behavior in any way. Subsequently, stockholders reelected Starr as the president of T.O.B.A. for the 1927–28 season, suggesting that the other board members did not mind this conflict as long as T.O.B.A. effectively functioned in some capacity. Throughout 1927 Starr intertwined his Bijou Amusement Company business with T.O.B.A.'s and wrote about the circuit's issues on Bijou Amusement letterhead.[52]

In 1928 Starr was not elected the T.O.B.A. board president for the first time since 1922. In his place the board elected African American St. Louis theater veteran Charles H. Turpin, praised for being a "shrewd politician and an astute businessman."[53] While Starr now had more time to pursue his "colored theater" motion picture empire after Turpin's election, he did not sever his T.O.B.A. ties; instead he moved to the vice president position. Turpin had been on the T.O.B.A. board since its creation, and his interracial institution organizing efforts went back to the onset of the Colored Consolidated Vaudeville Exchange in 1913. That the board had its first African American president was significant in that T.O.B.A was finally led by one of the "men of the race," as S. H. Dudley had desired in 1907, and his election could have represented a moment of black autonomy in black vaudeville. Yet, the circuit was in turmoil in 1928, and who knew what "Charley Turpin" had in store to attempt to restore T.O.B.A. Time to its glory?[54]

## PERFORMERS COMBAT MANAGEMENT

As the black entertainment world celebrated Charles Turpin as T.O.B.A.'s first African American president, the circuit performers had their own reactions to the decline of black vaudeville. When contracts shifted from a flat fee to a percentage of the door admissions as artist payment, T.O.B.A. troupers spoke out. Previously the C.A.U. had been the vehicle performers used to challenge management, but union strategies alone could no longer contain T.O.B.A.'s troubles.[55] In the circuit's Eastern District performers made specific complaints about Dudley's management style and argued that while agency advertisements promised forty weeks of work, *ten weeks* a season was more the reality by 1927. A trouper booked through the Washington, DC, office might receive "two weeks" in Baltimore, "four weeks" in Washington, and another "four in Virginia." Performers signed contracts that were "subject to change without notice," cancellation if managers saw fit, and required "as many as fifteen percentage" commission "on a percentage basis" of a theater house's receipts. In reality this meant that a performer could be contracted to sing at the Foraker Theatre in Washington, DC, and have their contract cancelled while traveling before they reached the actor's boarding house at the Summit Hotel. Theater professional George Tyler noted that the increasing instability of a trouper's salary in the Eastern District was "why actors are broke and shabbily dressed."[56]

As the next season brought no significant improvements, theater veteran and *Defender* entertainment columnist Salem Tutt Whitney used his platform to detail performer concerns and try to encourage improvement. In a witty New Year's poem Whitney chronicled how "we'd like to see the T.O.B.A. improve its theaters as well as they play/ With jumps that will give the producers a chance/ to live through the year without pawning their pants."[57] Whitney followed the New Year's column with a more serious plea that "we [the black entertainment world] need the T.O.B.A. and the association needs us . . . performers [should] play fairly" and the "association [should] deal squarely."[58]

Generally, the T.O.B.A. board met most performer complaints with the tried strategy of continued reassurance that "OLD TOBA is still in existence and WILL BE."[59] But the seemingly false promises of better shows, fewer jumps, and better salaries was all "such rot" to actor, producer, future film star, and Baltimore native Clarence Muse. In January 1928, Muse wished "the Colored Profession a prosperous theatrical season," but by summer 1928 openly criticized the circuit's management for its issues. To Muse, T.O.B.A.'s failure was not due to some racial or industry outsider, but the whole organization, African American and white. Muse critiqued incoming president "race man" Charles Turpin as the "great vandal of the colored show world" for continuing to rob performers of a livable wage. But Muse also lambasted white booking director Sam Reevin, who listened to artists' concerns and answered all inquiries but merely issued performers a "new contract," for what Muse hyperbolically argued was another "theatrical year of sorrow."[60]

Reevin immediately responded directly to Muse publicly, without waiting for new president Turpin to step into the fray. Reevin referred to Muse only as the newspaper's "correspondent" and questioned the specific amounts that Muse had cited as the supposedly exorbitant commission fees and damages clauses unjustly charged to T.O.B.A. performers. The booking manager wanted names of specific acts or artists who had been forced to pay these alleged fees. Reevin also contended he was "satisfied" that your "correspondent has a personal grudge against some individual or individuals connected with T.O.B.A." and was unjustly critiquing the "entire organization."[61]

Muse followed this rebuttal with a reproduced Midwest District T.O.B.A. contract to let readers decide for themselves what Muse alluded to as debt peonage or entertainment sharecropping. Performers produced the labor of entertaining the masses with a hope for a share or a percentage of the profits at the end of a series of performances, minus the expenses incurred for train tickets, baggage shipping, and lodging. "Any sound business man," Muse contended, would "readily see that the idea of keeping a show in debt and moving it each week with advances is but another way of exercising 'peonage.'"[62] The peonage and sharecropping comparisons would have negatively resonated with many audience members who just fled plantations and industry towns as migrants to find some economic prosperity.

Muse contended that "race actors" were like any other potentially exploited worker in America, a laborer who served the whims of an employer. Muse also maintained that he knew "hundreds of artists" who shared his complaints but were "afraid [to be] blackballed." This concept of repression and fear in the black vaudeville industry mirrored the same concerns that had arisen in white vaudeville in the FTC federal lawsuit in 1919. Muse's critiques demonstrated that some veteran performers were not afraid to speak their truths, even if it meant that black actors publicly chastised both white and black theater magnates. It also signaled an entertainment genre that could weaken if performers' concerns were not taken more seriously. Where would a disgruntled black vaudevillian go to find work? The emerging world of films might provide an answer.

## THE EFFECTS OF SOUND FILM

The rise of American motion pictures coincided with vaudeville's decline. When the T.O.B.A. circuit began in 1921, it controlled fifty-eight out of 122 black-serving vaudeville theaters.[63] Yet when the board elected Charles Turpin to lead in 1928, T.O.B.A. controlled forty-five black-serving vaudeville theaters. By comparison, the number of motion picture theaters rose to twenty-four thousand "four-walled" institutions in the country in 1930. Of these institutions only 2 percent, or 461, of theaters were black-serving institutions, absent of strict racial segregation.[64] When vaudeville spaces diminished dramatically as the 1920s closed, motion picture theaters took their place. Federal government reports estimated that Americans spent near $1.5 billion on motion picture admissions and $166 million on "theaters, concerts, and other entertainments" in 1928 alone. The estimated tax revenue garnered from these institutions in 1930 was $2,214,725,000 at the onset of the Great Depression. Show business was "big business" throughout the nation, and if T.O.B.A. was going to continue to have any stake in this "rising tide," it would not only be on the stage, but on the screen as well.[65]

T.O.B.A. and black vaudeville's connection to motion pictures was not a new development of the late 1920s. Many theater houses in the Dudley Circuit, Klein's Colored Consolidated Vaudeville Exchange, Reevin's Mutual Amusement Company, and Starr's Bijou Amusement Companies all had the capability to screen silent films, and silent films and vaudeville bills shared newspapers' entertainment sections. The house musicians that accompanied acts in large vaudeville theaters might also play alongside a silent film to add emotion and drama to the text on the screen.[66] When film was a young medium in the 1910s, theater managers held internal discussions on whether to wait to "see how they were doing with pictures" or put in some "crackerjack vaudeville shows" if a film reel failed to pack the house.[67] Both T.O.B.A., as well as the Southern Consolidated Vaudeville Company that it merged with in 1921, contained key clauses about developing "theatres for the purpose [of] motion picture entertainment and presenting motion picture films" in their charters and mission statements.[68] But T.O.B.A. was created to book live entertainers on stage, and despite these clauses there was the sense that films would *supplement* not *supersede* vaudeville and tab performances. Yet this vision of coexistence changed with the advent of sound films.

Film historian Donald Crafton chronicled sound experiments in the 1910s with newsreels and movie shorts by the Phonofilm, Movietone, and Vitaphone companies in the early 1920s. These experiments captured sound effects or individual words or sung phrases but were not full films that synchronized speaking, background sounds, and music with moving images.[69] While some film historians contend that "sound changed *everything,* how movies were made, but most importantly what films *were,*" others stress the difficulty and unpredictability of sound film technology that was not quickly overcome as filmmakers struggled to meet a public's new desires and tastes.[70] One of the most known films associated with the shift to sound film was *The Jazz Singer*.

In a story loosely based on famed vaudevillian Al Jolson, *The Jazz Singer* told a tale of Jakie Rabinowitz—soon-to-become Jack Robin—a Jewish immigrant performer torn between the duty to his Jewish traditions and fame on the American vaudeville stage. The plot was initially written by Samson Raphaelson as the short story "The Day of Atonement" in 1922 and was later produced on Broadway in 1925, starring vaudevillian George Jessel as Robins. Warner Brothers bought the rights to the story in 1927 and cast Al Jolson in Jessel's role.[71] As one of the first full-length features to include Vitaphone sound, *The Jazz Singer* premiered in October 1927 and furthered a new technological age where dialogue and music could be coordinated from the screen. Watching and *hearing* Jolson perform "Blue Skies" and "Kol Nidre" and conclude with the 1918 vaudeville song "Mammy" in *The Jazz Singer* was marketed as the "greatest drawing card on the screen."[72] However, the film only included approximately two-and-a-half minutes of talking across its entirety, and the costly technology needed to replicate such productions en masse was not yet widely available. *The Jazz Singer* was not a complete victory for "talking cinema" as much as it was "a triumph for Jolson" and Warner Brothers studios.[73]

That a film that helped modernize a mass entertainment genre did so by retrieving the vestiges of blackface minstrelsy and jazz- and blues-inflected music did not go unnoticed. African American critics who took any positive note of *The Jazz Singer* did so with the caveat that the film should be looked upon with interest by "colored performers," like former minstrels Bert Williams, S. T. Whitney, and S. H. Dudley, who would have been the stars of such a film "had they been able to register equally as well upon the screen as they have upon the stage."[74] Yet other critics commented on the "canned" or manufactured emotion of the movie and lamented that film sound technology replaced the need for a house orchestra accompanying the film, removing another job opportunity for vaudevillian musicians.[75]

T.O.B.A. board members invested financially and intellectually in motion pictures, even before 1927. Why would the T.O.B.A. elite invest in an enterprise that could eventually bring a significant end to much of their income stream? Investors did not really believe that live vaudeville theater would come to a complete end and speculated on the promise of a new potentially profitable enterprise. Although some film historians argue that black audiences were indifferent to early motion pictures, Jacqueline Stewart reveals that there was a growing black audience for silent films in the 1910s. In 1914–15 *Defender* listings for motion picture theaters alongside vaudeville theaters as well as brief film reviews suggested that a black public attended silent films in Chicago, and this viewership occurred in urban communities throughout the country.[76]

Never one to miss an entrepreneurial opportunity, S. H. Dudley simultaneously championed T.O.B.A. stage shows and independent film productions. In 1920, Dudley Enterprises invested in the Congressional Film Company, which planned to open studios in Silver Spring, Maryland, with Dudley as the company's first star in "Minister to Dahomey."[77] While the Congressional Film Company failed to materialize, this did not stop other African American T.O.B.A. investors from entering the movie arena. The First National Colored Film Corporation was developed in Durham, North Carolina, in 1926 with capital stock of $100,000. Both T.O.B.A. stockholders, F. K. Watkins, the African American "movie king" of Durham, and William S. Scales of Winston-Salem, planned the First National as a "new movement" of entertainment holdings by "race men." However, the realization of First National was plagued by a lack of willing actors thought to be "too slow" and "too poor" to leave vaudeville and leap into the film enterprise.[78]

Not dissuaded by Watkins and Scales's failed attempts, Dudley picked up the race film mantle once again in the mid-1920s. He proposed that investment in race films, or all black performer productions, was the next step in black entertainment success and wanted to create the Colored Players Film Corporation (CPFC), a silent black film production company.[79] Using the same entrepreneurial model he developed with the Dudley Circuit in the 1910s, he called out to entrepreneurs in Boston, DC, Cincinnati, Baltimore, and Chicago to help sustain his legacy and "finish the biggest and the greatest Negro enterprise in the history of the world."[80] Hyperbole aside, Dudley clearly saw the increased development in sound motion picture theaters and saw the comparably few sound "race films" as an opportunity to ask fellow actors and managers to join in the next "big thing." He asked African American audience members to "demand colored pictures at the theatre where you spend your money or spend your money with the theatres that play colored pictures." Dudley also appealed to all "loyal race lovers to become a part owner and booster of better colored pictures."[81] He also enjoyed the idea of being on the screen as well and eventually acted in the silent comedic production *Easy Money*.[82]

As an entrepreneur Dudley realized his race films dreams when the Colored Players Film Corporation was founded in Philadelphia in 1926. While CPFC letterhead listed Dudley as the corporation's president and he was heavily involved in CPFC marketing, manager David Starkman and the majority of the corporation's leadership was white, similar to the management makeup of several early race film companies. Film scholar Charles Musser explains the CPFC's significance in the race film arena by noting that it was in economic and ideological competition with the famed race film director Oscar Micheaux's film company. Between 1926 and 1929 the CPFC produced four silent black dramatic films, including *Children of Fate* and *Scar of Shame*, the latter of which film historian Thomas Cripps chronicles as one of the "finest examples" of class divisions within urban black communities.[83]

The economic potential of dividing investments between the stage and the screen was clearly articulated by Salem T. Whitney. Whitney rightly argued that African Americans were powerful consumers whom the film industry could benefit from and vice versa. Whitney estimated that four hundred theaters in the nation catered to African Americans and serviced a potential daily 160,000 "colored consumers." He further calculated that African Americans spent an average of $9,984,000 on race films and Hollywood productions. This near $10 million made from black consumers, Whitney argued, warranted that the motion picture industry should do "more to give our [black] actors more consideration."[84]

Despite T.O.B.A.'s efforts to support both artistic genres, film's popularity did indeed weaken vaudeville's success. The white manager of Macon's Douglass Theatre, Ben Stein, found it "impossible" to pay live acts what they were worth in late 1927 and diverted any funds he had to "playing a large picture program every week." Just six months later, Stein wired the T.O.B.A. main office saying it was "IMPOSSIBLE to get SHOWS."[85] As a T.O.B.A. performer Leonard Reed maintained "the movies hurt TOBA." After 1927 vaudeville acts or musical performances became only one part of an evening's entertainment at many live performance theaters. Spectators came to see a film followed by a "cartoon," a newsreel, and *then* perhaps the "show," a live theater act.[86] By the 1930s motion pictures slowly began to outpace mainstream vaudeville and T.O.B.A.

## "JIM CROW BAIT": OBEYING SEGREGATION

Despite the popularity and marketing of films like the *Crimson Skull* or *The Wages of Sin* with their "all-star colored" casts, black theater professionals commented that "the continued decline of the circuit" could not "all be blamed on the talkies."[87] In reality, a monumental factor in T.O.B.A.'s demise was the institution of segregation itself. Legal segregation and the "color line" in part fueled the existence of a separate circuit, otherwise black audiences may have been able enjoy black acts among a diverse playbill in safety and peace. Victoria Wolcott holds that recreation segregation battles "were part of a broader struggle for control and access to urban space."[88] "Separate but equal" was never equal, but it also was rarely entirely separate in the entertainment world. For example, when black-serving establishments in urban spaces booked popular high-profile acts like dancer Bill Robinson who attracted white and black patronage, the notion of black space was contested when white spectators visited T.O.B.A. theaters. Scholars of institutions built on segregated economies, like Negro League Baseball or black music recording companies, argue that these institutions and reserved black spaces eventually faded with legal integration because the "institutions, as designed, had no future."[89] It is true that integration in the mid-twentieth century dramatically altered African American attendance at black-serving theaters or concert halls. Yet 1920s T.O.B.A. concluded not because of segregation's demise, but oddly because of the reinforcement of its existence.

Although sanctioned by federal law, the practice of segregation in public accommodations in the United States did not happen instantaneously after 1896, nor did it look the same in every region of the nation. A city in Alabama might have not a single theater or amusement center open for black use, while white facilities in the District of Columbia might allow black patronage and have racially separate seating. When urban areas attempted to create fixed segregation statutes where there had been none previously, black civil rights advocates encouraged simply not "obeying segregation" as a resistance tactic.

When Washington, DC, passed local ordinances to formally segregate institutions like public accommodations in the 1910s, African American leaders encouraged their citizens to build their own exclusive institutions rather than submit to segregation. As discussed by Washington, DC, race relations scholars, if a white theater or opera house restricted African Americans to "colored balconies," then black residents were supposed to stay home in protest.[90] The black periodical the *Washington Bee* cheered "enterprising citizens" who used their resources to "build theaters of their own" and denounced Jim Crow. Black citizens who patronized white theaters in the District and sat in the seats reserved for "colored people" were labeled by the *Bee* as "menaces to civilization" and racial progress.[91]

In numerous national black press articles, race leaders implored black citizens to fight for *voluntary separation* and refuse to willingly adhere to segregation statutes, whether legally or socially enforced. But this tactic was not meant to dismantle racial inequality all together but rather foster the creation of a self-sufficient black community. Agitation for desegregation in theaters was not a widespread battle in the 1910s and '20s. When the Lafayette Theatre opened in 1913 on New York City's Seventh Avenue between 132nd and 133rd Streets in Harlem, the area was still racially mixed. Accordingly, the Lafayette, which served as the foundation for the legendary black-serving Apollo Theater, "was not built for the colored race," but for the white masses.[92] In the 1910s African Americans were forced to crowd into the Lafayette's segregated balcony in an area that was becoming a black neighborhood. Race patrons rightfully complained about their subjugation at the Lafayette but did not demand integration so as much as preservation of a black space in a growing black community. These patrons were eventually successful in their protests, and the theater became known for its black audiences after 1913.[93] Similarly, Atlanta race leaders encouraged black consumers to boycott segregated theater facilities by withholding their patronage. Rather than sit in the theater galleries "among the rats, mice, and dirt" and accept the "disgrace" of enforced segregation, uplift advocates contended that black patrons should "fight Jim Crowism" by staying home until they could champion their own establishments.[94] T.O.B.A. had developed precisely because of this resistance method of separate institution building.[95]

Even many white "progressive" reformers proposed maintaining racially separate institutions as a method of curtailing the racial clashes seen throughout the nation after World War I. In the aftermath of racial violence like the Chicago Riots in 1919, white community leaders did not promote better racial communication and a path to integration to solve the divide. Instead white leaders encouraged what historian Jeanne Theoharis refers to as "polite racism," or using more palatable language to define segregation and more efficient ways of separating racial groups.[96] White real estate brokers wanted to create "districts to be known as *exclusive* territory of Negroes" and suggested that "white men would be willing to come to the [financial] assistance of the colored" if African Americans only stayed in completely separate neighborhoods, schools, and theaters. Other white Chicagoans endorsed segregation and defined it not as "isolation" but the "*natural grouping* together of Negroes under wholesome conditions."[97]

Despite these simplistic and deceiving definitions of what became racial separation in the name of white supremacy, commercial black entertainment complicated proposed arguments for "exclusive Negro territories." What happened when there was money to be made in these segregated districts, and African Americans did not merely act as consumers but as owners of these establishments? In chapter 4, the details of the destruction of Tulsa's Dreamland Theatre in 1921 already revealed what could occur when a black-owned theater became more successful than a white theater amid Jim Crow. Black economic success was often seen as a challenge to racial hierarchies meant to keep African Americans in their subservient "place." But quite often the creation and consumption of art and culture permeated the color line, especially when black and white consumers both patronized high-profile African American acts.

When Nashville's Bijou Theatre booked Ethel Waters in 1926, the theater's owner and T.O.B.A. president Milton Starr knew that white patrons would also pay to see the "World's Greatest Colored Phonograph Star." Yet under Tennessee's enforcement of strict segregation, many theaters excluded black patrons altogether, and the Bijou was the only black-serving T.O.B.A. establishment in Nashville. Starr solved this issue by booking Waters at the Bijou and "presenting a midnight performance [for whites] on Friday night in a strictly colored theater."[98] This concept of a "midnight ramble," where white patrons visited exclusive black establishments after hours, further "insulted the race patrons" when Starr allowed black residents to attend the Waters performance in a temporarily segregated balcony in their own theater. Midnight rambles gave the illusion of following the letter of segregation law in Southern T.O.B.A. houses, but they rightfully angered black consumers. Nashville black residents "deplored" this "unprecedented" extension of race prejudice in the city and encouraged Waters and others to "refuse to play under such humiliating terms."[99] Not chastened by this public rebuke, in 1927 Starr and other theater owners continued to advocate for "white midnight shows" for tab shows, like Irvin C. Miller's "Brownskin Models," in other theaters within the Southern T.O.B.A. District, especially if these showings could be used to bolster overall floundering ticket sales.[100] Starr's actions worked against the purposes of T.O.B.A. and helped displace him as the circuit's president in 1928.

While Starr segregated African American patrons within black T.O.B.A. spaces in the South, predominantly white theaters in the Midwest and Eastern Districts booked African American acts by promising them better salary and improved conditions. Acts with crossover appeal, like famed dancer Bill "Bojangles" Robinson, opened in theaters on the Orpheum Circuit to racially mixed but often segregated audiences.[101] As black audiences followed the artists they enjoyed, they unwittingly supported segregation by sitting in second-tier, "colored only" seating. This was known as falling for "Jim Crow Bait" or paying for the façade of equal but very separate facilities in white institutions for cheaper admission than black-serving institutions. The baiting plan economically undercut the theaters of black entertainment marketplace and gave African American consumers "reason and opportunity" to purchase goods and services from white-owned establishments for less.[102] Admission at Philadelphia's T.O.B.A.-affiliated New Standard Theatre might cost the consumer between sixty cents and one dollar admission for one vaudeville performance. A balcony seat at "the Keith and Loew vaudeville houses" offered black patrons "six acts of vaudeville" and a motion picture for a "dime" as long as they made no attempt to come to the orchestra level and assert any social equality.[103]

T.O.B.A. leaders like Dudley implored audience members to "spend your money where it will be circulated among our people" and to come back to T.O.B.A. theaters.[104] In his entertainment columns, Whitney further lamented the theaters that could no longer book T.O.B.A. acts, like Baltimore's Royal or New Orleans' Lyric, because they could not secure the audiences to cover artists' salaries. Whitney chastised "the great majority of Race people [who] are not only willing to be segregated," but would "pay for the privilege of being humiliated" in black-only balconies that included "race ticket sellers, ushers, and maids [and] red plush cushions on the seats."[105] Even the Chattanooga headquarters braced itself as Sam Reevin, who openly denounced segregated seating, found "it difficult to compete with 'Jim Crow.'" Once special "accommodations extended to the Race people of Chattanooga by white theaters" commenced, black patrons stopped attending the Liberty Theatre in favor of theaters that had the hottest black acts, despite segregated seating. Whitney concluded that "as long as we submissively acquiesce to Jim Crow," the longer "it will be inflicted" upon black communities.[106]

Whitney and Dudley's economic black nationalist cries to support black institutions were not complete solutions to legally sanctioned and sometimes violently enforced segregation in public accommodations, nor did they address larger issues of political or economic inequality. Although race leaders and the National Association for the Advancement of Colored People (NAACP) rallied to protest the racist theatrical film *The Birth of a Nation*, widespread calls to *nationally* boycott segregated live performance theaters were not frequent.[107] Victoria Wolcott asserts that "when racial peace was valued above racial justice," protests against segregation were individually targeted occurrences. This quest for racial peace explains why Dudley or Gibson did not lead a national movement against segregated vaudeville theaters in the 1920s in the aftermath of Red Summer or other racial massacres.[108] T.O.B.A.'s presence made it possible to patronize separate all-black spaces as an alternative to complete exclusion from vaudeville theaters or being confined to the "colored balcony." By the late 1920s, a national economic depression affected the entire vaudeville industry, African American and white.

## THE GREAT DEPRESSION LOOMS

For many T.O.B.A. audience members, the Great Depression arrived in mid-1928. Working-class Americans experienced financial troubles that predated the stock market crashes of 1929. Although "1929 is when it [the Great Depression] hit banking and big business," sharecroppers and tenant farmers contended with poor environmental conditions that negatively affected large cash crop production, while miners and other laborers without work faced "suffering and starvation" long before the Depression's official start. Cheryl Greenberg highlighted the Depression stories of many African Americans whose experiences suggested that the onset of economic decline did not completely devastate many black communities because they were accustomed to fighting adversity.[109] Economic scarcity and employment restrictions were familiar to these communities that contended with racial oppression daily. Although black families were often skilled in stretching material and financial resources or working cooperatively, the onset of the Great Depression meant that a T.O.B.A. admission ticket priced at sixty cents to a dollar was a luxury expense spectators might no longer afford.

Just before the Depression's onset, T.O.B.A. management discussed the "future quality of shows" in what was labeled a meeting of "T.O.B.A. Big Guns" at the annual stockholder meeting in February 1928.[110] So fundamental was the circuit to the advancement of black variety entertainment that producers argued that "the success of the TOBA meant the success of Race show business generally," and the interests of all the stakeholders collided in these last meetings.[111] Management tried more radical solutions for increasing business, and soon the board planned for a merger to curtail their losses. The board agreed to merge with the Majestic Circuit of New York, owned and managed by white entrepreneurs Jack Goldberg and Charles H. Meyers. Although the Majestic Circuit board included black theater professionals James A. Jackson, Dr. J. A. C. Lattimore, and John T. Gibson—all T.O.B.A. veterans—the merger could subvert Turpin's authority.

Under the merger, T.O.B.A. would gain twelve additional theaters that were previously "white only" Majestic theaters reclaimed for black use. Additional theaters did not solve problems of underpaid actors who were not being booked as frequently or dwindling spectators who could not afford admission prices. The merger plan also did not include any discussion of extending franchises to additional black-owned theaters or plans to hire black managers, weakening African American influence at the management and theater employment levels of T.O.B.A.[112] The proposed merger only highlighted potential racial clashes within the organization. *Pittsburg Courier* black theater critic William Nunn angrily questioned why "MISTER Jack Goldberg," and not a race entrepreneur, was given a chance to revive T.O.B.A. Nunn remarked on the paucity of the circuit's acts, and audience members queried why more "Negro men of ability" weren't asked to come to the helm and put T.O.B.A. back on track.[113]

In August 1928 H. B. Miller, Martin Klein's brother-in-law and owner of the T.O.B.A. franchised Monogram Theatres in Chicago, refused to pay "$2,000 a year any longer" for a franchise in a floundering industry.[114] Midwest and Southern managers held a meeting in November 1928 and "unanimously decided to abolish the Chicago office" and effectively cancel the Majestic merger.[115] With no T.O.B.A. theater, Chicago lost its prominence in the circuit and Martin Klein, a T.O.B.A. founder, lost his job. The city held great significance in T.O.B.A.'s history, as it was where Dudley had initially publicized the need for an all-black theater circuit in 1907 after he realized the success and possibilities of the Pekin Theatre. It was also the location where Klein had tested the Colored Consolidated Vaudeville Exchange and proved that an interracially managed black vaudeville circuit could function. The close of the Chicago office meant that Sam Reevin took over the Midwest *and* Southern circuits. Reevin announced that he would "appreciate anything that might be said regarding the great co-operation of the other officials of the circuit—Charles Turpin, president, S.H. Dudley manager of Washington and [Milton] Starr—and their untiring efforts to place the TOBA circuit on a solid foundation."[116]

Further evidence of the potential decline of African American influence and authority in T.O.B.A.'s higher ranks can be seen in the Southern District and the deliberations on what to do with Macon's T.O.B.A. theater. In 1928, Ben Stein, white manager of the subleased Douglass Theatre, wanted to turn the site into a "Toby House for white people," effectively creating a theater that booked black artists for white only audiences, like conditions in Harlem's Cotton Club. L. D. Joel of the 1910s Southern Vaudeville Circuit warned Stein against this "awful gamble."[117] A "white Toby house" subverted the entire T.O.B.A. mission and would warrant protest from black audiences, who would not just be *segregated* within their own spaces but *excluded* from the town's predominantly black-serving theater. Still, Stein suggested this switch when profit losses were so rampant that even the ledger sheets in the Douglass Theatre were written on the backs of the white "big time" Keith-Orpheum-issued ledger sheets. If there was no money for paper and office supplies, there was definitely no money to pay higher wages or hire headliner acts in Macon. Ultimately, Stein's plan never came to fruition, and the Douglass remained a black-serving, albeit struggling, theater.

When 1929 began, T.O.B.A. was still listed as one of the Domestic Commerce corporations in the United States, with Sam Reevin then its secretary, treasurer, *and* booking director. The *Defender* praised Reevin and believed that, as he was "in full charge," T.O.B.A. conditions had "changed wonderfully."[118] A 1929 *Afro-American* survey of "Business and Industry" stated that "the Negro" was making an "intelligent effort" to find his place in American business circles. The article noted that the Department of Commerce listed T.O.B.A. as one of the twelve strong black businesses in the country, albeit with mixed leadership, in a list that included black banks, tailors, undertakers, and insurance agencies.[119] But arguably this Department of Commerce listing had more to do with black theater veteran J. A. Jackson's circuit boosterism in his position as director of the new Division of Negro Affairs in the Commerce Department, than with T.O.B.A.'s actual productivity.[120] At the February stockholder meeting in Louisville, Kentucky, the board reelected Turpin as circuit president, and Reevin was especially recognized for "keeping things moving smoothly" in the aftermath of the Chicago closure. The board promoted the belief that "1929 looks mighty good" with a new advertising campaign and plan for improved acts.[121] Yet in this same meeting long-standing member of the board E. S. Stone resigned and was replaced by African American Kentucky entrepreneur and esteemed physician Dr. J. A. C. Lattimore. Eastern Director Dudley, along with stockholders from Memphis and Birmingham, failed to attend.[122] The sparsely attended annual meeting said much more about the fraying state of the organization than the headlines of great meeting "success."

The stock market crash that marked the official beginning of the Great Depression economic disasters occurred between October 24 and October 29, 1929. T.O.B.A. did not immediately come to an end within the next month or even the next year of the Depression, but the effects of the financial downturn could not be avoided. Headlines critical of the circuit claimed the organization was the "laughing stock" of the country and that "actors and actresses" faced "starvation" as the public would not pay for "rotten shows."[123] By the 1929–30 season, the number of acts T.O.B.A. booked visibly decreased. Playbills moved from showcasing large tab shows, like the Silk Stocking Revue and the Mabel McGarr Company, alongside individual vaudeville acts in 1927, to highlighting smaller ensembles, like Butterbeans and Susie or Drake and Walker, alongside films by 1929.[124]

Additional evidence of economic decline can be found in the circuit's tax documents. In 1929, T.O.B.A. had a capital stock totaling $25,000, of which $13,300 or 133 shares had been issued. Those 133 shares represented approximately forty-four theaters that held the T.O.B.A. franchise.[125] In 1925 at least $18,200 of stock had been issued, which represented sixty T.O.B.A. franchised theaters, illustrating the decline in T.O.B.A. houses in just a four-year period. While Turpin was listed as president in the 1929 filing, there were no names listed for the board of directors, and the mission statement had been truncated to "booking theater plays."[126] Reevin reported just enough information to maintain the corporation's existence, and the robust and briefly thriving company that had been reported in 1925 documents was not seen in these new state filings. Corresponding summer newspaper reports echoed that in "all but a few places, the bottom seems to have fallen out of colored show business." The Southern route of T.O.B.A. was "shot to pieces," and even President Turpin's theater in St. Louis was only performing well enough to "keep the account on the right side of the ledger."[127] These reports were recorded months *before* the stock market crash and the official beginning of the Great Depression.

Board members' theater-related finances corroborate the tax documents. In 1928, S. H. Dudley began to shuffle his accounts amid the economic downturn. While Dudley's great wealth and social connection had been at the center of public scandal with his divorce petition in 1926, that wealth was not fixed. By 1929 T.O.B.A. was only a part of his overall business dealings, as he had a vast real estate portfolio. But a month before the crash Dudley began to borrow money from banks, friends, and business partners in an effort to bolster and maintain his theatrical enterprises. He took out a $3,000 loan from the Seventh Street Savings Bank and borrowed $1,500 from Henry G. Bergling.[128] Later as the Depression persisted, the *Pittsburgh Courier* even mistakenly reported that Dudley sold his Mid-City Theatre in Washington, DC, to a "white corporation."[129] These transactions illustrate that, although faring much better than average, T.O.B.A. spectators, even circuit management, braced for the worst with further economic setbacks on the horizon.

Although in these same years white Keith-Orpheum vaudeville houses evolved into Radio-Keith-Orpheum (RKO) Productions, Inc., "launching an era of electrical entertainment" in radio and film, the entire vaudeville industry faced a decline, and it was not entirely the fault of sound motion pictures, or the sparse diversity of playbill acts.[130] So serious were T.O.B.A.'s troubles that Sam Reevin left Chattanooga and traveled the circuit himself to determine why black entertainment audiences dwindled. Although Reevin did not address concerns of interracial leadership, after visiting Detroit, Indianapolis, Pittsburg, and several other cities, he determined the circuits' demise was "not due to poor shows." Rather, he revealed that poor theater attendance was "just a condition of where necessity comes ahead of luxury and amusements" amid economic decline. When black unemployment rose significantly during the Depression, T.O.B.A. followed the pattern of other institutions that relied on black consumers, like black insurance agencies or banks, and simply could not continue.[131]

A glimmer of hope for T.O.B.A. Time accompanied the semiannual stockholder meetings of February 1930. February's meeting lauded the new election of "three race men and one white man" as head of the circuit. Turpin was reelected president, S. H. Dudley was vice president, and Dr. J. A. C. Lattimore was secretary, with Reevin as treasurer and booking director. All the players in management were the same, yet this was the first time the president, vice president, and secretary were all African American.[132] William Nunn praised Reevin for his sincerity, honesty, and brutal frankness in stating that entire "show game" nationwide was "in crisis." Nunn also mistakenly believed that the talent and "inherent sense of race pride" among the remaining black T.O.B.A. members and musical producers would pull the organization through.[133] Black businesses often used race pride and solidarity as a rallying cry for black customers who might be tempted to patronize segregated white businesses, and race pride may have contributed to black audience members' continued interest in T.O.B.A. acts. Yet it was not enough to sustain longevity of the whole circuit. As a *Defender* headline plainly stated it, "folks were broke," and the last thing they had was money to spend on black vaudeville.[134]

Five months later, a 1931 retrospective of black entertainment remarked that, as national economic strife intensified, "business in the so-called Negro theaters was dull." The "old Howard" Theatre in Washington, DC, the "theater of the People" when it opened in 1910, was closed much of the 1930 season. With fewer venues to play and unstable contracts, troupers "scrapped this form of entertainment [vaudeville] for straight picture fare."[135] The organization was still officially listed as a corporation in 1931, but no tax filings can be located after 1930. At least forty theaters continued to hold the franchise through 1931, but many of the artists that had given life to T.O.B.A. stages eventually sought work beyond the circuit by the early 1930s.[136]

From 1926 through 1931, Toby Time withstood performer and management scandals, mismanagement woes, and the arrival of sound films. But it would be the menace of segregation during one of the worst economic disasters of the twentieth century that finally made theaters close and drop the T.O.B.A. franchise. Tellingly, one of the last official agency advertisements appeared in the twenty-fifth anniversary issue of the *Chicago Defender*'s entertainment page in May 1930. Amid Alberta Hunter advertisements and memorial tributes to the late Bert Williams, the "Greatest of All Our Stage Stars," was one more T.O.B.A. agency notice. It was a small advertisement declaring "T.O.B.A., Shows of All Kinds Wanted," without the fanfare or promise of multiple weeks of booking engagements that had been seen previously. Ironically, just across the page was a small column on Ethel Waters. The same T.O.B.A. star who had declared bankruptcy in 1928 was one of the "highest salaried women" of 1930 from her work in films, club appearances, and cabaret revues.[137] Although the circuit itself did not share this resiliency, "the sun would shine someday," as the artists and infrastructure that created T.O.B.A. Time persisted beyond black vaudeville and the Jazz Age.[138]

# EPILOGUE

## *T.O.B.A.'s Legacy*

I've seen it all my life in the show business, dancing marvelously, negro pianists originating haunting new songs and rhythms. As a showman dealing in talent, I've encountered ever so much that was extraordinary and fine in the gifts of our people.

—Clarence Muse as Dusty McClain in *Way Down South*

To know who you are and what you should be doing, you have to first know what your history is.

—August Wilson in *Ma Rainey's Black Bottom: A Legacy Brought to Screen*

*T.O.B.A. Time* has chronicled the 1920s journey of black vaudeville theater professionals who laid the foundations for hard-fought innovations in African American theater, dance, and music. In keeping with beliefs that history and the past must be known before one can understand the present or future, there has been a decided effort in recent years to memorialize the early-twentieth-century black entertainment environment with music tributes, documentaries, or feature films about artists like Bessie Smith, Count Basie, Sammy Davis Jr., or Ma Rainey. This study has been an effort to dispel the myths and gather the memories of T.O.B.A. Time to retrieve a history of black vaudeville and the Theater Owners' Booking Association's complicated fight for black autonomy in the American entertainment business in the early twentieth century.[1]

In the same decades that American laws and social customs sought to render African Americans as second-class citizens, T.O.B.A., organized by an interracial management company, allowed for a national transmission of African American entertainment into black-serving and black-owned theaters. The 1920s circuit was forged by black theater professionals who advanced racial uplift ideologies and believed that black business and theater ownership could equal racial progress and "overcome prejudice through accomplishments in art."[2]

Although many summaries of the circuit point to the racial tension and inequities in T.O.B.A.'s interracial management design, the circuit was not just a story of white management exploiting African American talent. T.O.B.A. was a "race" business that best functioned when African American entrepreneurs were included in its leadership. What began in the minds of African American and later white theater professionals evolved into a profitable corporation that centralized black vaudeville during the middle of the Jazz Age and the 1920s. When the circuit worked well it was often due in part to Sherman H. Dudley, a black theater professional who knew the business from the ground up and whom other artists, audiences, and theater managers trusted to have the best interests of black vaudeville at heart. But the institution also successfully functioned with the cooperation of a leader like Samuel Reevin, who, as a Russian Jewish immigrant, resisted national racial norms, was a skilled organizer, and from most accounts, treated black T.O.B.A. entertainers with respect. As a business, the circuit capitalized on its connection to a Southern market, grew from the strength of black consumers who participated in a segregated economy, and carefully used marketing and regional connections to reinforce that T.O.B.A. was the best circuit for "all companies and all acts" in order to develop a multimillion-dollar organization.

Although T.O.B.A. was indeed "tough" for artists, performing on the circuit strengthened the visibility, careers, and networks of black entertainers. Troupers contended with segregated travel, community critique, and gendered and racial hostility in order to obtain artistic education, travel, and earn incomes as performing artists. In turn, as jazz music and black social dances pervaded 1920s American popular culture and "record and roll sales girded the globe, bearing the voices" of black entertainers, it was these T.O.B.A. artists who captured the nation.[3] Despite fighting stereotypes of being buffoons, coons, or "wicked chorus girls" who transgressed the boundaries of respectability with their onstage material, many black vaudevillians fought for their places on the stage and joined entertainer unions to agitate for better physical and economic conditions. They were also powerful agents in transmitting black popular music culture to mass audiences through traveling theater performances, sheet music, and popular recorded music.[4]

Racial discrimination, segregation, and episodes of horrific racial violence greatly affected the entire circuit and only intensified in the 1920s, as exemplified by increased segregation statutes, the Tulsa Massacre, and the John Glover lynching at the Douglass Theatre. However, T.O.B.A. worked with regional press, transportation, and hospitality industries to try to mitigate racial strife. T.O.B.A. troupers disseminated black art and leisure across the country, while the institution forged business connections in black communities, brought the shows of major black urban centers to small towns, and furthered artistic and service industry employment opportunities for local African Americans. T.O.B.A. Time was the *only* time for many African American entertainers of the 1920s. Despite the internal and national factors that coincided with its end, black theater professionals off and onstage welcomed the opportunity to create a profitable business and share their talents in theaters that were "truly centers of black community life in the early twentieth century."[5]

The business of booking African American artists into black-serving venues did not end in 1931, and most of the T.O.B.A. board continued in entertainment management throughout the 1930s.[6] While some former T.O.B.A. theaters closed, others either independently booked acts or made the shift to motion pictures. Fortunately, audience members did not say farewell to many of their favorite acts, as several T.O.B.A. entertainers forged a path in black entertainment subsequent to the circuit's closing. Near the circuit's end some T.O.B.A. headliners worked in films, including Ethel Waters in *On With the Show,* Ernest "Sunshine Sammy" Morrison in the *Our Gang* shorts, and Clarence Muse in *Hearts of Dixie.* Even some blues queens ventured from T.O.B.A. Time to the screen like Bessie Smith did in the film short *St. Louis Blues* and Victoria Spivey in King Vidor's MGM film *Hallelujah* in 1929.[7] Circuit stars, including Bill Robinson and Hattie McDaniel, among others, rose to prominence in 1930s Hollywood films that, despite contested stereotypical images of black entertainers, offered African American men and women more entertainment employment opportunities in "distinct" and "visible" roles.[8] Vaudevillians, like Butterbeans and Susie or the Whitman Sisters, played formerly franchised theaters into the late 1930s. Other well-known stars, like Cab Calloway and others, garnered national and international acclaim on concert or Broadway stages, while lesser-known artists (the majority of T.O.B.A. entertainers) like dancers Leonard Reed and Bessie Dudley, who began this narrative, continued in cabarets, nightclubs, or were featured in motion picture shorts from the 1930s onward.

In the over one hundred years since the founding of the Theater Owners' Booking Association, at least three circuit theater buildings remain: the Howard Theatre in Washington, DC, the Walker Theatre (now the Madam Walker Legacy Center named for famed black hair care entrepreneur Madam C. J. Walker) in Indianapolis, and the Douglass Theatre in Macon. In the same way that T.O.B.A. theaters were often an anchor of 1920s black neighborhoods and "magnets for the entire community," these spaces showcase theatrical and musical entertainment and encourage patronage to black historic districts in their respective cities. The theaters' publicity packets acknowledge their historic origins as T.O.B.A. era sites. They also chronicle the difficulties in making these theaters viable and open

FIGURE 11. Howard Theatre, 2015 by Dhousch—
CC0, https://commons.wikimedia.org/w/index.php?curid=41870899.

FIGURE 12. Douglass Theatre, Macon, GA, 2014 (author's photos).

FIGURE 13. Walker Theatre, Indianapolis, IN, 2018 (author's photos).

spaces in some cases after years of neglect and racial discord in these urban black commercial centers. The Howard, Douglass, and Walker survived the closure of art spaces that came with the COVID-19 outbreak and, as late as 2022, were not only used for concerts or musical revues, but for private events, community programming, and arts education, similar to select T.O.B.A. theaters in the 1920s.[9]

While these theaters are some of the last physical reminders of T.O.B.A., perhaps the greater examples of the joy and humanity expressed by black vaudeville can be seen in entertainers' recollections. Former 1930s chorus dancer Alice Barker, who, when viewing retrieved footage of her own dancing film shorts in the 2010s, summarized that black vaudeville was simply "fabulous. It's absolutely fabulous to see and remember all these things that have happened." Lying in a nursing home bed, Barker bobbed her head and flashed a smile as she watched herself dance and reflected that she had been "paid to do something that I love doing," that she "would do for free, because it just felt so good doing it, because that music you know, I just get carried away in it . . ."[10] Although vaudeville as a genre and the Theater Owners' Booking Association as an entrepreneurial venture concluded in the 1930s, the legacy of the institution which S. H. Dudley argued "held sway longer than any colored booking organization ever organized," that "carried away" entrepreneurs, artists, and audiences, endures in the memories and narratives of T.O.B.A. Time.[11]

# APPENDIX

## *T.O.B.A. Circuit Theaters*

### T.O.B.A. Circuit Theaters, 1920–1931 by City

Listing compiled from circuit routings in *Chicago Defender* and *Baltimore Afro-American*; *Negro Year Book* (1922), *Official Theatrical World of Colored Artists Guide* (1928), and Eric Ledell Smith's *African American Theater Buildings* (2003).

# = Dudley Circuit
* = Black-Owned/Managed

| Location | Theater | Owner or Manager | Address | Date Joined |
|---|---|---|---|---|
| Alexandria, LA | Liberty | E. C. Holden / Tom Zantis | 821 Lee St. | 1921 |
| Asheville, NC | Eagle | Sam Reevin | 51 Eagle St. | |
| Atlanta, GA | 81 | Charles P. Bailey | 81 Decatur St. | |
| Atlanta, GA | Crystal | | | 1925 |
| Augusta, GA | Lenox | *J. A. Moffett | 1128 N Ninth St. | |
| Austin, TX | Lyric | E. H. Givens | 419 E Sixth St. | 1924 |
| Baltimore, MD | Lincoln | M. Flacks | 936 Pennsylvania Ave. | |
| Baltimore, MD | Regent | M. Horstein | 1627 Pennsylvania Ave. | |
| Baltimore, MD | Star | | 1531 E. Monument | |
| Baton Rouge, LA | Grand | Ernest Boehringer | 133 Liberty St. | |
| Beaumont, TX | Joyland | Lawrence Fontana | | |
| Beaumont, TX | Lincoln | Clemons Brothers | | 1921 |
| Bessemer, AL | Frolic | H. J. Hury / Ben Jaffe | 1916 First Ave. | 1928 |
| Birmingham, AL | Gay | H. J. Hury | 1722 N Fourth Ave. | 1921 |
| Birmingham, AL | Frolic | H. J. Hury | 312 N Eighteenth St. | |

| Location | Theater | Owner or Manager | Address | Date Joined |
|---|---|---|---|---|
| Birmingham, AL | Champion | Nathaniel Pressly | 306 N Eighteenth St. | |
| Charleston, SC | Milo | *J. J. Miller | 566 King St. | 1921 |
| Charleston, SC | Lincoln | *C. P. McClane | 601 King St. | |
| Charlotte, NC | Rex | S. W. Craver | | |
| Chattanooga, TN | Liberty | Sam Reevin | 310 E Ninth St. | 1921 |
| Chicago, IL | Monogram | H. B. Miller / Martin Klein | 3451 S State St. | 1921 |
| Chicago, IL | Grand | Martin Klein | 3110 S State St. | |
| Chicago, IL | Apollo | | 526 E Forty-Seventh St. | 1928 |
| Cincinnati, OH | Lyceum | *T. Spencer Finley / Lew Henry | | 1921 |
| Cincinnati, OH | Roosevelt | Jack Lustgarten | 425 Central Ave | |
| Cincinnati, OH | #Lincoln | *Lew Henry | 500 W Fifth St. | |
| Cleveland, OH | Temple | Bernard Bolansy | 2322 E Fifty-Fifth St. | |
| Cleveland, OH | Globe | M. B. Horowitz | 5217 Woodland Ave. | |
| Cleveland, OH | Grand Central | *O. T. Harris / Hyman Kaplan | 3543 Central Ave. | 1921 |
| Columbia, SC | Royal | H. W. Tolbutt | 1010 Washington | 1921 |
| Columbus, GA | Dream | G. S. Love | 1026 First Ave. | 1922 |
| Columbus, OH | #Dunbar | *J. A. Jackson | | |
| Columbus, OH | Pythian | Henry F. Eger | | |
| Dallas, TX | Ella B. Moore | *Chinz Moore / Ella B. Moore | 428 N Central Ave. | |
| Dallas, TX | Belmont | E. L. Cummings | 107 N Baylen | |
| Dallas, TX | Park | *Chinz Moore / Ella B. Moore | 424 Central | 1921 |
| Danville, VA | Hippodrome | James Henry / W. A. Donleavy | 215 N Union St. | 1922 |
| Dayton, OH | Palace | Lloyd H. Cox | 1125 W Fifth St. | 1927 |
| Detroit, MI | #Koppin | H. S. Koppin / Martin Klein | 528 Gratiot Ave. | |
| Detroit, MI | #Vaudette | *E. B. Dudley | 674 Gratiot Ave. | 1921 |
| Detroit, MI | Avenue | | | |
| Durham, NC | Wonderland | *F. K. Watkins / G. W. Logan | 418–422 Pettigrew St. | 1922 |
| East St. Louis, IL | Lincoln | Harry Hershenson | | |
| Ensley, AL | Palace | Milton Starr | 1810 D Ave. | 1926 |

| Location | Theater | Owner or Manager | Address | Date Joined |
|---|---|---|---|---|
| Gadsden, AL | Baker | | | |
| Galveston, TX | Lincoln | *Lee & Moore | 413–415 Twenty-Fifth St. | 1921 |
| Galveston, TX | Rialto | A. Martini | | |
| Gary, IN | Broadway | G. B. Young | 1678 Broadway | |
| Greensboro, NC | Palace | Charles Roth | | |
| Greenville, SC | Liberty | | | |
| Hot Springs, AK | Gem | | | |
| Hot Springs, AK | Truman | | | |
| Hot Springs, AK | Vendome | | 423 Malvern Ave. | |
| Houston, TX | American Theater | *C. H. Caffey | 609–11 San Felipe St. | 1921 |
| Houston, TX | Washington | Paul Barracco | 2711 Odin Ave. | |
| Houston, TX | Best | | 212 Main St. | |
| Indianapolis, IN | Washington | *Esmerelda S. Stone | 521 Indiana Ave. | |
| Indianapolis, IN | Walker | *Charles B. Erwin | 603–607 Indiana Ave. | 1927 |
| Jackson, MS | Lyric | | | 1921 |
| Jackson, TN | Gem | E. L. Drake | | |
| Jacksonville, FL | Strand | *W. J. Stiles | | 1921 |
| Kansas City, MO | New Rialto | | | |
| Kansas City, MO | Lincoln | Rubin Finklestein | | 1923 |
| Knoxville, TN | Gem | M. C. Kennedy | 102 E Vine | |
| LaGrange, GA | Strand | M. C. Kennedy | | |
| Little Rock, AK | Plaza | M. A. Lightman | | 1921 |
| Louisville, KY | Lincoln | *William Warley/ J. A. C. Lattimore | 914 W Walnut | 1921 |
| Macon, GA | Douglass | *Charles Douglass | | 1921 |
| Memphis, TN | Palace | A. Barrasso | 324–331 Beale St. | 1922 |
| Middletown, OH | Regal | | | 1929 |
| Mobile, AL | Pike | C. B. King | 256 Davis Ave. | 1922 |
| Monroe, LA | Liberty | | | |
| Montgomery, AL | Majestic | Bodreaux, Bennett, Gordon | 212 Bibb St. | 1921 |
| Muskogee, OK | Dreamland | *Loula T. Williams | | 1921 |
| Nashville, TN | Bijou | Milton Starr | 423 N Fourth Ave. | 1922 |
| New Bern, NC | Globe | E. L. Lewis | | 1921 |
| New Orleans, LA | Dauphene | | | |

| Location | Theater | Owner or Manager | Address | Date Joined |
|---|---|---|---|---|
| New Orleans, LA | Lyric | Morris Bordreaux / Clarence Bennett | 201 Burgundy St. | 1921 |
| Newport News, VA | Lincoln | | Twentieth St. and Jefferson Ave. | |
| Newport News, VA | Colonial | | 1414 Wanule Ave. | 1922 |
| Norfolk, VA | Palace | | 830 Church St. | |
| Oklahoma City, OK | Aldridge | *Zelia Breaux | 303–305 Second St. NE | 1921 |
| Okmulgee, OK | Dreamland | *Loula T. Williams | | |
| Pensacola, FL | Belmont | E. L. Cummings | 115 E Belmont St. | 1922 |
| Petersburg, VA | #S. H. Dudley | *S. H. Dudley | 109 Harrison St. | 1922 |
| Philadelphia, PA | New Standard | *John T. Gibson | 1124 South St. | |
| Philadelphia, PA | Dunbar | *John T. Gibson | Lombard & Broad St. | |
| Pittsburgh, PA | #Star | H. Tennebaum / *Charles Stinson | 1417 Wylie Ave. | 1922 |
| Pittsburgh, PA | Elmore | Ben Engleberg | 2312 Centre St. | 1929 |
| Pittsburgh, PA | Lando | Willliam Lando | | 1930 |
| Port Arthur, TX | Dreamland | Lawrence Fontana | | |
| Springfield, OH | Booker T. Washington | C. S. Olinger | 541 Fair St. | |
| Springfield, OH | Lincoln | *J. W. Hamilton | 618 S Center St. | |
| Savannah, GA | Pekin | *W. J. Stiles / A. G Monroe | 625 S Broad St. | 1921 |
| Shreveport, LA | Star | Charles Gordon | 1045 Texas Ave. | 1921 |
| St. Louis, MO | Booker T. Washington | *Charles Turpin | 2248 Market St. | 1921 |
| Tampa, FL | Palace | | Tampa & Zack St. | 1922 |
| Tulsa, OK | Dreamland | *Loula T. Williams | 133 N Greenwood St. | 1921 |
| Waco, TX | Gaiety | W. H. Leonard | 117 Bridge St. | 1921 |
| Washington, DC | #Blue Mouse | *Sherman Dudley | 2819 Twenty-Sixth St. NW | |
| Washington, DC | #Howard | *Andrew J. Thomas / Thomas Brothers | 626 T St. NW | 1922 |
| Washington, DC | #Dudley Theater (Minnehaha) | *Sherman Dudley | 1213 U St. | 1922 |

| Location | Theater | Owner or Manager | Address | Date Joined |
|---|---|---|---|---|
| Washington, DC | #Foraker | *Sherman Dudley, Raymond Murray, Rufus Byars | 1122 Twentieth St. NW | 1922 |
| Washington, DC | # Mid-City | *Sherman Dudley | 1223 Seventh Ave. NW | 1922 |
| Washington, DC | Rosalia | | 218–20 F Ave. SW | |
| Washington, DC | Strand | Ira Lamont | 5129–5131 Grant St. NE | |
| Wilmington, NC | Brooklyn | J. Wheeler | | 1921 |
| Winston-Salem, NC | New Lincoln | *William Scales | 311 Church St. | |
| Winston-Salem, NC | Lafayette | *William Scales | | 1921 |
| Winston-Salem, NC | Dunbar | R. A. Bottom | | |

# NOTES

## INTRODUCTION

1. Bessie Dudley interview by Robert O'Meally, June 29, 1992, Jazz Oral History Collection Program, Archives Center, National Museum of American History; Monroe N. Work, ed. *Negro Year Book: An Annual Encyclopedia of the Negro, 1922* (Tuskegee, AL: Negro Year Book Publishing Company, 1922), 303; "Black-serving" refers to institutions predominantly designed for the service and use of African American consumers. Note on terminology: "African American" and "black" are used interchangeably throughout the text. When quoting primary sources, I use the terms black people used to define themselves: "colored," "Negro," or members of the "Race."

2. W. C. Handy, "Careless Love," Pace and Handy Records, 1921; Alberta Hunter and Lovie Austin, "Downhearted Blues," 1922.

3. While author F. Scott Fitzgerald is often mistakenly credited with being the first to refer to 1920s America as the "Jazz Age" in 1922, the term also arose independently in black periodicals. I use "Jazz Age America" to refer to the contradictory era of the 1920s and early '30s when the popularity of African-American-based jazz music was on the rise at the same time the creators of this musical and cultural genre were being persecuted for their racial identity. The Jazz Age is intertwined with the Harlem Renaissance, Prohibition, and the New Negro era between 1919 and the early 1930s. Lucy Moore, *Anything Goes: A Biography of the Roaring Twenties* (Overlook, 2010), 66–67; "The Shimmy and the Jazz," *Afro American*, February 14, 1919.

4. Leonard Reed interview by Rusty Frank in 1993, Jazz Oral History Collection Program, Archives Center, National Museum of American History.

5. January–May 1902 Manager's Report Book, Tony Pastor Collection, Harry Ransom Center, University of Texas at Austin; Scrapbook, Billings-Merriam Family Vaudeville Scrapbooks, 1890–1913, Archives Center, National Museum of America History.

6. Anthony Slide, *Encyclopedia of Vaudeville* (Jackson, MS: University of Mississippi Press, 2012) xiv; Robert W. Snyder, *A Voice of the City: Vaudeville and Popular Culture in New York* (New York: Oxford University Press, 1989), xiii; Lawrence Levine, *Highbrow/Lowbrow: The Emergence of a Cultural Hierarchy in America* (Cambridge, MA: Harvard University Press, 1990), 77.

7. Proctors Theatre Handbill, 1896, Vaudeville Collection, Warshaw Collection of Business Americana, Archives Center, Smithsonian Museum of National American History.

8. Snyder, xv; Gillian M. Rodger, *Champagne Charlie and Pretty Jemima: Variety Theater in the Nineteenth Century* (Urbana: University of Illinois Press, 2010), 191–92.

9. Review of "Rollin' on the TOBA, A Tribute to the Last Days of Black Vaudeville," Playbill of *Bubbling Brown Sugar*, March 1976, http://www.playbill.com/production/bubbling-brown-sugar-anta-playhouse-vault-0000005259; "Review Roundup: Shuffle Along Opens on Broadway—All the Reviews!," BroadwayWorld.com, April 28, 2016; David Krasner, *Beautiful Pageant: African American Theatre, Drama and Performance in the Harlem Renaissance* (New York: Palgrave Macmillan, 2002), 240–49.

10. Peg Leg Bates by Rusty Frank, April 4, 1993, New York, Jazz Oral Histories Project, Archives Center, National Museum of American History; 1920s black vaudevillians more often used "Toby or T.O.B.A. Time" to describe the institution, rather than the "chitlin circuit." "Chitlins" or "chitterlings" are a black soul food staple that were often served in juke joints and clubs. Mid-to-late-twentieth-century urban theater productions also used "chitlin circuit" to describe the small, second-tier venues that showcased these predominantly black musicals and plays; Preston Lauterbach, *The Chitlin' Circuit and the Road to Rock 'n' Roll,* (W. W. Norton, 2011); Mel Watkins, *On the Real Side: A History of African American Comedy from Slavery to Chris Rock* (Chicago, IL: Chicago Review Press, 1999), 365.

11. Errol Hill, "Black Theatre in Form and Style," *The Black Scholar*, Vol. 10, No. 10 (July/August 1979), 29–31; Errol Hill, "Remarks on Black Theater History," *The Massachusetts Review*, Vol. 28, No. 4 (Winter 1987), 609–14; Nellie McKay, "Black Theater and Drama in the 1920s: Years of Growing Pains," *The Massachusetts Review*, Vol. 28, No. 4 (Winter 1987), 615–26; Allen Woll, *Black Musical Theater: From Coon Town to Dreamgirls* (Baton Rouge: Louisiana State University Press, 1989); Thomas Lawrence Riis, "Pink Morton's Theater, Black Vaudeville, the TOBA: Recovering the History, 1910–1930," in Josephine Wright, ed., *New Perspectives on Music: Essays in Honor of Eileen Southern* (Warren, MI: Harmonie Park Press, 1992); Henry Louis Gates Jr., "The Chitlin Circuit," in Harry J. Elam Jr. and David Krasner, *African American Performance and Theater History: A Critical Reader* (New York: Oxford University Press, 2001); David Krasner, *Beautiful Pageant: African American Theatre, Drama and Performance in the Harlem Renaissance* (New York: Palgrave Macmillan, 2002); Karen Sotiropoulos, *Staging Race: Black Performers in the Turn of the Century America* (Cambridge, MA: Harvard University Press, 2006); Camille F. Forbes, *Introducing Bert Williams: Burnt Cork, Broadway and the Story of America's First Black Star* (New York: Basic Civitas, 2008); Thomas Bauman, *The Pekin: The Rise and Fall of Chicago's First Black-Owned Theater* (Urbana: University of Illinois, 2014); Nadine George Graves, "Spreading the Sand: Understanding the Economic and Creative Impetus for the Black Vaudeville Industry," *Continuum: The Journal of African Diaspora Drama, Theatre and Performance*, Vol. 1, No. 1 (June 2014);

Henry Miller, "Valorizing Ancestor Discourse: Harlem Renaissance Criticism and Theatre Theory," *Continuum: The Journal of African Diaspora Drama, Theatre and Performance* Vol. 2, No. 2 (March 2016).

12. Nadine George-Graves, *The Royalty of Negro Vaudeville: The Whitman Sisters and the Negotiation of Race, Gender, and Class in African American Theater, 1900–1940* (New York: Palgrave Macmillan, 2000); Brenda Dixon Gottschild, *Waltzing in the Dark: African American Vaudeville and Race Politics in the Swing Era* (New York: Palgrave McMillan, 2002); Davarian L. Baldwin, *Chicago's New Negroes: Modernity, the Great Migration, and Black Urban Life* (Chapel Hill: University of North Carolina Press, 2007); Henry Sampson, *Blacks in Blackface: A Sourcebook on Early Black Musical Shows* (Lanham, MD: Scarecrow Press, 1980, 2013); Lynn Abbott and Doug Seroff, *The Original Blues: The Emergence of Blues in African American Vaudeville* (Jackson: University of Mississippi, 2017).

13. Errol G. Hill and James V. Hatch, *A History of African American Theatre* (New York: Cambridge Press, 2003), 206–8.

14. "Time" refers to the period of being a contracted T.O.B.A. employee. A performer could be on Dudley Time, Keith-Orpheum Time, etc.

15. C. A. Leonard, "Our Stage History, Almost Forgotten, Is Well Worth Knowing and Being Proud Of," *Chicago Defender*, August 10, 1929.

16. Ann Douglas, *Terrible Honesty: Mongrel Manhattan in the 1920s* (New York: Farrar, Straus and Giroux, 1995), 5–9; Baldwin, *Chicago's New Negroes*, 19.

17. Juliet E. K. Walker, *History of Black Business in America: Capitalism, Race, Entrepreneurship* (New York: Twayne Publishers, 1998), 183.

18. W. E. B. Du Bois, *The Negro in Business: Proceedings for the Fourth Conference for the Study of Negro Problems* (Atlanta, GA: Atlanta University, 1899), 5.

19. Booker T. Washington, *The Negro in Business* (Ohio: Hertel, Jenkins & Co., 1907), 18–19.

20. Shennette Garrett-Scott, *Banking on Freedom: Black Women in U.S. Finance Before the New Deal* (New York: Columbia University Press, 2019), 68–69; Other black women reformers believed that "colored women" and their "fine" business aptitudes should be in equal partnerships with their male counterparts. Fannie Barrier Williams, "The Woman's Part in a Man's Business," *Voice of the Negro* Vol. 1, No. 11 (1904), 546.

21. Rayford Logan, *The Negro in American Life and Thought: The Nadir, 1877–1901* (New York: Dial Press, 1954).

22. Walker, 183–84; Roberta Newman and Joel Nathan Rosen, *Black Baseball, Black Business: Race Enterprise and the Fate of the Segregated Dollar* (Jackson: University of Mississippi Press, 2014), 10–14.

23. Walker, xxiii–xxvi; Robert E. Weems and Jason Chambers, *Building the Black Metropolis: African American Entrepreneurship in Chicago* (Urbana: University of Illinois, 2017), 2–5.

24. Tim Owsley, "Show Business," *Defender*, June 25, 1927.

25. Weems & Chambers, 5–6.

26. The Harlem Renaissance was an era between 1920 and the mid-1930s of increased production of black literature, art, and music with the goal that black artistic production would disprove theories of black inferiority. Nathan Irvin Huggins, *Harlem Renaissance*

(New York: Oxford University Press, 1971); David Levering Lewis, *When Harlem Was in Vogue* (New York: Alfred A, Knopf, 1981).

27. W. E. B. Du Bois, "Opinion: Negro Art," *The Crisis*, June 1921, 55; Alain Locke, *The New Negro* (New York: Albert & Charles Boni, Inc., 1925); James Weldon Johnson, "Race Prejudice and the Negro Artist," 1928, quoted in Henry Louis Gates and Gene Andrew Jarrett, *The New Negro: Readings on Race, Representation and African American Culture, 1892–1938* (Princeton, NJ; Princeton University Press, 2007).

28. Locke, *The New Negro*, 349–50; James Weldon Johnson, *Black Manhattan* (New York: Alfred. A. Knopf, 1930), 186–88, 284.

29. Theophilus Lewis, "Survey of Negro Theatre III," *The Messenger*, October 1926; Langston Hughes, "The Negro Artist and the Racial Mountain," *The Nation* Vol. 122, No. 318, 693.

30. Hughes, 692–94.

31. Brothers Fayard and Harold Nicholas were child dance stars who developed their careers on the circuit in the late 1920s and early 1930s. Columbus, Georgia–born Gertrude "Ma Rainey" Pridgett was a vaudevillian and blues music star who began her career at the turn of the twentieth century. Her powerful voice and veteran status earned her the title "Mother of the Blues." Michael Martin, dir. *The Nicholas Brothers: We Sing and We Dance*, A&E Productions, 1992; Sandra R Lieb, *Mother of the Blues: A Study of Ma Rainey* (Amherst: University of Massachusetts Press, 1981).

32. W. Fitzhugh Brundage, ed., *Beyond Blackface: African Americans and the Creation of Popular Culture, 1890–1930* (Chapel Hill: University of North Carolina Press, 2011), 36; Davarian Baldwin, "Our Newcomers to the City: The Great Migration and the Making of Modern Mass Culture," in Brundage, 163.

33. LeRoy Ashby, *With Amusement for All: A History of American Popular Culture Since 1930* (Lexington: University Press of Kentucky, 2006), xxxv–xxxviii; Gillian M. Rodger, *Champagne Charlie and Pretty Jemima: Variety Theater in the Nineteenth Century* (Urbana: University of Illinois Press, 2010); Richard Butsch, *The Making of American Audiences: From Stage to Television, 1750–1990* (Cambridge, UK: Cambridge University Press, 2000); Lawrence W. Levine, "The Folklore of Industrial Society: Popular Culture and Its Audiences," *The American Historical Review*, Vol. 97, No. 5 (December 1992), 1369–99; Charles W. Stein, ed., *Vaudeville as Seen by Its Contemporaries* (New York: Alfred A. Knopf, 1984), xii–xiii.

34. Bessie Dudley interview by Robert O' Meally.

35. Rodger, 5.

36. Angel David Nieves and Leslie M. Alexander, eds., *We Shall Independent Be: African American Place Making and the Struggle to Claim Space in the United States* (Boulder: University of Colorado, 2008), 3–6.

37. Baldwin, *Chicago's New Negroes*, 5; Graves, "Spreading the Sand," 7.

38. Matthew Whittaker, *Race Work: The Rise of Civil Rights in the Urban West* (Lincoln: University of Nebraska Press, 2007), 3; Brundage, ed., *Beyond Blackface*, 2011; Lawrence Schenbeck, *Racial Uplift and American Music, 1878–1943* (Jackson: University of Mississippi Press, 2014).

39. W. E. B. Du Bois, "Krigwa Players Little Negro Theatre," *The Crisis*, Vol. 32, July 1926, 134–36.

40. Robert Weems, *Desegregating the Dollar; African American Consumerism in the Twentieth Century* (New York: New York University Press, 1998); Newman and Rosen, *Black Baseball, Black Business*, 2014.

41. Daphne Duval Harrison, *Black Pearls: Blues Queens of the 1920s* (New Brunswick, NJ: Rutgers University Press, 1988); Victoria W. Wolcott, *Remaking Respectability, African American Women in Interwar Detroit* (Chapel Hill: University of North Carolina Press, 2001); Sadiya Hartman, *Wayward Lives, Beautiful Experiments: Intimate Histories of Social Upheaval* (New York: W.W. Norton, 2019).

## CHAPTER 1. "WHISTLING COONS" NO MORE

1. S. H. Dudley, "From the Pen of S.H. Dudley," *Freeman*, December 15, 1906.

2. Ibid.

3. Ibid.

4. W. Fitzhugh Brundage, ed., *Beyond Blackface: African Americans and the Creation of Popular Culture, 1890–1930* (Chapel Hill: University of North Carolina Press, 2011), 2.

5. Nadine George Graves, "Spreading the Sand: Understanding the Economic and Creative Impetus for the Black Vaudeville Industry," *Continuum: The Journal of African Diaspora Drama, Theatre and Performance*, Vol. 1, No. 1 (June 2014), 13.

6. Annette Gordon-Reed, "Writing Early American Lives as Biography," *The William and Mary Quarterly*, Vol. 71, No. 4 (October 2014), 506–7; Lois W. Banner, "Biography as History," *The American Historical Review*, Vol. 114, No. 3 (June 2009), 581–82; Nick Salvatore, "Biography and Social History: An Intimate Relationship," *Labour History*, No. 87 (November 2004), 189–90.

7. Lawrence Schenbeck, *Racial Uplift and American Music, 1878–1943* (Jackson: University of Mississippi Press, 2012) 3–6; Kevin Gaines, *Uplifting the Race: Black Leadership, Politics, and Culture in the Twentieth Century* (Chapel Hill: University of North Carolina Press, 1996); Davarian Baldwin, "Our Newcomers to the City: The Great Migration and the Making of Modern Mass Culture," in Brundage, 171–73.

8. Gillian M. Rodger, *Champagne Charlie and Pretty Jemima: Variety Theater in the Nineteenth Century* (Urbana: University of Illinois Press, 2010), 5–7.

9. Joe Laurie Jr., *Vaudeville: From the Honky-Tonks to the Palace* (New York: Kennikat Press, 1972), 333–34; Robert M. Lewis, ed., *From Traveling Show to Vaudeville* (Baltimore, MD: Johns Hopkins University Press, 2003), 315–16.

10. "In Vaudeville: A Short History of This Popular Amusement," *Midway* (October 1905), 27; in Lewis, 321.

11. Lewis, 316–17; Forms of Variety Theater, http://memory.loc.gov/ammem/vshtml/vsforms.html, accessed October 3, 2012.

12. Pastor's Theater Handbill, 1879; Proctor's Theater Program, 1896 Warshaw Collection of Business Americana, Theater, Archives Center, National Museum of American History, Box 7, fldr 4; Laurie, 60–65.

13. "Promises in Vaudeville," *New York Times*, September 17, 1911.

14. Arthur Frank Wertheim, *Vaudeville Wars: How Keith-Albee and Orpheum Circuits Controlled the Big-Time and Its Performers* (New York: Palgrave Macmillan, 2009), 117–26; Robert W. Snyder, *The Voice of the City* (New York: Oxford University Press, 1989), 35–36.

15. Robert Grau, *Forty Years Observation of Music and Drama* (New York: Broadway Publishing Company, 1909), 14.

16. Arthur Frank Wertheim, *Vaudeville Wars: How Keith-Albee and Orpheum Circuits Controlled the Big-Time and Its Performers* (New York: Palgrave Macmillan, 2009), 172–73.

17. Salary List, American Vaudeville Circuit Inc., June-July 1914 in Vaudeville Series, Warshaw Collection of Business Americana, Archives Center, National Museum of America History.

18. Michael John Haupert, *The Entertainment Industry* (Westport, CT: Greenwood Press, 2006), 40; Brian Duryea, "Vaudeville: Where the Acts Come From, Why They Come, and What They Get for Coming," *Green Book Magazine*, July 1915, 547–48.

19. Leroy Ashby, *With Amusement for All: A History of American Popular Culture Since 1830* (Lexington: University of Kentucky Press, 2012), 121–25; Snyder, 43–44.

20. "King Rastus," *Virginian Pilot*, September 16, 1900.

21. Brian Duryea, "Vaudeville," 551–52.

22. Manager's Report Book, 1902, Tony Pastor Collection, Ransom Center, University of Texas at Austin; Proctor's Theater Program, Warshaw Collection of Business Americana, Theater, Archives Center, National Museum of American History, Box 7, fldr 4.

23. Manager's Report Book, 1902, Tony Pastor Collection, Ransom Center, University of Texas at Austin.

24. Larry Eugene Rivers and Canter Brown Jr., "The Art of Gathering a Crowd: Florida's Pat Chapelle and the Origins of Black-Owned Vaudeville," *The Journal of African American History*, Vol. 92, No. 2 (Spring 2007), 176–77; "Robert T. Motts, Owner and Manager of the Pekin Theater," *The Broad Ax*, July 15, 1911; One of the earliest African American-owned theaters was New York City's African Grove Theatre, which opened in 1821. Marvin McAllister, *White People Do Not Know How to Behave at Entertainments Designed for Ladies and Gentlemen of Colour: William Brown's African and American Theater* (Chapel Hill: University of North Carolina Press, 2002).

25. "Chicago to Have a Colored Theater," *Freeman*, August 3, 1901.

26. Thomas Bauman, *The Pekin: The Rise and Fall of Chicago's First Black-Owned Theater* (Urbana: University of Illinois Press, 2014), 16–17; "The Opening of the New Pekin Theatre," *Broad Ax*, March 24, 1906; "The New Pekin" *Cleveland Gazette*, April 7, 1906.

27. Bauman, 35, 42.

28. "The Profession in Chicago—Whose Who Along the Stroll," *Freeman*, July 9, 1910; Miller and Lyles were future authors of *Shuffle Along*, one of the longest-running early black Broadway musicals in the 1920s. David Krasner, *Beautiful Pageant: African American Theatre, Drama and Performance in the Harlem Renaissance* (New York: Palgrave Macmillan, 2002), 240–49.

29. Advertisements, *Broad Ax*, March 24, 1906; Bauman, 41.

30. Carle Browne Cooke, "Opening of the New Pekin," *Freeman*, April 14, 1906; *Lakeside Directory of Chicago*, 1910, 1736–37.

31. Bauman, 28–29, 46–47; Jacqueline Najuma Stewart, *Migrating to the Movies: Cinema and Black Urban Modernity* (Berkeley: University of California Press, 2005), 155–58; Paula Giddings, *Ida: A Sword Among Lions* (New York: Harper Collins, 2008), 456–57.

32. Bauman 153–54.

33. In 1900, the African American population in the United States totaled 8,803,535 people, of which 7,885,824 lived in the South Atlantic and the South Division. See *Statistical Abstract of the United States, 1901* (Washington, DC: Government Printing Office, 1902), 3–8.

34. C. L. Carrell to LaRell Trio, October 19, 1919, Falcon Vaudeville Trion Collection, Archives Center, NMAH; George's and Harts's Up to Date Scrapbook, Archives Center, NMAH.

35. Athelia Knight, "Sherman H. Dudley: He Paved the Way for the T. O. B. A.," *The Black Perspective in Music,* Vol. 15, No. 2 (Autumn 1987), 153–81.

36. Advertisement for the Dudley Circuit, *Freeman,* March 1912; R.W. Thompson, "Dudley in the Spotlight: Snapshot of the Premier Comedian of the Smart Set," *Freeman,* February 9, 1907.

37. 1880 Federal Census, Bossier, Louisiana, Roll 448, p 10D, 011.

38. Advertisement for the Dudley Circuit, *Indianapolis Freeman,* March 1912; Jean Baptiste Adoue, https://www.tshaonline.org/handbook/online/articles/fad14, accessed September 12, 2014; *Morrison and Fourmy's General Directory of the City of Dallas, Morrison and Fourmy's General Directory of the City of Galveston,* 1888–98.

39. "Remember the Mule: S.H. Dudley Dies at 66," *Pittsburgh Courier,* March 16, 1940; "S.H. Dudley," *The Messenger,* January 1925, 50.

40. Composite of Advertisements for Kickapoo Indian Sagwa, Indian Cough Cure, and German Liver Syrup in *Hopkinsville Kentuckian,* July 24, 1896; *Louisiana Democrat,* May 14, 1890; and *Worthington Advance,* March 27, 1890.

41. Mary Calhoun, *Medicine Show: Conning People and Making Them Like It* (New York: Harper and Row, 1976), 48–49.

42. History of Federal Food and Drugs Act of 1906, https://www.fda.gov/about-fda/das-evolving-regulatory-powers/part-i-1906-food-and-drugs-act-and-its-enforcement, accessed September 29, 2020.

43. Calhoun, 2–3; William H. Helfand, "Ephemera of the American Medicine Show," *Pharmacy in History,* Vol. 27, No. 4 (1985), 183–91.

44. Calhoun, 2–3; Athelia Knight, "He Paved the Way for the TOBA," 157.

45. *Morrison and Fourmy's General Directory of the City of Houston,* 1895, 146; *Morrison and Fourmy's General Directory of the City of Galveston,* 1899.

46. Frank Dumont, "The Golden Days of Minstrelsy," *New York Clipper,* December 12, 1914 in William L. Slout, *Burnt Cork and Tambourines: A Source Book for Negro Minstrelsy* (San Bernardino, CA: Borgo Press, 2007), 203.

47. Eric Lott, "Blackface and Blackness: The Minstrel Show in American Culture," in Annamarie Bean, et al., *Inside the Minstrel Mask: Readings in Nineteenth-Century Blackface Minstrelsy* (Hanover, NH: Wesleyan University Press, 1996), 18–27. Minstrelsy's origins and uses have been widely debated in such works as Robert Toll, *Blacking Up: The Minstrel Show in Nineteenth Century America* (New York: Oxford University Press, 1977); Eric Lott, *Love and Theft: Blackface Minstrelsy and the American Working Class* (New York: Oxford University Press, 1995); Annamarie Bean, et al., *Inside the Minstrel Mask: Readings in Nineteenth-Century Blackface Minstrelsy* (Hanover, NH: Wesleyan University Press, 1996); Dale Cockrell, *Demons*

*of Disorder: Early Blackface Minstrels and Their World* (Cambridge: Cambridge University Press, 1997); W. T. Lhamon Jr., *Raising Cain: Blackface Performance from Jim Crow to Hip Hop* (Cambridge, MA: Harvard University Press, 1998); Stephen Johnson, ed., *Burnt Cork: Traditions and Legacies of Blackface Minstrelsy* (Amherst: University of Massachusetts Press, 2012); Christopher Smith's *The Creolization of American Culture: William Sidney Mount and the Roots of Blackface Minstrelsy* (Urbana: University of Illinois, 2013); and Brian Roberts, *Blackface Nation: Race, Reform, and Identity in American Popular Music, 1812–1925* (Chicago: University of Chicago Press, 2017).

48. Bean, et al., *Inside the Minstrel Mask*, xiii-xiv.

49. Toll, *Blacking Up*, 198–99.

50. James Bland ad, 1864, Warshaw Collection of Business Americana, Archives Center, National Museum of American History, Smithsonian Institution, Theater, b11, f 48.

51. W. C. Handy, *Father of the Blues: An Autobiography* (New York: DeCapo Press, 1941), 34.

52. Handy, *Father of the Blues*, 33. Eileen Southern, *The Music of Black Americans: A History*, third edition (New York: W.W. Norton, 1997), 223–96.

53. *Freeman*, December 18, 1897; "Dudley's Georgia Minstrels," *Houston Daily Post*, January 4, 1897; "Georgia" in the troupe's title did not reveal its geographic or cultural origin, rather it was used to allude to a minstrel team of actual black performers. Being a "Georgia" was to have supposed connection to the "authentic" roots of blackface minstrelsy, and it had been used as a title as early as 1865 in Brooker and Clayton's Georgia Minstrels. See Toll, *Blacking Up*, 199, 276.

54. 1898 was the first full year Dudley joined a traveling group based outside of Texas. This also coincides with the last year his mother Margaret Dudley appeared in the Texas city directories. She is not listed in the 1900 federal census, which strongly suggests that she died in 1898 and S. H. left, no longer partly financially responsible for his mother's welfare.

55. "P.T. Wright," *Freeman*, December 18, 1897; R. W. Thompson, "Dudley in the Spotlight: Snapshot of the Premier Comedian of the Smart Set," *Freeman*, February 9, 1907.

56. *Indianapolis Freeman* via the *Iowa State Bystander*, January 28, 1898. Bernard Peterson, *The African American Theatre Directory, 1816–1960: A Comprehensive Guide to Early Black Theatre Organizations, Companies, Theatres, and Performing Groups* (Santa Barbara, CA: Greenwood Press, 1997), 143.

57. R. W. Thompson, "Dudley in the Spotlight: Snapshot of the Premier Comedian of the Smart Set," *Freeman*, February 9, 1907.

58. "The Stage," *Freeman*, November 7, 1903.

59. For more details and an analysis of the tragic Wright case, see the forthcoming article by Michelle R. Scott, "Good Business in Missouri: Violence, Minstrelsy, and the Case of Louis Wright," *Journal of African American History*, Fall 2022; Richards and Pringle's Famous Georgia Minstrels was a "colored" minstrel group active between 1880 and 1910. Owned by white O. E. Richards and Charles W. Pringle, the company employed 150 people in two separate companies, had six different bands, and traveled in six private Pullman rail cars. After a winter performance in New Madrid, Missouri, in 1902, town sheriffs arrested the entire costumed Georgia Minstrels troupe for alleged violent preperformance behavior and

supposedly shooting upon the crowd. The Wright case filled black press pages in 1902, and Dudley became the troupe's stage manager in October 1902. "The Stage," *Freeman*, October 25, 1902; Letterhead from Richards and Pringles, Rusco and Holland's *Big Minstrel Festival*, December 1, 1899; Minstrel Collections, Ransom Center; "Negro Minstrel Lynched," *New York Sun*, February 18, 1902; "Riot in Theater Leads to Lynching of Negro Minstrels," *St. Louis Republic*, February 18, 1902; "Missouri Mob Lynches Louis F. Wright, of Chicago," *Broad Ax*, February 22, 1902; "The Stage," *Freeman*, March 8, 1902; Flournoy E. Miller "My First Fifty Years," n. p. in the Flournoy Miller Collection, MARBL, Emory University.

60. "Miss Alberta H. Ormes," *Freeman*, October 18, 1902.

61. "The Stage," *Freeman*, August 25, 1900; "At the Theaters," *Baltimore Sunday Herald*, September 8, 1895; Isham was a producer of shows, such as 1895's *Octoroons* and 1897's *Oriental America*, light operatic revues that predated black musicals and highlighted the "exotic" draw of fair-skinned African American women. For greater discussion on Isham's practice of placing fair-skinned black women in his productions, see Jayna Brown, *Babylon Girls: Black Women Performers and the Shaping of the Modern* (Durham, NC: Duke University Press, 2008), 98–121.

62. *Colored American*, May 25, 1901.

63. "The Stage," *Freeman*, October 2, 1903; "The Stage," *Freeman*, November 28, 1903; Illinois, Cook County Birth Certificates, 1878–1922, Sherman Harry Dudley Jr., Chicago, 1904.

64. Dudley partnered with legendary heavyweight black boxer Jack Johnson and opened a café and bar on 2442 State Street in Chicago in 1904. As a fellow Texan, born in Galveston in 1878, Johnson and Dudley had risen from the ranks of obscurity together, with Dudley on stage and Johnson in the ring. "This One on Jack Johnson," *Afro-American*, September 18, 1909; Theresa Rundstedler, *Jack Johnson, Rebel Sojourner: Boxing in the Shadow of the Global Color Line* (Berkeley: University of California Press, 2013).

65. Nagol Mot, "The Stage," *Freeman* October 3, 1903.

66. Henry R. Sampson, *The Ghost Walks: A Chronological History of Blacks in Show Business, 1865–1910* (Metuchen, NJ: Scarecrow Press, Inc., 1988), 327; Lynn Abbott and Doug Seroff, *Ragged but Right: Black Traveling Shows, "Coon" Songs, and the Dark Pathway to Blues and Jazz* (Jackson: University of Mississippi, 2007), 87–107.

67. Abbott and Seroff, 81.

68. Knight, 157–58.

69. "The Stage," *Freeman*, April 19, 1902; "The Stage," *Richmond Planet*, July 14, 1906.

70. James Dorman, "Shaping the Popular Image of Post-Reconstruction American Blacks: The 'Coon Song' Phenomenon of the Gilded Age," *American Quarterly*, Vol. 40, No. 4 (December 1988), 450–51.

71. Susan Curtis, "Black Creativity and Black Stereotype: Rethinking Twentieth-Century Popular Music in America," in W. Fitzhugh Brundage, ed., *Beyond Blackface: African Americans and the Creation of Popular Culture, 1890–1930* (Chapel Hill: University of North Carolina Press, 2011), 136–38.

72. Catalog of Title Entries Third Quarter 1899, Vol. 20, U.S. Govt. Print. Off., 82.

73. Theatrical Advertising, *Washington Times*, November 28, 1906; *Lost Sounds: Blacks and the Birth of the Recording Industry, 1891–1922*, Archephone Records, 2006.

74. Rivers and Brown, 178–80, 187; Want Ads, *Indianapolis Freeman*, June 2, 1900. After auditioning for a company of "60 Colored Performers," "male, female, and juvenile," for his black-owned *A Rabbit's Foot* company, Chappelle's efforts fell through because of financial instability and regional and racial prejudice against the Jacksonville-based, African American theater manager. Yet he persisted with a restyled *Rabbit's Foot* minstrel show that toured the South from 1902 to 1911.

75. R. W. Thompson, "Dudley in the Spotlight: Snapshot of the Premier Comedian of the Smart Set," *Freeman*, February 9, 1907.

76. Ibid.

77. "S.H. Dudley to Become Theatrical Manager," *Freeman*, January 15, 1910.

78. Ibid.

79. The Colored Vaudeville Benevolent Association formed in 1909 in New York City with all male members as a mutual aid society for black entertainers. The C.V.B.A. dealt with performers' illnesses and burial funds and is discussed more fully in chapter 3. "Colored Vaudeville Performers Organize an Association," *The Clipper*, June 19, 1909; Tom Fletcher, *100 Years of the Negro in Show Business*, 195 (1954 repr., New York: Da Capo Press, 1984), 175–76.

80. Theatrical Ads, *Freeman*, March 1, 1911.

81. S. H. Dudley, "Letter to the Editor," *Freeman*, January 20, 1912.

82. Bauman, 138–42; "Robert T. Motts, Owner and Manager of the Pekin Theater," *Broad Ax*, July 15, 1911; The Pekin Theatre as an all-black venture closed in 1911 with the death of its owner Robert Motts.

83. Sylvester Russell, "The Immigration Questions," *Freeman*, February 28, 1903.

84. Amusements, *Washington Times*, September 10, 1900; "The Stage," *Freeman*, September 7, 1910; Abbott and Seroff, 87–107.

85. *Boyd's Directory of the District of Columbia, 1913*; Abstract of the Thirteenth Census—Population (Washington, DC, 1913), 82.

86. W. P. Bayless, "Passing Show at Washington, D.C.: Howard Theater," *Freeman*, December 3, 1910; "$100,000 Howard Theatre Opens for Negroes," *Baltimore Afro-American*, August 27, 1910. The National Amusement Company was granted a permit for one two-story brick, steel, and concrete theater at 622 T Street NW, with J. Edward Storck as architect and Henry Mass as builder, for $4,000. See Building Permits, *Evening Star*, February 25, 1910.

87. Building Permits, *Evening Star*, May 14, 1910; *Boyd's City Directories of the District of Columbia*, 1911–1913 (282); Those acquainted with the landscape of twenty-first-century Washington, DC, might be familiar with the business that now stands at 1213 U Street NW. Since 1958, 1213 U Street has been the site of the famed black eatery Ben's Chili Bowl. Remove the yellow and red "Washington's Landmark" sign from the façade, and a visitor can begin to see the Ben's Chili Bowl edifice as the S. H. Dudley's Playhouse of 1912.

88. *City Directory*, Washington, DC, 1914, 225.

89. *Boyd's City Directory of the District of Columbia*, 1914, 1706; Blair Ruble, *Washington's U Street: A Biography* (Baltimore: Johns Hopkins University Press, 2012), 70–72.

90. S. H. Dudley, "Letter to the Editor," *Freeman*, January 20, 1912; John R. Thomas, "Says a Chain of Colored Theaters Should Be Established," *Freeman*, February 3, 1912; Knight, "He Paved the Way," 159.

91. 1910; Census Place: *Chicago Ward 2, Cook, Illinois,* Roll: T624_242, Page: 8B, Enumeration District: 0190, FHL microfilm: 1374255; "Salem Tutt Whitney," *The New York Amsterdam News,* October 8, 1930.

92. "Musical and Dramatic," *Defender,* October 1, 1910; Russell might have also had a problem with the concept of "race work." In Russell's text, *The Amalgamation of America: Normal Solution of the Color and Inter-Marriage Problem* (1920), he pondered the question of the "color line" and espoused glorified views of intermarriage to the point where there would be no pure white race, but that blackness would be "absorbed."

93. Sylvester Russell, "The Most Important Issues of the Negro Stage Profession," *Freeman,* August 27, 1910.

94. Sylvester Russell, "Musical and Dramatic: Foremost Dramatic," *Defender,* October 1, 1910.

95. In 1911, Russell invited Dudley to meet Booker T. Washington in a discussion of the ongoing activities of Washington's National Negro Business League. Dudley was dedicated to black entrepreneurship and was eager to meet the race leader. After a Smart Set performance Dudley attended Washington's speech with his young son. Although Dudley Jr. caused no disturbance, Russell took offense to having a young child present in an evening for adults and told Dudley as much. Several weeks later Dudley demanded an apology for Russell's remarks about his fathering skills and upon receiving none, physically assaulted Russell. Russell later sued Dudley for $5,000 for assault. See "S.H. Dudley Sued by Sylvester Russell," *Defender,* March 11, 1911.

96. Sylvester Russell, "The Dudley Colored Theater Syndicate Project as a Problematical Discussion," *Freeman,* February 10, 1912.

97. "Howard—His Honor the Barber," *Washington Times,* March 30, 1911.

98. "The Dudley Circuit," *Defender,* August 17, 1912: Dudley Circuit, *Defender,* October 28, 1912.

99. Theatrical Advertisements, *Freeman,* February 8, 1913.

100. John R. Thomas, "Says a Chain of Colored Theaters Should Be Established," *Freeman,* February 3, 1912; "S.H. Dudley," *Broad Ax,* January 27, 1912.

101. "S.H. Dudley," *Messenger,* January 1925, 30.

102. *Broad Ax,* February 24, 1912.

103. Henry Sampson, *Blacks in Blackface: A Sourcebook on Early Black Musical Shows* (Lanham, MD: Scarecrow Press, 1980), 459; R. W. Thompson, "Washington News," *Defender,* June 24, 1916.

104. S. H. Dudley, *Broad Ax,* January 27, 1912.

105. "The Griffin Sisters," *Defender,* March 22, 1913; "On the Dudley Circuit," *Defender,* September 28, 1914, September 28, 1918.

106. *Colored Theatrical Guide and Business Directory of the United States,* (Brooklyn, NY 1915), 1; The *Guide* was heavily advertised by Sylvester Russell, who was listed as the guide's "special representative." By 1915 Russell realized that his misgivings about Dudley's business acumen were not completely grounded and supported Dudley in his professional if not personal success.

107. "Washington News," *Defender,* June 24, 1916.

108. S. H. Dudley, "Open Letter," *Defender,* December 15, 1917.

109. *1880 Saint Louis, St Louis (Independent City), Missouri*, Roll: 717, 1254717, Page: 193B, Enumeration District: 011, Image: 0531.

110. *1880 Saint Louis, St Louis (Independent City), Missouri*, Roll: 717, 1254717, Page: 193B-196, Enumeration District: 011. In 1880 African American residents made up 6 percent (22,256 people) of the city's overall population of just over 350,000 people. See: *Statistics of the Population of the United States at the Tenth Census* (Washington, DC: Government Printing Office, 1880), 399.

111. *Gould's City Directory of St. Louis*, 1885; *City Directory of St. Louis, 1891.*

112. *Gould's City Directory of St. Louis*, 1897; "Charles Turpin," *The Messenger*, January 1925. Turpin may have undertaken more stable work in 1897 to support his expanding family. His son, Charles Udell Turpin, was born in 1895. In 1897, C. H. still lived in the household with his immediate family and in 1900 was listed as single. Yet, Udell lived with his mother, Fannie, and grandparents in the same neighborhood and possessed the Turpin surname, which acknowledged Charles's paternity.

113. Gould's City Directory of St. Louis, 1901; Messenger, 1925, 49.

114. Rose M. Nolen, *Hoecakes, Hambone, and All That Jazz: African American Traditions in Missouri* (Columbia: University of Missouri Press, 2003), 78; Cyprian Clamorgan in Gerald Early, *Ain't But a Place: An Anthology of African American Writings about St. Louis,* (Columbia: Missouri Historical Society Press, 1998), 267–70.

115. Gould's City Directories of St. Louis, 1893–1894.

116. Handy, 29; Targee Street's atmosphere fueled the lyrics of the famed folk ballad "Frankie and Johnny," a tale of a failed love affair resulting in "Frankie" Baker shooting and killing her unfaithful "man" Allen "Johnny" Brit, who "did her wrong." Likewise, it was the basis of the storied woman "with a diamond ring," who "toted her man around by her apron strings," in W. C. Handy's "St. Louis Blues." Tim O'Neil, "Look Back: Frankie shot Johnnie in St. Louis, but didn't win her lawsuit," *St. Louis Dispatch*, October 17, 2010; Frank and Bert Leighton, "Frankie and Johnny," 1904.

117. Handy, 26.

118. Edward A. Berlin, *Ragtime: A Musical and Cultural History* (Berkeley: University of California Press, 1984), 23–24; John Hasse, *Ragtime: Its History, Composers, and Music* (New York: Schirmer Books, 1985), 2–3.

119. Berlin, *Ragtime*, 25–30. Tom Turpin published some of the earliest identifiable ragtime tunes, like 1897's "Harlem Rag"; Nathan B Young, *Your St. Louis and Mine* in Gerald Early, ed., *Ain't But a Place*, 341–45; Volume Catalog of Title Entries July–Dec 1897, No. 314, U.S. Govt. Print. Off., 72.

120. Early, 345; Edward A. Berlin, *King of Ragtime: Scott Joplin and His Era*, 2nd ed. (New York: Oxford University Press, 2016), 112–15, 151, 243.

121. Advertisements, *The Metronome*, May 1899, in Hazen Collection, Archives Center, National Museum of American History.

122. https://www.stlouis-mo.gov/government/departments/planning/cultural-resources/preservation-plan/Part-I-African-American-Experience.cfm, accessed May 1, 2017.

123. Eugene McQuillin, *The Municipal Code of St. Louis*, Approved April 3, 1900, Woodward & Tiernan, 1901. The constable system predated the creation of the St. Louis Police

Department and could be full of all of the corruption attached to electoral politics and the patronage system. It was phased out in the 1960s; "Armed Clash in Constable Fight Barely Averted," *St. Louis Post-Dispatch*, August 9, 1915; "Ministers and Business Men Endorse Phillips and Turpin," *St. Louis Argus*, August 2, 1918.

124. "Mound City Happenings," *Defender*, April 25, 1914; "C.H. Turpin," *The Messenger*, January 1925, 29; *Report of the Seventeenth Annual Session of the National Negro Business League*, Kansas City, MO, August 16, 17, 18, 1916, 161–62.

125. "Theater for Market Street," *St. Louis Post-Dispatch*, March 16, 1913; Walter Ehrlich, *Zion in the Valley: The Jewish Community in St. Louis* (Columbia: University of Missouri Press, 1997).

126. *Billboard*, June 28, 1913, 21.

127. "Mound City Happenings," *Defender*, April 25, 1914.

128. "C.H. Turpin," *The Messenger*, January 1925, 29.

129. See African Americans and Consumer Economy, http://lcweb2.1oc.gov:8081/ammem/amrlhtml/inafamer.html, accessed February 22, 2016.

130. Report of the Seventeenth Annual Session of the National Negro Business League, Kansas City, MO, August 16, 17, 18, 1916, 162.

131. *Ibid*, 162–63.

132. "Colored Consolidated Vaudeville Exchange Christmas Greetings," *Freeman*, December 20, 1913; *Colored Theatrical Guide*, 4.

133. Gibson's WWI draft card lists his birth date as 1878, while the 1900 Federal Census lists it as February 1871, and his death certificate notes February 3, 1872 as his date of birth.

134. *Wood's Baltimore City Directory, 1872–1876*; Between 1872 and 1876, George H. Gibson lived in Baltimore City just blocks away from Camden Yard and the harbor and changed his specific residence every year within that four-year period.

135. "John T. Gibson Laid to Rest in Philadelphia," *Defender*, July 3, 1937; *Harriet Driver (Hanni Diver) in Year: 1900*; Census Place: *Baltimore Ward 21, Baltimore City (Independent City), Maryland*, Roll: 617, Page: 10B, Enumeration District: 0276, FHL microfilm: 1240617.

136. *R.L Polk's Baltimore City Directory, 1890–1891*; At this point the city held over sixty-seven thousand African American residents, or just about 15 percent of the city's population, in enclaves throughout the region and represented one of the highest percentages of African Americans in the nation's urban sectors. See http://msa.maryland.gov/msa/stagser/s1259/121/6050/html/westbalt.html, accessed May 30, 2017; 1900 Census, Statistics of the Population.

137. Boyd's City Directory of Camden, 1895–1896.

138. Founded as Centenary Biblical Institute in 1867 by the Methodist Episcopal Church as a theological training school primarily for African American men, the renamed Morgan College was developed in 1890. Although the college had catered to male students, women were admitted by 1890 under the new charter, and the curriculum was "no longer exclusively or mainly Biblical." See Archives of Maryland, Session Laws, 1890, Chapter 326, 351; *Catalogue of Morgan College, 1890–1891* (Baltimore, MD, 1890); *Annual Catalogue of Morgan College and Branches, 1895–1896* (Baltimore, MD, 1895), 8.

139. W. E. B. Du Bois, *The Philadelphia Negro* (1899, repr., New York: Schocken Books, 1967), 75.

140. Ralph L. Lester, "Philadelphia Pioneers in Business," *The Crisis*, May 1944, 152; *Boyd's Directory of City of Philadelphia*, 1909, 1615; "Where to Find Colored Theaters," *Freeman*, June 4, 1910.

141. Dylan Gottlieb, "South Street," *The Encyclopedia of Greater Philadelphia* https://philadelphiaencyclopedia.org/archive/south-street/, accessed July 18, 2019.

142. "The Auditorium Theater at Philadelphia," *Freeman*, January 12, 1912; "The Auditorium Theater," *Freeman*, February 15, 1913; "The Auditorium Theater," *Freeman*, June 7, 1913.

143. W. E. B. Du Bois, *Philadelphia Negro* (original 1899, New York: Schoken Books, 1967), 122; "Trocadero and Circle Theaters," *Freeman*, June 11, 1910; "Trocadero and Circle Theaters," *Freeman*, March 1, 1913.

144. The Julius Cahn Theatrical Guide and Moving Picture Directory, 1910–1911.

145. Allen F. Davis, John F. Sutherland, and Helen Parrish, "Reform and Uplift among Philadelphia Negroes: The Diary of Helen Parrish, 1888," *The Pennsylvania Magazine of History and Biography*, Vol. 94, No. 4 (October 1970), 504.

146. Du Bois, *Philadelphia Negro*, 81.

147. Du Bois, *Philadelphia Negro*, 310–11, 391.

148. "Show Shops, Philadelphia, PA," *Freeman*, March 4, 1911.

149. "The Auditorium," *Freeman*, January 13, 1912; "The Auditorium," *Freeman*, February 15, 1913.

150. "Standard Theater," *Philadelphia Tribune*, February 22, 1913.

151. "New Standard Has Grand Opening," *Philadelphia Tribune*, April 26, 1913.

152. "New Theater at Philadelphia, PA," *Freeman*, January 14, 1914; "Gibson's New Standard, *Philadelphia Tribune*, February 28, 1914; "Standard Theatre," *Philadelphia Tribune*, March 14, 1914.

153. Du Bois, Philadelphia Negro, 7–8.

154. "John T. Gibson, One of Our Most Successful Theater Managers," *Philadelphia Tribune*, October 19, 1918.

155. Advertisements, *Philadelphia Tribune*, February 28, 1914; Interview with Leonard Reed, Jazz Oral Histories Collection, Archives Center, National Museum of American History.

156. "Standard Theatre Resumes Its Discrimination Tactics," *Philadelphia Tribune*, October 11, 1913.

157. "J.T. Gibson Breaks Up Discrimination," *Philadelphia Tribune*, January 17, 1914.

158. "Big Bill at Gibson's New Standard," *Philadelphia Tribune*, February 28, 1914.

159. "On the Dudley Circuit," *Defender*, January 25, 1915; "On the Dudley Circuit," *Defender*, February 13, 1915; *Colored Theatrical Guide*, 1–2; "John T. Gibson," *Philadelphia Tribune*, October 19, 1918.

160. Parts of this section were published in Michelle R. Scott's "These Ladies Do Business with a Capital B": The Griffin Sisters as Black Businesswomen in Early Vaudeville," *Journal of African American History*, Vol. 101, No. 4 (2017), 469–503.

161. "Griffin Sisters," *Freeman*, February 14, 1914.

162. Death Certificate for Emma Griffin, Illinois Deaths and Stillbirths, 1916–1947, FHL #1852630.

163. 1880 United States Federal Census, Louisville, Jefferson County, Roll 424, film 1254424, 424A.

164. *Caron's Directory of City of Louisville, 1894.*

165. "Emma Griffin Dead, Well Known on the Stage," *New York Age*, September 7, 1918; Emma Griffin, *Defender*, August 31, 1918.

166. "The Griffin Sisters: The First and Only Colored Women's Theatrical Booking Agency in the United States," *Freeman*, February 14, 2014; "Emma Griffin Dead," *New York Age*, September 7, 1918.

167. Lewis, *From Traveling Show to Vaudeville*, 29–31.

168. George Middleton, *Circus Memoirs* (Los Angeles: Rice and Sons, 1913), 69–71.

169. Middleton, *Circus Memoirs*, 71–74. For more on dime show performers of the nineteenth century, see Linda Frost, *Never One Nation: Freaks, Savages, and Whiteness in U.S. Popular Culture, 1850–1877* (Minneapolis: University of Minnesota Press, 2005); Robert Bodgan, *Freak Show: Presenting Human Oddities for Amusement and Profit* (Chicago, IL: University of Chicago Press, 2014).

170. James C. Crawford, "Colored Women Experience Difficulty in Getting Assailant into Court," *San Francisco Call*, February 21, 1906.

171. Entertainment Routings, *New York Tribune*, June 6, 1897, 7.

172. "At the Theaters," *Baltimore Sunday Herald*, September 8, 1895; for greater discussion on *The Creole Show* and the Octoroons, see Jayna Brown's *Babylon Girls*.

173. Emily Clark, *The Strange History of the American Quadroon* (Chapel Hill: University of North Carolina Press, 2013), 133–35, 184–87.

174. "Emma Griffin Dead, Well Known on the Stage," *New York Age*, September 7, 1918; "Emma Griffin Dies: Popular Actress Dies after a Protracted Illness," *Defender*, September 7, 1918.

175. Robert Grau, *The Business Man in the Amusement World* (Chicago, IL, 1910), 323; Wertheim, *Vaudeville Wars*, 122–23.

176. "The Griffin Sisters," *Freeman*, February 14, 2014.

177. "Musical and Dramatic," *Defender*, February 19, 1910; "Crown Garden," *Freeman*, September 10, 1910.

178. "Griffin Sisters," *Freeman*, February 14, 1914.

179. Department of Commerce and Labor, *Bulletin 8, Negroes in the United States* (Washington: Government Printing Office, 1900) 102, 164–65. 1,316,872 black females over age ten had wage positions in the country, with 582,001 women in agricultural labor, while 642,213 black women were cooks, laundresses, and domestic servants. Generally, black women who rose to business prominence were most notably in the catering, hospitality, or hair care industries, as seen in the lauded success of beauty care specialists Madame C. J. Walker and Annie Turnbo Malone; Monroe N. Work, ed., *Negro Year Book: An Annual Encyclopedia of the Negro, 1914–1915* (Tuskegee, AL: Negro Year Book Publishing Company, 1914), 7–8.

180. Henry T. Sampson, *Blacks in Blackface: A Sourcebook on Early Black Musical Shows*, 2nd ed. (Scarecrow Press, 2013), 1404–6; John Graziano, "The Early Life and Career of the 'Black Patti': The Odyssey of an African American Singer in the Late Nineteenth Century," *Journal of the American Musicological Society*, Vol. 53, No 3, (2000), 569.

181. "The Whitmans," *Defender*, January 26, 1918.
182. George Graves, *The Royalty of Negro Vaudeville*, 93–101.
183. "Griffin Sisters Helping the Stage," *Defender*, January 10, 1914.
184. "Griffin Sisters," *Freeman*, February 14, 1914.
185. "The Stage in Greater New York," *Broad Ax*, October 7, 1905.
186. "The Griffin Sisters," *Defender*, March 22, 1913.
187. "Griffin Sisters," *Freeman*, February 14, 1914.
188. Ibid.
189. Advertisements, *Freeman*, December 13, 1913.
190. Illinois Bureau of Labor Statistics, Annual Report of the Illinois Free Employment Offices, 1913, 1914; Griffin Sisters, *Freeman*, February 14, 1914; Classifieds, *Defender*, October 25, 1913; "Blacks in Chicago: Special Places," *Chicago Tribune*, January 22, 1978, 36.
191. "Griffin Sisters," *Freeman*, February 14, 1914.
192. "The Griffin Sisters Theatrical and Employment Agency," *Broad Ax*, January 3, 1914.
193. "The Alamo Theater," *Defender*, April 25, 1914.
194. Ar-W-Tee, "The Passing Show in Washington," *Freeman*, April 5, 1913. Emphasis mine.
195. Ibid.
196. "The Passing of the American Theater," *Defender*, December 5, 1914.
197. "The Griffin Sisters," *The Broad Ax*, May 22, 1915.
198. Sylvester Russell, "Actors Hold a Secret Session," *Freeman*, May 16, 1914.
199. Ibid.

## CHAPTER 2. "HEBREW, NEGRO, AND AMERICAN OWNERS"

1. "Passing Show," *Defender*, March 29, 1913; *Defender*, January 16, 1915.
2. "Consolidated Exchange a Big Success," *Freeman*, March 7, 1914.
3. Marie Gossett Harlow, "Our Race in the South," *Defender*, March 28, 1925.
4. "Industry and Business," *Afro American*, April 13, 1929.
5. Marvin McAllister, *Whiting Up: Whiteface Minstrels and Stage Europeans in African American Performance* (Chapel Hill: University of North Carolina Press, 2011), 76–78; Lawrence E. Mintz, "Humor and Ethnic Stereotypes in Vaudeville and Burlesque," *MELUS* Vol. 21, No. 4 (Winter 1996), 25–27; Robert W. Snyder, *The Voice of the City* (New York: Oxford University Press, 1989), 63.
6. Lauren Sklaroff, *Red Hot Mama: The Life of Sophie Tucker*, (Austin: University of Texas Press, 2018), 40–42; Pamela Brown Lavitt, "First of the Red Hot Mamas: The Jewish Ziegfeld Girl," *American Jewish History*, Vol. 87, No. 4 (December 1999), 258–260; Herbert G. Goldman, *Fanny Brice: The Original Funny Girl* (New York: Oxford University Press, 1992), 44–47; "Jottings," *American Israelite*, October 1, 1903.
7. Andrea Most, *Making Americans: Jews and the Broadway Musical* (Cambridge, MA: Harvard University Press, 2004), Vol. 26, 122; George and Hart's Up to Date Minstrels Scrapbook, National Museum of American History, Archives Center, box 2.
8. Jeffrey Melnick, *A Right to Sing the Blues: African Americans, Jews, and American Popular Song* (Cambridge, MA: Harvard University Press, 2001), 16–59; For greater discussion on Jews in American theater history, see Sidney Hecht, *Transposing Broadway: Jews, Assimilation*

*and the American Musical* (Palgrave MacMillan, 2014); Stewart Lane, *Jews on Broadway: A Historical Survey,* 2nd ed (New York: McFarland, 2017).

9. Nicholas Gebhardt, *Vaudeville Melodies: Popular Musicians and Mass Entertainment in American Culture* (Chicago: University of Chicago Press, 2017), 110–11; Karen Sotiropoulos, *Staging Race: Black Performers in Turn of the Century America* (Cambridge, MA: Harvard University Press, 2006), 224; Phillip Furia and Michael Lasser, *America's Songs: The Stories Behind the Songs of Broadway, Hollywood, and Tin Pan Alley* (New York: Routledge, 2006) 2–5; Irving Berlin, "Alexander's Ragtime Band," New York: Ted Snyder's Co. 1911.

10. Snyder, 60.

11. Eric Lott, *Love and Theft: Blackface Minstrelsy and the American Working Class* (New York: Oxford University Press, 1995), 6.

12. Irving Howe, "From the World of Our Fathers," in Mauriane Adams and John Bracey, eds., *Strangers and Neighbors: Relations Between Blacks & Jews in the United States* (Amherst: University of Massachusetts Press, 1999), 329.

13. Most, *Making Americans,* 26–27; "The Griffin Sisters: The First and Only Colored Women's Theatrical Booking Agency in the United States and Their Desires and Intentions," *Freeman,* February 14, 1914.

14. Vivienne, "Theater Folks and Theatergoers: Corkless Comedy," *Chicago Defender,* October 31, 1925.

15. "King Rastus," *Norfolk Virginia Pilot,* September 16, 1900.

16. Jacob Adler, *A Life on the Stage* (New York: Applause Books, 2001), xviii-xix; Stephan Kaner, *Stardust Lost: The Triumph, Tragedy, and Meshugas of the Yiddish Theater in America* (New York: Vintage, 2007), 44–53.

17. Registration State: *Illinois*; Registration County: Cook; Roll: 1439698; Draft Board: 08.

18. Ancestry.com. *Illinois, Marriage Index, 1860–1920* [database on-line]. Provo, UT, USA: Ancestry.com Operations, Inc., 2015; Year: 1900; Census Place: *Chicago Ward 5, Cook, Illinois*; Page: 5; Enumeration District: 0137; FHL microfilm: 1240249. The Kleins were part of a community of recent German Jewish immigrants who made Chicago their home at the onset of the height of European immigration to the United States in the nineteenth century. In the late 1870s, Phillip joined a community that amassed over four thousand residents out of over 350,000 Chicagoans. As the 1890s approached, Chicago Jewish communities took on an influx of Eastern European Jews, predominantly from the Russian Empire. While the numbers vary, approximately two million Eastern Europeans fled poverty, exile, and violence to settle in the United States between 1880 and 1910, and the Jewish population in Chicago grew from four thousand in the 1870s to two hundred thousand by the 1910s. Irving Cutler, *The Jews of Chicago: From Shetl to Suburb* (Urbana: IL, University of Illinois Press, 1996), 26–28; Robert Rockaway, *Words of the Uprooted: Jewish Immigrants in Early 20th Century America* (Ithaca, NY: Cornell University Press, 1998), 139; Cheryl Lynn Greenberg, *Troubling the Waters: Black-Jewish Relations in the American Century* (Princeton, NJ: Princeton University Press, 2006), 33.

19. Ancestry.com. *Cook County, Illinois, Marriages Index, 1871–1920* [database on-line]. Provo, UT, USA: Ancestry.com Operations, Inc., 2011; Federal Census, Year: 1880; Census Place: Port Huron, St Clair, Michigan; Roll: 605; Page: 346A; Enumeration District: 384.

20. Lillian's elder sister Fannie Nissel married German Jewish immigrant Henry "H.B." Miller in 1898 in Detroit and moved to Chicago in 1900. See Michigan Department of Community Health, Division of Vital Records and Health Statistics; Lansing, MI, USA; *Michigan, Marriage Records, 1867–1952*; Film: 64; Film Description: *1898 Wayne–1899 Emmet*: Year: 1900; Census Place: Chicago Ward 6, Cook, Illinois; Page: 6; Enumeration District: 0155; FHL microfilm: 1240250; *Lakeside Chicago City Directory*, 1900, 2438.

21. Year: 1910; Census Place: Chicago Ward 7, Cook, Illinois; Roll: T624_247; Page: 6A; Enumeration District: 0380; FHL microfilm: 1374260; Lakeside Directory of the City of Chicago, 1910, 916.

22. Lakeside Directory of the City of Chicago, 1910, 1737; Year: 1910; Census Place: Chicago Ward 5, Cook, Illinois; Roll: T624245; Page: 31A; Enumeration District: 0307; FHL microfilm: 1374258.

23. Statistical Abstracts, No. 22 Population of the Cities, 1930, 23.

24. Department of Commerce, *Negroes in the United States 1920–1932* (Washington, DC: Government Printing Office, 1935), 55; 65, 355 African Americans relocated to Chicago between 1910 and 1920; Moser, "Chicago Isn't Just Segregated, It Basically Invented Modern Segregation," *Chicago Magazine*, March 2017, See http://www.chicagomag.com/city-life/March-2017/Why-Is-Chicago-So-Segregated/) accessed August 5, 2018.

25. John Levy and Devra Hall, *Men, Women, and Girl Singers: My Life as a Musician Turned Talent Manager* (Silver Spring, MD: Beckham Publications, 2000), 14.

26. *The Negro in Chicago: A Study of Race Relations and a Riot* (Chicago Commission on Race Relations, 1922), 52; "Half a Million Darkies from Dixie Swarm to the North to Better Themselves," *Chicago Tribune*, May 15, 1917.

27. "East of State Street," *Chicago Defender*, May 30, 1914.

28. *Negro in Chicago*, 8, 106; Greenberg, 45–46.

29. Juliet E. K. Walker, *History of Black Business in America: Capitalism, Race, Entrepreneurship* (New York, 2009), 191.

30. Display Ad 18, *Defender*, December 31, 1910.

31. *The Negro in Chicago*, 232, 649.

32. *The Negro in Chicago*, 502.

33. "The Stage," *Freeman* January 23, 1909; "Kelly and Davis at the Monogram," *Franklin's Paper The Statesmen*, December 24, 1910; "Monogram," *Broad Ax*, January 20, 1912.

34. Dempsey J. Travis, "Chicago's Jazz Trial, 1893–1950," *Black Music Research Journal*, Vol. 10, No. 1 (Spring, 1990), 84–85.

35. Juli Jones, "Well Dahomey," *Freeman*, January 2, 1909. Dahomey is used to reference the African Kingdom of Dahomey that existed in eighteenth- and nineteenth-century Benin and is a description of the black presence on State Street. The black Broadway vehicle written by Will Marion Cook, Jesse Ship, and Paul Lawrence Dunbar that premiered in 1903 was also titled *In Dahomey*.

36. "The Profession in Chicago," *Freeman*, July 9, 1910.

37. "The Stage," *Freeman*, December 12, 1908.

38. Thomas Bauman, *The Pekin: The Rise and Fall of Chicago's First Black-Owned Theater* (Urbana: University of Illinois Press, 2014), 84; "Dahomey Stroll," *Freeman*, February 13, 1909.

39. Display Ads, *Freeman,* December 7, 1912; "Carita Day Turns People Away at the New Grand," *Freeman,* May 18, 1912.

40. "The Grand," *Freeman,* January 11, 1913.

41. Travis, "Chicago's Jazz Trail," 84.

42. Sylvester Russell, "Chicago Weekly Review," *Freeman,* May 11, 1912.

43. G. W. Walker, "Actor of the Famous Team Dead," *Defender,* January 14, 1911.

44. "Martin Klein in the City," *Freeman,* June 28, 1913.

45. Jacqueline Najuma Stewart, *Migrating to the Movies : Cinema and Black Urban Modernity* (Berkeley: University of California Press, 2005), 172–73."In Dahomey," *Freeman,* May 1, 1909; "Monogram," *Broad Ax,* September 9, 1916.

46. "The American Jew Fights Back," *Defender,* April 26, 1913; "Consistency Is Jewel," *Defender,* May 23, 1914.

47. "Consistency Is Jewel," *Defender,* May 23, 1914.

48. Greenberg, *Troubling the Waters,* 45–47.

49. "A Word for M Klein," *Freeman,* December 20, 1913.

50. "The New Monogram Theater Under the Ownership of H.B. Miller Continues to Run at Full Blast," *Broad Ax,* November 29, 1913.

51. "Boston Grand Opera House," *Jewish Advocate,* October 27, 1911.

52. "In Chicago and Suburbs," *Chicago Defender,* June 28, 1913; *Broad Ax,* June 28, 1913.

53. R. W. Thompson, "Dudley in the Spotlight: Snapshot of the Premier Comedian of the Smart Set," *Freeman,* February 9, 1907.

54. "Martin Klein in the City," *Freeman,* June 28, 1913.

55. Display Ad, *Freeman,* July 5, 1913.

56. "Christmas Advertisements," *Freeman,* December 20, 1913.

57. Display Ads, *Freeman,* March 21, 1914.

58. "The Griffin Sisters," *Freeman,* February 14, 1914.

59. Patricia Hill Collins, *Black Feminist Thought: Knowledge, Consciousness, and the Politics of Empowerment* (New York: Routledge Press, 1990), 69.

60. "Consolidated Exchange a Big Success," *Freeman* March 7, 1914.

61. The Stage, "Chicago Weekly Review," *Freeman,* March 7, 1914.

62. Sylvester Russell, "Chicago Weekly Review," *Freeman,* February 7, 1914.

63. The Stage, "Chicago Weekly Review," *Freeman,* March 7, 1914.

64. Shennette Garrett-Scott, *Banking on Freedom: Black Women in U.S. Finance Before the New Deal* (New York: Columbia University Press, 2019), 4–12; Fannie Barrier Williams, "The Woman's Part in a Man's Business," *Voice of the Negro* Vol. 1, No. 11 (1904), 543–47.

65. "The Griffin Sisters Theatrical and Employment Agency," *Broad Ax,* January 3, 1914; "Martin Klein Opens Employment Agency," *Defender,* February 6, 2015.

66. "Mr. Klein in Town," *Freeman,* October 2, 1915. Walter would become the second "Manager Klein" of Chicago by the late 1920s and early '30s; Walter D Klein, "Today with a Better Outlook, Flesh Shows Should Not Remain Extinct," *Defender,* May 22, 1937.

67. "Elite No. 1 to Expand," *Broad Ax,* October 28, 1916; "Consolidate Grows," *Defender,* September 15, 1917.

68. Theatrical Advertisements, "Notice, Notice, Notice" Ad, *Freeman* February 14, 1914.

69. Sylvester Russell, "Chicago Weekly Review, Consolidated Circuit Break Not Advisable," *Freeman*, November 14, 1914.

70. Tim E. Owsley, "What It Takes to Attend to Other People's Business Sylvester Russell Has It," *Freeman*, November 21, 1914.

71. Ibid.

72. Display Ad 10, *Defender*, October 20, 1917; S. H. Dudley, "Open Letter," *Defender*, December 15, 1917.

73. "Big Convention," *Defender*, June 8, 1918.

74. Joseph Gustaitis, *Chicago Transformed: World War and the Windy City* (Carbondale: Southern Illinois University Press, 2016), 260–66.

75. Milt Hinton interview by Billy Taylor, August 12–13, 1992, Jazz Oral History Collection Program, Archives Center, National Museum of American History.

76. Henry Gang Jines, "Liberty Theater," *Chicago Defender*, January 20, 1923.

77. The 81 Theatre was located south east of Five Points at 81 Decatur Street between Courtland and Ivy. The 1,500-seat theatre was erected in 1909 by Charles P. Bailey and L.D. Joel in Atlanta, GA.

78. Bernard L. Peterson, *The African American Theatre Directory, 1816–1960: A Comprehensive Guide to Early Black Theatre Organizations, Companies, Theatres, and Performing Groups* (Santa Barbara, CA: Greenwood Press, 1997), 194; http://historic-memphis.com/memphis-historic/moguls/moguls.html accessed 24 November 2014. The confusion that often appears in secondary works and in some of the recollections of black performers about TOBA's origins often results from the use of the same acronym for the 1920s national circuit and other short-lived circuits in the South.

79. 1900 United States Federal Census, Memphis Ward 2, Shelby Tennessee, Roll 1597, pg. 5A; US World War I Draft Registration Card for Anselmo Barrasso, June 5, 1917. Fred A. Barrasso died on June 25, 1911, see *R. L. Polk's & Co's Memphis City Directory*, 1912, 159; "Profession at Memphis," *The Freeman*, January 29, 1910; *R. L. Polk's & Co's Memphis City Directories*, 1912–1925; Anselmo Barrasso's Palace Theatre was later part of the 1920s T.O.B.A. circuit.

80. For more on Memphis's Beale Street see Preston Lauterbach, *Beale Street Dynasty: Sex Song and the Struggle for the Soul of Memphis* (New York: W.W. Norton, 2016).

81. Year: 1910; Census Place: Jacksonville Ward 7, Duval, Florida; Roll: T624_159; Page: 22A; Enumeration District: 0084; FHL microfilm: 1374172; Year: 1930; Census Place: Jacksonville, Duval, Florida; Page: 21B; Enumeration District: 0034; FHL microfilm: 2340048.

82. Theatrical Ads, *Freeman*, December 17, 1910.

83. Theatrical Ads, *Freeman*, December 28, 1912.

84. Clarence Muse, *Way Down South* (Los Angeles: David Graham Fischer), 22, 17, 40–43, 66.

85. "Warns the Performers," *Freeman*, January 2, 1912: The legendary complaints that both performers and managers had with Bailey will be chronicled more in chapters 4 and 5. While artists liked Joel, Bailey was chronicled as "a nothing butt cracker from the back woods of Georgia" who could not " stand [black] prosperity."

86. https://www.jewishvirtuallibrary.org/the-pale-of-settlement, accessed 17 November 2018.

87. https://www.jewishvirtuallibrary.org/pogroms-2.

88. https://www.myjewishlearning.com/article/jewish-emigration-in-the-19th-century/ by Shmuel Ettinger, accessed 16 November 2018.

89. National Archives and Records Administration; Washington, DC; ARC Title: *Petitions for Naturalization, compiled 1907–1974*; ARC Number: 1490568; Record Group Title: *Records of District Courts of the United States*; Record Group Number: 21; Staatsarchiv Hamburg; Hamburg, Deutschland; *Hamburger Passagierlisten*; Microfilm No.: K_1794.

90. Year: 1906; Arrival: New York, New York; Microfilm Serial: T715, 1897–1957; Microfilm Roll: Roll 0700; Line: 11; Page Number: 95; Robert Rockaway, *Words of the Uprooted: Jewish Immigrants in Early 20th Century America* (Cornell University Press, 1998), 1–39.

91. Susie McCarver Webster, *Historic City-Chattanooga* (McGowan & Cooke: Chattanooga, 1915), 13–14.

92. Webster, 7; "Chattanooga, In Honor of the 47th Annual Encampment of the Grand Army of the Republic," *Chattanooga Times*, 1913, 4.

93. Statistics of the Population, 1920, Table No. 32, p. 52, Table No. 37, p. 63.

94. George Berke, ed., *Diamond Jubilee: Congregation of B'nai Zion, 1888–1963* (Chattanooga, Tenn: s.n., 1963), 10–11; Rockaway, 142; A. Solomon to M. Goldstein, April 9, 1913 in Rockaway, 143–44.

95. A. Solomon to M. Goldstein, 9 April 1913 in Rockaway, 143–44.

96. National Archives and Records Administration, Washington, DC; ARC Title: *Petitions for Naturalization, compiled 1907–1974*; ARC Number: 1490568; Record Group Title: *Records of District Courts of the United States*; Record Group Number: 21.

97. Year: 1910; Census Place: Chattanooga Ward 7, Hamilton, Tennessee; Roll: T624_1503; Page: 12A; Enumeration District: 0067; FHL microfilm: 1375516; *U.S. City Directories, 1822–1995* [database on-line]. Provo, UT, USA: Ancestry.com Operations, Inc., 2011.

98. *U.S. City Directories, 1822–1995* [database on-line]. Provo, UT, USA: Ancestry.com Operations, Inc., 2011. (*U.S. City Directories, 1822–1995* [database on-line]. Provo, UT, USA: Ancestry.com Operations, Inc., 2011); Joy Effron Ableson Adams, *The Jewish Community of Chattanooga*, Arcadia, 1999, 67–73.

99. Yiddish was noted as Samuel's first language on the 1930 census, while Sara's first language was Russian, 1930; Census Place: Signal Mountain, Hamilton, Tennessee; Page: 6A; Enumeration District: 0072; FHL microfilm: 2341987.

100. Charter of Incorporation #173, 1920, Tennessee State Archives; Berke, *Diamond jubilee*; http://www.bnaizioncongregation.com/bz-history.htm (accessed January 9, 2019); The Maccabean: A Magazine of Jewish Life and Letters, Volumes 20–21. As a newcomer Reevin also affiliated with the B'Nai Zion community and even contributed a small donation to the Jewish Colonial Trust in 1910 alongside M. H. Silverman and his wife, Bessie. The Jewish Colonial Trust lasted between 1899 and 1934 and was the first Zionist bank "intended to be the financial instrument of the Zionist Organization," with a purpose "to obtain capital and credit to help attain a charter for Palestine." https://www.jewishvirtuallibrary.org/jewish-colonial-trust (accessed January 9, 2019).

101. *U.S. City Directories, 1822–1995* [database on-line]. Provo, UT, USA: Ancestry.com Operations, Inc., 2011, Chattanooga, 1914, p. 684.

102. Michelle R. Scott, *Blues Empress in Black Chattanooga: Bessie Smith and the Emerging Urban South* (Urbana: University of Illinois Press, 2008), 13–34.

103. Mark Curriden and Leroy Phillips Jr., *Contempt of Court: The Turn of the Century Lynching That Launched a Hundred Years of Federalism* (Anchor Books, 1999), 20–25, 198–218; "Race War Is Averted: Chattanooga Was Quiet in Morning," *Wilmington Daily Commercial*, March 21, 1906; The events of the Atlanta Riot of September 1906 were actually commented on by the Russian Empire who compared American race riots and programs "hoping that the United States will now cease to attribute the Russian excesses to official provocation, admitting instead that they are the result of *natural* racial animosity." See "Russia Hears of Atlanta," *New York Times*, October 3, 1906.

104. Steven Herzberg, "Jews and Blacks," in Adams and Bracey, eds., *Strangers and Neighbors*, 248.

105. In 1920 the black population reached 18,894 persons, 32 percent of the overall population; *Statistics of the Population*, 1930, Table 22, page 23.

106. "Hustling Chattanooga," *Nashville Globe*, June 24, 1910.

107. "Chattanooga, In Honor of the 47th Annual Encampment of the Grand Army of the Republic," *Chattanooga Times*, 1913, 50.

108. R.J. Crawford, "Business Negroes of Chattanooga," *Voice of the Negro*, November 1904; "Hustling Chattanooga," *Nashville Globe*, June 24, 1910.

109. Scott, *Blues Empress in Black Chattanooga*, 102.

110. "Hustling Chattanooga," *Nashville Globe*, June 24, 1910.

111. NNBL, Report of the 18th and 19th Annual Sessions, Chattanooga, Tenn. and Atlantic City, NJ, Washington DC, 1917, 2.

112. "Chattanooga, In Honor of the 47th Annual Encampment of the Grand Army of the Republic," *Chattanooga Times*, 1913, 64.

113. Advertisements, *Nashville Globe*, June 24, 1910; "Hustling Chattanooga," *Nashville Globe*, June 24, 1910; *Freeman* May 14, 1910.

114. *U.S. City Directories, 1822–1995* [database on-line]. Provo, UT, USA: Ancestry.com Operations, Inc., 2011, City Directories, Chattanooga City 1910–1914.

115. *U.S. City Directories, 1822–1995* [database on-line]. Provo, UT, USA: Ancestry.com Operations, Inc., 2011, 1914.

116. "Along the Color Line: Social Uplift," *The Crisis*, March 1912, 184; *Negro Year Book and Annual Encyclopedia of the Negro*, 1922, 306.

117. Theatrical Ads, *Freeman*, September 19, 1914.

118. Theatrical Ads, *Freeman*, February 6, 1915.

119. "Performers Beware of the Queen Theatre," *Freeman*, October 3, 1914; "Mr. Reevin of the Queen Theater Replies to Washburne and Piper," *Freeman*, October 31, 1914.

120. "Good Show at the Queen Theatre, Chattanooga, TN," *Freeman*, December 19, 1914.

121. Muse, *Way Down South*, 42.

122. Eric Goldstein, "Now Is the Time to Show Your True Colors: Southern Jews, Whiteness, and The Rise of Jim Crow," in Marcie Cohen Ferris and Mark Greenberg, eds. *Jewish Roots in Southern Soil: A New History* (New York: Brandeis University Press, 2006), 140–41; Sam E. Reevin, "Well Known and Popular Manager of T.O.B.A. Speaks," *Defender*, August 6, 1921.

123. "Files Articles of Incorporation," *The Moving Picture World*, September 14, 1918; "Do You Have Trouble With Your Film Delivery Service?," *Exhibitor's Trade Review*, Vol. 5, No. 20 (1919), 1528.

124. Display Ad, *Defender*, August 17, 1918.

125. Food Will Win the War advertisement, *Chattanooga Times*, 12 February 1918; Registers for the Draft for WWI (Registration State: Tennessee; Registration County: Hamilton; Roll: 1852926; Draft Board: 1) Livingood, Hamilton County, Tennessee, 355–356, 1920; Census Place: Chattanooga Ward 1, Hamilton, Tennessee; Roll: T625_1742; Page: 11B; Enumeration District: 157. As a new citizen Reevin also registered for the draft along with 6,811 others in the city.

126. "Gang," Liberty Theater, *Chicago Defender*, January 20, 1923.

127. "Well Done Work By Colored Singer," *Chattanooga News*, January 10, 1918; "Colored Veteran of Civil War to Lecture," *Chattanooga News*, April 13, 1918; "Negro Churches to Have Union Organ Recital," June 1, 1918; Announcements, *Chattanooga News*, May 21, 1918.

128. *G.M. Connelley & Co's Alphabetical Directory of Chattanooga*, Tennessee, 1919–1920.

129. "Here and There," *Afro American*, January 20, 1922; WR Arnold, "TOBA News," *Chicago Defender*, February 28, 1925; Henry Gang Jines, Liberty Theater, *Chicago Defender*, January 20, 1923.

130. Starr's file with the Bureau of Veteran's Affairs lists his birth date as June 26, 1896, while his application for Social Security offers the May date. See: Ancestry.com. *U.S., Department of Veterans Affairs BIRLS Death File, 1850–2010* [database on-line]. Provo, UT, USA: Ancestry.com Operations, Inc., 2011; Ancestry.com. *U.S., Social Security Death Index, 1935–2014* [database on-line]. Provo, UT, USA: Ancestry.com Operations Inc, 2014-Number: 415–14–1650; Issue State: Tennessee; Issue Date: Before 1951; Year: 1900; Census Place: Nashville Ward 6, Davidson, Tennessee; Page: 7; Enumeration District: 0082; FHL microfilm: 1241564.

131. Year: 1900; Census Place: Nashville Ward 6, Davidson, Tennessee; Page: 7; Enumeration District: 0082; FHL microfilm: 1241564; Fedora Small Frank, *Beginnings on Market Street; Nashville and Her Jewry 1861–1901*, (Jewish Community of Nashville and Middle Tennessee, 1976), 180.

132. Nashville City Directories, 1897; Year: 1900; Census Place: Nashville Ward 6, Davidson, Tennessee; Page: 7; Enumeration District: 0082; FHL microfilm: 1241564; See Death Certificate for Rachel Lusky in Tennessee State Library and Archives; Nashville, Tennessee; *Tennessee Death Records, 1908–1959*; Roll #: M-5; 1901 Nashville Business Directory in Fedora Small Frank, *Beginnings on Market Street; Nashville and Her Jewry, 1861–1901*, Jewish Community of Nashville and Middle Tennessee, 1976, 180.

133. Frank, *Beginnings on Market Street* 1–3, 90, 157–58; Nashville City Directories; Ida Clyde Clarke, *All About Nashville*, (Nashville, 1912), 158–59, 180.

134. "Annual Report of Nashville Public Schools," 1913, 31; Nashville City Directory, 1914; Milton Starr Obituary, *Washington Post*, June 10, 1976; Clark, *All About Nashville*, 118–19; Milton's admittance to Vanderbilt was rare, for among the twelve to thirteen universities in Nashville, Jewish students were only allowed entry at five: Vanderbilt, the University of Nashville, Peabody, Ward Seminary, and the Nashville College for Women. Frank, *Beginnings on Market Street*, 94. Only Milton Starr and John T. Gibson in Philadelphia transferred

their university skills in terms of organization over into theater management on the future T.O.B.A. circuit.

135. Goldstein, "Now Is The Time to Show Your True Colors: Southern Jews, Whiteness, and The Rise of Jim Crow," 144.

136. Statistics of the Population in 1920, Table 31, page 500.

137. Lovett, *The African American History of Nashville*, 20.

138. Ida Clarke, *All About Nashville*, 1912, 220–21.

139. Ibid.

140. Christopher M. Scribner, "Nashville Offers Opportunity: *The Nashville Globe* and Business as a Means of Uplift, 1907–1913," *Tennessee Historical Quarterly*, Vol. 54, No. 1 (Spring 1995), 55.

141. *National Negro Classified Business Directory* (Wilmington Delaware: National Negro Business Directory System Inc., 1919).

142. National Negro Business League, Report of the 18th and 19th Annual Sessions, Chattanooga, Tenn. and Atlantic City, NJ (Washington DC, 1917), 2.

143. Theatrical Ads, *Globe* April 4, 1913; Nashville City Directory, 1913.

144. *Marshall, Bruce & Polk Nashville Directory, 1914.*

145. "Star Theatre Manager Beats Up a Little Boy," *Nashville Globe*, November 21, 1913. Just months after opening the original Starr Theater, its black manager E. E. Rice accused J. Starr in the *Globe* of "beating up a little boy" in front of the theater," for being disruptive during a movie. Supposedly, when Rice confronted Starr about this incident, Starr allegedly claimed "what is a little niger [*sic*] anyhow . . . I will do as a I please, they will come on to the show just the same."

146. "Explanation of the Star Theater Affair," *Globe*, December 5, 1913. Starr's response appeared on the front page. Starr contended that indeed he removed a "rough" African American adolescent "in long pants" who disrespected upstanding black patrons. Yet Starr asserted that Rice had lied about the details of the incident in retaliation for being fired that day for incompetence.

147. "Explanation of the Star Theater Affair," *Globe*, December 5, 1913.

148. Greenberg, 47, Goldstein, "Now is the Time," 140–43.

149. *Marshall, Bruce & Polk Nashville Directory, 1915.*

150. *Marshall, Bruce & Polk Nashville Directory, 1916*; "Bijou Has Weekly Feature Night," *Moving Picture World*, Oct–Dec 1916.

151. "The Bijou," *Chicago Defender*, September 15, 1917.

152. Rose Long Gilmore, *Davidson County Women in the World War, 1914–1919* (Nashville: Foster and Parkes, 1923), 484; See: Ancestry.com. *U.S., Department of Veterans Affairs BIRLS Death File, 1850–2010* [database on-line]. Provo, UT, USA: Ancestry.com Operations, Inc., 2011.

153. Theatrical Ad, *Nashville Globe*, January 5, 1917, January 12, 1917.

154. Theatrical Ads, *Nashville Globe*, February 2, 1917.

155. "Bijou Theater Nashville," *Nashville Globe*, December 6, 1918.

156. Ibid.

157. Theatrical Ads, *Nashville Globe*, December 20, 1918; Ethel Waters and Charles Samuels, *His Eye Is on the Sparrow: An Autobiography of Ethel Waters* (New York: Da Capo Press, 1992), 160–61.

158. Nashville Directories, City Directories, 1918–1920, 1926; Year: 1920; Census Place: Nashville Ward 8, Davidson, Tennessee; Roll: T625_1734; Page: 2A; Enumeration District: 33. The city directory listed family patriarch Joseph as the custodian of the Bijou in 1920 further cementing the idea that the show business was the Starr family business, no matter how low-ranked the position.

159. "The Monogram," *Indianapolis Freeman,* January 11, 1913.

160. Death Certificate for Emma Griffin, Illinois Deaths and Stillbirths, 1916–1947, FHL #1852630.

161. "Explanation of the Star Theater Affair," *Globe,* December 5, 1913.

## CHAPTER 3. T.O.B.A. FORMS

1. "The Old and the New," *Defender,* January 3, 1920.

2. Display Ad 24, *Defender,* June 5, 1920; "To Incorporate Southern Consolidated Vaude," *Billboard,* July 31, 1920; "New Combine of Southern Negro Houses in Announced," *Billboard,* January 1, 1921.

3. E. Franklin Frazier, "La Bourgeoise Noire," in Henry L. Gates and Gene Jarrett, *The New Negro: Readings on Race, Representation, and African American Culture, 1892–1938* (Princeton, 2007), 139–40. The New Negro, both as a definition of a political era and as the character of individual African Americans of the interwar period, has been written on extensively. For more New Negro historical scholarship, see Davarian L. Baldwin, *Chicago's New Negroes: Modernity, the Great Migration, and Black Urban Life* (Chapel Hill: University of North Carolina Press, 2007); Henry Louis Gates and Gene Andrew Jarrett, *The New Negro: Readings on Race, Representation, and African American Culture, 1892–1938* (Princeton, NJ: Princeton University Press, 2007); Erin Chapman, *Prove It On Me: New Negroes, Sex, and Popular Culture* (New York: Oxford University Press, 2012).

4. Robert Weems, *Desegregating the Dollar: African American Consumerism in the Twentieth Century* (New York: NYU Press, 1998), 21–28.

5. Stanley R. Latshaw, "Educating the Upper Three-Sevenths: How Trade Associations Have Used and May Use National Advertising to Increase Demand for Their Products," *Advertising and Selling Magazine,* January 29, 1921, 16–17.

6. *The Annual Meeting of the National Negro Business League,* Sixteenth Annual Meeting 1915, Boston, Massachusetts, 76–79.

7. Sadie Tanner Mossell, "The Standard of Living Among One Hundred Negro Migrant Families in Philadelphia," University of Pennsylvania, Ph.D. Thesis, 1921, 12–13, 30–31.

8. Charter of Incorporation #173, 1920, Tennessee State Archives.

9. City Directory, Chattanooga, 1920; Michelle Scott, *Blues Empress in Black Chattanooga: Bessie Smith and the Emerging Urban South* (Urbana: University of Illinois Press, 2008), 82–100.

10. "The Stage," *Defender,* August 17, 2018; "Kentucky News Letter," *The Moving Picture World,* September 14, 1918, 1601.

11. Ike Stevens, "The Corporation: A codification of the laws governing the creating of Domestic Corporations," (Nashville, TN: McQuiddy Printing Company, 1917), 3; Reevin took over ownership of the Grand Theatre in 1926, further reducing Slabosky's role in the venture.

12. Henry "Gang" Jines, "Liberty Theater," *Defender*, January 20, 1923; Charter of Incorporation #173.

13. Charter of Incorporation #173.

14. Ibid.

15. Ike Stevens, "The Corporation," 66–67; John S. Parker, ed., *The Corporation Manual, 22nd Edition*, Corporate Forms and Precedents: Charter Clauses: Films (New York: United States Corporation Company, 1921), 2007–8.

16. Charter of Incorporation #173.

17. Harwell Wells, "The Purpose of a Corporation: A Brief History," *Temple 10 Q: Temple Business Law Magazine*, https://www2.1aw.temple.edu/10q/purpose-corporation-brief-history/.

18. Neal B. Spahr, *Baldwin's Cumulative Code Supplement Tennessee*, 1920, (Louisville, KY: Baldwin Law Book Company, 1929); Thompson's Shannon's code of Tennessee, 1918 (Louisville, KY, Baldwin Law Book Company, 1918).

19. W. E. B. Du Bois, *The Negro in Business: Proceedings for the Fourth Conference for the Study of Negro Problems* (Atlanta: Atlanta University, 1899), 15.

20. Domestic Corporation Annual Report for Year 1922, Nashville, TN.

21. "New Combine of Southern Negro House Announced," *Billboard*, January 21, 1921.

22. Milton Starr, "Milton Starr Makes Statement," *Defender*, February 12, 1921; Display Ad 24, Defender, June 5, 1920.

23. Robert E. Weems Jr., "Out of the Shadows: Business Enterprise and African American Historiography," *Business and Economic History*, Vol. 26, No. 1 (Fall 1997), 205. Weems argues that although Washington's activism was often critiqued for its failure to prioritize political and social equality, his pro-black business stance was as nationalistic as those of European immigrants who encouraged consumers to "patronize the stores of your countrymen" or as militant as black organizations, like the Universal Negro Improvement Association, that also promoted "black business."

24. Report of the Seventeenth Annual Session of the National Negro Business League, Kansas City, MO, August 16, 17, 18, 1916, 162.

25. Report of the Sixteenth Annual Conference, Boston, MA, 187–88.

26. Theatre Managers Form Organization, *Defender*, June 19, 1920; William Henry Harrison Jr., *Colored Girls' and Boys' Inspiring United States History, And a Heart to Heart Talk about White Folks* (1921), 240.

27. Display Ad 24, *Defender*, June 5, 1920; "Big Circuit," *Defender*, June 5, 1920.

28. "New Combine of Southern Negro Houses is Announced," *The Billboard*, January 1, 1921.

29. Milton Starr, "Milton Starr Makes Statement," *Defender*, February 12, 1921.

30. Display Ad 17, *Defender*, March 12, 1921.

31. Display Ad 24, *Defender*, June 5, 1920.

32. The race of the theater owners was determined by consulting 1920–21 city directories in which African Americans were designated with a "c" by their names or displayed in a "colored only" portion of the directory. Breaux and Williams's gender were also discovered by looking at local Oklahoma black city directories, where they were noted with their full names and a "Mrs." prefix. *Polk-Hoffine Directory Co's Tulsa City Directory*, 1921, 19.

33. "TOBA Doings," *Defender,* April 2, 1921; "TOBA Doings," *Defender,* May 21, 1921.

34. Frank Montgomery, "Frank's Dope," *Defender,* April 23, 1921; "The Griffin Sisters: The First and Only Colored Women's Theatrical Booking Agency in the United States and Their Desires and Intentions," *Indianapolis Freeman,* February 14, 1914.

35. James Grant, *The Forgotten Depression: 1921, The Crash That Cured Itself* (New York: Simon & Schuster, 2014), 5–6; Milton Starr, "A Statement," *Defender,* June 18, 1921.

36. Display Ad 19, *Defender,* July 30, 1921.

37. Frank Montgomery, "Frank's Dope," *Defender,* May 21, 1921.

38. "Note or Two," *Defender,* May 15, 1920.

39. Annual Report of the Secretary of the Commonwealth to the Governor of Virginia and General Assembly of Virginia for the year ending Sept. 30, 1920 (Richmond, VA, 1921), 366; "Plan for New Theater," *Washington Post,* June 13, 1920; T. J. Calloway, "Pageant of Progress," *The Crisis,* February 1921, 155.

40. "Big Circuit," *Defender,* June 5, 1920; Display Ad 24, *Defender,* June 12, 1920.

41. "To Incorporate Southern Consolidated Vaudeville Circuit," *Billboard,* July 31, 1920.

42. Ibid; "Cummings Leaves for Stockholders Meeting," *Pensacola Journal,* January 5, 1922. Cummings was the manager of one black vaudeville theater, the Belmont, from 1920 to 1925; was part of the T.O.B.A. board in 1922; and was a real estate agent by 1930. Manuscript Census, Year: 1920; Census Place: Pensacola, Escambia, Florida; Roll: T625_219; Page: 7B; Enumeration District: 3; Year: 1930; Census Place: Pensacola, Escambia, Florida; Page: 6A; Enumeration District: 0017; FHL microfilm: 2340050.

43. "To Incorporate Southern Consolidated Vaudeville Circuit," *Billboard,* July 31, 1920.

44. Frank Montgomery, "Frank's Dope," *Defender,* May 21, 1921.

45. W. Fitzhugh Brundage, ed., *Beyond Blackface: African Americans and the Creation of Popular Culture, 1890–1930* (Chapel Hill: University of North Carolina Press, 2011), 28.

46. Frank Montgomery, "Frank's Dope," *Defender,* May 21, 1921; "Important Developments in the Vaudeville World," *Defender,* May 21, 1921.

47. "New Circuits of Negro Houses and the Probable Effects," *Billboard,* January 21, 1921.

48. Ibid.

49. "War at End," *Defender,* May 28, 1921; "Signs of Truce in War of Colored Circuit," *Afro-American,* June 3, 1921.

50. "Important Developments in the Vaudeville World," *Defender,* May 21, 1921; Display Ad 24, *Defender,* May 28, 1921.

51. "TOBA Meets Thursday," *Afro-American,* January 26, 1923.

52. Merger news did not settle until two years after the chartering of the organization, with frequent notices of clandestine meetings in Chattanooga. There was continued discussion of T.O.B.A. assuming the theaters of the Southern Vaudeville Consolidated and a merger with the Managers and Performers Consolidated Circuit ("Struggle for Supremacy," *Billboard,* April 1, 1922). Eventually the smaller circuits were left to their own devices and the M & P-controlled theaters in Pensacola; Jacksonville; St. Petersburg; Tampa; Miami; Ocola; Savannah, Augusta, and Columbus, Georgia; Houston; Mobile; Greenville; Spartanburg, South Carolina; and Gulf Port, Mississippi. See "Circuits Join," *Defender,* November 11, 1922.

53. "Air of Mystery," *Billboard,* October 1921; "New Circuit Exposed," *Defender,* March 25, 1922.

54. Domestic Corporation Annual Report for 1922, #2788, July 1922, Tennessee State Library.

55. "News from New Orleans, Louisiana," *Broad Ax*, January 21, 1922; "New Orleans Man to Head $5,000,000 Theatre Circuit," *Dallas Express*, January 28, 1922; Five million dollars in 1922 is about $77.2 million in 2020 dollars. https://www.measuringworth.com/calculators/uscompare/relativevalue.php, accessed August 24, 2021.

56. Tim Owsley, "Show Business," *Defender*, June 25, 1927.

57. S. H. Dudley, "Open Letter," *Defender*, December 15, 1917.

58. "TOBA to Have Try Out House," *Afro-American*, April 1924.

59. Juliet E. K. Walker, *History of Black Business in America: Capitalism, Race, Entrepreneurship*, (New York, 2009), 185–86, 193; "Industry and Business," *Afro-American*, April 13, 1929.

60. National Negro Business League, Sixteenth Annual Meeting 1915, 74–78.

61. "Theatre Moguls Now in Session," *Afro-American*, June 6, 1922.

62. Display Ad 2, *Philadelphia Tribune*, May 23, 1925.

63. Jason Chambers, *Madison Avenue and The Color Line: African Americans in the Advertising Industry* (Philadelphia: University of Pennsylvania Press, 2011), 28–29.

64. "The Stage," *Freeman*, April 17, 1915.

65. Display Ad, *Defender*, January 19, 1924.

66. "$5000 Suit," *Defender*, June 10, 1922; Display Ad 32, *Defender*, January 13, 1923.

67. Monroe Nathan Work, ed., *Negro Year Book and Annual Encyclopedia of the Negro 1921–1922* (Tuskegee, AL: Negro Year Book Publishing Co., 1922), 303–12.

68. Display Ad 26, *Defender*, June 10, 1922.

69. Weems, *Desegregating the Dollar*, 11–14.

70. Southern Newspapers Publishing Association advertisement, *Advertising and Selling*, January 15, 1921, 1.

71. Clarence Muse, *Way Down South* (Los Angeles: David Graham Fischer, 1932), 107.

72. Muse, *Way Down South*, 50, 77–78.

73. Theater Handbills, 1927, in Charles Henry Douglass Business Records, Middle Georgia State Archives, Washington Library; Ads, *Evening Star*, April 8, 1923.

74. Contract, Charles M. Russell (Ma Rainey and Her Paramount Steppers), Douglass Theater, February 10, 1928, in Charles Henry Douglass Business Records, Middle Georgia State Archives, Washington Library.

75. Letter from Bartling Norfolk to Douglass, October 5, 1927; Letter from Joseph Douglass to C. H. Douglass, April 16, 1928, Charles Henry Douglass Business Records, Middle Georgia State Archives, Washington Library.

76. "New Act," *Defender*, July 24, 1926.

77. Reevin to Douglass, March 10, 1925, Charles Henry Douglass Business Records, Middle Georgia State Archives, Washington Library.

78. Reevin to Stein, September 19, 1927, Charles Henry Douglass Business Records, Middle Georgia State Archives, Washington Library.

79. Uncle Dudley, "T.O.B.A. Improving to Use Any Miller Show," *Defender*, January 1, 1927; "Additional Stage News: On the T.O.B.A.," *Defender*, December 18, 1926.

80. Leonard Reed interviewed by Rusty Frank, February 27, 1993, Jazz Oral History Collection Program, Archives Center, National Museum of American History.

81. Vaudeville, or classic blues, refers to songs that stemmed from Southern black communities and had a twelve- or sixteen-bar format, an AAB lyric pattern, and were initiated by black women vocalists on the vaudeville or tent show stage in the 1910s to 1920s. Vocalists were often backed by an ensemble of drums, brass, and piano. For a technical discussion, see "Blues" by David Evans in Mellonee V. Burnim and Portia K. Maultsby, eds., *African American Music: An Introduction* (Routledge, 2015), 127–31.

82. Daphne Duval Harrison, *Black Pearls: Blues Queens of the 1920s* (New Brunswick, NJ: Rutgers University Press, 1988), 31–41.

83. James A. Jackson, "Showfolks More than Entertainers," *Messenger* (1925), 16.

84. Display Ad, *Defender*, January 19, 1924; Display Ad 31, *Defender*, April 11, 1925; Display Ad 35, *Defender*, February 7, 1925; Reevin to Douglass, May 27, 1925, Charles Henry Douglass Business Records, Middle Georgia State Archives, Washington Library.

85. Amusements, *Washington Evening Star*, April 1, 1923; Display Ad 2, *Philadelphia Tribune*, May 23, 1925.

86. "Bennett Optimistic: President of T.O.B.A. Looks Forward to Better Conditions," *Defender*, January 28, 1922; "TOBA Meets," *Defender*, February 9, 1924; "Reevin Optimistic," *Defender*, February 14, 1925; "TOBA Meets," *Defender*, December 12, 1925.

87. Domestic Corporation, Annual Report to the State of Tennessee #02944, 1925.

88. Jack L. Cooper, "Colored Actors Union and T.O.B.A. Heads Hold Premier Session," *Defender*, March 28, 1925.

89. Cooper, "Colored Actors Union and T.O.B.A.," March 28, 1925.

90. Rodgers in Gates and Jarrett, 130.

91. Uncle Rad Kees, "Colored Vaudeville Benevolent Association: Its Purpose, Possibilities and Faults," *Freeman*, February 19, 1910; Karen Sotiropoulos, *Staging Race: Black Performers in the Turn of the Century America* (Cambridge, MA: Harvard University Press, 2006), 201–3.

92. "C. V. B. A. Show," *Defender*, April 22, 1922.

93. "Clarence Powell of the Georgia Minstrels, Praises His Former Friend and Benefactor," *Defender*, April 22, 1911; "Actor Dies Suddenly," *Afro-American*, February 16, 1923; "Final Curtain Rung Down on Gilpin," *New York Amsterdam News*, May 14, 1930; Certificate of Incorporation of the Negro Actors' Guild of America, October 14, 1936, Negro Actors' Guild of America records, box 1, Schomburg Center for Research in Black Culture, New York Public Library.

94. Alfred L. Berheim, *The Business of the Theater* (New York: Actor's Equity Association, 1932), 1.

95. George Fuller Golden, *My Lady Vaudeville and Her White Rats*, New York, 1909, 80–81; Constitution and By-Laws of White Rats Actors' Union of America, Inc., 1912.

96. Charter member George Fuller Golden alluded to the clear racial exclusion in discussing the naming of the organization that was inspired by the British vaudevillian society, the Water Rats of London. "Rats" as a title was the inverted form of "star," but the American selection of "white" was based in part of the advanced age of some of its members (with their supposed white hair), but "for other reasons as well," that afterwards "were thought by many to have been a mistake." George Fuller Golden, *My Lady Vaudeville and Her White Rats* (New York, 1909), 73.

97. Alfred L. Berheim, *The Business of the Theater* (New York: Actor's Equity Association, 1932), 132–33.

98. Chas. Berry, "CAU Facts," *Defender,* October 29, 1921.

99. *Federal Trade Commission vs. Vaudeville Managers' Protective Association,* et al., Stenographic transcript [of proceedings] before the Federal Trade Commission, New York City. Docket no. 128. United States, Washington, Galt & Williams, 1919, 15–16.

100. Federal Trade Commission vs. Vaudeville Managers' Protective Association, 11–13; "Palmer to Examine Vaudeville Evidence," *New York Times,* April 2, 1920.

101. "Vaudeville Heads Win Final Victory," *New York Times,* April 4, 1920. E. F. Albee argued that the March 1920 decision was of "greatest importance to the entire theatrical business in all its branches." (See "Vaudeville Heads Win Final Victory," *New York Times,* April 4, 1920). Between July and August 1919, the actors prevailed against the theater monopoly after a thirty-day strike that closed theaters in eight states for lack of performers and was supported by stage managers, stage hands, musicians, truck drivers, and handbill posters. The Actors' Equity Association of the 4As or "Equity" became the representative union for American theater actors; an eight-performance work week became standard and rehearsing without pay would be limited, among other labor concerns. Alfred L. Berheim, *The Business of the Theater,* (New York, Actor's Equity Association, 1932) 135, http://www.actorsequity.org/AboutEquity/timeline/timeline_1919.html.

102. J. A. Jackson, "Colored Actors' Union," *Messenger,* November 1, 1925.

103. Kennard Williams, "South's Amusements Need General Housecleaning," *Afro-American,* November 22, 1924.

104. "Dud's Dope," *Defender,* March 8, 1924.

105. Nadine George Graves, "Spreading the Sand," 12; J. A. Jackson, "The Colored Actors Union," *Messenger,* November 1, 1925.

106. "Colored Actors Union Is Campaigning for Members," *Billboard,* March 29, 1924.

107. Telfair, "How the Union Stands," *Defender,* March 29, 1924.

108. Cooper, "Colored Actors Union and T.O.B.A.," March 28, 1925.

109. Local chapters of the American Federation of Musicians succeeded in closing DC's Howard Theatre for an evening in March 1925 over a dispute of nonpayment of salary to the stage crew and the unionized orchestra. "Police Called in to Settle Actors' Strike," *Afro-American,* March 21, 1925.

110. Cooper, "Colored Actors Union and T.O.B.A.," March 28, 1925.

111. "TOBA Directors Hold Meeting," *Pittsburgh Courier,* July 25, 1925.

112. "J. A. Jackson Newspaperman to Lay Actors' Claims Before Theatrical Owners Booking Association," *Afro-American,* December 19, 1925.

113. "TOBA Meets," *Afro-American,* December 12, 1925.

114. Cooper, "Colored Actors Union and T.O.B.A.," March 28, 1925.

## CHAPTER 4. THE MULTIPLE MEANINGS OF T.O.B.A.

1. Alyn Shipton, *Hi-De-Ho: The Life of Cab Calloway* (New York: Oxford University Press, 2010), 6–9; "'Shuffle Along,'" Race Musical Comedy, Is Real Broadway 'Wow,'" *Defender,*

August 27, 1921; *Shuffle Along* playbill, Chicago Theater Collection-Historic Programs [Olympic 1922–12–17], Special Collections, Chicago Public Library.

2. Calloway by Driggs; "Cab with 'Plantation Days,'" *Afro-American*, March 19, 1927.

3. C. A. Leonard, "Our Stage History, Almost Forgotten Is Well Worth Knowing and Being Proud Of," *Defender*, August 10, 1929.

4. Daphne Duval Harrison, *Black Pearls: Blues Queens of the 1920s* (New Brunswick, NJ: Rutgers University Press, 1988), 23.

5. "W. R. Arnold Quits T.O.B.A. to Travel," *Defender*, November 14, 1925.

6. "T.O.B.A. Actors Struggle to Live," *Afro-American*, February 7, 1925.

7. The flapper figure was the social representation of the New Woman between the ages of eighteen and twenty-four, who openly smoked, drank, danced, and engaged in premarital sexual activity, while the cake eater was the effeminate man who adopted a polished fashion style, did not engage in manual labor, and did not fit stereotypical images of "rugged" masculinity. See Joshua Zeitz, *Flapper: A Madcap Story of Sex, Style, Celebrity, and the Women Who Made America Modern* (New York: Broadway Books, 2007) and Stephen Duncombe and Andrew Mattson, *The Bobbed Hair Bandit: A Story of Crime and Celebrity in 1920s New York* (New York: Mortalis, 2007), 93, 149.

8. Lucy Moore, *Anything Goes: A Biography of the Roaring Twenties* (New York: Overlook Press, 2011), 15.

9. For details on the racial violence during the summer of World War I's aftermath, see Cameron McWhirter, *Red Summer: The Summer of 1919 and the Awakening of Black America*, (New York: Henry Holt and Co., 2011).

10. "Walls of Hell," *Half Century Magazine*, April 1919.

11. Alain Locke, ed. *The New Negro: Voices of the Harlem Renaissance* (New York: Albert & Charles Boni, Inc., 1925), 5–12.

12. Henry T. Sampson, *Blacks in Blackface: A Sourcebook on Early Black Musical Shows* (Lanham, MD: Scarecrow Press, 1980), 133.

13. W. R. Arnold, T.O.B.A. News, *Defender*, February 28, 1925.

14. Display Ad 24, *Defender*, June 5, 1920, "To Incorporate Southern Consolidated Vaude," *Billboard*, July 31, 1920; New Combine of Southern Negro Houses in Announced, *Billboard*, January 1, 1921.

15. "Thespianism in Louisville, Kentucky," *Freeman*, July 6, 1912.

16. Tom Fletcher, *100 Years of the Negro in Show Business* (1954, New York: DeCapo Press, 1984), 6–9.

17. Theatrical Advertisements, *Defender*, July 30, 1921.

18. Bessie Dudley interviewed by Robert O'Meally, June 29, 1992, Jazz Oral History Collection Program, Archives Center, National Museum of American History.

19. Saidiya Hartman, *Wayward Lives, Beautiful Experiments: Intimate Histories of Social Upheaval* (New York: W.W. Norton & Co., 2019), 302–3.

20. Bessie Dudley interviewed by Robert O' Meally; "Lincoln, Vaudeville and Pictures," *Afro-American*, January 12, 1923.

21. Sadie Goodson interviewed by Lolis Eric Eli, January 29, 1993, Jazz Oral History Collection Program, Archives Center, National Museum of American History; "Sadie Good-

son" in Year: 1920; Census Place: Pensacola, Escambia, Florida; Roll: T625_220; Page: 19A; Enumeration District: 36.

22. Peg Leg Bates interviewed by Rusty Frank, April 4, 1993, Jazz Oral History Collection Program, Archives Center, National Museum of American History.

23. Fletcher, 22.

24. Mary Beth Swetnam Mathews, *Doctrine and Race: African American Evangelicals and Fundamentalism* (Tuscaloosa: University of Alabama Press, 2017), 99–103.

25. Vivienne, "Theater Folks and Theatergoers: Stage Aspirant," *Defender*, February 6, 1926; Vivienne, "Theater Folks and Theatergoers: Our Belief in God," *Defender*, April 24, 1926.

26. Charles H. Wesley, "The Religious Attitudes of Negro Youth: A Preliminary Study of Opinion in an Urban and a Rural Community," *The Journal of Negro History*, Vol. 21, No. 4 (October 1936), 383–84.

27. Bessie Dudley interviewed by Robert O' Meally.

28. Albert Murray, *Stomping the Blues* (New York: DeCapo Press, 1976), 23–44; Harrison, *Black Pearls*, 30–37, 111; Victoria W. Wolcott, *Remaking Respectability, African American Women in Interwar Detroit* (Chapel Hill: University of North Carolina Press, 2001), 35–37.

29. Fourteenth Census of the United States, 1920. Records of the Bureau of the Census, Record Group 29. National Archives, Washington, DC, Census Place: Pensacola, Escambia, Florida; Roll: T625 220; Page: 19A; Enumeration District: 36.

30. Sadie Goodson interviewed by Lolis Eric Eli.

31. Clarence Williams, "Gulf Coast Blues" (New York: Clarence Williams Publishing, 1923).

32. Lawrence Levine, *Highbrow/Lowbrow: The Emergence of Cultural Hierarchy in America* (Cambridge, MA: Harvard University Press, 1990), 77.

33. Willard B. Gatewood, *Aristocrats of Color: The Black Elite* (Fayetteville: University of Arkansas Press, 2000), 187–95; Evelyn Higginbotham, *Righteous Discontent: The Women's Movement in the Black Baptist Church, 1880–1920* (Cambridge, MA: Harvard University Press, 1993), 187.

34. Gillian M. Rodger, *Champagne Charlie and Pretty Jemima: Variety Theater in the Nineteenth Century* (Urbana: University of Illinois Press, 2010), 5–7; Karen Sotiropoulos, *Staging Race: Black Performers in the Turn of the Century America* (Cambridge, MA: Harvard University Press, 2006), 163–65.

35. Fourteenth Census of the United States, 1920. Records of the Bureau of the Census, Record Group 29. National Archives, Washington, DC, Year: 1920; Census Place: Baltimore Ward 14, Baltimore (Independent City), Maryland; Roll: T625_663; Page: 7B; Enumeration District: 238; Shipton 16–17.

36. Cab Calloway interviewed by Frank Driggs.

37. Peg Leg Bates interviewed by Rusty Frank; Jacqui Malone, *Steppin' on the Blues: The Visible Rhythms of African American Dance* (Urbana: University of Illinois, 1996), 55.

38. Peg Leg Bates interviewed by Rusty Frank; "Emma Bates, Clayton Bates" in Year: 1910; Census Place: Fairview, Greenville, South Carolina; Roll: T624_1460; Page: 12A; Enumeration District: 0012; FHL microfilm: 1375473.

39. Marshall Royal interviewed by Patricia Willard, October 25, 1977, Jazz Oral History Collection Program, Archives Center, National Museum of American History.

40. Marshall Royal interviewed by Patricia Willard.

41. Kennard Williams, "T.O.B.A. Actors Struggle to Live," *Afro-American*, February 7, 1925.

42. Department of Commerce, *Statistical Abstract of the United States, 1925*, (Washington Government Printing Office, 1926), 54. "Showmen" refers to circus performers and entertainers who might have performed acrobatic and novelty acts rather than solely acting or singing on the vaudeville or dramatic stage.

43. W. R. Arnold, "Conditions on T.O.B.A. Bright," *Defender*, February 7, 1925.

44. Vivienne, "Theater Folks and Theatergoers: Stage Struck," *Defender*, November 7, 1925.

45. Harrison, 33.

46. Vivienne, "Theater Folks and Theatergoers: Stage Struck," *Defender*, November 7, 1925.

47. "New Act," *Defender*, July 24, 1926; "New Sister Team," *Defender*, July 17, 1926.

48. Cab with "Plantation Days," *Afro-American*, March 19, 1927.

49. Cab Calloway interviewed by Frank Driggs; Transcript of Danny Barker interview by Michael White, July 21–22, 1992, Jazz Oral History Collection Program, Archives Center, National Museum of American History, 85.

50. "T.O.BA. Head Sees Optimism in the South," *Defender*, August 21, 1926.

51. LeRoy Ashby, *With Amusement for All: A History of American Popular Culture Since 1830* (Lexington: University Press of Kentucky, 2006), 195–97.

52. Amy Henderson, "Media and the Rise of Celebrity Culture," *OAH Magazine of History*, Vol. 6, No. 4, *Communication in History: The Key to Understanding* (Spring 1992), 50–52.

53. Marlis Schweitzer, "The Mad Search for Beauty: Actresses' Testimonials, the Cosmetics Industry, and the 'Democratization of Beauty,'" *The Journal of the Gilded Age and Progressive Era*, Vol. 4, No. 3 (July 2005), 285–87; Davarian Baldwin, "Chicago's New Negroes," *American Studies*, Vol. 44, No. 1 New Voices in American Studies (Spring/Summer 2003), 137; Susannah Walker, *Style and Status: Selling Beauty to African American Women, 1920–1975* (Lexington: University of Kentucky Press, 2007), 72–76.

54. Display Ad 8, *Afro-American*, September 24, 1927.

55. Zakiya A. Adair, "Respectable Vamp: A Black Feminist Analysis of Florence Mills' Career in Early Vaudeville Theater," *Journal of African American Studies*, Vol. 17, No. 1 Special Issue: *Black Girls' and Women's Resistance Strategies* (March 2013) 11–14; Display Ad 26, *Defender*, March 31, 1928; Display Ads, *Afro-American*, December 22, 1928.

56. Display Ad 31, *Afro-American*, June 15, 1929.

57. Display Ad 24, *Defender*, February 11, 1926.

58. Leonard Reed interviewed by Rusty Frank, February 27, 1993, Jazz Oral History Collection Program, Archives Center, National Museum of American History.

59. David Kyvig, *Daily Life in the United States, 1920–1940* (Chicago: Ivan R. Dee, 2002), 12.

60. Contract, DeWayman Niles and C. H. Douglass, December 16, 1924, in Charles Henry Douglass Business Records, Middle Georgia Archives, Washington Library, Macon, GA.

61. A scene in *Bessie* dramatizes how Rainey accounted all the salary allotted to her in her contract. Actual contracts with Rainey reveal the inequities of a contract that promised only "50% of (the house) Receipts" for an ensemble of 23 people for three separate dates. With this large number of people in the cast, there would have to be a full house each night just for Rainey to be able to pay the cast, let alone clear any profit. Dee Rees dir. *Bessie*, HBO, 2015; Contracts, Charles M. Russell (for Ma Rainey) to Ben Stein, February 10, 1928, in Charles Henry Douglass Business Records, Middle Georgia State Archives, Washington Library.

62. Clifford Edward Watkins, *Showman: The Life and Music of Perry George Lowery* (Jackson: University of Mississippi Press, 2003), 79.

63. Cab Calloway interview by Frank Driggs; Transcript, Leonard Reed interviewed by Rusty Frank, February 27, 1993, Jazz Oral History Collection Program, Archives Center, National Museum of American History, 39.

64. Forty-eight weeks is the estimate for full-time work, as T.O.B.A. offered between forty and sixty weeks of work barring a downturn in the season. In 1929 the average farmworker made $44.52 monthly for a seven-month season, totaling $311.64. In 1926 a coal miner who worked by "hand or picked" could make $120.62 a month or $1447.44 a year. See *BLS Monthly Labor Review*, July 1939, 59; *Hours & Earnings in Bitumonous Coal Mining*, 1929: Bulletin of the United States Bureau Labor of Statistics, No. 516, 2; Mary Elizabeth Pidgeon, *Wages of Women in 13 States* (Washington, DC: United States Government Publishing Office, 1931), 142–43.

65. Contracts, Theaters, Charles Henry Douglass Business Records, Middle Georgia Archives, Washington Library, Macon, GA.

66. Leonard Reed interviewed by Rusty Frank.

67. Jesse Cobb and C. H. Douglass, Contract, December 15, 1924, in Charles Henry Douglass Business Records, Middle Georgia Archives, Washington Library, Macon, GA.

68. Ledger, 1931–1934, in Frank Schiffman Apollo Theater Collection, Archives Center, National Museum of American History. See historical comparison calculators at https://www.measuringworth.com/calculators/uscompare/relativevalue.php, accessed August 12, 2021.

69. Transcript of Danny Barker interview by Michael White, July 21–22, 1992, Jazz Oral History Collection Program, Archives Center, National Museum of American History, 85.

70. Elizabeth Stordeur Pryor, *Colored Travelers: Mobility and the Fight for Citizenship before the Civil War* (Baltimore: Johns Hopkins Press, 2016).

71. The Great Migration was a demographic shift in which an estimated 1.2 million African Americans moved from rural and urban Southern centers to urban Northern centers between 1915 to 1930. Eric Arnesen, *Black Protest and the Great Migration: A Brief History with Documents*, Bedford/ St Martin's, 1; Isabel Wilkerson, *The Warmth of Other Suns: The Epic Story of the Great Migration* (New York: Random House, 2010), 178–79.

72. Pigmeat Markham interview by Tony Bruno, City College New York, April 17–18, 1972, in Camille Billops and James V. Hatch Archives, Stuart A. Rose Manuscript, Archives, and Rare Book Library, Emory University.

73. Vivienne, "Theater Folks and Theatergoers: Parents' Opinion," *Defender*, November 14, 1925.

74. Hartman, 301.

75. Vivienne, "Theater Folks and Theatergoers: Stage Struck," *Defender*, November 7, 1925.

76. Clarence Muse, *Way Down South*, (Los Angeles: David Graham Fischer, 1932), 17.

77. Adolphus "Doc" Cheatham interviewed by Frank Driggs, December 7–8, 1992, Jazz Oral History Collection Program, Archives Center, National Museum of American History; "Charles Neal, In Oh Kay-See," *Defender*, February 13, 1926.

78. Michael W. Harris, *The Rise of Gospel Blues: The Music of Thomas Andrew Dorsey in the Urban Church* (New York: Oxford University Press, 1992), 39–44, 148–49; Thomas Dorsey and Hudson Whittaker, "Its Tight Like That," *Vocalian*, 1928.

79. Malone, 80–82.

80. Michelle R. Scott, *Blues Empress in Black Chattanooga: Bessie Smith and the Emerging Urban South* (Urbana: University of Illinois, 2008), 121–23; Jill Watts, *Hattie McDaniel: Black Ambition, White Hollywood* (Amistad Press, 2005), 61–63.

81. Leonard Reed interviewed by Rusty Frank.

82. Transcript of Fayard Nicholas interview by Rusty E. Frank, June 8, 1992, Jazz Oral History Project Archives Center, National Museum of American History, 112.

83. Malone, 81; Sharon Ammen, *May Irwin, Singing Shouting and the Shadow Minstrelsy*, (Urbana: University of Illinois Press, 2017), 90–114; "Mammy's Carolina Twins: A Southern Lullaby," 1898 in Samuel DeVincent Sheet Music Collection, Archives Center, National Museum of American History.

84. "Sammy Davis, Jr.: I've Gotta Be Me," dir. by Sam Pollard, *American Masters*, 2017.

85. Child Entertainer Laws, https://www.dol.gov/whd/state/childentertain.htm, accessed September 27, 2017; See Nancy Pride, "Incidents Preceding the Louisiana Child Labor Law of 1912," *Louisiana History: The Journal of the Louisiana Historical Association*, Vol. 19 (Autumn 1978), 437–45.

86. Jane Addams, Henry Baird Favill, and Jean M. Gordon, "Child Labor on the Stage: A Symposium," *The Annals of the American Academy of Political and Social Science*, Vol. 38, *Uniform Child Labor Laws* (July 1911), 62.

87. Marshal Royal had formal music training with a private tutor in the 1920s, Cab Calloway took music lessons at Douglass High School in Baltimore, and the Nicholas Brothers had no formal dance training but were academically tutored on the road. The 1940 census lists both Fayard and Harold Nicholas as having completed the fourth year of high school, and they had been professionally performing since 1929. United States of America, Bureau of the Census. Sixteenth Census of the United States, 1940. Washington, DC: National Archives and Records Administration, 1940 Census Place: New York, New York, New York; Roll: T627_2667; Page: 10A; Enumeration District: 31–1809.

88. "Valada the Great," *Freeman*, January 11, 1913; Mark Miller, *High Hat, Trumpet and Rhythm: The Life and Music of Valaida Snow* (Toronto: Mercury Press, 2007).

89. "Gibson Family Sextet Rehearses," *Cleveland Call and Post*, October 4, 1941.

90. Marshal Royal Jr. interviewed by Patricia Willard, 1977, Jazz Oral History Collection Program, Archives Center, National Museum of American History; Marshal Royal and Claire Gordon, *Marshal Royal: A Jazz Survivor* (London: Bloomsbury Academic, 2001).

91. Transcript of Fayard Nicholas interview by Rusty E. Frank, June 8, 1992, Jazz Oral History Project Archives Center, National Museum of American History.

92. Donald Bogle, *Bright Boulevards, Bold Dreams: The Story of Black Hollywood* (New York: Ballantine Books, 2005), 113–14, 185–91.

93. Bogle, 26–27.

94. Richard Lewis Ward, *A History of Hal Roach Studios* (Carbondale: Southern Illinois University Press, 2005); "Sammy Gets New Movie Contract," *Afro-American*, July 17, 1926.

95. Interview with Pigmeat Markham by Tony Bruno.

96. Milton Starr, "A Statement," *Defender*, June 18, 1921.

97. Annual meeting details were covered in both industry and black periodicals as discussed in chapter 4. See "Bennett Heads T.O.B.A. Circuit of Colored Houses," *Billboard*, January 14, 1922; "T.O.B.A. Directors in Season Meeting; Book Bigger Shows," *Afro-American*, August 27, 1927; "T.O.B.A. Doings," *Defender*, April 2, 1921; "T.O.B.A. Doings," *Defender*, April 30, 1921.

98. Salem Whitney Tutt, "Observations," *Defender*, February 6, 1926.

99. Leonard Reed interviewed by Rusty Frank.

100. Kennard Williams, "T.O.B.A. Actors Struggle to Live," *Afro-American*, February 7, 1925.

101. G. M. Howell to Ben Stein, November 26, 1927, Charles Henry Douglass Business Records, Middle Georgia Archives, Washington Library, Macon, GA.

102. "Bijou Theater, Equal of Any Other Colored Theater," *Nashville Globe*, December 6, 1918.

103. Tony Langston, "Western Vaudeville Managers' Association Sets Example for Circuit Using 'Our' People," *Defender*, December 6, 1924.

104. S. H. Dudley, "Uncle Dud Writes," *Defender*, December 13, 1924.

105. Tony Langston, "Western Vaudeville Managers' Association Sets Example for Circuit Using 'Our' People," *Defender*, December 6, 1924; Salem Tutt Whitney, "Observations," *Defender*, June 5, 1926.

106. Salem Tutt Whitney, "Observations," *Defender*, June 5, 1926.

107. Whitney, "Observations," June 5, 1926.

108. "Cover the Stage," *Baltimore Afro-American*, May 16, 1924; Salem Tutt Whitney, "Observations," *Defender*, June 5, 1926.

109. Salem Whitney Tutt, "Observations," *Defender*, February 6, 1926.

110. "Riot in Theater Leads to Lynching of Negro Minstrels," *St. Louis Republic*, February 18, 1902; Ferdinand Barnett, "The Lynch Law," *Lewiston Daily Sun*, May 24, 1902; "Negro Minstrels Are Mobbed in Arkansas," *San Francisco Call*, January 15, 1911.

111. Muse, *Way Down South*, 62; Harrison, *Black Pearls*, 25; "Griffin Sisters Helping the Stage," *Defender*, January 10, 1914.

112. Reevin to Douglass, December 5, 1924; Reevin to Smith, January 22, 1925, Manager Correspondence, Charles Henry Douglass Business Records, Middle Georgia Archives, Washington Library, Macon, GA.

113. Ethel Waters and Charles Samuels, *His Eye Is on the Sparrow: An Autobiography of Ethel Waters* (New York: Da Capo Press, 1992), 167–72.

114. Starr to Stein, November 15, 1925, in Charles Henry Douglass Business Records, Washington Library, Macon, GA.

115. John Levy interviewed by John Mitchell, December 10–11, 2006, Jazz Oral History Collection Program, Archives Center, National Museum of American History. Levy recalled the story of attempting to end a performance in Cicero, Illinois, at 3 a.m. only to stare down the barrel of gun and hear "Hey, kid, take that thing (bass) off; we're gonna have a show."; "Actor Dies from Blows of Central Park Officer: Man Left Dying," *The New York Amsterdam News*, September 1, 1926.

116. The Tulsa Massacre has been a renewed focus of documentaries and popular television productions between 2019 and 2021, including HBO's *The Watchmen* and *Lovecraft Country*. Samuel Spencer, "Lovecraft Country: The True Story of the 1921 Tulsa Massacre," *Newsweek*, October 12, 2020, https://www.newsweek.com/lovecraft-country-episode-9-1921-tulsa-massacre-riot-real-life-true-story-hbo-1538238; Jennifer Vineyard, "The Tulsa Race Massacre Happened 99 Years Ago," *New York Times*, October 21, 2019, https://www.nytimes.com/2019/10/21/arts/television/watchmen-tulsa-race-riot.html.

117. Scott Ellsworth, *Death in a Promised Land: The Tulsa Race Riot of 1921* (Baton Rouge: Louisiana State University Press, 1982), 13–15.

118. "Colored Business Directory," *Tulsa Star*, February 7, 1920.

119. Ellsworth, *Death in a Promised Land*, 3; Advertisements, *Half Century Magazine*, 1918.

120. "What's at the Dreamland Theater-Tulsa, OK?" *Freeman*, February 6, 1915.

121. "T.O.B.A. Doings," *Defender*, April 23, 1921.

122. Ibid; "T.O.B.A. Doings," *Defender*, March 19, 1921; "An Open Letter: Southern Theater Manager Tells the Whole World a Mouthful," *Defender*, May 14, 1921.

123. This Week, *Afro American*, January 21, 1921.

124. Cameron McWhirter, *Red Summer: The Summer of 1919 and the Awakening of Black America* (New York: Henry Holt and Co., 2011); Harper Barnes, *Never Been a Time: The 1917 Race Riot That Sparked the Civil Rights Movement* (London: Walker Books, 2008); Charles Lumpkin, *American Pogrom: The East St. Louis Race Riot and Black Politics* (Athens: Ohio University Press, 2008). The script for most of these instances was the same: rumors that savage African American men or boys attacked a white woman swirled around a city's white community until vigilante white men avenged the virtue of white womanhood by lynching the supposed attackers and destroying the black community at large. Another key catalyst to white supremacist violence was African American economic success. The results in each of these previous cases were similar: white mobs destroyed black-owned residential and commercial property and injured or murdered Africans American citizens while sustaining few injuries or deaths of their own, all in an attempt to assert white dominance.

125. Alfred L. Brophy, *Reconstructing the Dreamland: The Tulsa Riot of 1921: Race, Reparations, and Reconciliation* (New York: Oxford University Press, 2002), xvii.

126. Ellsworth, *Death in a Promised Land*, 45–47; Alfred L. Brophy, *Reconstructing the Dreamland*, 26–36.

127. Ellsworth, 51–53.

128. "Leading Men Lost Lives in Tulsa," *Afro-American*, June 10, 1921; Brophy, 53.

129. "Police Aided Tulsa Rioters," *Defender*, June 11, 1921; Brophy 53–55.

130. Tulsa Chapter Red Cross Disaster Relief, Condensed Report, December 31, 1921, 3.

131. "Former Morgan Teacher Tells of Tulsa Riot," *Afro-American*, June 17, 1921.

132. "Tulsa Riot Ruins," *Afro-American*, July 1, 1921.

133. "Leading Men Lost Lives in Tulsa," *Afro-American*, June 10, 1921.

134. Walter F. White, "Tulsa's Shame Due to Corrupt Rule," *Defender*, June 18, 1921; The Dixieland Theatre was managed by William Redfern and, although not as heavily patronized as the Dreamland, was also damaged as a property in the Greenwood District. See *Polk-Hoffhine Directory Co's Tulsa City Directory*, 1921, 19.

135. Maurice Williams, *Disaster Relief Report, June 1921*, 4. In 1920 renewed efforts were made to locate mass unmarked graves of the Massacre's black victims. Tony Simpson and Jenny Wagon Courts, "Mass Grave Discovered in Search for 1921 Tulsa Race Massacre Victims," October 22, 2020. https://abcnews.go.com/US/mass-grave-discovered-search-1921-tulsa-race-massacre/story?id=73771538.

136. "T.O.B.A. Doings," *Defender*, July 2, 1921; Mitchell and Joseph Carmouche continued their careers through the 1930s until they relocated to Georgia and retired in Brunswick, where they opened a grocery store. See United States of America, Bureau of the Census. Sixteenth Census of the United States, 1940. Washington, DC: National Archives and Records Administration, 1940. T627, Census Place: Brunswick, Glynn, Georgia; Roll: T627_678; Page: 3B; Enumeration District: 63–10.

137. "Merry Christmas and Happy New Year Everybody!" *Indianapolis Freeman*, December 28, 1912; "A Note or Two," *Defender*, March 25, 1922; *J.W. Williams V. the City of Tulsa*, May 31, 1923.

138. Jayna Brown, *Babylon Girls: Black Women Performers and the Shaping of the Modern* (Durham, NC: Duke University Press, 2008), 92–121. Brown carefully contextualizes the popularity of the fair-skinned black women of Jack's and Isham's productions in relationship to the "sexual commodification of the mulatta" at the moment of 1890s American "urban development as well as imperial expansion."

139. Claudia Johnson, "The Guilty Third Tier: Prostitution in Nineteenth-Century American Theaters," *American Quarterly* Vol. 27, No. 5 (December 1975), 577–78.

140. Mary Church Terrell, "The Progress of Colored Women," *The Voice of the Negro*, July 1904, 291–94.

141. "Those Wicked Chorus Girls," *Freeman*, June 28, 1902.

142. "Ramblings," *Freeman*, November 13, 1909.

143. "Ramblings," *Freeman*, December 4, 1909; Joshua Zeitz, *Flapper: A Madcap Story of Sex, Style, Celebrity, and the Women Who Made America Modern* (New York: Broadway Books, 2007), 6–9, 193–96; Martha H. Patterson, *Beyond the Gibson Girl: Reimagining the American New Woman, 1895–1915* (Urbana: University of Illinois Press, 2005); Erin Chapman, *Prove It On Me: New Negroes, Sex and Popular Culture in the 1920s* (New York: Oxford University Press, 2012), 9–14; Treva B. Lindsey, *Colored No More: Reinventing Black Womanhood in Washington DC* (Urbana: University of Illinois Press, 2017), 2–18.

144. 1910–1919 Contracts, Musical Spillers Collection, Moreland-Spingarn Archives, Howard University.

145. Charles H. Turpin, "Turpin Weeps," *Defender*, April 1, 1922.

146. Benton Overstreet, "Letter to the Editor," *Defender*, April 8, 1922.

147. Boots Hope and Clarence Williams, "Brown Skin Gal," 1925; Bessie Dudley interview by Robert O'Meally.

148. Draft Card, Ulysses Nicholas, Ancestry.com. U.S., World War I Draft Registration Cards, 1917–1918 [database online]. Provo, UT, USA: Ancestry.com Operations Inc, 2005. Registration State: Alabama; Registration County: Mobile; Roll: 1509442; Draft Board: 2; Watts, *Hattie McDaniel*, 55–62; Scott, *Blues Empress*, 76.

149. "Stage Girls Not Wanted as Servants: Unemployed Women of Stage Seek Domestic Work in Vain," *Defender*, April 29, 1922.

150. Ann Petry, *The Street* (New York: Houghton Mifflin, 1946), 34; For more on domestic laborers and sexual assault, see Danielle McGuire, *At the Dark End of The Street: Black Women, Rape, and Resistance* (New York: Vintage Books, 2010); Cheryl D. Hicks, *Talk with You Like a Woman: African American Women, Justice, and Reform in New York, 1890–1935* (Chapel Hill: University of North Carolina Press, 2010); LaShawn Harris, *Sex Workers, Psychics and Number Runners: Black Women in New York City's Underground Economy*, (Urbana: University of Illinois Press, 2016).

151. "T.O.B.A. Actors Struggle to Live," *Afro-American*, February 7, 1925.

152. Hartman, 337.

153. Bessie Dudley interview by Robert O'Meally.

154. Bessie Dudley interview by Robert O'Meally; Passenger Lists of Vessels Arriving at New York, New York, 1820–1897. Record of Dudley leaving for Paris in Records of the US Customs Service, Record Group 36. National Archives at Washington, DC, 1931; Arrival: New York, New York; Roll 5054; Line: 16; Page Number: 42.

155. Robin Bachin, ed. *Big Bosses: A Working Girl's Memoir of Jazz Age America*, Althea McDowell Altemus (Chicago: University of Chicago Press, 2016).

156. Chris Alberston, *Bessie* (New Haven, CT: Yale University Press, 2003), 95–96.

157. Vivienne, "Theater Folks and Theatergoers: Chorus Girls Over the Top," *Defender*, October 10, 1925.

158. Peg Leg Bates interviewed by Rusty Frank.

159. Vivienne, "Theater Folks and Theatergoers: Back Line Chorus Girls," *Defender*, October 17, 1925.

160. Vivienne, "Theater Folks and Theatergoers: Stage Vulgarity," *Defender*, October 24, 1925.

161. Vivienne, "Theater Folks and Theatergoers: Chorus Girls Over the Top," *Defender*, October 10, 1925.

162. "Theatrical Notes," *Defender*, August 7, 1926.

163. Sotiropoulos, *Staging Race*, 196.

164. James A. Jackson, "Showfolks: More the Entertainers," *Messenger*, March 1925.

165. Howard Phelps, "The Negro Needs to Clean House," *Half Century Magazine*, January 1919.

166. Vivienne, "Theater Folks and Theatergoers: Stage Vulgarity," *Defender*, October 24, 1925.

167. Sampson, *Blacks in Blackface*, 79–80, 278; Camille F. Forbes, *Introducing Bert Williams: Burnt Cork, Broadway and the Story of America's First Black Star* (New York: Basic Civitas, 2008).

168. Vivienne, "Theater Folks and Theatergoers: Corkless Comedy," *Defender*, October 31, 1925.

169. Scott, *Blues Empress*, 132.

170. Thomas Dorsey and Hudson Whittaker, "It's Tight Like That," *Vocalian*, 1928; Jodie Edwards, "He Likes It Slow," Okeh, 1926; Katrina Hazzard-Gordon, *Jookin: The Rise of Social Dance Formations in African-American Culture* (Philadelphia: Temple University Press, 1990), 82–88; Tera Hunter, *To 'Joy My Freedom: Southern Black Women's Lives and Labors After the Civil War* (Cambridge, MA: Harvard University Press, 1997), 175–86; Roberta Schwartz, "How Blue Can You Get? It's Tight Like That and the Hokum Blues," *American Music* Vol. 36, No. 3 (Fall 2018), 377–82.

171. George Allen, "Letter to Editor: Stage Vulgarity," *Defender*, May 7, 1927.

172. Tosh Hammed, Clarence Williams, "I Want a Hot Dog for My Roll," Discography of American Historical Recordings, s.v. "OKeh matrix W80686. I want a hot dog for my roll / Butterbeans & Susie," https://adp.library.ucsb.edu/index.php/matrix/detail/2000207327/W80686-I_want_a_hot_dog_for_my_roll, accessed August 7, 2019.

173. Sampson, *Blacks in Blackface*, 350–51.

174. S. H. Dudley, *Broad Ax*, January 27, 1912; S. H. Dudley, "Wants an Overlord for Vaudeville Acts," *Afro-American*, February 9, 1923.

175. J. A. Jackson, "T.O.B.A. Circuit to Have Try Out House," *Afro-American*, April 19, 1924.

176. Babe Townsend, "Letter to Editor," *Defender*, August 1, 1925.

177. S. H. Dudley, "TAB Shows," *Defender*, June 5, 1926.

178. Sampson, *Blacks in Blackface*, 133.

179. *Douglass to Reevin*, September 1, 1926, Manager Correspondence, Theaters, Charles Henry Douglass Business Records, Middle Georgia Archives, Washington Library, Macon, GA.

180. Lewis, *From Traveling Show to Vaudeville*, 323; United Booking Offices of America Contract, December 10, 1914, Falcon Trio Collection, Archives Center, National Museum of America History, box 3, folder 6.

181. Contract, Bessie Smith to C. H. Douglass, March 16, 1925, Contracts, Charles Henry Douglass Business Records, Middle Georgia Archives, Washington Library, Macon, GA.

182. Reevin to Douglass, March 25, 1925, Manager Correspondence, Theaters, Charles Henry Douglass Business Records, Middle Georgia Archives, Washington Library, Macon, GA.

183. Gray to Douglass, January 23, 1925, Correspondence, Theaters, Charles Henry Douglass Business Records, Middle Georgia Archives, Washington Library, Macon, GA; "Lonnie Fisher TOBA Comic," *Afro-American*, May 16, 1924.

184. Vivienne, "Theater Folks and Theatergoers," *Defender*, October 24, 1925; "Chicago Theatrical News," *Defender*, August 28, 1926.

185. Cab Calloway interview by Frank Driggs.

186. S. T. Whitney, "Observations," *Defender*, July 11, 1926.

## CHAPTER 5. A "RESPONSIBILITY" TO COMMUNITY

1. Transcript of Danny Barker Interview by Michael White, July 21–23, 1992, Archives Center, National Museum of American History, Smithsonian Institution, 28–30.

2. Idelle Truitt Elsey interviewed by Charles Hardy, June 29, 1984, "Goin North: Tales of the Great Migration," Oral History Collection, Louie B. Nunn Center for Oral History, University of Kentucky Libraries.

3. Viola Turner interviewed by Walter Weare, April 15, 1979, Interview number C-0015 in the Southern Oral History Program Collection (#4007) at the Southern Historical Collection, The Louis Round Wilson Special Collections Library, UNC-Chapel Hill.

4. Kennard Williams, "South's Amusements Need General Housecleaning," *Afro-American*, November 22, 1924.

5. Williams, "The South's Amusements Need General Housecleaning."

6. Viola Turner interviewed by Walter Weare, April 15, 1979.

7. Sadie Tanner Mossell, "The Standard of Living Among One Hundred Negro Migrant Families in Philadelphia," University of Pennsylvania, PhD Thesis, 1921, 12–13, 30–31; Five hundred dollars in 1920 would be worth $6,460 in 2020. The average migrant salary in 1920 equates to $9,690 to $24,500 in 2020. See https://www.measuringworth.com/calculators/uscompare/relativevalue.php.

8. Robin Kelly, "We Are Not What We Seem: Rethinking Black Working Class Opposition in the Jim Crow South," *The Journal of American History*, Vol. 80, No. 1 (June 1993), 84–87; Jacqueline Najuma Stewart, *Migrating to the Movies: Cinema and Black Urban Modernity* (Berkeley: University of California Press, 2005), 143–50.

9. Richard Butsch, *The Making of American Audiences: From Stage to Television 1750–1990* (Cambridge, UK: Cambridge University Press, 2000), 115–16.

10. Ethel Waters and Charles Samuels, *His Eye Is on the Sparrow: An Autobiography of Ethel Waters* (New York: Da Capo Press, 1992), 74; Vivienne, "Theater Folks and Theatergoers: The Power of Applause," *Defender*, November 28, 1925.

11. Daphne Duval Harrison, *Black Pearls: Blues Queens of the 1920s* (New Jersey: Rutgers University Press, 1988), 37, 53; Henry Cole, "Black Mountain Blues," 1930, *Discography of American Historical Recordings*, s.v. "Columbia matrix W150658. Black Mountain blues/Bessie Smith," accessed January 13, 2021.

12. Oral History T-0023 interview with Nathaniel Sweets, interviewed by Dr. Richard Resh, Black Community Leaders Project, July 20, 1970; Graves, 32–33; Jacqui Malone, *Steppin' on the Blues: The Visible Rhythms of African American Dance* (Urbana: University of Illinois, 1996), 77–81.

13. Ralph Ellison, *Shadow and Act* (New York: Vintage Books, 1995), 253.

14. Albert Murray, *Stomping the Blues* (New York: DeCapo Press, 1976), 20, 38.

15. *Billboard*, April 7, 1917, 3.

16. Anthony Duane Hill, J. A. Jackson's Page in "Billboard: A Voice for Black Performance During the Harlem Renaissance between 1920–1925" (PhD diss. New York University, 1988), 115–20.

17. The *New York Clipper* was a weekly theatrical magazine that operated from 1853 to 1924 and advertised itself as the "oldest amusement newspaper in America." *Variety* is a currently published entertainment periodical and was founded in 1905 as the premier vaudeville trade magazine. *Variety*'s mission was "an aim to make" the periodical an "artists' paper, a medium, a *complete* directory, a paper to which *anyone* interested in the theatrical world

may read." Yet breadth in coverage meant that *Variety* was regionally and racially superficial in its early reporting. Its first edition mentioned eight "colored" related theatrical activities within its nearly fifty-page issue. *Variety*, December 16, 1905, 2.

18. Report of the 16th Annual Convention of the National Negro Business League (Boston, MA, 1915), 73–74.

19. "TOBA Doings," *Defender*, February 9, 1929.

20. Jason Chambers, *Madison Avenue and the Color Line: African Americans in the Advertising Industry* (Philadelphia: University of Pennsylvania Press, 2011), 21.

21. "The Stage," *Freeman*, January 6, 1900.

22. Walker-Drake Trio Ad, December 26, 1914, "The Stage," *Freeman*, February 7, 1903.

23. Theater advertisements, *Freeman*, August 5, 1899.

24. Mail List, *Freeman*, September 1, 1900; Mail List, *Freeman*, September 21, 1912.

25. Sylvester Russell, "Tenth Annual Review," *Freeman*, December 5, 1909.

26. "Stage Page," *Defender*, January 5, 1924; "The Movie and Stage Department," *Defender*, October 10, 1925; "The Movie and Stage Department," *Defender*, October 17, 1925; "Williams Quits Afro American," *New York Amsterdam News*, July 18, 1926.

27. "W. R. Arnold Quits T.O.B.A. to Travel," *Defender*, November 14, 1925; "W.R. Arnold Not With T.O.B.A. Now," *Pittsburgh Courier*, February 11, 1928.

28. Reevin to Douglass, June 8, 1925, Charles Henry Douglass Business Records, Middle Georgia State Archives, Washington Library.

29. "TOBA Directors Hold Meeting," *Pittsburgh Courier*, July 25, 1925.

30. "On the TOBA Circuit," *Defender*, September 25, 1925.

31. *The Official Theatrical World of Colored Artists Guide* (New York: Theatrical World Publishing, 1928), 83, 67–69. This guide was a directory of black-serving theaters, actors' hotels, restaurants, and shipping companies in the country. It also listed black active entertainers by genre as well as posted individual act's advertising cards. It was unfortunately only published in this national edition in 1928; "Stage Page," *Afro-American*, January 21, 1927.

32. Christopher Reed, *The Rise of Chicago's Black Metropolis, 1920–1929*, (Urbana: University of Illinois Press, 2011), 102.

33. Kennard Williams, "The South's Amusements Need General Housecleaning," *Afro-American*, November 22, 1924.

34. "Contrasts," *Defender*, November 5, 1927.

35. "Howard Theater Gets New Manager," *Afro-American*, October 6, 1928.

36. Interview with Nathaniel Sweets, interviewed by Dr. Richard Resh, Black Community Leaders Project, July 20, 1970, Oral History Collection, State Historical Society of Missouri.

37. Edward Renton, *The Vaudeville Theatre, Building, Operation, and Management* (New York: Gotham Press, Inc., 1918), 129, 158–59.

38. Bestowing black women with formal titles was a sign of respect and dignity, particularly in the generations after enslavement, as many black women attempted to define themselves as "ladies" worthy of citizenship. Darlene Clark Hine and Kathleen Thompson, *A Shining Thread of Hope: The History of Black Women in America* (New York: Broadway Books, 1999), 147–53.

39. "New Crown," *Freeman*, December 20, 1913; "Bijou Theatre, Nashville, Tenn., the Equal of Any Colored Theatre in the Country," *Nashville Globe*, December 6, 1918.

40. Howard Program, May 22, 1920, in Programs and Playbills, 1920s, Negro Actors Guild of America records, box 36, folder 3, Schomburg Center for Research in Black Culture, The New York Public Library.

41. Colored Hotels Badly Needed, *Afro-American,* August 31, 1923.

42. Call Sheet Gus Hill Enterprises 1917, "Jolly" John Larkin scrapbook, Stuart A. Rose Manuscript, Archives, and Rare Book Library, Emory University.

43. Tom Fletcher, *100 Years of the Negro in Show Business* (New York: DeCapo Press, 1984), 57, 64; James W. Loewen, *Sundown Towns: A Hidden Dimension of American Racism* (New York: New Press, 2005), 4–10.

44. *The Negro Motorist Green Book* (New York: Victor H. Green Publications, 1949), 1.

45. *Julius Cahn-Gus Hill Theater and Moving Picture Directory* (Orange, NJ: Chronicle Press, 1922), 124–39.

46. William Basie, *Good Morning Blues: The Autobiography of Count Basie as told to Albert Murray* (New York: Random House, 1985), 94.

47. Christopher Reed, *The Rise of Chicago's Black Metropolis, 1920–1929,* 72, 81–103; Commissioned by African American banker and entrepreneur Anthony Overton in 1922, the Overton Building was a multiple-purpose center that held the Overton Hygienic Cosmetics factory and a host of other black-operated establishments. It was a true hallmark of Chicago's black entrepreneurial community. "TOBA Agency Advertisements," *Defender,* November 18, 1922; January 19, 1924; February 7, 1925; "Honor Chicago Banker at Banquet," *Defender,* December 25, 1926.

48. *Julius Cahn-Gus Hill Theatrical Guide* (Orange, NJ: Chronicle Publishing, 1922), 134.

49. Charles S. Johnson, "Illinois: Mecca of the Migrant Mob," December 1923 in Tom Lutz and Susanna Ashton ed., *These Colored United States* (New Brunswick, NJ: Rutgers University Press, 1996), 111–112; Demographic reports mention that the city's black population grew from forty-four thousand people in 1910 to 109,000 to 112,000 people by 1920; *Statistical Abstracts,* 1930, Table 22, 23–34.

50. "T.O.B.A Bookings," *Defender,* September 5, 1925.

51. "TOBA Folks Struggle To Live," *Afro-American,* February 7, 1925.

52. *OTWCAG,* 32, 67–68: Display Ad 23, *Defender,* February 16, 1924; Michelle R. Scott, "Alberta Hunter: She Had the World in A Jug, With the Stopper in Her Hand," in Sarah Wilkerson Freeman, ed., *Tennessee Women: Their Lives and Times* (Athens: University of Georgia Press, 2009), 106.

53. Basie, 96; Dempsey J. Travis, "Chicago's Jazz Trail, 1893–1950," *Black Music Research Journal,* Vol. 10, No. 1 (Spring 1990), 82–85; William Howland Kenney III, "The Influence of Black Vaudeville on Early Jazz," *The Black Perspective in Music,* Vol. 14, No. 3 (Autumn, 1986), 238; Born in 1904, Red Bank, New Jersey, native William "Count" Basie honed his instrumentalist and bandleading talents in New York and on T.O.B.A. in the 1920s before becoming an internationally popular swing jazz band leader.

54. Clarence Muse, *Way Down South* (Los Angeles: David Graham Fischer, 1932), 16–18; Transcript of Danny Barker interview, 70.

55. Muse, 25–26; Clarence Muse, black actor, producer, and Baltimore native, was born in 1889 and worked in New York theater and T.O.B.A. productions before becoming an actor in Hollywood films.

56. Muse, 17; *OTWCAG*, 39.

57. Muse, 2; Basie, 100.

58. Scott, *Blues Empress*, 81–83; Chattanooga City Directory, 1922.

59. Map of Southern Railway, 1913 in Warshaw Collection of Business Americana, Railroads, box 88, Archives Center, NMAH.

60. Kenneth W. Mack, "Law, Society, Identity, and the Making of the Jim Crow South: Travel and Segregation on Tennessee Railroads, 1875–1905," *Law & Social Inquiry*, Vol. 24, No. 2 (Spring, 1999) 380; Mia Bay, *Traveling Black: A Story of Race and Resistance* (Cambridge, MA: Harvard University Press, 2021).

61. William Logan Martin, Commissioner, *The Code of Alabama, Adopted by Act of the General Assembly of the State of Alabama*, Approved February 16, 1897, Vol. 1 (Atlanta, 1897), 2 vols. *The Making of Modern Law: Primary Sources*; William Hemingway, *The Annotated Mississippi Code Showing the General Statutes in Force*, August 1, 1917, Vol. 2 Indianapolis, 1917, 3 vols. *The Making of Modern Law: Primary Sources.*

62. Bowe and Lindell to C. H. Douglass, December 15, 1926, in the Charles Henry Douglass Business Records, Middle Georgia Archives, Washington Library, Macon, GA.

63. Oral history interview with Viola Turner, April 17, 1979. Interview C-0016. Southern Oral History Program Collection (#4007) in the Southern Oral History Program Collection, Southern Historical Collection, Wilson Library, University of North Carolina at Chapel Hill.

64. Mack, 403; Chris Albertson, *Bessie* (New Haven, CT: Yale University Press, 2003), 105.

65. Salem Tutt Whitney, "Timely Topics: Black Inconsistency," *Defender*, February 18, 1928.

66. A. C. Barnes, Southern Railway System to Stein, Douglass Theatre, September 12, 1927, Douglass Collection.

67. Basie. 100–101; Muse, 61; Waters and Samuels, 168; Dancer and instrumentalist Gonzelle White was one of the few black women who managed her own troupe of twenty to twenty-five artists throughout T.O.B.A.'s tenure. Ethel Waters, famed "colored" vaudevillian as she defined herself, began as teenage vocalist "Sweet Mama Stringbean" in the 1910s before becoming a blues vocalist, a T.O.B.A. headliner, and a Broadway star in the 1920s to 1950s.

68. Myra B. Young Armstead, "Revisiting Hotels and Other Lodgings: American Tourist Spaces through the Lens of Black Pleasure-Travelers, 1880–1950," *The Journal of Decorative and Propaganda Arts*, Vol. 25 (2005), 141; "Colored Hotels Badly Needed," *Afro-American*, August 31, 1923.

69. "Chattanooga, Tenn," *Freeman*, January 24, 1914; "T.O.B.A. Dope," *Afro-American*, February 5, 1927; *Chattanooga City Directories 1926.*

70. Muse, 43, 50.

71. Milton Starr, "Milton Starr Makes Statement," *Defender*, February 12, 1921; "100,000 Theatre Found in Macon," *Afro-American*, October 14, 1921.

72. Fritz to Douglass, Personal Correspondence, March 11, 1926, Douglass Hotel Stationary, Douglass Theater Handbill for 1927, in Charles Henry Douglass Business Records,

Middle Georgia State Archives, Washington Library; J. A. Jackson, "100,000 Theatre Found in Macon," *Afro American*, October 14, 1921.

73. Interview transcript with Viola Turner by Walter Weare, April 17, 1979.

74. Peg Leg Bates interviewed by Rusty Frank, April 4, 1993, Jazz Oral History Collection Program, Archives Center, National Museum of American History.

75. *OTWCAG*, 95.

76. "TOBA Actors Struggle To Live," *Afro-American*, February 7, 1925.

77. "John Gibson Makes Former College Gift of $5000," *Afro-American*, December 27, 1924.

78. Interview transcript with Viola Turner by Walter Weare, April 17, 1979; Sadie Tanner Mossell, "The Standard of Living Among One Hundred Negro Migrant Families in Philadelphia," dissertation University of Pennsylvania, 1921, 30–31.

79. Mabley to Schiffman telegram, September 9, 1938, Frank Schiffman Collection, box 1, Archives Center, National Museum of American History; *OTWCAG*, 81.

80. Milt Hinton interviewed by Billy Taylor, August 12–13, 1992, Jazz Oral History Collection Program, Archives Center, National Museum of American History; "Addie Havelow" in Census Place: Philadelphia, Philadelphia, Pennsylvania; Page: 5B; Enumeration District: United States of America, Bureau of the Census. *Fifteenth Census of the United States, 1930*. Washington, DC: National Archives and Records Administration, 1930. T626, 2,667 rolls; African American widow Addie Havelow turned her private home into a well-known vaudeville and big band "haunt." The price of the room included use of the piano and a meal and in return Mrs. Havelow, a Virginia migrant, earned an independent income to support her daughter Willie May.

81. Basie, 94.

82. T.O.B.A. Letterhead, Manager Correspondence, November 15, 1925, Charles Henry Douglass Business Records, Middle Georgia State Archives, Washington Library; Display Ads *Defender*, September 2, 1922; Langston Hughes, *The Big Sea* (New York: Hill and Wang, 1993), 208–9.

83. *Statistical Abstracts 1930*, 25; Monroe Work, ed. *The Negro Year Book and Annual Encyclopedia of the Negro* (Tuskegee, AL: Negro Year Book Publishing Company, 1922) 305; Jones, *Recreational Amusements in Washington, DC*, 1927, 115–20; The five theaters associated with T.O.B.A. between 1921 and 1928 included the Foraker at 1112 Twentieth Street NW, the Blue Mouse on Twenty-Sixth and M Streets NW, the S. H. Dudley Theatre at 1213 U Street, Mid-City Theatre at 1223 Seventh Street, and the famed Howard Theatre at Sixth and T Streets.

84. Billy Pierce, "Colored Agents," *Variety*, July 27, 1927.

85. *OTWCAG*, 85.

86. Jack L. Cooper, "Colored Actors Union and T.O.B.A. Heads Hold Premier Session," *Defender*, March 28, 1925.

87. "Actor's Hotel Opens," *Afro-American*, July 17, 1926; In an unusual switch, rather than a black woman taking in boarders, Jules McGarr maintained the theatrical lodgers and Mabel McGarr went to the stage in the position of being "one of the few women able to direct the activities of a company of ten unassisted"; "Managing a Show Difficult Job Says Mabel McGarr," *Afro-American*, March 19, 1927.

88. The Whitelaw Hotel opened in DC in 1919 and served the black elite while being financed by African American entrepreneurs. It fell into disrepair in the 1970s, only to be reopened as low-income housing in the 1990s. See Joseph D. Whitaker, "Whitelaw Hotel Is Closing After Checkered History," *Washington Post*, July 4, 1977; 1930 Federal Census, Washington, DC, sheet 10A.

89. *OTWCAG*, 39; Lease No. 42, May 19, 1922, Washington, DC.

90. Oral history interview with Asa T. Spaulding, April 13, 1979, Southern Oral History Program Collection, Wilson Library, UNC Chapel Hill.

91. St. Louis Argus, July 6, 1917; Charles Lumpkins, *American Pogrom: The East St. Louis Race Riot and Black Politics* (Columbus: Ohio University Press, 2008).

92. Bobby Lovett, *African American History of Nashville, Tennessee, 1780–1930* (Fayetteville: Arkansas Press, 1999), 102.

93. Alfred L. Brophy, *Reconstructing the Dreamland: The Tulsa Riot of 1921: Race, Reparations, and Reconciliation* (New York: Oxford University Press, 2002), 21.

94. Waters, 169; "Lawless Mobs Reign 3 Days in Macon," *Afro-American*, August 4, 1922; "Giant Cop Brutal to Young Boy," *Defender*, August 12, 1922; "Alleged Lynchers Found Not Guilty," *Pensacola Journal*, September 13, 1922; The Dyer Bill was crafted in 1919 to make lynching and mob violence a federal crime. It passed in the House of Representatives in January 1922 but was stalled in the Senate in summer 1922. One hundred years later the Dyer Bill evolved into the Emmett Till Antilynching Act passed on March 29, 2022. https://naacp.org/find-resources/history-explained/legislative-milestones/dyer-anti-lynching-bill; https://www.congress.gov/bill/117th-congress/house-bill/55/text, accessed April 22, 2022.

95. St. John's Open Forum, *Philadelphia Tribune*, December 22, 1923; Finely Wilson and Mayor Mackey Douglass Speakers, *Pittsburgh Courier*, February 4, 1928; Frederick Jerome Taylor, "Black Musicians in the *Philadelphia Tribune*, 1912–20," *The Black Perspective in Music* vol 1, No. 1 / 2 (1990), 130–31.

96. "Play Cast Announced," *Evening Star*, December 22, 1924; *Evening Star*, December 30, 1924.

97. "T.O.B.A. Houses in Flood Districts," *Afro-American*, May 7, 1927; "Theaters to Help Flood Refugees," *Afro-American*, May 14, 1927, 18; Robert Mizzelle, *Backwater Blues: The Mississippi Flood of 1927 in the African American Imagination* (Minneapolis: University of Minnesota Press, 2014).

98. Stewart, 155.

99. Transcript of Danny Barker, 28–30.

## CHAPTER 6. "TROUBLE IN MIND"

1. "Movie and Stage Department," *Defender*, October 13, 1928.

2. "Began Career in Baltimore: Ethel Waters Started on the Road to Fame Here in Baltimore," *Afro-American*, December 2, 1921; Ethel Waters and Charles Samuels, *His Eye Is on the Sparrow: An Autobiography of Ethel Waters* (New York: Da Capo Press, 1992), 199; Salem Tutt Whitney, "Timely Topics: Pride of Race," *Defender*, November 10, 1928; Harry Keller, "Ethel Waters Has Company of 60 in Newest Show," *Afro-American*, July 16, 1927.

3. "Ethel Waters Co. Closes in Strike," *Afro-American*, May 12, 1928; "Ethel Waters of Africana Files Petition of Bankruptcy," *New York Amsterdam News*, September 26, 1928; Waters and Samuels, *His Eye Is on the Sparrow*, 189–190; Donald Bogle, *Bright Boulevards, Bold Dreams: The Story of Black Hollywood* (New York: Ballantine Books, 2005), 83–86.

4. "Chicago Theatrical News," *Defender*, May 28, 1927.

5. Display Ad, *Defender*, November 24, 1928.

6. "S. H. Dudley to C. H. Douglass," February 15, 1926, in Charles Henry Douglass Business Records, box 21A, folder 212.

7. "S. H. Dudley," *The Messenger*, January 1925, 62.

8. "Dudley Denies Divorce Rumor," *Afro-American*, March 27, 1926.

9. Desdemona Barnett was a black migrant from an educated black family in Floyd, Georgia. Barnett's father, William, was an attorney and her mother, Ella, a schoolteacher. After relocating to Washington, DC after her father's death in mid-1910, a teenage Desdemona trained as a stenographer to help support her family. Year: 1900; Census Place: Rome Ward 5, Floyd, Georgia; Page: 3; Enumeration District: 0122; FHL microfilm: 1240196; Year: 1920; Census Place: Washington, Washington, District of Columbia; Roll: T625_211; Page: 9B; Enumeration District: 199 U.S. City Directories, 1822–1995 [database online]. Provo, UT, USA: Ancestry.com Operations, Inc., 2011; Boyds' Directories of the City of District of Columbia, 1909–1920. *U.S. City Directories, 1822–1995* [database online]. Provo, UT, USA: Ancestry.com Operations, Inc., 2011.

10. The fear of the young female clerical worker of the 1920s either being seduced by or seducing her elder male employer is discussed in the period memoir by Althea McDowell Altemus, Robin Bachin ed., *Big Bosses: A Working Girls Memoir of Jazz Age America* (Chicago: University of Chicago Press, 2016); "Her Husband Charges Misconduct," *Norfolk New Journal and Guide*, May 15, 1926; Dudley and Barnett had a long-term professional relationship. Barnett was listed as a legal partner in Dudley's business dealings prior to when the two wed, as "D. W. Barnett" was often the only woman partner listed alongside black male entrepreneurs; "A Note or Two," *Defender*, September 20, 1919; "Notes," *Washington Herald*, June 27, 1920.

11. Only 7.5 percent of American women per 1,000 had filed for divorce in 1926. See "100 Years of Marriage and Divorce Statistics in the United States," Department of Health and Welfare, 1973, 24. The survey also notes that 92 percent of women over the age of fifteen were in marital relationships in the US in 1920.

12. *Afro-American*, May 15, 1926; *Defender*, May 15, 1926; *Norfolk New Journal and Guide*, May 15, 1926; "S.H. Dudley in Sensational Suit: Scandal Rocks DC as Dudley Demands Divorce," *Afro-American*, May 15, 1926.

13. "S.H. Dudley in Sensational Suit."

14. Ibid.

15. "$100 a Week Whiskey Bill, Mrs. Dudley," *Afro-American*, May 20, 1926; "Alimony for Mrs. Dudley $150," *Afro-American*, August 14, 1926. Barnett-Dudley argued that at times S. H. had punched her, blackened her eye, threw her downstairs, kicked her in her stomach, and even threatened her with a revolver. In this era, even when domestic violence was coded in claims about drunkenness, poverty, and ethnicity, accusations that the famed S. H. Dudley

was a potential "wife-beater" were definitely newsworthy and damning. See Linda Gordon, *Heroes of Their Own Lives: The Politics and History of Family Violence in Boston, 1880–1960* (Urbana: University of Illinois, 2002), 254–63. Dudley's lawyers did a careful accounting of his financial holdings, including his T.O.B.A. properties, to counter Barnett-Dudley's inflated contentions about his wealth. This accounting revealed that Dudley was not quite the mogul Barnett-Dudley claimed, but he was indeed quite wealthy. Ownership of the Mid-City Theatre and investment in T.O.B.A. allowed him to buy single-family homes, apartment buildings, and undeveloped property in Washington, DC, and Maryland, yet he was not worth as much as Mrs. Dudley contended.

16. S. H. Dudley, "Tab Shows," *Defender*, June 5, 1926.

17. "Wife of S.H. Dudley Slain By Lover," *Pittsburgh Courier*, September 25, 1926.

18. "Wife of S.H. Dudley Slain By Lover"; Louis R Lautier, "Friend Tried to Warn Mrs. Dudley of Death Threat," *Defender*, October 2, 1926; "Mrs. S. Dudley Slain After Reconciliation," *Afro-American*, September 25, 1926; "Mrs. Dudley's Slayer Faces," *Defender*, May 21, 1927; "20 Year Prison Term for Former Policeman," *Washington Post*, May 21, 1927; Davis immediately attempted suicide but instead blinded and paralyzed himself. He recovered a year later and was sentenced to a twenty-year term for murder.

19. "Mrs. S. Dudley Slain After Reconciliation," *Afro-American*, September 25, 1926; "Mrs. Dudley's Slayer Faces," *Defender*, May 21, 1927; Society, *Afro-American*, October 2, 1926; "20 Year Prison Term for Former Policeman," *Washington Post*, May 21, 1927; "Sues Hubby Who Would Imitate DC Killer Cop," *Afro-American*, July 15, 1927; The divorce and criminal details left a legacy on how other 1920s African American women dealt with domestic abuse and divorce in Washington, DC. Even after George Davis pled guilty to second-degree murder and was sentenced to twenty years in prison, local DC cases evoked Davis's name and, by extension, Dudley and T.O.B.A. In 1927 when a Mrs. Hattie Brown charged her husband, Charles H. Brown, with cruelty and attempted to divorce him, she did so claiming that Charles stated he was going to "do as Davis did" if she left him. Mrs. Brown was granted the divorce. "Sues Hubby Who Would Imitate DC Killer Cop," *Afro-American*, July 15, 1927.

20. "Clarence Muse Accused By Chorus Girl," *Afro-American*, July 17, 1926; "Actress Drops Suit Against Clarence Muse," *Afro-American*, July 24, 1926.

21. Bill Potter, "Theatrical Comment," *Defender*, September 26, 1925.

22. Bogle, *Bright Boulevards, Bold Dreams*, 54.

23. Angela Davis, *Blues Legacies and Black Feminisms* (New York: Vintage Books, 1999), 277–78, 281–82.

24. W. R. Arnold, "Bessie Smith Stabbed," *Defender*, March 7, 1925; W. R. Arnold, "Bessie Smith, Nationally Known Singer Is Stabbed by Highwayman," *Pittsburgh Courier*, March 7, 1925; Chris Alberston, *Bessie* (New Haven, CT: Yale University Press, 2003), 92–93.

25. "Colored Actors Kills Co Worker," *Variety*, January 27, 1927.

26. "Convict Man Who Slew His Wife's Admirer," *New Journal and Guide*, May 14, 1927; Estate of Dudley, Sherman, Estate No. RE06980, January 1, 1937, Register of Wills for Prince George's County; Haynes later became one of the NAACP attorneys who worked with Thurgood Marshall on the *Brown v. Board of Education* case.

27. "20 Year Prison Term for Former Policeman," *Washington Post*, May 21, 1927.

28. Booking Sheets, Ma Rainey, February 14, 1928; Ida Cox, March 9, 1928, Charles Henry Douglass Business Records, Washington Library, Macon, GA.

29. Reevin to Douglass, May 28, 1925, in Charles Henry Douglass Business Records, Washington Library, Macon, GA.

30. Reevin to Douglass, June 18, 1925, in Charles Henry Douglass Business Records, Washington Library, Macon, GA.

31. City Directories, Chattanooga, 1924; Manager Correspondence, Reevin (Nason) to Douglass, November 27, 1925, in Charles Henry Douglass Business Records, Washington Library, Macon, GA.

32. City Directories of Chattanooga, 1924.

33. "W.R. Arnold Writes from Nashville," *Afro-American*, July 10, 1926; "Vaudeville: Ill and Injured," *Variety*, October 13, 1926; Muse, *Way Down South*, 42.

34. "Sam E Reevin Improving," *Defender*, July 17, 1926; Article 1, *American Israelite*, June 3, 1926.

35. Nason to Douglass, November 27, 1925; Douglass Letters, May–July 1926 in Charles Henry Douglass Business Records, Washington Library, Macon, GA.

36. Mrs. Nason worked for T.O.B.A. out of financial necessity, and her employment was not merely supplemental. Her husband, Roy Sewall Nason, a Maine native, was listed as divorced in his death certificate in 1931, and his will, filed in 1926, entrusted all his property to a Mabel Alexander. *Executor's Bonds and Letters, 1879–1932; Administrator's Bonds and Letters, 1878–1928*; Author: *Tennessee Probate Court (Hamilton County)*; Probate Place: *Hamilton, Tennessee* Ancestry.com. *Tennessee, Deaths and Burials Index, 1874–1955* [database online]. Provo, UT, USA: Ancestry.com Operations, Inc., 2011. File # 1876783.

37. Muse, *Way Down South*, 42.

38. Ibid.

39. "Chicago Theatrical News," *Defender*, May 28, 1927.

40. Douglass Expense Ledger, August 6, 1927. Receipts for the week of August 6, 1927, showed a profit of $5,169.18 but expenses of $5,933.07, for a total loss of $763.89.

41. "T.O.B.A. Routings," *Defender*, October 24, 1925; W. R. Arnold, "T.O.B.A. Dope," *Afro-American*, April 23, 1927.

42. "Georgia Theater Owner Takes Rap at T.O.B.A.," *Pittsburgh Courier*, March 19, 1927.

43. Douglass to Reevin, September 1, 1926.

44. Starr to Douglass, September 7, 1927; Douglass resumed control of the theater in 1930.

45. "Chicago Theatrical News," *Defender*, May 28, 1927.

46. Tim Owsley, "Show Business," *Defender*, June 25, 1927.

47. "1927 Worst Theater Season Since Panic," *Defender*, December 31, 1927.

48. "The New Circuit," *Defender*, January 16, 1926.

49. Starr to Stein, November 15, 1925, in Charles Henry Douglass Business Records, Washington Library, Macon, GA.

50. "Starr Buys Theatre in Augusta, GA," *Pittsburgh Courier*, July 25, 1925.

51. "Reevin and Dudley to Jar Milton Starr," *Pittsburgh Courier*, January 23, 1926.

52. Starr to Stein, September 10, 1927, in Charles Henry Douglass Business Records, Washington Library, Macon, GA.

53. "We'd Like to See, Timely Topics," *Defender*, January 7, 1928; "T.O.B.A. Big Guns Meet at Trenier," *Afro-American*, February 4, 1928.

54. ORAL HISTORY T-0023, Interview with Nathaniel Sweets interviewed by Dr. Richard Resh, Black Community Leaders Project July 20, 1970, in Oral History Collection (S0829), State Historical Society of Missouri.

55. S. H. Dudley, "Dud's Dope," *Afro-American*, April 30, 1927.

56. George Tyler, "Tyler Tells About 'Inside' of Stage," *Afro-American*, July 9, 1927.

57. Salem Tutt Whitney, "We'd Like to See, Timely Topics," *Defender*, January 7, 1928.

58. Salem Tutt Whitney, "Timely Topics: One Thing and Another," *Defender*, February 25, 1928.

59. S. H. Dudley, "1927 Worst Theater Season Since Panic," *Defender*, December 31, 1927.

60. "Muse's Letter," *Defender*, January 14, 1928; Clarence Muse, "Muse Tells Actor's Side," *New York Amsterdam News*, August 22, 1928.

61. Sam E. Reevin, "T.O.B.A. Circuit, Helps Race Actors, Claim Loop Manager," *Pittsburgh Courier*, August 25, 1928.

62. "TOBA's Guarantee to Shows Impossible," *Pittsburgh Courier*, September 1, 1928; Clarence Muse, "T.O.B.A. Needs Better Understanding With Race Actors," *Pittsburgh Courier*, September 8, 1928.

63. There were an additional 224 black-serving motion picture theaters in the nation in 1921. Eric Ledell Smith, *African American Theater Buildings: An Illustrated Guide* (Jefferson, NC: McFarland, 2011), 239.

64. Colored Theatrical Guide, 17–18; http://www.umsl.edu/~gradyf/film/theatre.htm; Eric Ledell Smith, *African American Theater Buildings: An Illustrated Guide* (Jefferson, NC: McFarland, 2011), 239.

65. J. F. Steiner, "Recreation and Leisure Time Activities," *Recent Social Trends* Vol. 2 (1933), 951–53.

66. "Amusements," *Evening Star*, April 1, 1923; Scott Eyman, *The Speed of Sound: Hollywood and the Talkie Revolution, 1926–1930* (New York: Simon & Schuster, 1997), 18–22.

67. Walter Glimmer to R. M. Colt, Gloversville, NY, June 22, 1914, in Vaudeville, Warshaw Business Americana, Box 15, f 2, Archives Center, National Museum of American History.

68. Charter of Incorporation #173, 1920, Tennessee State Archives; "To Incorporate Southern Consolidated Vaude," *Billboard*, July 31, 1920.

69. David Crafton, *The Talkies: American Cinema's Transition to Sound, 1926–1931* (Berkeley: University of California Press, 1999), 65–69, 89.

70. Scott Eyman, *The Speed of Sound: Hollywood and the Talkie Revolution, 1926–1930* (New York: Simon & Schuster, 1997), 20; Crafton, 6–7.

71. "The Jazz Singer Al Jolson's Own Life Story," *Jewish Advocate*, March 22, 1928; Eyman, 129–37.

72. "Advertisements," *Variety*, November 30, 1927; Thomas Cripps, *A Slow Fade to Black: The Negro in American Film, 1900–1942* (New York: Oxford University Press, 1977), 220.

73. Crafton, 8, 108–10; Cass Warner Sperling, dir., *The Brothers Warner*, Warner Sisters Productions, 2008.

74. George Perry, "Al Jolson to Attempt Screen Role," *Pittsburgh Courier*, June 25, 1925.

75. J. Edgar Stanley, "Mourns Loss of Orchestra," *Afro-American*, June 9, 1928; Mary Carbine, "The Finest Outside the Loop: Motion Picture Exhibition in Chicago's Metropolis, 1905–1928," *Camera Obscura: Feminism, Culture and Media Studies*, 1990, Vol. 8, No. 2 (23), 34.

76. Cripps, 11; Jacqueline Najuma Stewart, *Migrating to the Movies: Cinema and Black Urban Modernity* (Berkeley: University of California Press, 2005), 130–31; Gregory A. Waller, "Another Audience: Black Moviegoing," 1907–16, *Cinema Journal*, Vol. 31, No. 2 (Winter 1992), 3–25; Allyson Nadia Field, *Uplift Cinema: The Emergence of African American Film and the Possibility of Black Modernity* (Durham, NC: Duke University Press, 2015); Pearl Bowser et al., *Oscar Micheaux and His African American Filmmaking and Race Cinema of the Silent Era* (Bloomington: Indiana University Press, 2016).

77. Congressional Corp., *Variety*, June 5, 1920; Congressional Film Corp., *Billboard*, June 5, 1920.

78. "Durham Has a Film Corporation," *Pittsburgh Courier*, January 23, 1926; Charlene Regester, "From the Buzzard's Roost: Black Movie-Going in Durham and Other North Carolina Cities," *Film History*, Vol. 17, No. 1, local film (2005), 117–20.

79. Uncle Dudley, "TOBA Improving," *Afro-American*, January 1, 1927.

80. S. H. Dudley, "Dud's Dope: Race Pictures," *Defender*, May 21, 1927.

81. "Uncle Dud's Dope: Dudley Proposed to Spend Your Money in the Right Place," *Pittsburgh Courier*, July 16, 1927.

82. Dudley to Douglass, February 15, 1926; Macmanan to Douglass, February 1, 1927; Dudley to Douglass, October 28, 1927, in Charles Henry Douglass Business Records, Washington Library, Macon, GA, box 20, fld 174.

83. S. H. Dudley, "T.O.B.A. Broadcasts," *Pittsburgh Courier*, March 24, 1928; Charles Musser, "Colored Players Film Corporation: An Alternative to Micheaux," in Bowser et al., *Oscar Micheaux and His Circle*, 176–82; Charles Musser, "Race Cinema and the Color Line," in Charles Musser and Jaqueline Najuma Stewart, eds., *Pioneers of African American Cinema: Film Notes* (New York: King Lorber, 2016), 20–22; *City Directory of Philadelphia, 1925*; Cripps, 196–98.

84. Salem T. Whitney, "Timely Topics: One Thing and Another," *Defender*, February 25, 1928.

85. Stein to Reevin, September 2, 1927; Reevin to Stein (telegram Cablegram), March 17, 1928, in Charles Henry Douglass Business Records, Washington Library, Macon, GA.

86. Leonard Reed interviewed by Rusty Frank, February 27, 1993, Jazz Oral History Collection Program, Archives Center, National Museum of American History.

87. Movie handbills, Charles Henry Douglass Business Records, Washington Library, Macon, GA; "Salem Tutt Whitney Blames Theater Owners and Managers for Decline in Show Business," *Defender*, July 27, 1929.

88. Victoria Wolcott, *Race, Riots, and Rollercoasters: The Struggle Over Segregated Recreation in America* (Philadelphia: University of Pennsylvania Press, 2012), 3.

89. Roberta Newman and Joel Nathan Rosen, *Black Baseball, Black Business: Race Enterprise and the Fate of the Segregated Dollar* (Jackson: University of Mississippi Press, 2014), 188–89.

90. Chris Myers Asch and George Derek Musgrove, *Chocolate City: A History of Race and Democracy in the Nation's Capital* (Chapel Hill: University of North Carolina Press, 2017), 208–15.

91. "The Capital City," *Washington Bee*, February 12, 1910.

92. "Lafayette Theater, between 132 and 133rd and 7th Avenue not for Colored," *Freeman*, January 4, 1913; Richard Carlin, et al., *Ain't Nothing Like the Real Thing: The Apollo Theater and American Entertainment* (Washington, DC: Smithsonian Books, 2010).

93. Romeo Daughtery, "Lafayette Theatre, New York, A Negro Institution Whether They Want It That Way or Not," n.d. in Lester Walton Collection, Schomburg Center for Black Research, Box 6, fld 7.

94. John Cameron Rogers to Editor, *Half Century Magazine*, December 3, 1919.

95. "J.T. Gibson Breaks Up Discrimination," *Philadelphia Tribune*, January 17, 1914.

96. Jeanne Theoharis, *A More Beautiful and Terrible History: The Uses and Misuses of Civil Rights History* (New York: Beacon Press, 2019), 89.

97. *The Negro in Chicago: A Study of Race Relations and a Riot*, Chicago Commission on Race Relations, 1922, 224, 486; Emphasis mine.

98. "President of T.O.B.A. Jim Crows Patrons in Nashville," *Pittsburgh Courier*, May 8, 1926.

99. Ibid. For more on midnight rambles, see Charlene Regester, "From the Buzzard's Roost: Black Movie-Going in Durham and Other North Carolina Cities," *Film History* Vol. 17, No. 1, local film (2005), 117–20; Randy Gue, "The Assertion of Cultural Difference at Atlanta's 81 Theatre, 1934–1937," *Film History* vol. 8 (1996), 209–18.

100. Starr to Stein, December 15, 1927, in Charles Henry Douglass Business Records, Washington Library, Macon, GA.

101. "A Note or Two," *Defender*, May 14, 1927.

102. W. Fitzhugh Brundage, ed., *Beyond Blackface: African Americans and the Creation of Popular Culture, 1890–1930* (Chapel Hill: University of North Carolina Press, 2011), 25.

103. Display Ad 2, *Philadelphia Tribune*, May 23, 1925; Salem Tutt Whitney, "Timely Topics: Jim Crow Bait," *Defender*, September 3, 1927.

104. "Uncle Dud's Dope," Dudley Proposed to Spend Your Money in the Right Place, *Pittsburgh Courier*, July 16, 1927.

105. Salem Tutt Whitney, "Timely Topics: What Would You Do: Save Your Sympathy," *Defender*, December 17, 1927.

106. Salem Tutt Whitney, "Timely Topics: Black Inconsistency," *Defender*, February 18, 1928.

107. Melvin Stokes, *D.W. Griffith's Birth of a Nation: A History of the Most Controversial Motion Picture of All Time* (New York: Oxford University Press, 2008).

108. Wolcott, *Race, Riots, and Rollercoasters*, 29–30.

109. Studs Terkel, *Hard Times: An Oral History of the Great Depression* (1970, New York: The New Press, 2005), 122, 82; Cheryl Lynn Greenberg, *To Ask for an Equal Chance: African Americans in the Great Depression* (Rowman and Littlefield, 2010), 1–3.

110. "T.O.B.A. Big Guns Meet at Trenier," *Afro-American*, February 4, 1928.

111. Salem T. Whitney, "Timely Topics: One Thing and Another," *Defender*, February 25, 1928.

112. W. R. Arnold, "New Circuit Closes Deal for 12 Houses," *Afro-American*, July 21, 1928.

113. William G. Nunn, "TOBA Circuit Responsible for Poor Calibre of Road Shows," *Pittsburgh Courier*, December 21, 1929.

114. "Sylvester Russell's Review," *Pittsburgh Courier*, August 25, 1928.

115. W. R. Arnold, "T.O.B.A. Abolishes Its Chicago Office," *Afro-American*, November 24, 1928; "Closes Chicago Office of T.O.B.A.," *Defender*, November 24, 1928.

116. "New TOBA Policy," *Defender*, December 29, 1928.

117. Jim Haskins, *The Cotton Club* (1977, New York: Hippocrene Books, 1994); L. D. Joel to Ben Stein, July 9, 1928, in Charles Henry Douglass Business Records, Washington Library, Macon, GA.

118. Commercial and Industrial Organizations of the United States, 1929 edition, Domestic Commerce Series, No. 5; "Sam Reevin: A Hustler," *Defender*, February 16, 1929.

119. "Industry and Business," *Afro-American*, April 13, 1929.

120. As previously discussed, before his 1927 appointment into federal service, theater veteran Jackson covered T.O.B.A. for *Billboard* and was involved in creating black theater directories and the Colored Actors' Union; Robert Weems and Lewis Randolph, *Business in Black and White: American Presidents and Black Entrepreneurs in the Twentieth Century* (New York University Press, 2009), 4–28.

121. "T.O.B.A. Officials Meeting Is Success," *Pittsburgh Courier*, February 16, 1929.

122. "T.O.B.A. Doings," *Defender*, February 9, 1929; "TOBA Officials Hold Confab in the Falls City," *Indianapolis Recorder*, February 9, 1929.

123. William G. Nunn, "TOBA Circuit Responsible for Poor Calibre of Road Shows," *Pittsburgh Courier*, December 21, 1929.

124. "T.O.B.A. Routings," *Afro-Americans*, March 12, 1927; "T.O.B.A. Bookings," *Defender*, November 23, 1929.

125. Each theater holder had to own at least three shares of stock at one hundred dollars a share to equal one franchised theater; Domestic Cooperation Annual Report, August 19, 1929, Tennessee State Archives, Nashville.

126. Domestic Cooperation Annual Report, August 19, 1929, Tennessee State Archives, Nashville.

127. "Salem Tutt Whitney Blames Theater Owners and Managers for Decline in Show Business," *Defender*, July 27, 1929.

128. Deed of Trust, Dudley Desdemona B., Dudley Sherman H. to Howard John D., Shreve Charles, September 23, 1929, doc #192909230117.

129. While the Depression contributed to Dudley leasing his Mid-City property theater to the Lichtman Realty Company in 1937 for "$12,000," Dudley held on to the deed and actually willed the Mid-City Theater to his son Sherman H. Dudley Jr. and granddaughter Shirley H. Dudley. Land Lease from Dudley Sherman H. to Lichtman Realty Company, 3/27/1937, Doc #1937008561 in Washington, DC, Office of the Recorder of Deeds; Estate of Dudley, Sherman, Estate No. RE06980, January 1, 1937, Register of Wills for Prince George's County.

130. Advertisements, *Billboard*, June 15, 1929; "The Forum," *Billboard*, January 25, 1930, 42, 4.

131. "Small Audiences; Folks Broke, Says TOBA Manager," *Defender*, January 25, 1930; Walker, *History of Black Business in America: Capitalism, Race, Entrepreneurship* (Chapel Hill, NC: University of North Carolina Press 2009), 225–26.

132. "T.O.B.A. officials Discuss Crisis in Show Game," *Pittsburgh Courier*, February 15, 1930.

133. William Nunn, "Hard Times Cause Scarcity of Good Road Shows," *Pittsburgh Courier*, January 4, 1930.

134. Robert E. Weems Jr. "Out of the Shadows: Business Enterprise and African American Historiography," *Business and Economic History* Vol. 26, No. 1 (Fall 1997), 207–8; "Small Audiences; Folks Broke, Says TOBA Manager," *Defender*, January 25, 1930; "T.O.B.A. Leaders Hold Meeting in Cincinnati," *Defender*, August 23, 1930; William G. Nunn, "T.O.B.A. Facing the Biggest Crisis of Its Career This Year," *Pittsburgh Courier*, August 23, 1930.

135. "1930 Saw Progress and Retrogression in the Field of Theatricals," *Afro-American*, January 3, 1931.

136. With little to promote, T.O.B.A. publicist W. R. Arnold announced his resignation in May 1930. In 1930 T.O.B.A.'s listed authorized capital stock was $20,000, down from $25,000 from the filing in 1929. The corporation was still engaged in "booking plays"; "T.O.B.A. to Lose Arnold's Help," *Defender*, May 31, 1930; Commercial and Industrial Organizations of the United States, Department of Commerce, September 1931, 60; Domestic Cooperation Annual Report, 1930 Tennessee State Archives, Nashville; Gue, 214.

137. "State, Music, Movies," *Defender*, May 3, 1930.

138. Richard M. Jones, "Trouble in Mind," 1924.

## EPILOGUE

1. Dee Rees, dir., *Bessie*. HBO, 2015; Jeremy Marre, dir., *Count Basie: Through His Own Eyes*, Eagle Rock Productions, 2018; Sam Pollard, dir., *Sammy Davis, Jr.: I've Gotta Be Me*, American Masters, 2019; George C. Wolfe, dir., *Ma Rainey's Black Bottom*, Netflix, 2020.

2. Muse, *Way Down South*, 145.

3. James A. Jackson, "Showfolks More than Entertainers," *The Messenger*, March 1925.

4. William Howland Kenney III, "The Influence of Black Vaudeville on Early Jazz," *The Black Perspective in Music* Vol. 14, No. 3 (Autumn 1986), 238.

5. Eric Ledell Smith, *African American Theater Buildings: An Illustrated Guide* (Jefferson, NC: McFarland, 2011), 6.

6. "Hear Regal to Join Vaudeville Chain: Critics Think 'Legit' Houses Are Returning," *Defender*, November 21, 1935; Martin Klein died in Chicago at age forty-seven on June 7, 1931. His son, Walter, took up the mantle of booking black theater entertainers and productions until the 1940s. Charles H. Turpin died in December 1935. Mourners lauded him as "the first of the race to operate a legitimate theater" in St. Louis and as "Justice Turpin," leaving an imprint on the St. Louis entertainment landscape. John T. Gibson passed in 1937 and was nationally revered for using his wealth to upbuild the Philadelphia black community through economic fortunes made from black vaudeville. Sherman H. Dudley died in Oxon Hill, Maryland, on February 29, 1940. In the years after T.O.B.A., Dudley remained a prominent black entrepreneur in Washington, DC, retained as much property as possible during the Great Depression, and became involved with local black politics and benevolent societies. After 1937, Samuel Reevin cut public ties with show business but remained a champion of black civil rights. He passed in 1975. Finally, Martin Starr died in Washington, DC, in June

1976. The *Washington Post* noted Starr for his continued and contested contributions to black theater through T.O.B.A. and, forty years after Toby Time's close, applauded him for his circuit work and for "furthering the careers of Bessie Smith and Ethel Waters." See "Here and There With Bob Hayes," *Defender*, July 6, 1929; Year: 1930; Census Place: Detroit, Wayne, Michigan; Page: 4A; Enumeration District: 0218; FHL microfilm: 2340774; "Martin Klein Ill," *Defender*, December 11, 1926; Walter D. Klein, "Today, With the Outlook Better, Flesh Shows Will Not Remain Extinct," *Defender*, May 22, 1937; "Insect Bite Fatal to St. Louis Judge," *Philadelphia Tribune*, January 2, 1936; "R.C. Fisher, Bite Fatal to Judge Turpin," *Defender*, January 4, 1935; Interview with Nathaniel Sweets interviewed by Dr. Richard Resh, Black Community Leaders Project, July 20, 1970, in Oral History Collection (S0829), the State Historical Society of Missouri; Certificate of Death, Commonwealth of Pennsylvania, Department of Health, Bureau of Vital Statistics, No. 57062; "John T. Gibson Dies in Philly," *Afro-American*, June 19, 1937; "John T. Gibson Boosted Bessie Smith to Stardom," *Afro-American*, October 2, 1937; Social Security Administration; Washington, DC, USA; *Social Security Death Index, Master File*; Ralph Matthews, "Watching the Big Parade," *Afro-American*, March 16, 1940; "S.H. Dudley, Famous Comic, Dies in Maryland," *Afro-American*, March 9, 1940; "Dudley Funeral at D. C. Church," *Afro-American* March 16, 1940; "Remember the Mule," *Pittsburgh Courier*, March 9, 1940; "Attack on Negroes Denounced By Jews," *Chicago Defender*, July 20, 1946; Samuel E. Reevin, "Answer to A Part or Apart," *American Jewish Times*, June 1947; "Milton Starr, 80, Owned Theaters, Aided Arts," *Washington Post*, June 10, 1976.

7. Randy Gue, "It Seems That Everything Looks Good Nowadays As Long As It Is in the Flesh & Brownskin," *Film History* Vol. 8, 1996, 214; Donald Bogle, *Bright Boulevards, Bold Dreams: The Story of Black Hollywood* (New York: Ballantine Books, 2005), 26–28, 33–37, 82–85, 89–90.

8. Miriam Petty, *Stealing the Show: African American Performers and Audiences in 1930s Hollywood* (Berkeley: University of California Press, 2016), 5; Al Moses, "Footlight Flickers," *Afro-American*, October 2, 1937; McDaniel rose from blues belter to the first African American to win an Academy Award for her contentious role of Mammy in *Gone with the Wind* within a decade after T.O.B.A.'s close. "The Academy Award of Hattie McDaniel," *Atlanta Daily World*, March 12, 1940; Bogle, 102–83.

9. https://madamwalkerlegacycenter.com/; https://www.thehowardtheatre.com/about; https://www.douglasstheatre.org/index.php?option=com_content&view=article&id=55&Itemid=60, accessed October 18, 2021.

10. Alice Barker, April 20, 2015, https://youtu.be/bktozJWbLQg.

11. S. H. Dudley, "Formation of New Circuit Is Pressing Need," *Afro-American*, December 28, 1929.

# BIBLIOGRAPHY

## PRIMARY SOURCES

### *Manuscript Collections*

**Archives Center, National Museum of America History (NMAH)**
Billings-Merriam Family Vaudeville Scrapbooks, 1890–1913
Samuel DeVincent Collection of Sheet Music
Falcon Vaudeville Trio Collection
George and Hart's Up-to-Date Minstrels Scrapbook
Hazen Collection of Band Photographs and Ephemera
Jazz Oral History Program Collection
Jeni LeGon Collection
John Levy Papers
Dewey Michael's Burlesque Collection
Musical History Documents and Graphics, 1872–1984
Philadelphia Theater Plat Book
Duncan Scheidt Collection
Frank Schiffman Apollo Theater Collection
Robert Scurlock Collection of Photography
Bobby Short Papers
George Sidney Collection
Ernie Smith Jazz Film Collection
Oscar Sullivan Papers, 1900–1960
WANN Radio Station Collection
Warshaw Collection of Business Americana

**Smithsonian Libraries, NMAH**
Trade Catalog Collection

**Harry Ransom Center, University of Texas at Austin (Ransom)**
Minstrel Collection
Tony Pastor Collection
Florenz Ziegfield Collection

**Moorland Spingarn Research Center, Howard University, Washington, DC**
C. Glenn Carrington Scrapbooks
Freeman Henry Morris Murray Papers
Isabele Taliaferro Spiller Papers
Leigh R. Whipper Papers

**Manuscript, Archives, and Rare Books Library, Emory University, Atlanta, GA (MARBL)**
Camille Billops and James Hatch Collection (Artist and Influence Oral Histories)
Bricktop (Ada Beatrice Smith) Papers, 1894–1984
Jolly John Larkin Scrapbook
Flournoy Miller Papers
Victory Spivey Papers

**Schomburg Center for Black Research, New York, New York**
Helen Armstead-Johnson Miscellaneous Theater Collections, 1831–1993
Flournoy E. Miller Collection
Negro Actors Guild Collection
Edith Spencer Scrapbook
Lester Walton Papers

**Tennessee State Archives, Nashville, TN**
Domestic Corporation Annual Reports, 1920–31

**Washington Memorial Library, Macon, GA**
Charles H. Douglass Business Records

**Reports, Court Proceedings, & Directories**
"100 Years of Marriage and Divorce Statistics in the United States," Department of Health and Welfare, 1973
*Abstract of the Thirteenth Census-Population,* Washington, DC, 1913
Atlanta University Press, *Atlanta University Publications, No. 1, 2, 4, 8, 9, 11, 13, 14, 15, 16, 17, 18,* New York: Arno Press and the New York Times, 1968
Berheim, Alfred L., *The Business of the Theater,* New York: Actor's Equity Association, 1932
Clarke, Ida, *All About Nashville,* 1912
*Colored Theatrical Guide and Business Directory,* Brooklyn, NY, 1915
*Commercial and Industrial Organizations of the United States,* Department of Commerce, September 1931
*Commercial and Industrial Organizations of the United States,* Domestic Commerce Series, No. 5, 1929

Department of Commerce, Bureau of the Census, *Thirteenth Census of the United States, 1910-Population, Vol. I-III,* Washington, DC: Government Publishing Office, 1913

Department of Commerce and Labor, Bureau of the Census, *Twelfth Census of the United States: 1900—Population,* Hamilton County, Chattanooga City, 1900

Department of Commerce and Labor, Bureau of the Census, *Statistics of Women At Work,* Washington, DC: Government Publishing Office, 1907

*Diamond Jubilee: Congregation of B'nai Zion, 1888–1963,* Chattanooga, Tenn: s.n., 1963

Du Bois, W. E. B., *The Negro in Business: Proceedings for the Fourth Conference for the Study of Negro Problems,* Atlanta: Atlanta University, 1899

Dumont, Frank, *The Witmark Amateur Minstrel Guide and Burnt Cork Encyclopedia,* Chicago: M. Witmark & Sons, 1899

*Federal Trade Commission vs. Vaudeville Managers' Protective Association,* et al. Stenographic transcript [of proceedings] before the Federal Trade Commission, New York City. Docket no. 128. United States, Washington, DC: Galt & Williams, 1919

Grau, Robert, *The Business Man in the Amusement World,* Chicago, 1910

Grau, Robert, *Forty Years Observation of Music and Drama,* New York: Broadway Publishing, 1909

*Gus Hill National Theater Directory* 1900–1915

*Julius Cahn-Gus Hill Theatrical Guide and Moving Picture Supplement,* 1922

*Julius Cahn Official Theatrical Guides,* 1908–1915

Harrison, William Henry, Jr., *Colored Girls' and Boys' Inspiring United States History, And a Heart to Heart Talk about White Folks,* 1921

*National Negro Classified Business Directory,* Wilmington, DE: National Negro Business Directory System Inc., 1919

*Negroes in the United States, 1920–32,* Department of Commerce and Labor, Bureau of the Census, 1934

*The Negro in Chicago: A Study of Race Relations and a Riot,* Chicago Commission on Race Relations, 1922

*Official Theatrical World Of Colored Artists: National Directory and Guide,* 1928

*Proceedings of the National Negro Business League,* Boston, August 23–24, 1900

*Public Acts of the State of Tennessee,* 1921

Renton, Edward, *The Vaudeville Theatre, Building, Operation, and Management,* Gotham Press, Inc., 1918

*Report of the Sixteenth Annual Meeting of the National Negro Business League,* Boston, 1915

*Report of the Seventeenth Annual Session of the National Negro Business League,* Kansas City, MO, August 16, 17, 18, 1916

*Report on Population of the United States, Eleventh Census of the United States,* 1890, Washington, DC: Government Publishing Office, 1895

Rice, Edward LeRoy, *Monarchs of Minstrelsy: From Daddy Rice to Date,* New York: Kenny Publishing, 1911

*Statistics on Population of the United States at the 10th Census,* Washington, DC: U.S. Government Printing Office, 1880

*Tulsa Chapter Red Cross Disaster Relief, Condensed Report*, Tulsa, Oklahoma: December 31, 1921
Webster, Susie McCarver, *Historic City-Chattanooga*, Chattanooga: McGowan & Cooke, 1915
Work, Monroe N., *Negro Year Book: Annual Encyclopedia of the Negro*, 1912–1922

**City Directories & Commerce Guides**

*Boyd's City Directory of Camden*, 1895–1896
*Boyd's City Directories of the District of Columbia*, 1900–1930
*Chattanooga Business & Professional Directory*, Galligan & Crowley Publishing Co., 1919
*G. M. Connelley & Co's Alphabetical Directory of Chattanooga, Tennessee*, Chattanooga, TN: G.M. Connelly & Co, 1901–1930
*Gould's City Directories of St. Louis*, 1893–1894
*Lakeside Directory of Chicago*, 1900–1910
*Marshall-Bruce-Polk Co.'s Nashville City Directories*, 1900–1929
*Morrison and Fourmy's General Directory for the City of Dallas*, 1888–91
*Morrison and Fourmy's General Directory for the City of Galveston*, 1890–94
*Polk-Hoffhine Directory Co.'s Tulsa City Directory*, 1914–27
*Wood's Baltimore City Directory*, 1872–76

**Newspapers & Periodicals**

*Advertising and Selling*
Baltimore *Afro-American*
*Billboard*
*Chicago Defender*
Chicago *Broad Ax*
*Colored American Magazine*
*Crisis*
*Exhibitor's Trade Review*
*The Green Book Magazine*
*Half Century Magazine*
*Indianapolis Freeman*
*Jewish Advocate*
*The Messenger*
*Metronome*
*Moving Picture World*
Nashville *Globe*
*The Nation*
New York *Amsterdam News*
New York *Clipper*
New York *Interstate Tattler*
*New York Times*
*Opportunity*
*Philadelphia Tribune*
*Pittsburgh Courier*
*St. Louis Argus*

*St. Louis Republic*
*Voice of the Negro*
Washington *Bee*
Washington *Evening Star*
*Washington Post*
*Variety*

## SECONDARY SOURCES

Abbott, Lynn, and Doug Seroff. *The Original Blues: The Emergence of Blues in African American Vaudeville.* Jackson, MS: University of Mississippi, 2017.

Abbott, Lynn, and Doug Seroff. *Ragged but Right: Black Traveling Shows, "Coon" Songs and the Dark Pathway to Blues and Jazz.* Jackson, MS: University of Mississippi, 2007.

Abbott, Lynn, and Per Oldaeus. "For Ofays Only: An Annotated Calendar of Midnight Frolics at the Lyric Theater," *The Jazz Archivist* Vol. XVII (2003).

Adair, Zakiya R. "Respectable Vamp: A Black Feminist Analysis of Florence Mills Early Career," *Journal of African American Studies* Vol. 17, No. 1 (March 2013), 7–21.

Adams, Mauriane, and John Bracey, eds. *Strangers and Neighbors: Relations Between Blacks & Jews in the United States.* Amherst: University of Massachusetts Press, 1999.

Alberston, Chris. *Bessie.* New Haven, CT: Yale University Press, 2003.

Altemus, Althea McDowell. *Big Bosses: A Working Girl's Memoir of Jazz Age America.* Edited by Robin Bachin, Chicago: University of Chicago Press, 2016.

Ammen, Sharon. *May Irwin: Singing, Shouting, and the Shadow of Minstrelsy.* Urbana: University of Illinois Press, 2017.

Asch, Chris Myers, and George Derek Musgrove. *Chocolate City: A History of Race and Democracy in the Nation's Capital.* Chapel Hill: University of North Carolina Press, 2017.

Ashby, Leroy. *With Amusement for All: A History of American Popular Culture Since 1930.* Lexington: University Press of Kentucky, 2006.

Baldwin, Davarian. "Chicago's New Negroes," *American Studies* Vol. 44, No. 1/2 New Voices in American Studies (Spring/Summer 2003).

Baldwin, Davarian L. *Chicago's New Negroes: Modernity, The Great Migration, and Black Urban Life.* Chapel Hill: University of North Carolina Press, 2007.

Barlow, William. *Looking Up and Down: The Emergence of Blues Culture.* Philadelphia: Temple University Press, 1989.

Basie, William. *Good Morning Blues: The Autobiography of Count Basie as told to Albert Murray.* New York: Random House, 1985.

Bauman, Thomas. *The Pekin: The Rise and Fall of Chicago's First Black-Owned Theater.* Urbana: University of Illinois, 2014.

Bay, Mia. *Traveling Black: A Story of Race and Resistance.* Cambridge, MA: Harvard University Press, 2021.

Bean, Annamarie, James V. Hatch, and Brooks McNamara. *Inside the Minstrel Mask: Readings in Nineteenth-Century Blackface Minstrelsy.* Hanover: Wesleyan University Press, 1996.

Beresford, Mark. *That's Got 'Em: The Life and Music of Wilbur Sweatman.* Jackson: University of Mississippi Press, 2010.

Berlin, Edward A. *King of Ragtime: Scott Joplin and His Era*, 2nd ed. New York: Oxford University Press, 2016.

Berlin, Edward A. *Ragtime: A Musical and Cultural History*. Berkeley: University of California Press, 1980.

Bernhardt, Clyde E. B. as told to Sheldon Harris. *I Remember: Eighty Years of Black Entertainment, Big Bands, and the Blues.* Philadelphia: University of Pennsylvania Press, 1986.

Bjorn, Lars. *Before Motown: A History of Jazz in Detroit.* Ann Arbor: University of Michigan Press, 2001.

Black, Timuel D., Jr. *Bridges of Memory: Chicago's First Wave of Black Migration*. Evanston, IL: Northwestern University Press, 2003.

Bodgan, Robert. *Freak Show: Presenting Human Oddities for Amusement and Profit.* Chicago: University of Chicago Press, 2014.

Bogle, Donald. *Bright Boulevards, Bold Dreams: The Story of Black Hollywood*. New York: Ballentine Books, 2005.

Bogle, Donald. *Toms, Coons, Mulattoes, Mammies, and Bucks: An Interpretative History of Blacks in Films* 4th ed. London: Bloomsbury Academic, 2001.

Bowser, Pearl, Jane Gaines, and Charles Musser. *Oscar Micheaux and His African American Filmmaking and Race Cinema of the Silent Era.* Bloomington: Indiana University Press, 2016.

Bradford, John. "The Problem of Child Entertainment," *Journal of Education*, Vol. 81, No. 3 (2013) (January 21, 1915), 63–64.

Brophy, Alfred L. *Reconstructing the Dreamland: The Tulsa Riot of 1921: Race, Reparations, and Reconciliation*. New York: Oxford University Press, 2002.

Brown, Jayna. *Babylon Girls: Black Women Performers and the Shaping of the Modern*. Raleigh, NC: Duke University Press, 2008.

Browner, Tara, and Thomas L. Riis, eds. *Rethinking American Music*. Urbana: University of Illinois Press, 2019.

Brundage, W. Fitzhugh, ed., *Beyond Blackface: African Americans and the Creation of Popular Culture, 1890–1930*. Chapel Hill: University of North Carolina Press, 2011.

Burnim, Mellonee V., and Portia K. Maultsby, eds. *African American Music: An Introduction.* New York: Routledge, 2015.

Butsch, Richard, ed. *For Fun and Profit: The Transformation of Leisure into Consumption.* Philadelphia: Temple University Press, 1990.

Butsch, Richard. *The Making of American Audiences: From Stage to Television 1750–1990*. Cambridge, UK: Cambridge University Press, 2000.

Cadoo, Cara. *Envisioning Freedom: Cinema and the Building of Black Modern Life*. Cambridge, MA: Harvard University Press, 2014.

Calhoun, Mary. *Medicine Show: Conning People and Making Them Like It.* New York: Harper and Row, 1976.

Carbine, Mary. "The Finest Outside the Loop: Motion Picture Exhibition in Chicago's Metropolis, 1905–1928," *Camera Obscura: Feminism, Culture and Media Studies* Vol. 8, No. 2 (23), (1990), 8–41.

Carlin, Richard, et al. *Ain't Nothing Like the Real Thing: The Apollo Theater and American Entertainment.* Washington, DC: Smithsonian Books, 2010.

Chafe, William et al., *Remembering Jim Crow: African Americans Tell About Life in the Segregated South*. New York: New Press, 2001.

Chambers, Jason. *Madison Avenue and the Color Line: African Americans in the Advertising Industry*. Philadelphia: University of Pennsylvania Press, 2011.

Chapman, Erin. *Prove It On Me: New Negroes, Sex, and Popular Culture in the 1920s*. New York: Oxford University Press, 2012.

Christiansen, Richard. *A Theater of Our Own: A History and a Memoir of 1001 Nights in Chicago*. Evanston, IL: Northwestern University Press, 2004.

Collins, Patricia Hill. *Black Feminist Thought: Knowledge, Consciousness, and the Politics of Empowerment*. New York: Routledge Press, 1990.

Crafton, David. *The Talkies: American Cinema's Transition to Sound, 1926–1931*. Berkeley: University of California Press, 1999.

Cripps, Thomas. *A Slow Fade to Black: The Negro in American Film, 1900–1942*. New York: Oxford University Press, 1977.

Cuney-Hare, Maud. *Negro Musicians and Their Music*. Washington, DC: Associated Publishers, 1936.

Curriden, Mark, and Leroy Phillips Jr. *Contempt of Court: The Turn of the Century Lynching That Launched 100 Years of Federalism*. New York: Faber and Faber, 1999.

Curtis, Susan. *Colored Memories: A Biographer's Quest for the Elusive Lester A. Walton*. Columbia: University of Missouri Press, 2008.

Cutler, Irving. *The Jews of Chicago: From Shtetl to Suburb*. Urbana: University of Illinois Press, 1996.

Davis, Angela. *Blues Legacies and Black Feminism: Gertrude 'Ma' Rainey, Bessie Smith, and Billie Holiday*. New York: Random House, 1998.

Dorman, James. "Shaping the Popular Image of Post-Reconstruction American Blacks: The 'Coon Song' Phenomenon of the Gilded Age," *American Quarterly* Vol. 40, No. 4 (December 1988), 450–451.

Du Bois, W. E. B. *The Gift of Black Folk: The Negroes in the Making of America*. Boston: Stratford, 1924.

Du Bois, W. E. B. *Philadelphia Negro*, 1899, repr., New York: Schoken Books, 1967.

Early, Gerald. *Ain't But a Place: An Anthology of African American Writings about St. Louis*. St. Louis: Missouri Historical Society Press, 1998.

Elam, Harry J., Jr., and David Krasner. *African American Performance and Theater History: A Critical Reader*. New York: Oxford University Press, 2001.

Ellison, Ralph. *Shadow and Act*. New York: Quality Paperback Book Club, 1994.

Ellsworth, Scott. *Death in a Promised Land: The Tulsa Race Riot of 1921*. Baton Rouge: Louisiana State University Press, 1982.

Erdman, Andrew. *Queen of Vaudeville: The Story of Eva Tanguay*. Ithaca, NY: Cornell University Press, 2012.

Eyman, Scott. *The Speed of Sound: Hollywood and the Talkie Revolution, 1926–1930*. New York: Simon & Schuster, 1997.

Ferris, Marcie Cohen, and Mark Greenberg, eds. *Jewish Roots in Southern Soil: A New History*. New York: Brandeis University Press, 2006.

Field, Allyson Nadia. *Uplift Cinema: The Emergence of African American Film and the Possibility of Black Modernity*. Durham, NC: Duke University Press, 2015.

Fletcher, Tom. *100 Years of the Negro in Show Business!* New York: Burdge & Co., 1954.

Floyd, Samuel A. *The Power of Black Music: Interpreting Its History from Africa to the United States*. New York: Oxford University Press, 1995.

Floyd, Samuel A., and Marsha J. Reisser. "Social Dance Music of Black Composers in the Nineteenth Century and the Emergence of Classic Ragtime," *The Black Perspective in Music* Vol. 8, No. 2 (Autumn 1980), 161–193.

Forbes, Camille F. *Introducing Bert Williams: Burnt Cork, Broadway, and the Story of America's First Black Star*. New York: Basic Civitas, 2008.

Frank, Fedora Small. *Beginnings on Market Street: Nashville and Her Jewry, 1861–1901*. Nashville, TN: Jewish Community of Nashville and Middle Tennessee, 1976.

Furia, Phillip, and Michael Lasser. *America's Songs: The Stories Behind the Songs of Broadway, Hollywood, and Tin Pan Alley*. London: Routledge Press, 2006.

Gaines, Kevin. *Uplifting the Race: Black Leadership, Politics, and Culture in the Twentieth Century*. Chapel Hill: University of North Carolina Press, 1996.

Garrett-Scott, Shennette. *Banking on Freedom: Black Women in U.S. Finance Before the New Deal*. New York: Columbia University Press, 2019.

Gates, Henry Louis, and Gene Andrew Jarret. *The New Negro: Readings on Race, Representation and African American Culture, 1892–1938*. Princeton, NJ: Princeton University Press, 2007.

George-Graves, Nadine. *The Royalty of Negro Vaudeville: The Whitman Sisters and the Negotiation of Race, Gender, and Class in African American Theater, 1900–1940*. New York: Palgrave Macmillan, 2000.

George Graves, Nadine. "Spreading the Sand: Understanding the Economic and Creative Impetus for the Black Vaudeville Industry," *Continuum: The Journal of African Diaspora Drama, Theatre and Performance* Vol. 1, No. 1 (June 2014), 1–17.

Giddings, Paula. *When and Where I Enter: The Impact of Black Women on Race and Sex in America*. New York: Quill William Morrow, 1996.

Gilbert, Douglas. *American Vaudeville: Its Life and Times*. New York: Dover Publications, 1940.

Golden, George Fuller. *My Lady Vaudeville and Her White Rats*. New York: Broadway Publishing Company, 1909.

Gordon, Linda. *Heroes of Their Own Lives: The Politics and History of Family Violence in Boston, 1880–1960*. Urbana: University of Illinois Press, 2002.

Gottschild, Brenda Dixon. *Waltzing in the Dark: African American Vaudeville and Race Politics in the Swing Era*. New York: Palgrave Macmillan, 2002.

Grant, James. *The Forgotten Depression: 1921, The Crash That Cured Itself*. New York: Simon & Schuster, 2014.

Graziano, John. "The Early Life and Career of the 'Black Patti': The Odyssey of an African American Singer in the Late Nineteenth Century," *Journal of the American Musicological Society* Vol. 53, No. 3 (2000), 543–96.

Greenberg, Cheryl Lynn. *To Ask for an Equal Chance: African Americans in the Great Depression*, Lanham, MD: Rowman and Littlefield, 2010.

Greenberg, Cheryl Lynn. *Troubling the Waters: Black-Jewish Relations in the American Century*. Princeton, NJ: Princeton University Press, 2006.

Gue, Randy. "It Seems That Everything Looks Good Nowadays As Long As It Is in the Flesh & Brownskin," *Film History* Vol. 8 (1996), 209–28.

Gussow, Adam. *Seems Like Murder Here: Southern Violence and the Blues*. Chicago: University of Chicago Press, 2002.

Gustaitis, Joseph. *Chicago Transformed: World War and the Windy City*. Carbondale: Southern Illinois University Press, 2016.

Handy, W. C. *Father of the Blues: An Autobiography*. New York: Macmillan, 1941.

Harris, Abram. *The Negro as Capitalist: A Study of Banking and Business among American Negroes*. Philadelphia: American Academy of Political and Social Science, 1936.

Harris, Michael W. *The Rise of Gospel Blues: The Music of Thomas Andrew Dorsey in the Urban Church*. New York: Oxford University Press, 1992.

Harrison, Daphne Duval. *Black Pearls: Blues Queens of the 1920's*. New Brunswick, NJ: Rutgers University Press, 1988.

Hartman, Sadiya. *Wayward Lives, Beautiful Experiments: Intimate Histories of Social Upheaval*. New York: W. W. Norton, 2019.

Hasse, John. *Ragtime: Its History, Composers, and Music*. New York: Schirmer Books, 1985.

Haupert, Michael John. *The Entertainment Industry*. Westport, CT: Greenwood Press, 2006.

Helfand, William H. "Ephemera of the American Medicine Show," *Pharmacy in History* Vol. 27, No. 4 (1985), 183–191.

Higginbotham, Evelyn Brooks. *Righteous Discontent: The Women's Movement in the Black Baptist Church, 1880–1920*. Cambridge, MA: Harvard University Press, 1993.

Higham, John. "Social Discrimination against Jews in America, 1830–1930," *Publications of the American Jewish Historical Society* Vol. 47, No. 1 (September 1957), 1–33.

Hill, Errol. "Black Theatre in Form and Style," *The Black Scholar*, July/August 1979, Vol. 10, No. 10, 29–31.

Hill, Errol. "Remarks on Black Theater History," *The Massachusetts Review* Vol. 28, No. 4 (Winter 1987), 609–14.

Hill, Errol G., and James V. Hatch. *A History of African American Theatre*, Cambridge: Cambridge University Press, 2003.

Huggins, Nathan Irvin. *Harlem Renaissance*. New York: Oxford University Press, 1971.

Hughes, Langston. *The Big Sea: An Autobiography*. New York: Hill and Wang, 1993.

Hughes, Langston. "The Negro Artist and the Racial Mountain." *Nation*, June 23, 1926.

Hughes, Langston, and Milton Meltzer. *Black Magic: A History of the African-American in the Performing Arts*. New York: DeCapo Press, 1990, original in 1967.

Hunter, Tera. *To 'Joy My Freedom: Southern Black Women's Lives and Labors after the Civil War*. Cambridge, MA: Harvard University Press, 1997.

Jansen, David A., and Gene Jones. *Spreadin' Rhythm Around: Black Popular Songwriters, 1880–1930*. New York: Schirmer Books, 1998.

Johnson, Claudia. "The Guilty Third Tier: Prostitution in Nineteenth-Century American Theaters," *American Quarterly* Vol. 27, No. 5 (December 1975), 575–84.

Johnson, James Weldon. *Black Manhattan*. New York: Alfred. A. Knopf, 1930.

Johnson, J. Rosamond. "Why They Call American Music Ragtime," *The Black Perspective in Music* Vol. 4, No. 2 Bicentennial Number (July 1976), 260–64.

Johnson, Stephen, ed. *Burnt Cork: Traditions and Legacies of Blackface Minstrelsy*. Amherst: University of Massachusetts Press, 2012.

Jones, William H. *Recreation and Amusement Among Negroes in Washington, D.C.: A Sociological Analysis of the Negro in an Urban Environment*. Washington, DC: Howard University Press, 1927.

Kelly, Robin D. G. "We are Not What We Seem: Rethinking Black Working Class Opposition in the Jim Crow South," *The Journal of American History* Vol. 80, No. 1 (June 1993), 75–112.

Kenney, William Howland, III. "The Influence of Black Vaudeville on Early Jazz," *The Black Perspective in Music* Vol. 14, No. 3 (Autumn 1986), 233–48.

Kenzer, Robert C. "Black Businessmen in Post-Civil War Tennessee," *Journal of East Tennessee History* 66 (1994), 59–80.

Kibler, M. Alison. "Rank Ladies, Ladies of Rank: The Elinore Sisters in Vaudeville," *American Studies* Vol. 38, No. 1 (Spring 1997), 97–115.

Knight, Athelia. "He Paved the Way for T. O. B. A.," *The Black Perspective in Music*, Vol. 15, No. 2 (Autumn 1987), 153–81.

Krasner, David. *Beautiful Pageant: African American Theatre, Drama, and Performance in the Harlem Renaissance*. New York: Palgrave Macmillan, 2002.

Lavitt, Pamela Brown. "First of the Red Hot Mamas: The Jewish Ziegfeld Girl," *American Jewish History* Vol. 87, No. 4 (December 1999), 258–60.

Lauterbach, Preston. *Beale Street Dynasty: Sex, Song, and the Struggle for the Soul of Memphis.* New York: W. W. Norton, 2016.

Laurie, Joe Jr. *Vaudeville from Honky Tonks to the Palace*. New York: Broadway Publishing, 1953.

Lauterbach, Preston. *The Chitlin' Circuit and the Road to Rock 'n' Roll,* New York: W. W. Norton, 2011.

Leavitt, Michael Bennett. *Fifty Years in Theatrical Management*. New York: Broadway Publishing, 1912.

Levine, Lawrence W. "The Folklore of Industrial Society: Popular Culture and Its Audiences." *The American Historical Review* Vol. 97, No. 5 (December 1992), 1369–99.

Levine, Lawrence W. *Highbrow/Lowbrow: The Emergence of Cultural Hierarchy in America.* Cambridge, MA: Harvard University Press, 1990.

Levy, John, and Devra Hall. *Men, Women, and Girl Singers: My Life as a Musician Turned Talent Manager*. Silver Spring, MD: Beckham Publications, 2000.

Lewis, Robert M., ed. *From Traveling Show to Vaudeville: Theatrical Spectacle in America, 1830–1910*. Baltimore: John Hopkins Press, 2003.

Lhamon, W. T., Jr. *Jump Jim Crow: Lost Plays, Lyrics, and Street Prose of the First Atlantic Popular Culture*. Cambridge, MA: Harvard University Press, 2003.

Lhamon, W. T., Jr. *Raising Cain: Blackface Performance from Jim Crow to Hip Hop*. Cambridge, MA: Harvard University Press, 1998.

Lieb, Sandra R. *Mother of the Blues: A Study of Ma Rainey*. Amherst: University of Massachusetts Press, 1981.

Lindsey, Treva B. *Colored No More: Reinventing Black Womanhood in Washington DC*. Urbana: University of Illinois Press, 2017.

Locke, Alain Leroy. *The New Negro*. New York: Albert & Charles Boni, 1925.

Logan, Rayford. *The Negro in American Life and Thought: The Nadir, 1877–1901*. New York: Dial Press, 1954.

Lott, Eric. *Love and Theft: Blackface Minstrelsy and the American Working Class*. New York: Oxford University Press, 1995.

Lovett, Bobby L. *The African American History of Nashville, 1780–1930*. Fayetteville: University of Arkansas Press, 1999.

Lutz, Tom, and Susanna Ashton ed. *These Colored United States*. New Brunswick, NJ: Rutgers University Press, 1996.

McAllister, Marvin. *White People Do Not Know How to Behave at Entertainments Designed for Ladies and Gentlemen of Colour: William Brown's African and American Theater*. Chapel Hill: University of North Carolina Press, 2002.

McAllister, Marvin. *Whiting Up: Whiteface Minstrels and Stage Europeans in African American Performance*. Chapel Hill: University of North Carolina Press, 2011.

McWhirter, Cameron. *Red Summer: The Summer of 1919 and the Awakening of Black America*. Henry Holt and Co., 2011.

Moore, Lucy. *Anything Goes: A Biography of the Roaring Twenties*, New York: Overlook Press, 2011.

Melnick, Jeffrey. *A Right to Sing the Blues: African Americans, Jews, and American Popular Song*. Cambridge, MA: Harvard University Press, 2001.

Middleton, George. *Circus Memoirs: Reminiscences of George Middleton as Told to and Written by His Wife*. Los Angeles: George Rice & Sons Printers, 1912.

Moser, Whet. "Chicago Isn't Just Segregated, It Basically Invented Modern Segregation," *Chicago Magazine*, March 2017.

Most, Andrea. *Making Americans: Jews and the Broadway Musical*. Cambridge, MA: Harvard University Press, 2004.

Murray, Albert. *Stomping the Blues*. New York: DeCapo Press, 1976.

Muse, Clarence. *Way Down South*. Los Angeles: David Graham Fischer, 1932.

Musser, Charles, and Jacqueline Najuma Stewart. *Pioneers of African American Cinema: Film Notes*. New York: King Lorber, 2016.

Newman, Roberta, and Joel Nathan Rosen. *Black Baseball, Black Business: Race Enterprise and the Fate of the Segregated Dollar*. Jackson: University of Mississippi Press, 2014.

Nieves, Angel David, and Leslie M. Alexander, eds. *We Shall Independent Be: African American Place Making and the Struggle to Claim Space in the United States*. Boulder: University of Colorado, 2008.

Nolen, Rose M. *Hoecakes, Hambone, and All That Jazz: African American Traditions in Missouri*. Columbia: University of Missouri Press, 2003.

Peiss, Kathy. "Vital Industry and Women's Ventures: Conceptualizing Gender in Twentieth Century Business History," *The Business History Review* Vol. 72, No. 2 Gender and Business (Summer 1998), 218–41.

Peterson, Bernard L. *The African American Theatre Directory, 1816–1960: A Comprehensive Guide to Early Black Theatre Organizations, Companies, Theatres, and Performing Groups*. Santa Barbara: Greenwood Press, 1997.

Petty, Miriam. *Stealing the Show: African American Performers and Audiences in 1930s Hollywood.* Berkeley: University of California Press, 2016.

Powell, Herbert Preston. *The World's Best Book of Minstrelsy*. Philadelphia: Penn Publishing Company, 1926.

Pryor, Elizabeth Stordeur. *Colored Travelers: Mobility and the Fight for Citizenship before the Civil War*, Baltimore: Johns Hopkins Press, 2016.

Reed, Christopher Robert. *Black Chicago's First Century, Vol. 1, 1833–1900*. Columbia: University of Missouri Press, 2005.

Reed, Christopher Robert. *The Rise of Chicago's Black Metropolis, 1920–1929*. Urbana: University of Illinois Press, 2011.

Regester, Charlene. "From the Buzzard's Roost: Black Movie-Going in Durham and Other North Carolina Cities," *Film History* Vol. 17, No. 1, local film (2005), 113–24.

Riis, Thomas Lawrence. "Pink Morton's Theater, Black Vaudeville, the TOBA: Recovering the History, 1910–1930," in Josephine Wright ed., *New Perspectives on Music: Essays in Honor of Eileen Southern*. Warren, MI: Harmonie Park Press, 1992.

Riis, Thomas L. *Just Before Jazz: Black Musical Theater in New York, 1890 to 1915*. Washington, DC: Smithsonian Institution Press, 1994.

Rivers, Larry Eugene, and Canter Brown Jr. "The Art of Gathering a Crowd: Florida's Pat Chapelle and the Origins of Black-Owned Vaudeville," *The Journal of African American History* Vol. 92, No. 2 (Spring 2007), 169–90.

Roberts, Brian. *Blackface Nation: Race, Reform, and Identity in American Popular Music, 1812–1925*. Chicago: University of Chicago Press, 2017.

Robertson, David. *W.C. Handy: The Life and Times of the Man Who Made the Blues*. New York: Knopf, 2009.

Robinson, Cedric. *Forgeries of Memory and Meaning: Blacks and the Regimes of Race in American Theater and Film before World War II*. Chapel Hill, NC: University of North Carolina, 2007.

Robinson, Edward A. "The Pekin: The Genesis of American Black Theater," *Black American Literature Forum* Vol. 16, No. 4 (Winter 1982), 136–38.

Rockaway, Robert. *Words of the Uprooted: Jewish Immigrants in Early 20th Century America*. Ithaca, NY: Cornell University Press, 1998.

Rodger, Gillian M. *Champagne Charlie and Pretty Jemima: Variety Theater in the Nineteenth Century*. Urbana: University of Illinois Press, 2010.

Ruble, Blair. "Seventh Street, Black D.C's Music Mecca," *Washington History*, Vol. 26, Jazz in Washington (Spring 2014), viii, 1–11.

Ruble, Blair. *Washington's U Street: A Biography*. Baltimore: Johns Hopkins Press, 2012.

Rundstedler, Theresa. *Jack Johnson, Rebel Sojourner: Boxing in the Shadow of the Global Color Line*. Berkeley: University of California Press, 2013.

Sampson, Henry T. *Blacks in Blackface: A Source on Early Black Musical Shows*. Metuchen, NJ: Scarecrow Press, Inc., 1980, 2nd edition, 2013.

Sampson, Henry T. *The Ghost Walks: A Chronological History of Blacks in Show Business, 1865–1910*. Metuchen, NJ: Scarecrow Press, Inc., 1988.

Schenbeck, Lawrence. "Music, Gender, and 'Uplift' in the 'Chicago Defender,' 1927–1937," *The Musical Quarterly* Vol. 81, No. 3 (1997), 344–70.

Schenbeck, Lawrence. *Racial Uplift and American Music, 1878–1943*. Jackson: University of Mississippi Press, 2014.

Schwartz, Roberta Freund. "How Blue Can You Get? It's Tight Like That and the Hokum Blues," *American Music* Vol. 36, No. 3 (Fall 2018), 367–93.

Schweitzer, Marlis. "'The Mad Search for Beauty': Actresses' Testimonials, the Cosmetics Industry, and the 'Democratization of Beauty,'" *Journal of the Gilded Age and Progressive Era*, Vol. 4, No. 3 (July 2005), 255–92.

Scott, Michelle R. *Blues Empress in Black Chattanooga: Bessie Smith and the Emerging Urban South*. Urbana: University of Illinois, 2008.

Scott, Michelle R. "'These Ladies Do Business with a Capital B': The Griffin Sisters and Black Businesswomen in Early Vaudeville." *Journal of African American History* Vol. 101, No. 4 (2016), 469–503.

Scott, Michelle R. "To Help Enlighten Our People: Theater Folks and Stage Advice Columns in the 1920s *Chicago Defender*," *American Studies with American Studies International (AMSJ)* Vol. 53, No. 3 (2020), 55–76.

Scribner, Christopher M. "Nashville Offers Opportunity: *The Nashville Globe* and Business as a Means of Uplift, 1907–1913," *Tennessee Historical Quarterly* Vol. 54, No. 1 (Spring 1995), 55.

Semmes, Clovis E. *The Regal Theater and Black Culture*. New York: Palgrave Macmillan, 2006.

Seniors, Paula Marie. *Beyond Lift Every Voice and Sing: The Culture of Uplift, Identity, and Politics in Black Musical Theater*. Columbus: University of Ohio Press, 2009.

Shapiro, Nat, and Nat Hentoff, ed. *Hear Me Talkin' To Ya: The Story of Jazz as Told by the Men Who Made It*. New York: Penguin Books, 1962.

Shaw, Arnold. *The Jazz Age: Popular Music in the 1920's*. New York: Oxford University Press, 1987.

Slout, William. *Burnt Cork and Tamborines: A Source Book for Negro Minstrelsy*. San Bernardino, CA: Borgo Press, 2007.

Slide, Anthony. *Encyclopedia of Vaudeville*, Jackson: University of Mississippi Press, 2012.

Smith, Eric Ledell. *African American Theater Buildings: An Illustrated Guide*. Jefferson, NC: McFarland, 2011.

Snyder, Robert. *A Voice of the City: Vaudeville and Popular Culture in New York*, second edition. New York: Ivan R. Dee, 2000.

Sotiropolous, Karen. *Staging Race: Black Performers in Turn of the Century America*. Cambridge, MA: Harvard University Press, 2006.

Southern, Eileen. *The Music of Black Americans: A History*. New York: W. W. Norton Co., 1997.

Spencer, Jon Michael. *The New Negroes and Their Music*. Knoxville: University of Tennessee Press, 1997.

Springhall, John. *The Genesis of Mass Culture: Show Business Live in America, 1840–1940*. New York: Palgrave Macmillan, 2008.

Stein, Charles W., ed. *Vaudeville as Seen by Its Contemporaries*. New York: Alfred A. Knopf, 1984.

Stevens, Ronald Smokey. *The First 60 Years: The History of Afro American Musical Theater and Entertainment, 1865–1930*. New York: Avid Reader Press, 2013.

Stewart, Jacqueline Najuma. *Migrating to the Movies: Cinema and Black Urban Modernity*. Berkeley: University of California Press, 2005.

Stokes, Melvin. *D.W. Griffith's Birth of a Nation: A History of the Most Controversial Motion Picture of All Time*. Cambridge, MA: Oxford University Press, 2008.

Taylor, Yuval, and Jake Austen. *Darkest America: Black Minstrelsy from Slavery to Hip Hop*. New York: W.W. Norton & Company, 2012.

Theoharis, Jeanne. *A More Beautiful and Terrible History: The Uses and Misuses of Civil Rights History*. New York: Beacon Press, 2019.

Toll, Robert. *Blacking Up: The Minstrel Show in Nineteenth Century America*. New York: Oxford University Press, 1977.

Travis, Dempsey J. "Chicago's Jazz Trail, 1893–1950," *Black Music Research Journal* Vol. 10, No. 1 (Spring 1990), 82–85.

Tye, Larry. *Rising From the Rails: Pullman Porters and the Making of the Black Middle Class*. New York: Henry Holt and Co., 2004.

Walker, Juliet E. K. "Black Entrepreneurship: An Historical Inquiry," *Business and Economic History* 12 (1983), 37–55. www.jstor.org/stable/23702738.

Walker, Juliet E. K. *History of Black Business in America: Capitalism, Race, Entrepreneurship*. Chapel Hill: University of North Carolina Press, 2009.

Walker, Juliet E. K. "War, Women, Song: The Tectonics of Black Business and Entrepreneurship, 1939–2001," *Review of Black Political Economy* Vol. 31, No. 3 (2004), 65–116.

Walker, Susannah. *Style and Status: Selling Beauty to African American Women, 1920–1975*. Lexington: University of Kentucky Press, 2007.

Walton, Lester A. "The Future of the Negro on the Stage," *Colored American Magazine*, May and June, 1903.

Washington, Booker T. *The Negro in Business*, Boston, MA: Hertel, Jenkins & Co, 1907.

Waters, Ethel, and Charles Samuels. *His Eye Is on the Sparrow: An Autobiography of Ethel Waters*. New York: Da Capo Press, 1992.

Watkins, Clifford Edward. *Showman: The Life and Music of Perry George Lowery*. Jackson: University of Mississippi Press, 2003.

Watkins, Mel. *On the Real Side: A History of African American Comedy*. Chicago: Chicago Review Press, 1999.

Watts, Jill. *Mae West: An Icon in Black and White*. New York: Oxford University Press, 2001.

Weems, Robert. *Desegregating the Dollar: African American Consumerism in the Twentieth Century*. New York: New York University Press, 1998.

Weems, Robert E., Jr. *Business in Black and White: American Presidents and Black Entrepreneurs in the Twentieth Century*. New York: New York University Press, 2009.

Weems, Robert E., Jr. "Out of the Shadows: Business Enterprise and African American Historiography," *Business and Economic History*, Fall 1997, Vol. 26, No. 1, Papers Presented at a Conference on "The Future of Business History" Hagley Museum and Library (Fall 1997), 200–212.

Weems, Robert E., Jr., and Jason Chambers. *Building the Black Metropolis: African American Entrepreneurship in Chicago*. Urbana: University of Illinois, 2017.

Weems, Robert E., Jr., and Lewis A. Randolph. "The Right Man: James A. Jackson and the Origins of U.S. Government Interest in Black Business," *Enterprise & Society* Vol. 6, No. 2 (2005), 254–77.

Wertheim, Arthur Frank. *Vaudeville Wars: How Keith-Albee and Orpheum Circuits Controlled the Big-Time and Its Performers*. New York: Palgrave Macmillan, 2009.

Williams, Edward Christopher. *When Washington Was in Vogue: A Lost Novel of the Harlem Renaissance.* New York: Harper Perennial Reprint, 2005.

Williams, Fannie Barrier. "The Club Movement Among the Colored Women," *The Voice of the Negro*, March 1904.

Wolcott, Victoria W. *Race, Riots, and Rollercoasters: The Struggle Over Segregated Recreation in America*. Philadelphia: University of Pennsylvania Press, 2012.

Wolcott, Victoria W. *Remaking Respectability, African American Women in Interwar Detroit*, Chapel Hill: University of North Carolina Press, 2001.

Woll, Allen. *Black Musical Theater: From Coon Town to Dreamgirls.* Baton Rouge: Louisiana State University Press, 1989.

Zeitz, Joshua. *Flapper: A Madcap Story of Sex, Style, Celebrity, and the Women Who Made America Modern*. New York: Broadway Books, 2007.

### Theses and Dissertations

Ellerbee, Jason L. "African American Theaters in Georgia: Preserving an Entertainment Legacy." Master's Thesis in Historic Preservation, Athens: University of Georgia, 2004.

Hill, Anthony Duane. "J. A. Jackson's Page in Billboard: A Voice for Black Performance During the Harlem Renaissance between 1920–1925." PhD diss. New York: New York University, 1988.

Mossell, Sadie Tanner, "The Standard of Living Among One Hundred Negro Migrant Families in Philadelphia," PhD diss. Philadelphia: University of Pennsylvania, 1921.

Pride, Armistead Scott. "A Register and History of Negro Newspapers in the United States: 1827–1950." PhD diss. Evanston, IL: Northwestern University, 1950.

### Films

Binney, Josh, dir. *Boarding House Blues*, All American News, 1948.

Cooper, Ralph, and William Nolte, dir. *The Duke is Tops*, Million Dollar Productions, 1938.

Dahl, Christine, dir. *Wild Women Don't Have the Blues*. California Newsreel, 1987.

Garner, Rosemary and Greg Palmer, dir. *Vaudeville*, Thirteen/WNET, 1997.

Goldberg, Whoopi, dir. *Whoopi Goldberg Presents Moms Mabley*, HBO, 2013.

Hamilton, Robin, dir. *Howard Theater: A Century in Song*, DCW50, 2011.

Martin, Michael, dir. *The Nicholas Brothers: We Sing We Dance*, A&E Productions, 1992.

Nelson, Stanley, dir. *Boss: The Black Experience in Business*, Firelight Films, 2019.

Pollard, Sam, dir. *Sammy Davis, Jr.: I've Gotta Be Me*, American Masters, 2019.

Rees, Dee, dir. *Bessie*, HBO, 2015.

Stone, Andrew, dir. *Stormy Weather*, 20th Century Fox, 1943.

Williams, Roger Ross, dir. *The Apollo*, HBO, 2019.

Wise, Jason, dir. *Wait For Your Laugh*, Forgotten Man Films, 2017.

Zemickis, Leslie, dir. *Bound By Flesh: Story of Violet and Daisy Hilton, Mistress, Inc.*, 2012.

# INDEX

*Page references in italics refer to illustrations.*

**Michelle R. Scott** is an associate professor of history at the University of Maryland, Baltimore County. She is the author of *Blues Empress in Black Chattanooga: Bessie Smith and the Emerging Urban South.*

The University of Illinois Press
is a founding member of the
Association of University Presses.

---

University of Illinois Press
1325 South Oak Street
Champaign, IL 61820-6903
www.press.uillinois.edu